ORGANIZATIONAL COMMUNICATION

BALANCING CREATIVITY
AND CONSTRAINT

ORGANIZATIONAL COMMUNICATION

BALANCING CREATIVITY
AND CONSTRAINT

Eric M. Eisenberg
University of Southern California

H. L. Goodall, Jr.
Clemson University

ST. MARTIN'S PRESS
New York

TO ALL OUR STUDENTS AND COLLEAGUES ON THE VERGE

Editor: Jane Lambert
Managing editor: Patricia Mansfield Phelan
Project editor: Suzanne Holt
Production supervisor: Katherine Battiste
Art director: Sheree Goodman
Text design: Laura Ierardi
Graphics: TCSystems
Cover design and art: Marjory Dressler

For information, write:
St. Martin's Press, Inc.
175 Fifth Avenue
New York, NY 10010

ISBN: 0-312-06847-6

ACKNOWLEDGMENTS

Table 3.3, from *Complex Organizations: A Critical Essay*, 3d ed., by Charles Perrow, © 1986. Reprinted by permission of McGraw-Hill, Inc.
Table 3.5, from *The Organization Man*. Copyright © 1956, 1984 by William H. Whyte, Jr. Reprinted by permission of Simon & Schuster.
Figure 3.4, "The Needs Hierarchy," from *Motivation and Personality* by Abraham Maslow, © 1954. Reprinted by permission of HarperCollins Publishers.

Acknowledgments and copyrights are continued at the back of the book on page 363, which constitutes an extension of the copyright page.

PREFACE

Signposts in a Strange Land

If you drive across America today, you will notice historical markers that point out roads we no longer use. These roads are variously called paths, trails, routes, runs, traces, pikes, and passages. They answered important questions for our forebears—how and where the mail should be delivered, how explorers could best cross the midlands and arrive at the Pacific coast, where the cattle drives ran from Texas to Denver and Kansas City, and even how outlaws could escape into Mexico or Canada. Today, all we have left of these roads are signs that show us—because we no longer use these paths—which answers and approaches no longer work.

Over time, the old roads gave way to lanes, avenues, and turnpikes. The new roads were joined by railroads, then superhighways. Planes flew overhead. Rural farms and small towns developed into cities with suburbs connected by expressways and commuter trains. We are left only with markers: the Boston Post Road, the Chesapeake and Ohio Canal Bridge, the Mason-Dixon Line, the Pecos Trail, U.S. 1, Route 66. These markers stand as signposts in a strange land, made strange by the fact that what we see now was once never envisioned, what we take for granted was once unknown. A person crossing America on foot or on horseback saw a different country than most of us do today.

Organizational landscapes are also littered with numerous roads and passages, some not taken, some once well traveled but abandoned, others still enjoying brisk traffic. What gives organizations their character is the nature of these juxtapositions among answers that once worked but that are now obsolete, and current answers that eventually end up in the dustbin. What is more, each organization comprises multiple answers or alternative ways of seeing reality. Organizational communication is the process by which ways of seeing—or answers—are expressed, suppressed, and negotiated by organizational members.

Good communication skills have always been in demand in business, but the precise definition of such skills changes over time. Whereas early twentieth-century definitions of effective communication focused on the giving and taking of orders, toward the middle of the century the focus shifted toward honesty and self-disclosure. In the 1970s, definitions of effective communication were tied to judgments of appropriateness—that is, saying the right thing at the right time to the right person. Today, effectiveness connotes the ability to advocate positions and to empower lower-level employees. The specific meaning of effective organizational communication is always relative to changing historical, cultural, social, political, and technological contexts.

The purpose of *Organizational Communication*, then, is to describe the role and importance of organizational communication within an evolving social context. In doing so, we point out the tried and true business pathways that are now dead ends, as well as those routes that lead in promising future directions. Our goal is to provide a comprehensive text that focuses on current business practices, while at the same time offering a thorough reconsideration of the history, theories, and research on communication and organizations.

Plan of the Text

The text is presented in two parts:

- In Part I, "Theories of Organization and Communication," Chapters 1 and 2 begin our discussion of the role of communication in business, and the evolution of theories of communication in our understanding of organizations. Chapters 3 through 6 explore theories of organizations and communication within the historical and cultural periods that produced them.
- In Part II, "Contexts," Chapters 7 through 9 analyze current organizational communication practice at three levels: the individual, the relationship, and the group. Chapters 10 and 11 explore the connections between communication and the financial viability of a business, along with the future of organizational communication in general.

Part I: Theories of Organization and Communication

Chapter 1 places the study of organizational communication in the context of current global economic, social, political, and cultural trends and events. We use these ideas to discuss the various continuities, changes, and new values and priorities affecting communication at work. Chapter 2 offers four definitions of communication applicable to organizations: communication as (1) information transfer; (2) transactional process; (3) strategic control; and (4) balancing creativity and constraint. We then delineate three elements of all communication relationships—self, other, and contexts—that provide a framework for understanding how meaning is created through social interaction. We use these three elements to propose that people act as individuals situated among various contexts and guided by the goal of authentic dialogue.

Chapters 3 through 6 present a detailed historical narrative about the major theories of organizations, society, and communication from the Industrial Revolution to the present day. Chapter 3 reviews two founding perspectives on organizational communication that continue to be influential—scientific management and human relations. Our text is unique in the distinction it makes between human relations and human resources approaches. Chapter 4 introduces the systems perspective on organizational communication, situating the study of organizational systems within compatible advances in engineering, biology, sociology, and information science. The chapter concludes with a discussion of management theorist Karl Weick (1979), whose work is a hybrid of systems and cultural approaches.

Chapter 5 takes a fresh look at cultural studies of organizations and communication. The chapter begins with an appreciation of the role of language in the workplace. Next, we provide a framework for interpreting cultural performance through an analysis of four interrelated terms: actions, practices, narratives, and dialogues that reveal competing interests, voices, and values within organizations. We close the chapter with the question, Can (and should) an organization's culture be managed?

Chapter 6 explores two emerging perspectives on organizational communication: critical theory and postmodernism. These formerly radical approaches have of late entered the mainstream of academic theory. We show how both critical and postmodern approaches offer useful ways of seeing organizational advocacy, empowerment, dialogue, productivity, and effectiveness. We offer examples of how both approaches are already having an impact on practice in real organizations.

In summary, Chapters 3 through 6 offer an alternative reading of what has become standard fare in most introductory organizational communication textbooks. This alternative reading is unique in its attention to the social context in which the theories were developed and applied. Furthermore, our approach works to explain theories and concepts by focusing on concrete business applications.

Part II: Contexts

Chapters 7 through 9 extend and apply the theoretical frameworks to specific organizational issues and contexts. We move systematically from a consideration of the personal experience of individual employees, to the formation of relationships, to the uses of groups, networks, and teams in organizations.

Chapter 7 explores a significant and often overlooked perspective—the experience of work from the standpoint of the individual employee. We start by describing the competing interests of work life: while companies expect commitment and cooperation, employees seek identity and creativity. We discuss research on organizational entry and assimilation; on cooperation and resistance to organizational goals; and on new directions for work organization that potentially may improve the individual experience of work.

Chapter 8 begins with the question, Why do relationships matter so much in organizations? We argue that in many jobs today, interpersonal competence is no longer a luxury but a bona fide qualification for effective job performance. We show how relational communication provides individuals with increased resources for amassing influence, achieving goals, and obtaining social support on the job. We then detail the importance of interpersonal relationships with superiors, subordinates, peers, and external customers and suppliers. Of note is the fact that this is the first text published in organizational communication with the word *customer* featured prominently in the index. Next, we discuss romance and sexual harassment and their impact on organizational communication. Finally, we provide suggestions for improving interpersonal competence through assertiveness, active listening, and responsible communication.

Chapter 9 provides a new treatment of the role of groups in organizations, focusing not only on small-group research but also on informal, emergent networks and various types of teams. Specifically, we examine issues of advocacy, cross-functional coordination, and empowerment within the team context.

The final two chapters explore the future of organizational communication both in practice and as a field of study. Chapter 10 takes a comprehensive look at organizations as profit-making entities and makes some clear connections between communication and bottom-line financial performance. Ours is the first treatment of organizational communication that takes seriously the relationship between effective communication and profitability. Of course, we would not endorse some of the many ways of becoming profitable. Toward this end, we have integrated questions of ethics throughout the text, in the form of "Ethics Boxes" that raise ethical questions relevant to each chapter, and we present an extended section on morality and responsibility in the final chapter. Chapter 11 emphasizes the need for organizations to learn from past mistakes and to find ways to keep on learning as conditions change. We address the issue of what must be learned in these successful organizations—basic skills, new technologies, and new ways of organizing—as well as their implications for society and for the planet. At the close of this chapter, we return to our central metaphor—that of striking a balance between creativity and constraint—to question the different ways individuals can position themselves in the world through communication and in so doing take responsibility for our future.

To facilitate application of course materials, we have included unique case studies at the close of each chapter that guide application. These cases are drawn from our consulting experiences, yet they are accessible to undergraduates. We don't believe in cases that have "right" answers; therefore, our case studies encourage dialogue about possible alternative solutions that should help students develop their own ideas about what makes the greatest difference in thinking about organizational communication.

Finally, we offer an *Instructor's Manual* as a pedagogical resource to be used with this text. This manual provides course syllabi, test items, and assignments as well as practical advice on how to teach each chapter. In addition, the glossary of terms at the end of the manual may be photocopied and distributed to students if desired.

Acknowledgments

Organizational Communication is the product of a joint venture between the authors and the publisher. Because what we have done departs in significant ways from traditional organizational communication texts, we thank our editors, Cathy Pusateri and Jane Lambert, for sponsoring the project, and our project editor, Suzanne Holt, for seeing it through to completion. Thanks, also, to Melissa Levine, editorial assistant at St. Martin's Press, for creating the glossary of terms in Appendix E of the *Instructor's Manual*. Special thanks must be extended to Betty Pessagno, whose extraordinary copyediting job greatly contributed to the quality of the text you have before you. We also wish to acknowledge the many people in business who have graciously invited us into their companies and taught us much over the years about the nature of organizational communication as it is lived each day.

In addition, we'd like to thank the following reviewers for their helpful suggestions and insights: Stephen P. Banks, University of Idaho; Carol Berteotti, University of Wisconsin–La Crosse; Stan Deetz, Rutgers University; Katherine Miller, Arizona State University; Peter Monge, University of Southern California; and Dennis Mumby, Purdue University.

We are especially grateful to our colleagues who have supported this project from the beginning and who have in some cases volunteered to teach sections of the text while it was being developed, providing us with rich feedback. We specifically thank Peter Kellett, Doreen Geddes, Lindsley Armstrong, Lora Sager, Eddie Smith, and Fran Marrus at Clemson University; Patricia Geist at San Diego State University; Connie Bullis, Mary

Strine, Len Hawes, and Jim Anderson at the University of Utah; Steve Smith at the University of Arkansas; Stan Deetz at Rutgers University; Rita Whillock at Southern Methodist University; Stewart Auyash at Ithaca College; David Payne at the University of South Florida; Bruce Hyde at St. Cloud State University; John Stewart at the University of Washington; Fred Steier at Old Dominion University; Karen Altman, Walter Fisher, Everett Rogers, Gwen Brown, Candise Chaudoir, and Gelya Frank at the University of Southern California; and the participants of the Alta Conferences on Interpretive Approaches to Organizational Communication. We are especially grateful to Peter Monge, whose close reading of an early draft of the text was critical in the preparation of the final manuscript, and to Patricia Riley, whose keen insights about organizational communication regularly appear in these pages.

We could not have written this book without the enthusiastic and loving support of each other and our families: Lori Roscoe, Evan and Joel Eisenberg, Sandra and Nicolas Goodall, and Martha, Clarence, Kate, and Rick Bray. During the drafting of these chapters, children were born into both households, and one of us changed jobs and moved from Utah to South Carolina via an extended summer stay with his in-laws in Alabama. These changes made the "question of balance" so central to these pages especially poignant. Through it all, our spouses and children never failed to provide us with the often extraordinary levels of support we needed to complete this project.

Finally, we dedicate this book to our students and colleagues, the community with whom we identify, the people who both constrain our actions and provide an enthusiastic forum for our most wildly creative ideas. Inasmuch as we live in a time of great intellectual, social, political, economic, and spiritual turmoil, we never take for granted those individuals who in the face of all this uncertainty have made a commitment to continue the dialogue.

Eric M. Eisenberg
H. L. Goodall, Jr.

CONTENTS

PART TWO

CONTEXTS
193

CHAPTER 7
THE EXPERIENCE OF WORK   195

CHAPTER 10
COMMUNICATION AND ORGANIZATIONAL EFFECTIVENESS   **290**

PART ONE

THEORIES OF ORGANIZATION AND COMMUNICATION

THE
CHANGING WORLD
OF WORK

You are so young, so before all beginning . . . be patient toward all that is unsolved in your heart and try to love the questions themselves like locked rooms and like books that are written in a very foreign tongue. Do not now seek the answers, which cannot be given you because you would not be able to live them. And the point is, to live everything. Live the questions now. Perhaps you will then gradually, without noticing it, live along some distant day into the answer.

Resolve to be always beginning—to be a beginner!

—Rainer Maria Rilke, 1984

Individuals just embarking on careers harbor many misconceptions about the world of work. Most of our students report feeling shocked upon starting their first "real" job. They expected work to be serious and orderly, and they trusted that managers would be competent and fair. Then they discovered that reality did not always fit their expectations.

Students are surprised to learn that the questions asked most frequently about organizational communication lack simple answers. For example, even the most straightforward questions, such as "What is the best way to supervise employees?", "What is the best way to attract and keep customers?", or "What is effective organizational communication?" can only be answered after a host of situational and historical factors have been specified (Eisenberg & Phillips, 1991). In other words, the very definition of effective communication is not constant; rather, it varies by type of company, type of people involved, timing, and culture.

Answers to questions about organizational communication are highly situated and relatively perishable. They are situated because the kind of communication that works for, say, a small start-up clothing manufacturer, is most likely inappropriate for a mature film-production company. Answers about organizational communication are perishable because patterns of interaction that were effective even five years ago may be out of date today owing to changes in jargon, technology, or the nature of the industry. Those who fail to see these attributes of organizational communication and who cling to what they know as dogma often perish as well.

As an example of an organization clinging to old answers, we cite our experience with a machine shop in California. The general manager is a Marine Corps veteran;

management systems and structures in the organization are modeled after the military. While this model may have been effective some years back (and even then, only in certain places and in selected industries—see Morgan, 1986), it no longer works for this company. Neither management nor employees are willing to put up with a rigid hierarchy and an intimidating management style. In addition, the current business environment requires flexibility. Rapid changes in the social, economic, and political climate demand speedy, flexible responses, which is not a strength of the military model. For example, even General Electric is reconsidering the wisdom of its autocratic management style under Jack Welch, its CEO (Chief Executive Officer). In the 1990s, GE has begun to question whether the benefits of such an approach outweigh the costs in employee morale, turnover, and productivity.

When we first taught classes in organizational communication 15 years ago, three industries—banking, air transportation, and fast food—were held up as noncompetitive. Today, they are three of the most fiercely competitive industries in the world. If space permitted, we could provide other examples of where the commonsense wisdom of even a decade ago no longer fits. Thus, instead of a book of right answers about organizational communication, we will focus here on enabling you to ask good questions about organizations, the answers to which will change over time.

Despite these caveats, we do have opinions about what constitutes good organizational communication in most companies most of the time. From time to time in this book, we offer such opinions, but as possibilities to be considered, not rigid laws. We feel strongly that what most distinguishes successful executives, consultants, researchers, managers, and employees from unsuccessful ones is a consistent ability to ask good questions of a situation. The lessons of experience are not a tablet of yellowed truths, but the sensitive approach that an intelligent, well-informed human being brings to a situation. Over time, the way an individual sees and interprets a situation guides his or her actions. The best preparation for organizational life is to keep one's mind open to multiple ways of interpreting equivocal situations.

People who are capable of considering a wide range of questions or a large number of competing interpretations for a situation are successful because they are not locked into one way of doing things or into one set of answers. As a consequence, they are able to manage conflict and diversity, and in general to adapt to a fast-paced business environment. They can reinvent themselves and their organizations in response to, and sometimes in anticipation of, changing times.

We pose a number of questions in this book: Why do people work? How can workplaces be improved? Can work be both fun and profitable? Are all workplaces basically the same, and, if not, how do companies and industries differ? What should be the relationship between a person's work life and personal life? Do all kinds of people have an equal voice in decision making? Should they? How should an organization present itself to the outside world? What role do leaders play in promoting organizational effectiveness? And most important: How can knowledge of communication help us to understand and perform better at work?

Although none of these questions has a definite answer, we want to emphasize that they are all good questions. People who repeatedly ask such questions—regardless of whether they work in business, the university, or anywhere else—are singularly capable of dealing with the exceptionally fast rate of change in the business world. This is because they are primarily engaged in interpreting organizational communication—and it is their openness to the possible meanings of work that makes them both the designers and inheritors of our collective future.

THE CHANGING WORLD OF WORK

This first chapter outlines the ways that work has changed in recent years. In an attempt to situate the study of organizational communication within a timely, practical, real-world context, we focus our attention on major themes and trends. Our remarks suggest above all the inexorable rate of change in the business environment. But not everything about business conditions today is completely new. Two continuities are especially worth noting. First, success in business has always been and continues to be hard-won and difficult to maintain. Only 4 percent of the businesses operating in 1900 are around today. There are many reasons for this minute percentage: changing technology, changing customer tastes, poor management, and the difficulty of keeping a successful business profitable over a long period of time. Second, an antagonism persists between the mainly economic concerns of businesses and the personal concerns of employees. Managers and academics have shown an increasing interest in improving the quality of the employee's work life. However, when the good of the company clashes with the good of an individual employee, the company inevitably prevails. As a result, in recent years considerable interest has been shown in designing and maintaining organizations that are both pro-profit and pro-people. But such organizations are by no means commonplace, and the challenge to remain both profitable and a good place to work is, if anything, getting harder.

Next, we focus on two broad categories of issues facing contemporary organizations: increased competitive pressure and new priorities and values regarding work.

Increased Competitive Pressure

Several years ago, we would have written this section very differently. Specifically, we would have talked about economic cycles, boom and bust times for certain industries and for the economy as a whole, and their impact on people and on communication. This approach is not possible today because we are in the midst of an historic period of global social and economic change. In this revolutionary era, the focus is directly on learning how to live and work in a world of real (economic, ecological, personal) limits. This is not a temporary, cyclical correction. Clearly the slack has gone out of business, and the evidence is all around us. Severe competitive pressures have led to widespread layoffs and plant closings. What is more, bankruptcies are routine. The abuses of credit by government, private industry, consumers, and lending institutions in the 1980s were supplanted in the 1990s by a much more conservative lending attitude. The people who provide the money for organizations—customers, stockholders, and the public—are in no mood for risky business. Venture capitalists, who invest in start-up companies, have become ultraconservative in their investment choices. The result is less slack in the system and a slimmer margin for error.

This economic belt-tightening is the price for the overspending and excesses of the

1980s. Unlike previous economic downturns, however, in this one businesses are not simply bouncing back, leaving organizations relatively intact. Instead, as is already becoming evident, we are witnessing fundamental changes in the structure of organizations, communities, and societies.

Focus on Quality and Customer Service   Economic pressures are not the sole motivation for companies to reexamine their structures and processes. Another motivation is the customers' increased sophistication and expectation of quality products and services. With few exceptions, U.S. companies are obsessed with quality and customer satisfaction. This preoccupation has been largely the result of foreign competition, mainly from Japan, and the realization that to survive the United States must compete in a global marketplace. Whatever the reason, today virtually every workplace has a special program designed to bring about total quality or total customer satisfaction based on the ideas of W. Edwards Deming, Philip Crosby, Karl Albrecht, and others. Business efforts to improve quality and customer service are often targeted at winning the coveted Baldrige Award for quality (named for former U.S. Secretary of Commerce Malcolm Baldrige).

One company currently struggling to survive the pressure is American Honda, which by all accounts is a successful car company. A key measure of its success is the JD Powers Customer Satisfaction Index. Over a recent five-year period (1987–1991), Honda seriously slipped in the index, from third all the way to sixteenth. (We are referring specifically to Honda—their Acura spinoff continues at number one, but is in almost every way a separate company.) Interestingly, in most years that Honda's standing relative to its competitors has fallen, its absolute level of customer satisfaction has improved. In other words, simply getting better is not good enough. Worse still, for American Honda, simply getting better is a losing strategy.

This emphasis on customer satisfaction has not been limited to retail or even to the private sector. Hospitals and universities, for example, have become more patient- and student-focused, respectively. Medical residents at Long Beach Memorial Hospital in California, for example, are required to spend one full day as "patients," complete with hospital gowns and intravenous tubes, to help them learn to empathize with patients. Major changes are under way at universities as well. Stanford University has been leading the effort to reexamine the basic mission of the university with regard to its primary customers, undergraduate students. Stanford, Yale, and Columbia are moving to restructure their operations both to respond to current economic concerns and to better serve the needs of customer-students. In some cases, this has meant staff layoffs and the closing of academic departments. Increasingly, hospital and university presidents are using the language of businesspeople to exhort their employees to achieve higher quality, to promote customer satisfaction, and in general to do more with less.

A Recipe for Stress   The pressures for improved quality and customer service have coincided precisely with the strained economic conditions and the disappearance of slack from business. This is a recipe for stress. Blue- and pink-collar workers are urged to work smarter *and* harder while at the same time watching their job security evaporate. For white-collar workers, disappearing job security has been accompanied by confusion and anxiety about the changing nature of their jobs and of their ability to meet new responsibilities. Contrary to the older conceptions of managers as logical, reflective planners and coordinators, research suggests that the new managers need expertise mainly in brief, informal, face-to-face interactions (Kanter, 1989; Mintzberg, 1973). Today, management has more to do with communication and relations with people than with planning and application of technical knowledge. Managerial personnel who lack these newer skills soon find that their jobs are in jeopardy.

Management practice in the late twentieth century, regardless of company or industry, is often called firefighting. This reactive style of management is designed to deal first with the "hot" issue that is currently foremost on an organization's agenda. This approach avoids the long view and is oblivious to the unanticipated (usually negative) consequences of short-term solutions. Interestingly, this metaphor is not fair to real firefighters, who think of fires as projects and do a great deal of planning to combat them. The best firefighters are least likely to sacrifice long-term outcomes for short-term gains. The paradox remains: Just when it is most important to take the time to make the best decision since so little slack exists, people feel least able to do so.

Turbulent Organizational Environments   The environments in which all organizations exist vary in both character and complexity. In a classic article, Fred Emery and Eric Trist (1965) used a weather metaphor to describe these variations. At one extreme is the turbulent environment, which is dense, complicated, and hard to predict. An organization with such an environment lives in constant fear of environmental jolts (unexpected occurrences that can deeply affect the business). Moreover, it has difficulty forecasting the likely consequences of organizational actions, such as a new marketing strategy, distribution policy, or the look of a product. For example, a company that makes computer software for businesses can never stop worrying about changes in hardware, software, government regulations, and competitors' products, most of which are not under their control.

At the opposite extreme is the placid environment, in which events are regular, calm, and predictable. Companies with placid environments are less fearful not only about unexpected events but also about unanticipated consequences of organizational actions. Public utilities remain among the increasingly rare companies that can still make decisions and set policies without fear of significant repercussions (although this is becoming less true daily).

Unexpected Interdependencies   Contemporary hospitals exist in a turbulent environment. Changes in technology, research, demographics, government regulations, and insurance all have had profound ripple effects on hospitals. For example, not long ago, a warm tropical current (El Niño) increased the price of a hospital stay. It did so in the following circuitous way. The storm destroyed the Peruvian anchovy crop, which in turn increased the price of gelatin, which is composed in large part of anchovy bones. Gelatin is a major component of X-ray film. As this example shows, no organization should underestimate the complex, interdependent connections that exist within its environment. Unanticipated consequences are the rule in organizational decision making. This is what Karl Weick (1979) meant when he said that managers get into trouble when they fail to "think in circles."

Turbulence and Boundary Spanners   The unpredictability of environmental occurrences has led organizations to place a premium on rapid retrieval of information. They can stay informed about environmental conditions in many ways, ranging from simple and more traditional methods (e.g., market research, customer feedback, and newspaper reading) to complex and innovative approaches (e.g., through computer databases and elaborate executive information systems). In recent years, companies have dramatically increased their environmental scanning efforts, but generally most firms still do much less in this area than they should.

Perhaps the simplest, and most often overlooked, way for an organization to keep in touch with its external environment is through its boundary spanners (Adams, 1980). These are company employees who have direct contact with the public, and they include bank tellers, telephone receptionists, repair technicians, market researchers, salespeople, and customer service representatives. These personnel can provide a key intelligence link to the outside world. According to J. Stacy Adams (1980), boundary spanners serve at least three functions. First, they can pay careful attention to the opinions of people outside the organization, using that information to guide organizational decision making. This is an obvious function for a market researcher but may be equally applicable to a cashier or salesperson. Second, they keep alert to broader, more subtle trends in the environment, serving as a kind of early warning system against environmental jolts. For example, a customer service representative might notice a growing concern about the recyclability of certain products or packaging. Third, boundary spanners are important representatives of the organization to its environment. Customer impressions of a restaurant, for example, are based largely on the behavior of its waiters and waitresses.

Turbulence and Giantism   What happens to information about the environment once it is inside a company? If customers complain to a car dealer about product quality, or if a middle manager of a hotel chain notices a disturbing trend that might affect business, can the company do anything with the information? When companies fail to respond to environmental information, employees quickly become discouraged. According to Tom Peters (1987), some companies are unresponsive to such information because Americans have a bias in favor of giantism; that is, they have a long-held belief that bigger is better. Quality and flexibility, which are the hallmarks of successful companies today, are difficult to maintain once a business grows beyond a certain size. According to Peters, the big company has rarely, if ever, been more efficient or more innovative than its smaller competitors. In fact, the "winning" organization must be flatter (with fewer levels of hierarchy), promote more sharing of power among employees, be oriented toward niche markets (deciding what it does best and sticking to it), and in general be flexible and responsive in its pursuit of total quality and excellent customer service.

Naturally, bigness does have some important advantages; increased financial stability and reduced competition have prompted many strategic mergers and acquisitions. Overall, however, there is no effective way to manage a company once it grows beyond, say, 10,000 employees. It is therefore easy to understand why IBM has splintered into independent business units; why Japanese car companies opted to introduce their luxury autos (e.g., Lexus) through separate companies; and why, in general, small, flexible, entrepreneurial businesses employ most working Americans and will continue to play a critical role in the United States' economic future (Drucker, 1992).

Shifting Power Bases   Prior to 1900, power in society often rested with the person who owned the most tangible resources—land, equipment, oil, and, during the era of slavery, even other people. At the turn of the century, those who controlled these resources wielded the greatest power. The second half of the twentieth century has seen a dramatic shift away from tangible resources toward less tangible information resources. Indeed, today we are commonly said to be living in an information society. Over 50 percent of the U.S. labor force is currently involved in the transfer, reprocessing, or transmittal of information (SCA, 1991). In specific instances, companies like TRW and American Airlines have discovered that the information aspects of their business (for TRW, credit verification; for American, a computerized reservation system) represent their greatest financial successes (Davis & Davidson, 1991). More so than tangible resources, today information is power, and those who have quickest access to the best information are most likely to succeed.

The Power of Relationships   Some would say that having the right information is not sufficient to achieve and maintain power. According to Rosabeth Moss Kanter (1989), for example, informal interpersonal relationships and communication networks are the most dynamic sources of power in organizations today. The reason is, once again, related to the turbulent business environment. In this environment, formal relationships are slower and less trustworthy sources of information than informal relationships. Most decision makers rely heavily on verbal information from people they trust. Informal relationships allow employees to get things done across functions within organizations, across organizations, and between business, government, and other stakeholders. For example, the fact that billionnaire presidential hopeful Ross Perot (formerly head of Electronic Data Systems) exploited informal, personal relationships with both the governor of Texas and the presidents of major high-technology electronic firms was one determining factor in making Austin, Texas, the high-tech town it has become (Gibson & Rogers, 1993).

A relational power base can be frightening to the average employee; by contrast, the idea of information as power seems at least vaguely democratic. Some may object that the idea of informal relationships as power is simply a restatement of the old cliché, "It's not *what* you know but *who* you know." Worse yet, some believe that the growing relational basis of power has unfavorable implications for women and minorities, as well as for others who may lack connections with those in power. Although such fears are not wholly unjustified, a return to the homogeneous and blatantly discriminatory workplaces of the past is unlikely. Informal relationships will no doubt keep much of the power concentrated in traditional hands, and yet a growing acceptance of diversity by formerly closed insider networks will take place. Today nearly every company with more than 300 employees offers workshops in cultural diversity. Such workshops are intended to help employees of differing ethnic backgrounds to understand one another. For example, they may help white clinical directors to understand the social norms and motivations of Filipino nurses, or Latino factory supervisors to become familiar with the language and interpersonal style of black mechanics.

Globalization   Business is moving to create a global marketplace, a world economy in which the United States is only one—and increasingly not the major—participant. Over 100,000 American companies do business abroad, and about a third of the profits of U.S. companies, as well as one-sixth of the nation's jobs, come from international business (Cascio, 1986; Offerman & Gowing, 1990). Whether or not this is good news, it is inevitable. Specifically, half of Xerox's 110,000 employees work overseas. Half of Sony's employees are not Japanese. The "American" car you buy is assembled here, but the parts may have come from around the world. Conversely, a late-model Mazda was recently classified as a domestic car because over 70 percent of its parts were made in America. Musicians like David Byrne and Paul Simon import world music to the United States, while American music, films, and television command large markets elsewhere. Three regions will be dominant in the twenty-first century: North America, the Pacific Rim, and Europe. The breakup of the Soviet Union means the potential for a Euro-Asian-Russian confederacy, but it will take some time before such a group will become a leading economic force. The good news about globalization is that it brings the United States an expanded market for products and services. The bad news is that it threatens the potential erosion of business because of foreign competition.

Other problems are associated with globalization. For example, differences in trade policies, import/export quotas, and tariffs can create serious problems for countries that feel they are being harmed by unfair global competition. The emergence of a global labor force has sent business owners and managers in search of the lowest possible labor costs. Typically, this means sending jobs overseas. Such practices have been commonplace for years in textiles and certain kinds of manufacturing, but in the past they were confined almost exclusively to repetitive, blue-collar jobs. Today, however, white-collar jobs are also affected. For example, U.S. firms like Arthur Andersen have recently turned to companies in the Philippines for such white-collar work as computer software engineering.

What are the consequences of U.S. companies employing less expensive workers from around the globe? In 1988, we asked the CEO of AT&T to justify closing a plant in New Jersey and moving thousands of jobs to Singapore. His reason for the move at that time was to increase profitability, for which he was unapologetic. From his perspective, his job was to protect the best interests of AT&T stockholders. Similarly, in the movie *Roger and Me*, director Michael Moore goes to Flint, Michigan—birthplace of General Motors (GM) and the United Auto Workers Union—to assess the impact of major GM plant closings and the resulting widespread unemployment (which at one point was near 20 percent). The purpose of his visit is to find Roger Smith, the president of GM, and to ask him whether General Motors had any responsibility to the people of Flint even if it made good business sense to move plants elsewhere. Smith didn't answer the question, but guessing from his nonverbal behavior in the film, his answer was "no."

Not everyone in business, however, believes that people and profits are incompatible. Although changes have not been dramatic, the standard view that gives primacy to *stock*holders is being extended somewhat to the notion of *stake*holders. An organizational stakeholder is anyone, including investors, managers, employees, customers, and suppliers, as well as portions of the general public, who has a significant interest in the actions and fate of the company. From this perspective, organizational decision making is not simply a matter of maximizing profits (or of trading off short- versus long-term returns). Instead, it involves satisfying multiple, competing audiences with often opposing goals.

This is a divisive, difficult issue, operating at an ideological, moral level. For many managers, defending the interests of stockholders and protecting shareholder value is a sacred imperative in a capitalist society. "Can't you see," these people say, "we have no other choice but to downsize by 50 percent if we are going to make our earnings targets." Though seductive, such a single-minded approach is a bit shortsighted. If profitability is the only criterion for success, the risks of unanticipated consequences are great. Furthermore, while it may not be profitable, for example, to recruit and promote physically challenged and minority candidates, or to conform to environmental regulations, many companies do so out of a sense of moral rightness. A growing number of companies worldwide have managed to strike a balance among stakeholder interests and have achieved at least some success in becoming both pro-profit and pro-people.

Inadequately Educated Labor Pool   Recently, the Hudson Institute published a comprehensive study referred to as *Workforce 2000* (Johnston & Parker, 1987), which projects the needs and character of our workforce at the turn of the century. None of the news is good. At the same time that our population is aging, with more people moving out of the active labor pool (Odiorne, 1986), the youth of America are less well prepared to take over their jobs. This lack of preparation runs deep, as is evidenced by a startlingly high rate of illiteracy among U.S. workers (as high as 25 percent in some industries). A recent survey by the Educational Testing Service conducted for the National Assessment of Educational Progress (NAEP) concluded that

only 24 percent of whites, 20 percent of Hispanics, and 8 percent of Blacks of the 3699 21–25 year-olds surveyed could figure out the tip and change for a two-item restaurant meal (Hamilton, 1988). The present concern with the level of literacy and basic skills of today's entry level workers is compounded by the realization that virtually all prognostications of the nature of work in the years ahead project an increase in that level of skill needed to perform well. Computer software can check the spelling of words in an article but cannot proofread for meaning and context. As robots take over routine assembly work from people, jobs will open requiring the monitoring and troubleshooting of computerized equipment. Yet the NAEP finds that among their 21–25 year-old sample, only 25 percent of Whites, 7 percent of Hispanics, and 3 percent of Blacks can interpret a complex bus schedule. It should not be surprising, then, to find that U.S. businesses are spending a record 210 billion dollars for on-the-job training and education, an effort about equal in size to public elementary, secondary, and higher education institutions combined (Offerman & Gowing, 1990, p. 96).

There is no shortage of evidence for these serious educational deficits. Layoffs from certain key industries, like automobile manufacturing and defense, reveal that thousands of people are unqualified to perform any comparable paying job. Standardized test scores are falling steadily, and teachers at all levels are frustrated with the inadequate preparation of students.

Education and Ethnicity   The educational crisis in the United States is a time bomb exacerbated by the ethnic split in the nation. In the upcoming decades, "the proportion of White members of this entry-level workforce will decline, and the proportion of minority populations will increase significantly" (Goldstein & Gilliam, 1990, p. 137). By the middle of the twenty-first century, Anglos (whites) will be a minority in the United States, and the emergent nonwhite majority (blacks, Latinos, Asians) will be expected to assume the burden of support for the elderly white retirees. Whether they will have the ability to take on this burden is debatable. According to one point of view, owing to historical deficits and unequal opportunity, the emergent nonwhite majority will not be sufficiently productive to carry the cost of Medicare and social security (Hayes-Bautista, 1988). A more radical view suggests that blood would flow before the emergent nonwhite majority would ever support the aging Anglos. In either case, good economic sense dictates that we educate all our young people and that we not turn our backs on currently disadvantaged minority groups on whose success or failure the future of our society will turn.

New Priorities and Values Regarding Work

At the same time that competitiveness is increasing and managers are demanding more from employees, another potentially contradictory trend has begun. According to Lynn Offerman and Marilyn Gowing (1990):

> The changing demographics discussed earlier are being accompanied by modifications in employee attitudes, motivations, and values (Odiorne, 1986). Increased desire for autonomy, self-development, and balance between work and family life is surfacing among many workers (Hall, 1986). People are seeking more meaningful work experiences, as well as more involvement in the decisions pertaining to themselves (London & Strumpf, 1986). Furthermore, there is evidence that compared with past generations of workers, today's workers have a growing perception of entitlement to such meaning and involvement in their work (p. 98).

In short, many Americans are changing the way they think about success. No longer willing to abandon everything else in life for their jobs, people are taking a stand on their new priorities. With some exceptions (notably entrepreneurs and some senior executives), work, career, and individual goal achievement are being placed within a set of priorities that also include family and community (Bellah et al., 1985). Many people are struggling to find, or to rediscover, some sense of balance in their lives.

Two factors have led to this questioning of priorities. First, high-paying, unionized manufacturing jobs have disappeared in the United States, making two-career families much more prevalent than in the past. Over 40 percent of the workforce is comprised of dual-earner couples (Zedeck & Mosier, 1990). Second, grandparents and other members of extended families rarely live nearby, so new child-care arrangements are needed and are being negotiated at a brisk rate (Wolfe, 1991). With both parents working outside of the home and child care becoming more difficult to arrange, issues of family well-being have appeared on the national political agenda. Nevertheless, the motivations for change are not solely economic; they also mark a retreat from the extreme materialism and individualism of the 1970s and 1980s.

Recovery from Workaholism   Not long ago, the model American employee came to work early, stayed late, and was willing to travel anywhere at a moment's notice. Getting ahead meant putting the job and career first, and everyone else—in particular, the family—was expected to understand. Recent discussions of a "glass ceiling" and a "Mommy track" for women in business sent a similar message: If work wasn't a woman's top priority, she would only go so far. Regrettably, this remains true for most women (Silverstein, 1992), even though some reach the top and still manage to balance all the commitments in their lives (Ferguson & Dunphy, 1992).

Certainly, many middle-aged men and women are redefining just how far they wish to go in their careers and are questioning where they were going in the first place. The motivations of individuals who are just entering the workforce are less clear. While some are willing to work as hard as they need to get ahead, others seem to be planning a more balanced life. Many people are seeking to meet their achievement needs and at the same

—————— **ETHICS BOX 1.1** ——————

ORGANIZATIONAL STRUCTURE AND INDIVIDUAL HEALTH

Workaholism is a term used to describe an individual who becomes unnaturally preoccupied with work. Typically, a workaholic spends long hours every day, including nights and weekends, at work. Family and friendships are often abandoned in favor of relationships at work or friendships with persons who share the same commitment to work. In some cases, workaholics like their jobs, but in most cases they worry that there is always more work to do and somebody has to do it.

Like alcoholism (from which the term *workaholism* was derived), this disease redefines the individual's quality of life as a daily dependence—in this case, dependence on work. And like the alcoholic, the workaholic is perhaps best understood as someone suffering from a disease. (Note: *disease* can also be understood as "dis-ease," a condition brought about by feeling deeply uncomfortable with the way things are.)

Although our society has made positive strides toward understanding alcoholism as a disease and the alcoholic as a victim, there is still a tendency to blame the victim for having the disease. The same is true of workaholics. We see a person who dedicates his or her life—often at the expense of health, family, and friendships—to the job as someone who has *decided* to behave in this way. In some cases, organizations employing workaholics see their hard work and long hours as signs of a close, personal identification with the job and company as well as increased productivity—in other words, as positive, desirable attributes.

Recently, however, some organizational theorists (see Alvesson, 1987; Deetz, 1991; Karasek, 1979) have proposed a new and different way of understanding workaholism as a "dis-ease," a condition brought about by the profound influences organizations have over our definitions of who we are, what we do, and our sense of self-worth and self-esteem. These theorists argue that *organizational power structures*—particularly the power structures inherent to organizational bureaucracies—and the adult/child dependence fostered by these "rational" work arrangements tend to destabilize individual personalities and produce unhealthy dependencies. Specifically, unhealthy work conditions tend to include:

1. Authoritarian and detailed supervision.
2. Tasks characterized by severe restrictions on employees' abilities to utilize resources.
3. Work production systems that do not provide opportunities for employees to contribute initiative, responsibility, or personal knowledge to the job.
4. Limited opportunities for employees to exercise influence on the planning or organization of tasks.
5. Tasks that deprive the individual of the self-determination of work rate and methods of carrying out the work.
6. Tasks that limit human contacts during work.

Furthermore, studies have shown that structures of power and everyday working conditions that deprive individuals of the ability to make decisions—and yet require high levels of performance or output—correlate highly with symptoms of depression, irritation, and anxiety (see Karasek, 1979; Katz & Kahn, 1978).

Clearly, to define an overworked, unhealthy person as a workaholic is in many ways like blaming the victim for the dis-ease. These symptoms of dis-ease that tend to be fostered by unhealthy working environments, dependent power structures, and rigid control of tasks and relationships are *ethical* problems. Put simply—as organizational theorist Stan Deetz poignantly argues—"It is wrong

─────────────────────── **ETHICS BOX 1.1** (*continued*) ───────────────────────

to knowingly do physical or psychological harm to others" (1991, p. 38). Given Deetz's statement, consider these ethical questions:

1. Do organizations intentionally or unintentionally reward unhealthy, but potentially productive, behavior as a way of maximizing worker output?
2. If you were a manager and suddenly realized that your organization rewarded unhealthy employee behavior, what steps could you take to do something about it? What new questions would you have to ask? Who would you take these issues to?
3. If you were an employee and discovered that the above list of unhealthy conditions was prevalent at your work site, what could you do about it? Who would you talk to?
4. Assume you work in a company where there is a workaholic. Assume further that workaholics, like alcoholics, cannot do anything about their disease until they admit they have a problem. Do you—as a co-worker or manager or friend—have an ethical obligation to help this person understand her or his problem? What would you do?

time have a rewarding personal life. Bit by bit, businesses are moving to accommodate these desires with sponsored child care, flexible working hours, and parental leave (Moskowitz & Townsend, 1991; Zedeck & Mosier, 1990).

Still, not all companies are similarly inclined, and some have shown something of a backlash. A general manager of a giant computer company once told us that he was tired of all the "dead wood" who left at 4:30 and acted as if they had assured jobs until they retired. "There are going to be some changes made," he vowed. "If a project needs to get done, I expect people to stay here around the clock to do it, even if it means days here without sleep." Maybe—but who's going to change the diapers?

Meaning and the Democratization of the Workplace   Not all the new values being espoused today involve a retreat from work. In fact, some involve a transformation of work from drudgery to a site of meaning and significance. Predictably, people want to feel that the time they spend on the job is worthwhile, and not just a way to draw a paycheck. A lot of misconceptions have arisen over this point. Often, white-collar workers and college students believe that blue-collar workers are motivated primarily by money, job security, and benefits. Actually, friendly co-workers and a supportive boss are far more important incentives to all workers. Opportunities to participate in decisions and the quality of interpersonal relationships at work are major determinants of job satisfaction; without them, stress and burnout may result (Miller et al., 1990). Work has considerable social significance for most Americans, who spend far more time on the job than they do with their families. Even when a person dislikes their co-workers, they comprise a significant network of support.

Work, Identity, and Meaning   Work relationships are more important to one's well-being than most people realize. Perhaps this is why so many people become ill or die soon after retiring or being laid off. They have lost their sense of belonging, their sense of identity. Some people continue driving to work long after they have retired, because they don't know where else to go—or more to the point, who else to be. The movement to enrich the meaning of work is, therefore, strong, though often unrecognized. It shows up in the informal connections people make to get work done; in the strong informal groups that form over long periods of time that, by their actions, determine how things "really work around here"; and in the significant emphasis on and desire for input into decision making. For work to be meaningful, employees must feel that they are respected and that their opinions matter; for reasons we will enumerate, both are rare in business today.

Popular wisdom holds that power in organizations is being shared more with employees, that decisions are being delegated to lower levels, and that managers are allowing employees considerable input into how they do their jobs. In many cases, however, work does not get done this way. True, some managers have had good experiences with sharing power with employees, facilitating semiautonomous work teams or process improvement teams in their organizations (Lawler, 1986). Undoubtedly, this is the right direction for business to take. Unfortunately, however, day-to-day management realities present formidable obstacles to real democratization and empowerment.

One specific obstacle is management style. Managers with the most power today—people mainly in their fifties—learned their jobs the old-fashioned way, which meant "be direct," stay "in control," and "kick ass and take names" if people don't comply. This style worked well when the labor pool was broader and it was possible to succeed simply by working harder and longer. It doesn't work very well anymore, but old styles die hard. Change is especially difficult when the managers in question are under extreme pressure from their superiors. Even under the best conditions, it's hard to surrender control over an operation, especially if a mistake might cost the manager his or her job.

A more subtle example of the conflict between democratization and management control is provided in the manufacturing department of a major U.S. defense contractor. This company is committed to employee involvement and teamwork, but like most of its competitors, it is engaged in a struggle for survival. A major advantage this company had was the low cost of its products. It had been able to keep costs low because the manufacturing manager had broken down every job into its smallest components, hired the least skilled employees and worked them as hard as he could. From a purely economic standpoint, his strategy worked—but was it the right thing to do? Or more to the point, were these cost-cutting efforts at survival in conflict with an empowered, team-based environment?

Empowerment   Practically speaking, empowerment is the biggest part of a manager's job. This process involves giving employees sufficient direction to know *where* they are going, but leaving choices about *how* to get there largely in their hands. After all, organizations instituted hierarchical division of labor to expand on the amount of work a simple collection of individuals working independently could do. The cardinal mistake that overcontrolling managers make is failing to trust employees enough to empower them to do their work. Managers who fail to empower employees inevitably end up micromanaging every detail of their employees' work, (i.e., doing both their own and the employees' jobs), which makes employees resentful.

Empowerment is one of the most critical processes in organizations, but it is also one of the most difficult to achieve. First, the manager has to have the communication skills to provide employees with clear direction while at the same time leaving specified areas of freedom for creativity. This is what Peters and Waterman (1982) call managing the loose-tight paradox. In addition, managers must first be empowered by *their* bosses before they can in turn empower their employees. If a supervisor is given no latitude in doing her job, how can she give the employee any in his?

Empowerment and Trust   No employee can tolerate being treated as if he or she is stupid and cannot be trusted. For example, a middle-manager at a bank once told us: "My secretary insists on reading and commenting on every letter I write! She wants to know what the context is for everything she does!" Our reaction was: "Of course she does. She is—and wishes to be treated like—an intelligent human being. What you have is a blessing, a person who wants more information to make her work meaningful. Take advantage of it." Besides, the person who actually does the job usually knows best how to improve it.

Empowerment and Identification   In the next few decades, there will be an accelerated reduction in the kinds of jobs that don't require humans to do them. The positive side of automation is its elimination of jobs that lack personal significance. For work to be meaningful, employees must be given the opportunity to think, and to voice their opinions. Whenever possible, an employee or team of employees should be able to complete a whole product or service. Failing this, when people understand "the big picture"—where their work fits into the whole product or service the company pro-vides—it gives them pride, allows them to identify with the company, and enables them to talk about what they do in significant terms.

In the near future, efforts to make work more meaningful and rewarding will be commonplace. The most productive workers are balanced, motivated individuals whose brains are switched on. When the new standard is "work smarter, not harder," the employee best able to do so must both feel appreciated and capable of acting from a stable personal foundation. In the short run, broader participation in decision making will not be easily achieved, as managers learn the value of consulting with employees and employ-ees come to feel freer about speaking up to management. In the long run, however, greater empowerment may be an inevitable result of economic pressures. As one senior manager of an electronics firm said: "I can't manage this place anymore. Maybe my employees can." Table 1.1 is a summary of the continuities, changes, and new values and priorities affecting organizations today.

Who Can Afford to Prioritize?   For many people, any sort of prioritization of work, family, or personal needs is an unimagined (and perhaps unimaginable) luxury. These people would laugh at much of what we have written so far. "Sure," they might say, "I want all these things, more input into decisions at work, more time for myself, more time with family and friends, but it's impossible. My boss is a jerk and I really need this job."

Our discussion of the quality of work life ought to be seen in light of the fact that many workers are subemployed, unemployed, or just barely employed. Today millions of people in the United States—men, women, and children—live below the poverty line. At the same time that we struggle to make work more meaningful, we should also aspire to improve the working and living conditions of those at the very bottom of the economic ladder. One of our new priorities about work should include improving the experience of work for *everyone*.

TABLE 1.1

SUMMARY OF THE CONTINUITIES, CHANGES, AND NEW VALUES AND PRIORITIES
AFFECTING THE WORLD OF WORK

THEME: Answers to questions about organizational communication are highly situated and relatively perishable.

Continuities	Changes	New Values and Priorities
Success in business has always been hard-won and hard to maintain. (Most businesses fail; only 4% of those in business in 1900 are still operating.)	Increased competitive pressures (lack of slack due to lack of "fat"; no room for complacency under market demands for continuously improving quality).	Old answers no longer work (big is not necessarily better; must accomplish more with less).
Persistent antagonism between the economic concerns of companies and the personal concerns of employees. (Can a business be both pro-profit and pro-people?)	Focus on quality and customer service (increased stress due to tension between detailed planning and immediacy of responding).	Recovery from "workaholism" (individuals and families plan for more balanced lives).
	Turbulent organizational environments (unexpected interdependencies; new reliance on boundary spanners, learning, and information; shifting power bases—not money but what to do with it; power of network relationships; multiculturalism).	Meaning and democracy in the workplace (demand for personally meaningful work experiences and democracy of decision making in organizations).
	Globalization (expanded markets and increased competition; differences in trade policies; *stake*holders replacing *stock*holders; new ethical and moral implications for doing business; inadequately educated labor pool).	Work, identity, and meaning (work relationships are important to well-being; move to enrich work experiences is constrained by traditional management styles).
		Empowerment of employees and managers (don't overcontrol; new dependence on mutual trust; need for employees to identify with the organizations they work for). Who can afford to prioritize? (not everyone has the economic freedom to make choices or seek empowerment).

WHY STUDY ORGANIZATIONAL COMMUNICATION?

The best reason to study organizational communication is to produce knowledge of the field that will permit everyone to play an active role in inventing the future. Too many people are content to live in daily frustration about red tape, dead-end careers, and lousy customer service. A better response is to remove some of the mystery from these things, and to retake control over the time we spend in organizations, which is, after all, most of our lives.

More specifically, a knowledge of organizational communication allows us to accomplish at least five useful objectives. First, it better equips us to ask informed questions about everyday business practices, such as why a person can't get a straight answer about a student loan. Second, it helps develop communication skills that are highly valued by others and will improve one's chances of success. Third, this information can improve the quality of work life through an enhanced understanding and application of knowledge about what makes work more satisfying. Fourth, it helps develop empathy for others who work at varying levels in different industries, empathy for their trials, frustrations, and triumphs. And fifth, knowledge and skill in communication can be applied to further promote organizational effectiveness.

SUMMARY

Studying organizational communication in the 1990s requires attention to historical continuities; to global political, economic, and social changes; and to the evolution of new values and priorities among employees. Given this turbulent background, old "stable" ways of doing business—and of communicating to get the job done—don't work very well, and the new questions we need to ask are highly situated and relatively perishable.

The substance of everyday organizational life is communication. The challenge of effective organizational communication poses an intriguing, evolving, meaning-centered quest for understandings and practices that can help us improve our everyday organizational lives. To do this requires achieving a productive balance between our individual needs for creativity and organizational demands for order. Human communication serves as the symbolic fulcrum on which the demands for balancing creativity and constraint are negotiated.

Why study communication as a source of symbolic leverage in a world of real organizational change? In addition to attaining an intellectual appreciation for how these changes have come about, the study of organizational communication offers the opportunity to learn how to ask informed questions, develop communication skills, improve the quality of work life, develop empathy for others who work, and promote organizational effectiveness. The study of communication, therefore, combines theory and application in ways that speak directly to one's personal experience of work life.

CASE STUDY

What Questions Should Anne Ask Now?

BACKGROUND

Anne Stone is a senior manager for a computer firm that produces IBM-compatible software. Her area of expertise is music learning systems that are manufactured primarily for schools and daycare centers. Since 1985, when the line of software was introduced, she has witnessed steady growth in her department to keep up with the burgeoning demand. Competition has been minimal, primarily because her chief competitor produced MAC-compatible software (not IBM). Both products, while essentially similar, were market-specific items that could not really compete with each other owing to their machine-dedicated architecture.

This year Anne has had to face the fact that the new generation of PCs is capable of reading either IBM or MAC software. Not only does this mean a dramatic increase in competition between the two firms now marketing essentially the same product, but it also means that Anne must downsize and restructure her department to cut costs and make it leaner. Because of her relatively small product line (in comparison with the rest of the company) and steady but modest profits, she fears that a decision may be made at the highest levels of the company to do away with her product line, and perhaps with it, Anne's job.

Anne is in a tough position, but she is used to finding creative solutions to problems and has no intention of giving up what she has spent the last several years developing and improving. She knows her counterpart at the MAC-compatible company is in the same position with her firm.

Anne has retained your services as a consultant. Using the data below, your task is to help her figure out what she needs to do.

DATA

Anne's department consists of 15 employees:

1 Administrative Assistant to Anne
10 Software Engineers (3 Senior Engineers on Software Development and Refinement Team; 4 Documentation Specialists/Software Engineers and 3 Documentation Specialists on Technical Documentation Team)
1 Secretary/Word Processing Operator to the Software Engineers
2 Marketing Specialists (1 for Current Accounts; 1 Telemarketing and Direct Mail)
1 Secretary to the Marketing Specialists

Anne runs a user-friendly office, but prefers to maintain a rather strict chain of command. When you asked her to draw an organizational chart for her department, this is what she produced:

Anne Stone, Senior Manager
Eva Johannson, Administrative Assistant

Software Development and Refinement Team	Technical Documentation Team	Marketing Specialists
Manuel Gonzalez, Senior Engineer	Candace Williams, Documentation Specialist/ Software Engineer	Phil Davis, Current Accounts
Carol Jones, Senior Engineer	Robert Noriega, Documentation Specialist/ Software Engineer	Brad Ellis, Telemarketing and Direct Mail
Al Alberts, Senior Engineer	Marie Culbertson, Documentation Specialist/ Software Engineer	
	Frank Fitzsimmons, Documentation Specialist/ Software Engineer Engineer	
	Eddie Smith, Documentation Specialist	
	Fran Jacobs, Documentation Specialist	
	Lincoln Forbes, Documentation Specialist	

Vivian Edwards, Secretary   Mark Phillips, Secretary

Anne also explains that there has been some difficulty between the Software Development Team and the Technical Documentation Team. She sees this as "part of what happens in this kind of department" because of "status differences between engineers and documentation specialists," and because of "language differences." The Marketing Specialists stay out of any conflicts between the two teams, and the two men plus their secretary have formed a tight-knit group. Anne feels that communication among the groups is "good, but could be improved."

Anne also defines herself as a perfectionist. She arrives at work early, stays late, and often works at the office or at home on weekends. She thinks that her closest allies in the department are Manuel and Candace because they, too, share this level of commitment to their work. Often these three go out to lunch or dinner together, something Anne seldom does with other members of her department.

Finally, Anne explains that she believes (although she has no direct evidence) that her competitor at the MAC-compatible firm has been recruiting her senior software engineers. She also suspects that the people in Marketing see what is happening in the industry and are probably making new plans for the future. Nobody talks about any of this, but she senses it. "Things have changed," she sighs.

SITUATING
ORGANIZATIONAL
COMMUNICATION

The illusion of novelty is a perceptual impairment associated with historical innocence. It can induce, for example, the supposition that the concepts studied by contemporary researchers—empathic listening, accuracy of serial transmission, superior-subordinate relations, and the like—are inventions of the twentieth century. . . . A persuasive argument can be made that the world's first bureaucracies—staffed as they were by armies of scribes generating untold thousands of written records—were the administrative organizations established under the pharaohs of ancient Egypt.

Especially noteworthy is the fact that the oldest surviving literary work should be a book on communication and human relations in the organizational context: The *Precepts* of Ptahhotep.

—*W. C. Redding & Philip Tompkins, 1988, p. 8*

Questions about organizational communication are as old as humanity. In the above quote, W. Charles Redding and Philip Tompkins argue that issues of most interest to communicators—concerning how and when to speak and listen to others—have changed very little throughout history. As noted in Chapter 1, answers about effective communication have come and gone while key questions endure. James G. March (1965) makes a similar observation: "In many respects, Dale Carnegie appears to have been rediscovering the truths of Machiavelli. And if one reads a treatise on management by a modern-day successful manager, one is frequently struck by the extent to which Aristotle probably said it better and apparently understood it more" (p. xiii). It is not hard to see why organizational communication should be an ongoing concern. Humans coordinate their activities to accomplish goals, whether they be hunting, gathering, cooking, caring for children, or building airplanes. We are social and symbolic animals and are distinguishable from other creatures in our reliance on language as a means of relating to and controlling our physical and social environment. The use of language to communicate with others to achieve coordinated action is at the core of what it means to be a functional human being.

But while the focus on communication has endured, approaches to understanding communication have changed over time. This chapter traces these changes beginning with information transfer models of communication and concluding with a model of organizational communication as dialogue.

APPROACHING ORGANIZATIONAL COMMUNICATION: EVOLVING DEFINITIONS

Definitions are never true or false; they are only more or less useful. Literally hundreds of definitions of the term *communication* have been offered over the years, and each has served a purpose for its adherents. This section organizes these definitions into meaningful groups that reflect the most influential approaches. Specifically, we identify four major definitions of communication that are applicable to organizations: (1) communication as *information transfer;* (2) communication as *transactional process;* (3) communication as *strategic control;* and (4) communication as *balancing creativity and constraint.*

Definition One:
Communication as Information Transfer

Communication is most commonly visualized as a metaphorical pipeline through which information is transferred from one person to another (Axley, 1984; Reddy, 1979). A manager has communicated well when he or she has transferred what is in his or her head to a subordinate, with minimal spillage along the way (Eisenberg & Phillips, 1991). Steven Axley (1984) concludes that most talk about communication in English contains one or more of the following assumptions:

1. Language *transfers* thoughts and feelings from person to person.
2. Speakers and writers *insert* thoughts and feelings in words.
3. Words *contain* the thoughts and feelings.
4. Listeners or readers *extract* the thoughts and feelings from the words (p. 429).

These assumptions form the basis of the conduit metaphor of communication, which reflects the instrumental, machinelike view of organizations as complex tools that individuals use to accomplish their goals and objectives. It is also in line with what Redding and Tompkins (1988) call the formulary-prescriptive phase of development of organizational communication; during this phase, clear, one-way communication was emphasized as a means of impressing and influencing others. This perspective is typically defined as follows: "Communication is the exchange of information and the transmission of meaning, and it is the lifeblood of an organization" (Dessler, 1982, p. 94).

This first perspective on communication has been further characterized as the information engineering approach. In this approach, information is regarded as a tool for accomplishing goals, but the actual process of transmission is not seen as problematic; that is, "if I say it, and you can hear it, you ought to understand it" (Feldman & March, 1981). From this point of view, we might say that *miscommunication* occurs either when no message is received (e.g., due to some distracting psychological or physical noise), or when the message that is received is not what the sender intended. Approached this way, typical communication problems include information overload, distortion, and ambiguity.

Information overload (Farace, Monge, & Russell, 1977) occurs when the receiver is overwhelmed by the information he or she has to process. Three sources of problems contribute to overload: (1) amount, or the absolute quantity of information to be processed; (2) rate, or the speed at which the information presents itself; and (3) complexity, the amount of work it takes to interpret and process the information. It is easy to imagine different kinds of overload situations that vary along these dimensions. A government worker in a severely understaffed bureaucracy, for example, may have to deal with mountains of simple, steady work. In contrast, a police officer on patrol is faced with varying amounts of complex information that often come in at a lightning-fast rate.

Distortion refers to what happens when noise interferes with the receiver's ability to process the message. Noise can be (1) semantic (i.e., the words of the message have different meanings for sender and receiver); (2) physical (i.e., outside interferences exist such as doors slamming, static on the telephone line, or jets passing overhead; or (3) contextual (i.e., the sender and receiver have differing frameworks or perspectives that contribute to miscommunication between them).

Finally, ambiguity is the presence of multiple possible interpretations for a message that make it difficult for a receiver to determine what the sender intended. Ambiguity is inevitable given the nature of language and meaning. Abstract language is open to multiple interpretations (e.g., "truth," "beauty," or "good job") and the most important meanings people have for words are not in the dictionary but in their own connotations. For this reason telling each of two employees to work a little bit harder could result in one putting in an extra half-hour a day and the other working all night long.

David Berlo (1960) offered a communication model that reflects the information engineering approach. According to Berlo's SMCR model, communication occurs when a sender (S) transmits a message (M) through a channel (C) to a receiver (R). The sender encodes an intended meaning into words; the receiver decodes the message when he or she receives it. Berlo was by no means the sole proponent of this view. In his best-selling management textbook, Keith Davis (1972) offered a similar definition: "Two-way communication has a back-and-forth pattern similar to the exchange of play between tennis players. The speaker sends a message, and the receiver's responses come back to the speaker."

The information transfer model can be used to explain a supervisor giving an employee instructions for doing a task. Imagine that an advertising agency has just received a new food account. The senior account representative calls a meeting and gives assignments to the junior people to put together some initial ideas for the client. One of the junior people on the team has trouble figuring out what is required of him because his boss is very disorganized in his presentation, and people keep coming in and out of the room, interrupting the meeting. When the due date rolls around, none of the assignments has been completed. Communication is said to have broken down because the meaning intended by the sender (in this case the senior representative) didn't get through clearly to the junior employee.

The first criticism of the information transfer approach is that it is overly simple and incomplete, and makes communication appear to be one-way, or at best sequential—that is, "I throw you a message, then you throw one back." A second perceived problem of this model is that it sees the message receiver as passive and uninvolved in constructing the meaning of the message. Like Alice in Wonderland, it assumes that words mean exactly what (the sender) wants them to mean, no more, no less. These dissatisfactions with the information transfer approach to communication led to the development of the transactional model.

Definition Two:
Communication as Transactional Process

The transactional view begins with the assertion that in actual communication situations, rarely are clear distinctions made between senders and receivers. People play both roles and often at the same time. "All persons are engaged in sending (encoding) and receiving (decoding) messages simultaneously. Each person is constantly sharing in the encoding and decoding processes, and each person is affecting the other" (Wenberg & Wilmot, 1973, p. 5). This approach highlights the importance of feedback (information about how a message was received), and in particular of nonverbal feedback, which either accompanies or substitutes for verbal feedback.

A familiar example is the messages students send to the teacher (verbally and nonverbally) during a lecture to indicate their degree of attention and comprehension. The importance of nonverbal communication is perhaps best captured by Watzlawick et al.'s (1967) famous axiom: "You cannot not communicate." By this they mean that even when a person is sitting down saying nothing, he or she is communicating something nonverbally through silence. Or to put it differently: Any behavior is a potential message (Redding, 1972).

The transactional model differs significantly from the information transfer approach because of the presumed location of the meaning of the message. In the information transfer model, the meaning of a given message resides with the person sending the message, and the challenge of communication is to transmit this meaning to another individual or group. The transactional model rejects this idea and focuses instead on the person receiving the message, and particularly on the construction of meanings for messages in the listener's mind (Axley, 1984). Thus, an expression commonly associated with the transactional approach is: "Meanings are in people, not words" (Richards, 1936). This shift in emphasis from the sender of the message to the interpretive processes of receivers reveals why misunderstandings are so common. Steven Axley (1984) goes so far as to say that "Miscommunication is the normal state of affairs in human communication . . . miscommunication and unintentional communication are to be expected, for they are the norm" (p. 432).

One area in which the transactional model might be fruitfully applied is leadership. As we describe later, ideas about leadership have evolved significantly from the belief that certain people are born leaders, to the acknowledgment that leadership is a relationship or transaction between a leader and his or her followers. In other words, a leader's ability to lead is a function of his or her ability to mobilize the meanings that followers have in their own minds for what the leader says or does. Leadership is the transactional management of meaning between leaders and followers.

One persistent criticism of the transactional view is its emphasis on the creation of shared meaning through communication (Bochner, 1982; Eisenberg, 1984; Parks, 1982). For example: "Human communication is the process of constructing shared realities—

creating shared meanings" (Shockley-Zalabak, 1991, p. 29), or: Communication is "shared meaning created among two or more people through verbal and nonverbal transaction" (Daniels & Spiker, 1991, p. 46). Critics of this approach hold that the bias toward clarity, openness, and shared meanings is based more on ideology than on empirical reality. Moreover, not only is degree of shared meaning ultimately unverifiable, but also much organizational communication is characterized by ambiguity, deception, and diversity of points of view (Conrad, 1985; cf. Eisenberg, 1984; Weick, 1979).

Definition Three:
Communication as Strategic Control

Implicit in the transactional model of communication is the presumption that effective communicators are usually clear and open in their efforts to promote understanding and shared meaning. Alternatively, the strategic control perspective (Parks, 1982) regards human communication as a tool individuals use for controlling their environment. In contrast to earlier models, it recognizes that in many situations, for personal, relational, or political reasons, greater clarity is not the only or even the main goal in interaction. The strategic perspective sees communicators as having multiple goals in situations. In a performance review, for example, a supervisor might want both to be clearly understood *and* preserve a positive working relationship (Goodall et al., 1986). From this perspective, a competent communicator is one who chooses strategies appropriate for the situation and consequently accomplishes multiple goals. In addition, this perspective recognizes that, although people often have reasons for their behavior, they should not be expected to communicate in any objectively rational way. Communicative choices—who to tell what, how much to tell, what kind of data to share, and what to hide—are socially, politically, and ethically motivated. We expect others to break the communicative rules of clarity and honesty when it is in their own best interests to do so (Conrad, 1985; Okabe, 1983).

Recognizing the limits of overly general, prescriptive statements about what constitutes effective communication, researchers began focusing on communication as goal-attainment, as accomplishing one's ends through adaptation and saying what is appropriate for the situation (Phillips & Wood, 1982; Wood, 1977). Communicators must be "rhetorically sensitive" (Hart & Burks, 1972) and be both able to read the constraints of the situation and adapt to multiple goals simultaneously, such as being clear, assertive, and respectful of the other person (Tracy & Eisenberg, 1991).

An extended example of the strategic perspective applied to organizational communication deals with the strategic use of ambiguity (Eisenberg, 1984). This concept describes the ways in which individuals may be unclear and still accomplish their goals. Specifically, strategic ambiguity

1. Promotes unified diversity
2. Preserves privileged positions
3. Is deniable
4. Facilitates organizational change

Strategic ambiguity takes advantage of the diversity of meanings that people often give to the same message. Unified diversity can be encouraged by an organization's mission statement. A statement like "Quality is Job One" is sufficiently ambiguous so that all employees at Ford can read their own meanings into it. By contrast, a more specific statement (e.g., "Quality through cutting-edge engineering") is much less inclusive and less likely to inspire unity, particularly in the manufacturing and administrative ranks of the company.

Ambiguity preserves privileged positions by shielding persons with power from close scrutiny. A seasoned diplomat or professor emeritus giving a speech, for example, is traditionally given the benefit of the doubt by supporters who fill in the blanks when he or she speaks. By being less than clear, employees can protect confidentiality, avoid conflict, and not reveal key information that may afford a competitive advantage. In this sense strategic ambiguity is deniable: the words that are used seem to be saying something, which under pressure, can be made to appear to mean something else.

Finally, ambiguity can facilitate organizational change by allowing groups and individuals the interpretive room to change their activities while appearing to remain consistent. A good example comes from the history of transatlantic ocean liners. With the advent of air travel, companies that provided overseas passage by ship were faced with a major challenge to their service. Those firms that defined themselves as *transportation* found themselves quickly out of business. Those firms that saw their business more broadly (and ambiguously) as *entertainment* survived and developed vacation or leisure cruises. McDonalds' commitment to becoming the "world's community restaurant" is similarly ambiguous and has created the possibility for many other businesses other than food, such as their new children's playgrounds "Leaps and Bounds."

Contrary to previous perspectives, the strategic view is specifically opposed to shared meaning as the primary basis or motivation for communication. Quite to the contrary, this approach maintains that shared meaning is an empirically unverifiable concept (Krippendorff, 1985) and that the primary goal of communication should be organized action, not shared understanding (Donnellon, Gray, & Bougon, 1986; Eisenberg, 1986, 1990; Eisenberg & Riley, 1988). If we accept the idea that the meaning one person creates may not correspond to the meaning that another person gives to the same communication, it is less important that the two people fully understand or agree with each other than it is that they act in mutually satisfying ways.

Although the strategic control perspective materially advances our appreciation of the subtleties of communication, it is not without significant problems. First, this perspective minimizes the importance of ethics. While strategic ambiguity is commonplace in organizations, it is often used to escape blame. Along these lines, *Fortune* magazine quoted an executive's definition of effective communication: "All you have to remember is . . . let the language be ambiguous enough that if the job is successfully carried out, all credit can be claimed, and if not, a technical alibi [can] be found" (Whyte, 1948).

A second important limitation of the strategic approach is its strong emphasis on the behavior of individuals—on an individual controlling his or her environment through communication—often at the expense of the community. The focus on individuals blinds us to systemic issues of cooperation, coordination, power and inequality, and in general to the interdependencies that exist among individuals and groups. Of the two, this criticism concerning individual bias has been the more damaging. The strategic control model suggests that the world is comprised of independent communicators, each working

ETHICS BOX 2.1

THE ETHICS OF QUALITY: ORGANIZATIONAL AMBIGUITY IN ACTION

The strategic uses of ambiguity can have positive or negative influences on the quality of organizational life. Viewed positively, for example, strategic ambiguity can encourage individuals to define corporate vision statements, objectives, and goals in personal and often productive ways. When Ford says "Quality is Job One," everyone from line assembly workers to top management is encouraged to take the initiative to ensure that every aspect of their jobs involves quality, and that attaining quality is their first and foremost priority.

On the other hand, ambiguous statements used to define performance objectives can have negative or prejudicial applications. *Quality* is, after all, an ambiguous term. Left solely to the discretion of individual managers and employees to define and to use to guide work decisions, the term can and does lead to misunderstandings. Similarly, because rewards based on quality attainments are still subject to organizational power relationships, there remains the potential for abuse through favoritism and inequitable applications of quality standards.

These general issues raise important ethical dimensions for communication. Consider the following questions:

1. Assume you are a manager charged with the responsibility for implementing a Total Quality Commitment program in your company. You have taken a preparatory training seminar and learned that part of what makes quality programs work well is the ability of those who implement them to leave determinations of quality standards to employees. You worry that if you follow this prescription there will be differences of opinion among employees about what constitutes quality and how it should be measured. What steps could you take to make productive use of the ambiguity while preserving equity among employees? Should the process begin with your definition of quality or not? Why?

2. Assume you work for a company that has recently adopted a Total Quality Commitment program. Your boss is unhappy about this decision because he sees it as "just another fashion statement," a way to "jump on the Quality bandwagon." He tells you, privately, that he intends to sabotage the program by using it to reward only those employees who work overtime and weekends. He believes that he can use this plan to make employees see how ridiculous this ambiguous term is, and why the company should return to the tried-and-true old ways of managing performance. You are shocked because of his devious plan but also because you believe the program will improve the workplace. Do you have an ethical obligation to confront him with your feelings? Do you have an ethical obligation to inform co-workers about his intentions? Do you have an ethical obligation to report him to his superiors? What would you do?

to control his or her own environment. It also implies, much as the transactional model does, that meaning is something that exists in people's heads. The strategic control perspective overemphasizes both the role and the power of individuals to create meaning through communication. For a summary of the three definitions of communication discussed to this point, see Table 2.1, page 28.

TABLE 2.1

SUMMARY OF EVOLVING DEFINITIONS OF ORGANIZATIONAL COMMUNICATION:
PRELIMINARY PERSPECTIVES

Communication as Information Transfer	Communication as Transactional Process	Communication as Strategic Control
Metaphor: Pipeline or conduit; sender transmits a message to a receiver.	*Metaphor:* Process; communication is a process that creates relationships; "You cannot not communicate."	*Metaphor:* Control; individuals attempt to control their environments.
Assumptions: (1) Language transfers thoughts and feelings from person to person; (2) speakers and writers insert thoughts and feelings into words; (3) words contain the thoughts and feelings; and (4) listeners or readers extract the thoughts and feelings from the words.	*Assumptions:* (1) There are rarely clear distinctions between senders and receivers; (2) nonverbal feedback accompanies or substitutes for verbal messages; (3) meanings are in people, not words.	*Assumptions:* Strategic ambiguity gains control because it (1) promotes unified diversity, (2) preserves privileged positions, (3) is deniable, and (4) facilitates organizational change.
Description: Source transmits a message through a channel (air or light) to a receiver. Communication is instrumental—a tool people use to accomplish objectives.	*Description:* Person receiving the message constructs its meaning; idea is for senders to adapt their messages to the needs and expectations of their listeners.	*Description:* Strategic ambiguity takes advantage of the diversity of meanings people often give to the same message; choices of what to say are socially, politically, and ethically motivated; strategies can be selected to accomplish multiple goals.
Measure of effectiveness: Receiver of communication understands (or does) precisely what the speaker intended.	*Measure of effectiveness:* Shared meaning.	*Measure of effectiveness:* Coordinated actions accomplished through diverse interpretations of meanings.
Limitations: (1) Overly simplifies communication: treats transmission of the message as linear/sequential and unproblematic; (2) sees the receiver as a passive receptor uninvolved with the construction of the meaning of the message; (3) does not account for differences in interpretation between speaker and listener.	*Limitations:* (1) Emphasis on shared meaning is problematic and ultimately unverifiable; (2) bias toward clarity and openness denies political realities; (3) does not account for ambiguity, deception, or diversity in points of view.	*Limitations:* (1) Can minimize the importance of ethics; (2) places strong emphasis on individuals over communities; (3) overemphasizes both the role and power of individuals to create meaning through communication.

Definition Four:
Communication as Balancing Creativity and Constraint

Our final approach to communication in organizations is closely linked to sociological theories concerning the individual and society. Since the late 1960s, the central problem in social theory has been the relationship between the individual and society, which is sometimes cast as a tension between micro and macro perspectives. Generally speaking, the macro perspective sees individuals as molded, controlled, ordered, shaped, and constrained by society and social institutions. In contrast, the micro perspective sees individuals as creating society and social systems. From this latter viewpoint, while we no doubt do conform and keep to routines and habits, "we are rule and system *users* and rule and system *breakers* as well" (Wentworth, 1980, p. 40). This perhaps false dichotomy has obvious implications for organizational communication, depending on whether the emphasis is placed on how individuals communicate to create and shape organizations, or on the constraints organizations place on individual communication.

A foundational text in the development of these questions about individual-social relationships is Peter Berger and Thomas Luckmann's *The Social Construction of Reality* (1967). In this book, the authors maintain that social organization is constructed over time as individuals act in patterned ways; then individuals take these patterns for granted as their reality. Few of the things that we take for granted in organizations are in the same category as laws of nature. Indeed, most were created or constructed through symbolic behavior and human choices. Over time, routines develop, and members amass a general stock of knowledge that indicates "how things are done around here." What follows is a never-ending tension between the need to maintain order and the need to promote change (Morrill, 1991).

While other writers have contributed significantly to this line of questioning (e.g., Alexander & Giesen, 1987; Gouldner, 1971; Knorr-Cetina & Cicourel, 1981), Anthony Giddens's (1979) theory of structuration is perhaps most relevant for students of organizational communication. In an attempt to describe the relationships between individual communication and social systems and structures, Giddens focuses on both the creative and constraining aspects of structure, which he calls the duality of structure. The designer of advertising for a new product, for example, is always bound by various rules, norms, and assumptions in the industry. At the same time, it is possible to transcend these existing structures in designing a creative ad. Similarly, the process of putting together a budget for a department is limited by rules of finance and the norms of the organization. At the same time, individuals have latitude in the planning process to suggest creative ways of putting the budget together.

By creative we mean that social systems are literally created through communication. Communication is not a process that goes on inside of organizations; rather, it is how people organize (Barnard, 1968; Farace, Monge, & Russell, 1977; Johnson, 1977). This is not to imply that the process is always deliberate or rational; on the contrary, much of what comes to be taken for granted as organizational reality is an unintended consequence of action. Put differently, although we might want to believe that we create social reality through communication, we only do so in an ironic sense—we rarely get the reality we set out to create (Ortner, 1980). Structuration theory sees human behavior as an unresolvable tension between creativity and constraint. As a result, all people are both determined and free, and while some things change, others will surely stay the same (cf. Eisenberg & Phillips, 1991).

Writing about socialization, William Wentworth (1980) describes the tension between creativity and constraint as a conflict between an under- and oversocialized image of humans. For Wentworth, neither approach offers a complete characterization of the relationships between the individual and society. Instead, socialization is a matter of balancing between creativity and constraint, between constructing social reality and being constrained by these constructions. For Wentworth communication is the primary site of this balancing act.

At this point in our discussion, it is appropriate to introduce our own definition of organizational communication. We believe that *communication is the moment-to-moment working out of the tension between individual creativity and organizational constraint.* When we use the phrase "moment-to-moment working out of the tension" we are referring specifically to the balancing act that positions creativity as a strategic response to organizational constraints and organizational constraints as the constructions of reality that limit our choices of how to make those strategic responses.

Let us focus for a moment on the weekly staff meetings held in most traditional organizations. We attended regular meetings at a company that manufactured hydraulic lifts for use in construction. In these meetings, the company president sat at the head of the table and ran the meeting according to an agenda that he controlled. Most of the talk at these meetings was in the form of short briefings on such topics as major new sales, personnel changes, and capital equipment expenditures. Little actual decision making took place in these sessions because the president would not permit opposing ideas—he saw disagreement as a sign of disloyalty. This was true even though the executives in the room were all experienced and capable decision makers. Such meetings illustrate the ongoing tension between creativity and constraint that exists in organizations, as well as how this tension is constructed through communication. In this case, soon after being hired, new employees heard the president called the "little general" because he embarrassed employees who disagreed with him. Nearly everyone had a similar experience: when they tried to take independent action, they were bullied or abused. Over time, nonconfrontation was taken for granted and employees came to believe this was simply "the way things were." In Berger and Luckmann's terms (1967), what had started out as a human construction had now been reified into accepted organizational reality.

This isn't the end of our story. Although the constraints on communication were strong at this company, not everyone was willing to tow the line. The norm of nonconfrontation is constantly reproduced through communication. This norm was occasionally countered by creative attempts at autonomy and individuation, such as the attempt to introduce a topic that was not on the agenda or to present new data suggesting that some current or past decision by the president was misguided. A videotape of these meetings would show this happening, specifically through such evidence as who spoke and who didn't, about what, in what ways, and when. By observing communication, we can find evidence of creativity and constraint. Rules, norms, and procedures that are taken for granted are either applied and reproduced or challenged and modified in talk.

Earlier we suggested that this balancing act activates creativity as a strategic response to organizational constraints. In our example, the staff members acted on information they already had to guide their choices of when to speak. Unfortunately for them, the president's interpretive framework for constructing reality (e.g., "anyone who objects to what I say is disloyal") limited their strategic choices and ability to respond. Because he was seemingly unable to respond to their initiatives differently, and because they were unable to get him to alter his construction of reality, the balance was tipped toward constraint and away from creativity. Because of this lack of balance, staff meetings were always one-sided affairs characterized by the president's domination and the staff's periodic resistance. Not much was ever accomplished.

Having reviewed the history of definitions of communication from information transfer, to transactional process, to goal-attainment, and now to balance, we wish to take the best concepts from each perspective—for example, context, process, and balance—and develop in more detail our own model of organizations as dialogues. Figure 2.1 on page 32 summarizes our progress thus far.

CREATIVITY AND CONSTRAINT
AS INTERPRETATION IN CONTEXT

This section contains one of the most important points we will make in this book. We have introduced the concept of balance between the individual and the organization. We now make a strong connection between communication as balancing creativity and constraint and the plight of individual employees who are continuously trying to make sense out of what is going on around them. Individuals in organizations develop interpretations of their work lives and, in turn, communicate and act on these dynamic, evolving interpretations. By making this connection, we draw on an intellectual movement called symbolic interactionism. This movement (Blumer, 1969; Mead, 1934) begins with the assumption that life is primarily a search for meaning. Meaning is found in social interaction. In fact, neither who we are nor the whole idea of having a self is ever achieved in isolation.

> The self is not presented to the world in isolation but in consort with other selves. . . .
> This view of a self as an actor within webs of relationships reveals that knowledge
> about the self is always interdependent with knowledge about others. It also reveals the
> centrality of communication as a bridge between or among selves and places at the
> forefront of communication theory the issue of linguistic representation of human
> experience. Knowledge of how a person, a self, interacts with a particular web should
> proceed dialectically within an evolving context (Goodall, 1991, p. 25).

Self, Others, and Contexts:
The Elements of Communication Relationships

Self   The self is constructed out of our social relationships with others and is constituted in language (Bakhtin, 1981; Blumer, 1969; Jackson, 1989; Mead, 1934). According to George Herbert Mead, the self comprises two facets: (1) the "I," or the creative, relatively unpredictable part of a person, and (2) the "me," or the socially constrained, relatively consistent part of the person that is shared with others. The "I" is impulsive; the "me" strives to control the impulsiveness to fit into society. The creative aspect of the self (I)

Metaphor: Balance

Assumptions:

1. The duality of structure: Individuals are molded, controlled, ordered, and shaped by society and social institutions; individuals also create society and social institutions.

2. Communication is the moment-to-moment working out of the tensions between our need to maintain order (constraint) and the need to promote change (creativity) as such, communication is the material manifestation of consciousness of

    a. Institutional constraints

    b. Creative potential

    c. Contexts of interpretation

Representative model:

Creativity ———————————————————————— **Constraint**

Communication

Description:

Creativity	*Communication*	*Constraint*
Interpretations of meanings; all forms of initiative; new ways of organizing tasks and understanding relationships; resistance to institutional forms of dominance; uses of storytelling and dialogue to alter perceptions; uses of social constructions of reality to forge new agreements and shape coordinated actions at work.	Reveals interpretations of contexts; asks questions about resources for creativity and the presence of constraints; suggests the possibility of dialogue.	Social and institutional forms, laws, rules, procedures, slogans, management styles designed to gain compliance and limit dialogue at all costs; top-down decision making and problem solving.

FIGURE 2.1

Communication as Balancing Creativity and Constraint

is the driving force of our actions with others, while the constraining aspect of the self (me) guides and directs those actions.

At the heart of our definition of organizational communication as the balancing of creativity and constraint is how the self interacts with others. The self in communication with others is, therefore, the site of this important balancing act. The balancing is accomplished through speaking the self or giving voice to our experiences. In part this means that a person can see—and respond to—the self as he or she does toward others.

We hold internal conversations with our self, we feel good or bad, happy or sad, about our self, and we try to balance our desire for creativity with our understanding of organizational and social constraints. This is mainly how the self deals with the world. Consider the following related observation: "[A]t the heart of all modes of understanding . . . lies the need to assure ourselves that the world out there is coherent and built on a scale which is compatible with and manageable by us. Only then can we enter into a relationship with it; only then can our sense of self be stabilized" (Jackson, 1989, p. 36).

But the self, however stabilized through our internal conversations, is never fixed. It is constantly revised through our experiences with others. As anthropologist Michael Jackson puts it: "The 'self' cannot, therefore, be treated as a thing among things; it is a function of our involvement with others in a world of diverse and ever-altering interests and situations" (1989, p. 3).

The implications of this definition of the self are important for interpreting organizational communication. First, because the self is constructed out of our need to balance creativity and constraint in our experiences with others, the self is necessarily "dialogic" (Bakhtin, 1981; Goodall, 1991; Holquist, 1990). We engage in conversations at work that affect our perceptions of the constructed social reality. We retell stories that have been told to us by others, and we use and comment on others' constructions of who we are (Blumer, 1969; Laing, 1965). We make use of both real and imagined characters and relationships (Phillips & Goodall, 1983). Our "voice," therefore, is multilayered with the inflections of many different people—co-workers, relatives, friends, teachers, students, enemies, fictional characters, TV stars, heroes, and villains (Conquergood, 1991). Every self in an organization, then, is multidimensional.

A second important aspect of this dialogic view of the self concerns the monitoring of our choices of organizational experiences. As Herbert Blumer puts it, "the actor selects, checks, suspends, regroups, and transforms the meanings in light of the situation in which he [sic] is placed and the direction of his actions" (1969, p. 5). Put another way, because the self is constructed from our experiences with others, those experiences have a great deal to do with the person we become. We try to choose wisely, sometimes asserting ourselves and taking risks, other times retreating to the comfort of known limits. Of course, we don't choose all of our experiences; accidents do happen and inevitably play a part in constructing our future. But where we can exercise judgment and control, we usually do so.

Third, and perhaps most important, a dialogic view of the self encourages us to take communication with others seriously. This does not mean that we must always be serious when engaging in conversation. Rather, it means that we should at least be as concerned about what conversations do to our sense of self—that always delicate balancing act—as we are about what food we put into our bodies. Furthermore, this principle comes equipped with an ethical dimension: "Do unto others (in conversation) what you would have them do unto you." We should realize that other selves are also engaged in a similar balancing act. Consider the following example:

Mark is a friend of ours who works as a systems programmer for Intergraph. He has been with this Fortune 500 company since he graduated from college about ten years ago. During his employment at Intergraph, Mark moved quickly through the ranks, became a manager and then gave up those responsibilities to get back to his heart: customizing large-

scale CAD-CAM (Computer-Aided Design–Computer-Aided Manufacturing) systems for Intergraph's international corporate customers.

Lately, Mark has been concerned about relationships with the other team members at work. On a recent trip to Atlanta, we asked him to talk candidly about those relationships. His description, in our view, typifies some of the major concerns most people have about their work relationships. Here is what he said: "I have enormous respect for our team members. We work in an extraordinarily stressful environment and have a solid track record, but there is always tension among us. I think a lot of this is due to the fact that we are three different people with three different ideas about how to get the job done. Unfortunately, we have to coordinate our work because there is only one way that can be used to write the architecture for the overall program.

"Recently all of this tension came to a head. Sally was in the running to be promoted to a high-level managerial job, and she thought I also wanted it. Truth is, I didn't and had already taken myself out of the competition. I had already been a manager and had no desire to reacquire those responsibilities. But I didn't tell her that. Ortez is the third member of our team, and he is a complete computer junkie. He has no interest in anything other than what he calls intricate, elegant programs, so when the rumor mill had it that he was also in the running for this job, Sally felt surrounded. She felt that she had to prove herself.

"Ortez responded by playing a sort of game with Sally and me. He pretended to want the job, even though we both knew he didn't. All of this happened, by the way, during a crucial stage in a large project, the stage where one of us had to get our way on how the architecture would be written. I tell you honestly that I woke up most mornings dreading to go to work, and this is a job I really, really like.

"I sort of got sucked in to this stupid game. I guess you would say I was just acting in a compliant way. I allowed it to happen, watched it go on, and did nothing very much to stop it. So the conflict escalated. Everything we did or said was subtle, but its broader meanings were clear to all of us. Every comment was scrutinized for some sort of hidden meaning, every move on the project became a battleground. In the end, Sally got the promotion because she would have anyway, Ortez got to lead us through the project, and I ended up trying—after the fact—to heal everyone's wounds. These were—and are—the roles we played for each other.

"Now Sally doesn't trust me. And she feels guilty because she still thinks I wanted the job, no matter what I say about it. So we have this power thing. Ortez has retreated back to the sanctity of his workstation. And it will happen all over again. It always does.

"But this is '90's Atlanta. This is the place where everyone drives as hard and as fast as they can get away with, and it is very uncool to ever honk your horn. The message here is to just deal with it. Maybe this is a metaphor for doing business, or for how we do relationships at work. Just deal with it. I don't know."

In Mark's story we can see three selves struggling to achieve some sense of balance in their work through their experiences and interactions with each other. By playing games with each other, they significantly altered each other's perceptions of work realities, and then they had to deal with what they had constructed. By taking roles that constrained talk among themselves to what was only in their own self-interest, they tipped the balance away from any creativity that could have helped them work out their differences. Individually, each "I" was in internal conflict with each "me"; collectively, the selves expanded the conflict to include all dimensions of their work experiences and feelings about each other.

Mark's example also points out the multidimensional nature of each self. Sally, Ortez, and Mark are all complex individuals. At work, their complexities are multiplied by the demands of work, by the demands they place on each other, and by their individual interpretations of the meanings available within their shared context of interpretations. None of them is entirely "stable," nor are their individual identities completely determined. They achieve selfhood through interactions with each other, which brings us to our second concept: others.

Others   The symbolic interactionist concept of *others* includes much more than simply a mirror image of the self. Over time, our perceptions of others develop out of a relationship between who we are and our experience with others in the world. This relational interpretation of the other is important for two reasons. First, it allows us to locate the other as a complex extension of the self. Consider the following statement:

> The human speaker can speak to the other precisely because he himself [*sic*] is not purely self, but is somehow also other. His own "I" is haunted by the shadow of a "thou" which itself casts and which it can never exorcise. . . . It reveals a rift, a limitation inside our own beings, but a rift which is our only hope of salvation—it is a rift which comes from our being vicariously within ourselves the other with whom we must commune, and who must commune with us, too, and thereby compensates for the rift, the limitation in our persons. The other within must hear all, for he already knows all, and only if the other, this *thou* hears will I become comprehensible to myself (Ong, 1958, pp. 58–59).

How we talk about others says a lot about our deepest sense of self. We construct the other in relation to our conception of self. Although we may like to believe that these constructions of others are individual and creative, they too are constrained by the self's culture (e.g., American, Japanese, European, African), race (e.g., Native American, white, black, Mexican), gender (e.g., female, male), and subconscious. In this sense, then, the self's symbolic construction of the other is always multilayered, partially determined, variously inflected, and dialogic.

The role of others in our understanding of organizations is interesting. Recall from our previous discussion how the information transfer, transactional process, and strategic control models are biased in favor of how a sender (self) acts toward receivers (others). More often than not, the sender was conceptualized as a manager and the other as a subordinate. In this sense, our literature on organizations and communication has long reflected a managerial bias (Putnam, 1982). Employees were viewed as others to be acted on, communicated to, ordered, and controlled rather than as interdependent partners capable of having their own voices with which to influence the organizational dialogue.

Finally, the concept of others as partners to the dialogue contains the important idea of plurality. Plurality refers to the fact that selves and others mutually construct the meanings they have for contexts and for each other. It also refers to the idea, discussed in detail in the following section, that there are always multiple interpretations of any context and that neither the self nor the other alone controls those interpretations. To accept the plurality of interpretations of meaning and the plurality of selves in communication with others is to ask new questions about the idea of contexts.

Context(s)   A context refers to where communication occurs (e.g., the physical setting) and to the interpretive frameworks used to make sense of the exchange between self and other. Because the idea of context is vital to our conception of organizational communication, the following section details (1) how contexts shape interpretations, (2) why mutiple contexts are always available, and (3) what the concept of context tells us about organizational dialogues. There is no meaning without context (Bateson, 1972). If we think of any message as a text, the con-text is information that goes with and helps make sense of the text. For example, if we overheard a friend calling someone we didn't know an "idiot!" how would we know what he or she really meant? We would most certainly need to know more about the relationship between our friend and the other person, and about what was happening just before our friend made the comment. Relationship and situation are two basic aspects of context. If they are close friends, and if they have been teasing each other all day, the comment could easily be seen as a sign of friendship or as one of a personal attack.

The way context works in this simple example is the rule, not the exception. We cannot fully understand the meaning of a message without first examining the relationship, its history, and the immediate situation for clues. This is especially true in organizations, where lines of authority, personal relationships, politics, the business situation, and many other factors can potentially affect the interpretation of any instance of communication.

Individuals in organizations never communicate in isolation—they communicate in contexts. Contexts are not, however, stable. According to the *Oxford English Dictionary*, the term *context* originated as a verb and meant "to weave together, interweave, join together, compose." We favor this older definition because it highlights context as "a verbal process aimed at the manufacture of something . . . the seaming together of otherwise disparate elements, perceptions, fabrics or words, the piecing together of a whole out of the sum of its parts" (Goodall, 1991, p. 64).

When we suggest that individuals communicate in contexts, we are using the term to refer both to the definition a person has of a situation at a given moment in time and to the process of altering this definition over time. Note that this definition reflects the duality of structure. People both create context through communication and are constrained by those contexts once created. (E.g., my impulsive decision to tell off my boss will constrain future interactions I have with her.) Or as Linda Putnam (1985) puts it: "People establish the context, use the context to interpret messages, and use the messages to change the context" (p. 152). Over time, what we define as context becomes our taken-for-granted, constructed reality. So when we say that individuals communicate in context, we mean that individuals communicate in accord with their constructions of reality, their interpretations of the evolving situation.

What we are doing here, somewhat subtly, is redefining what it means to work in an organization. Rather than seeing employees as either a cog in some giant machine or the product of a corporate culture, we believe that a great deal of work is, quite literally, interpretation of contexts. This is perhaps obvious for white-collar jobs, but it applies to blue-collar work as well. How individuals think and talk about work, the relationships between themselves, their work, others in the organization (managers, co-workers), and the enterprise as a whole have a significant impact on their choices for behavior, and ultimately on the performance of the organization.

Ben Hamper's book *Rivethead* (1991), which recounts life in a General Motors factory in Flint, Michigan, provides some examples of how differences in interpretation affect people's actions. This book gives us a look into the lives of factory workers, each of whom sees the plant, their work, and GM differently. There are tough-talking bigoted guys who work hard and follow the rules; even harder-working family men and women who drink themselves into oblivion; and people like Hamper who try to beat the system by keeping a psychological distance. But the message is clear. There is no single definition of work. Instead, each self brings to bear its own context for interpretation, which in turn informs and shapes its behavior. Even so, there are limits to the kinds of interpretations any individual can construct. Organizations are collections of individuals each striving to create meanings, but constrained by contexts constructed in part by other individuals who are similarly engaged in sense-making. Interpretation is what allows us to connect our individual dots to the larger puzzles of the universe. Interpretation is the continuing quest toward making sense of who we are and what we do for a living. Interpretation is not free; it is always constrained by other interpreters.

Imagine that you are a supervisor in a large bank. During lunch break, you accidentally run into one of your employees sobbing in the rest room. What should you do or say? The first challenge is to interpret the situation. You search the room and your memory for context. What do you know about this person that will help make sense of his behavior? There are many possibilities—personal problems, layoffs at work, stress. The point is that the crying itself—and in fact any behavior or communication—makes sense only in context. You suddenly remember that the employee's mother was seriously ill. You inquire about his family and discover that his mother is near death. This context then allows you to offer an appropriate response.

The example doesn't end here. The fact that you have shared this moment will have a profound effect on future interaction. The effect will differ among individuals. Some people would be enormously embarrassed to be caught crying by the boss and might remain aloof in the future. Others might use the occasion to become more friendly. Whatever the outcome, it is clear not only that context is necessary to make sense out of communication, but also that communication constructs the context for making sense of future interactions.

Multiple Contexts and the Situated Individual

Multiple contexts exist for interpreting communication. What are they? Consider this statement from Goran Ahrne:

> From birth every human being is affiliated to a family and a nation-state. Children's first experiences of the exercise of power occur within the family. After some years all children will have to yield to the power of the nation-state in the form of school. Growing up, children will slowly get to know the world outside the family, and the school. Gradually the everyday world will be larger, adolescence being the typical time for activities in groups or gangs of various kinds . . . . Having married and settled down and started to work, people fill their everyday lives with organizational affiliations. In the course of their lives individuals orient themselves within the existing organizations in the social landscape. Every individual attempts to establish a domain within this landscape, balancing between different organizational influences and leaving some unorganized space (Ahrne, 1990, p. 72).

In other words, we grow up and learn about life in relationship to a variety of evolving and related contexts. Each context has its associated constraints—rules, norms, and expected understandings—that make it unique. These constraints play a dual role. First, they limit creativity and individual freedom. Second, each set of constraints (context) suggests a particular construction of reality, and thus assists individual interpretation. If a co-worker leans over and kisses you (against your wishes), it is clear from the business context (rules, norms) that the behavior is inappropriate and a strong reaction on your part is warranted. On the other hand, if a family member does the same thing, the meaning is entirely different, and your response will most likely differ as well.

But now consider the privately held family business, or the husband and wife who work together. Both are examples of interpretation complicated by multiple contexts. We're sure you can imagine the conversations—"Dad, you can talk to me that way at home, but not here in front of the other employees!" or "How could you, my spouse, vote against me in the meeting!" Different contexts suggest different rules for action and interpretation. Even within a small organization, multiple contexts are always available for interpretation.

In conducting performance appraisals, for example, how tough should supervisors be on marginal performers? Seen in the context of the business as a financial entity accountable primarily to shareholders, they should be direct and tough. In a relational context (the relationship between supervisor and employee must go on, and after all, they're only human and make mistakes), one might justify being more understanding. And what if the employee is a member of an underrepresented minority group? Will this (contextual) information affect supervisors' communication, influencing their efforts to avoid being accused of discrimination? Making these kinds of choices—interpreting and communicating in multiple contexts—is the real stuff of organizational life.

This brings us to another key point: All individuals who work are situated in multiple contexts. In a broad sense, this means that behaviors are both guided and constrained by the types of organizations with which we affiliate, whether they be capitalist enterprises, voluntary associations, nation-states, or families (Ahrne, 1990). More specifically, all of our behavior is situated in smaller, more local contexts:

> The situated individual is a person who is constructing the everyday business of the
> maintenance and construction of the social realities in which we live. The situated
> individual is connected to others through a network of shared, mutually negotiated, and
> maintained meanings. These meanings provide location, identity, action, and purpose
> to the individual. They tell me where I am, who I am, what I am doing, how to do it, and
> why. . . . The network of meanings is not independent of the situated individual. It
> is the product of the interaction among situated individuals (Anderson, 1987, p. 268).

Little difficulty is encountered when the multiple contexts impinging on an individual suggest similar or consistent communication or behavior. Things get tough when they suggest conflicting actions. For example, top management of some companies in the United States has spent years cultivating close relationships with their employees. These relationships have resulted in a history of success, loyalty, and commitment. Lately, however, management is being pushed to fire or lay off long-standing employees to remain economically viable. As a manager approaches a conversation with such an employee, she is caught between the business and a more personal context, and no communication is likely to satisfy the demands of both.

A study of Disneyland's corporate culture provides a detailed example of multiple conflicting contexts for interpretation (Smith & Eisenberg, 1987). In the early days of the theme park, employees most often used two metaphors in their speaking—"the show" and the Disney "family." These metaphors were subtle keys to larger contexts. Thinking of Disneyland as a show or drama suggests that employees are actors playing parts. Consequently, they can be scripted by the "director" to act in particular ways because of "box office concerns" (e.g., smile more, cut your hair). Interpreting Disneyland as a family, on the other hand, suggests different and in many cases opposing contexts—that management, like a concerned parent, takes care of its employees and provides a nurturing environment. When Disneyland employees went on strike in the mid-1980s, it was as much over these two conflicting contexts for interpretation—whether work was to be seen as drama or family—as anything else. Recent reports (Van Maanen, 1991) suggest that the drama metaphor won out. Thus, the situated individual communicates in context and assists in the construction of contexts. The situated individual model of organizational communication may be summarized as follows:

1. The individual is an actor whose actions and communication are based on interpretations of contexts.
2. There is always more than one context that can be used to guide action or interpretation.
3. Communication is the sum of action and interpretation and as such can reveal sources of creativity, constraint, meaning, interpretation, and context.

An extended example will clarify the notion of a situated individual. Recently, one of us became involved with a customer service manager at a large travel agency. She asked for help in her struggle to convince her management that she needed a full-time accountant on her staff to assist with financial recordkeeping for customer service billings. Although she had initially received assurances from her boss that she could hire an accountant, she was suddenly told that her request was denied. The problem before her now was how to interpret this denial, and what, if anything, to do about it.

We may make sense out of (i.e., contextualize) this situation in many different ways. From the customer service manager's point of view (call her Laura), the problem was lack of expertise; no one in her department had the skills to do the job. The Finance Department, which was separate from Customer Service, saw the situation differently. The department had been trying to hire an accountant for four years, and it strongly resisted the idea that one might now be hired in Customer Service. Along these lines, rumors had surfaced in Finance about Laura's failings as a manager. The suggestion was that, if she were doing her job properly, she wouldn't need this new position. The general manager of the agency had a completely different view of the situation. For his part, he resisted hiring an accountant in Customer Service simply because none of the other companies he had worked for had one. The Board of Directors of the company saw the issue solely as an economic one: they weren't about to approve any new hires while there was a recession, because they believed it would look bad to the shareholders. Laura's peers took yet a different view. They perceived her as aloof and a loner, and not as a team player. Consequently, no informal group was inclined to help push her agenda to get an accountant. Had she been more involved in informal communication networks, she might not have faced this problem.

Believe it or not, this is a *simple* example of how multiple contexts can inform interpretation of selves, others, and action. The facts remain the same—whether or not to hire an accountant in Customer Service. However, the meanings of those facts are constructed differently depending on the context being applied. Because no one individual has access to all the potential contextual factors, each individual bases his or her own interpretations on a limited understanding of the reality being constructed. The information drawn on to build a context for interpretation is varied, multiple, and always limited. Furthermore, this is as good as it gets; upon close inspection, all the strictly rational models of work dissolve before our eyes. No decision is purely logical, and there is no one best way to do anything. The certainty we associate with any of our choices is not the result of access to any ultimate truth about the "right" way of doing things. All interpretations are, by definition, partial, partisan, and problematic (see Chapter 3 for details).

Fortunately, the limitations of any one person's interpretations are, as a rule, offset by others' perspectives. Sense-making is a social activity, more than one person is always doing the reality construction, and it is through communication that meanings are co-constructed. Individuals trying to coordinate their contexts, interpretations, communication, and actions are said to be organizing. One way of seeing this organizing process is as a dialogue.

ORGANIZATIONS AS DIALOGUES

Human beings are neither entirely social nor entirely private. To be human means to live in between, to establish a sense of self apart from the world (i.e., an identity) and a sense of self as part of the world (i.e., as a member of a community). Individual creativity constructs a sense of self, and social constraints reveal the position of self in relationship to others. Even if we could construct reality on our own, if our personal contexts were to prevail as truth, we would then be totally alone. Conversely, if our contexts for interpretation came entirely from others, we would lose our identity. The critical questions, then, are how we can accomplish both identity and community and how we can walk the narrow ridge between self and other (Buber, 1985). One route may be in dialogue.

Definitions of Dialogue

Continuing our theme of communication as balancing creativity and constraint, we maintain that dialogue is balanced communication, in which individuals each have a chance to speak and to be heard. There are three levels of definition within our conception of dialogue: (1) dialogue as equitable transaction; (2) dialogue as empathic conversation; and (3) dialogue as meeting.

Dialogue as Equitable Transaction   Not everyone in an organization has an equal say in making interpretations count. What is more, in traditional organizations many people are not encouraged to speak at all:

> Early in this century, organizations were quite controlling of communication . . . you
> could not interact with anybody in the organization unless you got permission from the supervisor,
> and then he wanted to know what you were going to talk about. So there's this notion in
> an organization that talking to people is not what your job is, that talking to people
> is interfering with the productivity and the work that has to be done (Evered &
> Tannenbaum, 1992, p. 48).

In organizations, some peoples' voices count more than others. These people are said to have power because they can back up what they say with rewards or sanctions. The extent to which one person has more weight than another in the dialogue is not always obvious to observers. This is because a deeper exercise of power is applied to the shaping of context. By shaping of context we mean that determinations of whose voice counts and whose doesn't are already established before we arrive on the scene. A host of contextual factors—the structure of rooms, arrangement of furniture, differences in dress and appearance, length of time scheduled for the meeting, who is invited (or not invited) to attend, norms and stories about prior communications and situations—all serve to give more weight to the points of view of certain individuals. Once in the situation, we may try to speak as if from a position of power, but it is an uphill battle when many of the contextual factors are stacked against us.

A good way of thinking about how individuals can participate in organizational dialogues is to ask questions about who gets to speak on organizational issues and who doesn't; when, where, and for how long; and who is listening. Some organizations, namely, dictatorships and traditional bureaucracies, are more like monologues than dialogues in that one individual or an elite group controls the context for communication. We see voice as the way an individual manifests self in public, in an ongoing struggle to express self to others. Voice is the realization of creativity or the ability of an individual or group to express itself in the ongoing organizational dialogue. In most organizations, a few voices are loud and clear (e.g., senior management) while others are muted or suppressed (e.g., janitorial or housekeeping staff; clerical staff). We are reminded of the insensitive (but unfortunately typical) manager who, upon walking into a suite of offices that was vacant except for the receptionist, looked her in the eye and exclaimed: "There's *nobody* here!"

In defining dialogue as equitable transaction, we wish to call attention to the issue of unequal voice in organizations. In the literature of organizations, voice has a specific meaning: it is an employee's decision to speak up against the status quo, as an alternative either to keeping quiet and staying (loyalty) or giving up and leaving (exit) (Hirschman, 1970). Most people recognize that in an ideal world achieving voice is the preferred option because it raises important issues and encourages creativity and commitment. In most companies, however, there are many barriers to voice. The suppression of employee voice within some organizations leads to "whistle-blowing," where frustrated employees take their concerns to outsiders—for example, to the media or to the courts (Redding, 1985).

At a minimum, then, dialogue requires that communicators be afforded equitable opportunities to speak. While the notion of dialogue as equitable transaction is a good starting point for thinking about communication in organizations, it stops short of addressing the quality of the resultant conversation. Even if multiple viewpoints (contexts) are represented, nothing guarantees how they will be considered or the process by which some views will take precedence over others.

Dialogue as Empathic Conversation   Empathy is the ability to stand in another's shoes and to imagine the world as that person has constructed it. Achieving empathy is extremely challenging both within and outside of organizations, because most people inevitably believe their view of reality to be the only correct view and all others' perceptions are mistaken or misguided. It takes an enormous perceptual shift to accept the validity of another person's perspective, especially if it differs from yours.

> We each have strongly held fixed notions, about both ourselves and the world, that form the background of the way we interact with the world, that we've been leaning on for a long time. There's the possibility of having some of those beliefs shift or dissolve away. In a sense, all of it is about yourself, since your beliefs are yours, and your *interpretive structure* is yours. But you've got to risk having some of that dissolve away. And that is, I guess, the exciting opportunity, and the potential risk, of a real dialog [sic] (Evered & Tannenbaum, 1992, p. 45).

However difficult, it is precisely such a shift in perspective that can transform organizations. Individuals in one department learn that what is on-center in their world is off-center in another department. Similarly, they come to see that to effectively manage diversity means primarily to acknowledge that different individuals and groups have differing perspectives on the organization. All perspectives are partial, none is right or has an inherent privilege over others. The challenge is both to accept and to be stimulated by these differences in interpretation without feeling pressured to seek greater homogeneity and agreement. Put differently: "Can I recognize the value of your [perspective] . . . without us having to somehow merge into something that's less rich than the community of differences?" (Evered & Tannenbaum, 1992, p. 52).

Just as the need for more diverse voices in organizations is hardly debatable, so, too, greater empathy is easily justified. But is empathy enough? Some philosophers, notably Martin Buber and Mikhail Bakhtin, say no. In critiquing empathy as the ideal of dialogue, these authorities have formulated a view of dialogue as meeting.

Dialogue as Meeting   For Buber and Bakhtin, the notion of empathy is insufficient for dialogue because it retains the idea of one individual experiencing the other as a kind of object, rather than fully recognizing the other as a complete being, not as a thing but as a fellow interpreter. As long as we are "only" being empathic, we may continue to see the dialogue as mainly instrumental in accomplishing our own personal and professional goals. One's empathy may be false or a means to a strategic end.

Beyond empathy, certain dialogues are valuable in and of themselves. This type of dialogue is described in detail by Buber, who distinguishes the interhuman (dialogue that has value for itself) from the social (dialogue that has value as a route to self-realization and individual fulfillment). In Buber's view, it is the bond between humans that is primary, expressed as an unresolvable balance:

> We are answerable neither to ourselves alone nor to society apart from ourselves but to that very bond between ourselves and others through which we again and again discover the direction in which we can authenticate our existence (Friedman, 1992, p. 6).

Next consider this quote from Bakhtin:

> A single consciousness is a contradiction in terms. Consciousness is essentially multiple . . . I am conscious of myself and become myself only when revealing myself for another, through another and with the help of another. . . . The very being of man [sic] is the *deepest* communion. To be means to communicate . . . to be means to be for another, and through the other, for onself (Bakhtin, in Emerson, 1983).

From this perspective, dialogue is what makes us human; it is the fundamental activity of our species. For human beings, life exists only in communion with other human beings. But do meetings in organizations ever resemble Buber's ideal? What might this communion in dialogue be like in practice? Buber characterizes it as a relationship between "I and Thou," where two individuals acknowledge fully that each is an interpreter and do not reduce the other to an object of interpretation within a context that has already been constructed.

Seeking dialogue because it has value for itself can sometimes result in positive consequences for the organization.

> [Dialog] is one of the richest activities that human beings can engage in. It is the thing that gives meaning to life, it's the sharing of humanity, it's creating something. And there is this magical thing in an organization, or in a team, or a group, where you get unrestricted interaction, unrestricted dialog, and this synergy happening that results in more productivity, and satisfaction, and seemingly magical levels of output from a team (Evered & Tannebaum, 1992, p. 48).

This definition of dialogue has an abstract, spiritual aspect, but it is also practical because its pursuit highlights deficiencies (and possibilities) in the ways we currently communicate. Are we open to the voices of others, recognizing that all views are partial and that each of us has the right to speak? Are we open to the possibility of real human connection in organizational life, to the kind of interaction in which we stand in relation to one another with mutual respect and openness of spirit?

For many people in organizations today, these questions are not easily answered. Although we may desire an open dialogue that responds to the mutuality of selves involved in constructing meanings, we may also feel constrained by learned behaviors that teach us to guard our most intimate understandings. We may also be constrained by considerations of the social, professional, and political consequences of our disclosures, as well as by the habit of separating our emotions from our work.

To establish dialogue as authentic meeting, we must learn to interpret communicative action as a dialogic process that occurs between and among individuals, rather than as something we do *to* one another. Both parties are responsible for the dialogue as well as for the risks taken. Only together do we make progress.

We engage in dialogue to learn more about our selves in context with others. Dialogue helps us attain new appreciations for the multilayered dimensions of every context and of every interpretation of a context. "The crucial point is to go into a dialog with the stance that there is something that I don't already know, with a mutual *openness* to learn. Through dialog we can learn, not merely receive information, but revise the way we see something. Something about the dialog honors *inquiry* and learning from the inquiry" (Evered & Tannenbaum, 1992, p. 45).

Authentic dialogue also provides a practical communication skill that is invaluable: We learn to speak from experience and to listen for experience. By sharing and risking the truth of our experience, we discover important questions that will guide our interpretation of contexts, of others, and finally, of ourselves. We gain access to the shaping forces of our own and other's experiences. These forces guide our individual and collective constructions of reality, teach us what counts as knowledge as well as how to value it, and influence how our evaluations of persons and things are generated.

Admittedly, authentic dialogue is difficult to attain and does not characterize most relationships, either in or outside of organizations. But it should be an important communicative goal for many individuals and groups. In the end, we believe that authentic dialogue creates the energy to transform organizations from places where people work to dynamic working places. Most people readily acknowledge the importance of equitable transactions and will settle for increased empathy across hierarchical levels and professional groups. But all of us dream of authentic dialogue, of individuality within community, of organizations that are both effective *and* enjoyable because they encourage the kinds of communication required for real human connection. In William Torbert's (1991) words, we should strive to create "liberating structures" through the "power of balance" (p. 97).

SUMMARY

Questions about communication and organization have been with us throughout history, and this chapter traces some alternative views of communication through the ages. The chapter also deals with shifting definitions of such terms as *meaning, context, self,* and *other,* culminating in our proposed model of organizations as dialogue that reveals important connections among these terms. For a summary of the different ways in which people have approached the idea of dialogue, see Table 2.2.

Central to all these discussions is the principle that in the pursuit of identity and community, people constantly strive to make sense out of the world. This sense or meaning is ever-changing and socially constructed. The process is not inherently democratic, for some people have more say than others in the rules, norms, and beliefs that become taken for granted. Most interesting from a communication perspective are the issues of how some people's ideas prevail in dialogue and how this balance of power may be altered.

Dialogue is not simply an abstract concept. As we will see in Chapters 3 to 6, the historical movement in theories of organization and communication has been toward including more and different voices at all levels of the organization. The shift from scientific management (Chapter 3) to high-involvement organizations (Chapter 5) and finally to postmodern organizational forms (Chapter 6) can be characterized as an evolution from monologue to dialogue, as well as a continuing effort to find workable models for organizational dialogue. Organizational communication theory and practice are increasingly focused on orchestrating diverse voices.

Chapters 7 to 11 provide contexts for interpretation which provide resources for dialogue. For example, Chapter 7 addresses the personal context, through which an individual interprets organizational reality in accord with his or her personality, background, attitudes, values, and beliefs. What we find meaningful outside of work colors or shapes what we find meaningful or important inside. Family responsibilities, physical characteristics, our personality type, religious and political beliefs, preferences for leisure activities, what we watch on television and hear on the radio, the music, theater, or dance we prefer, the cars we drive or the trains or buses we ride, the purchases we make—all of these factors define us as individuals at work. Taken together, they make up the "glasses" through which an individual interprets the world.

Our personal context affects not only our own interpretations, but also our dialogues with others. If an employee has children, for example, and works for a boss who is childless,

TABLE 2.2
SUMMARY OF CREATIVITY AND CONSTRAINT AS INTERPRETATION OF CONTEXTS

Context and Interpretation	Multiple Contexts and the Situated Individual	Organizations as Dialogues
Assumptions: (1) There is no meaning without context (Bateson); (2) relationship and situation shape context; (3) organizations are collectivities of contexts.	*Assumptions:* (1) There is always more than one context for interpreting the meaning of communication; (2) interpretations of meanings are shaped by constraints that (3) suggest a particular construction of reality; and (4) multiple contexts suggest multiple interpretations of reality.	*Assumptions:* (1) Humans are neither entirely social nor entirely private; (2) humans establish a sense of self as well as a sense of membership in a community; (3) the accomplishment of both selfhood and community is accomplished through dialogue with others.
Definitions: Context is the information that goes with and helps make sense out of the text.	*Definitions:* The situated individual communicates in contexts and assists in the construction of contexts.	*Definitions:* A dialogue is balanced communication in which participating individuals and groups each have a chance to speak and to be heard.
Feature: (1) Contexts are not stable (they are verbs rather than nouns); (2) contexts reveal the duality of structure; (3) contexts redefine work in organizations as interpretation of contexts.	*Features:* (1) The individual is an actor whose actions and communication are based on interpretations of contexts; (2) there is always more than one context that can be used to guide action or interpretation; and (3) communication is the sum of action and interpretation and as such can reveal sources of creativity, constraint, meaning, interpretation, and context.	*Features:* Three senses of dialogue apply to communication in organizations: (1) dialogue as equitable transaction; (2) dialogue as empathic conversation; and (3) dialogue as authentic meeting.

the differences in their lives and responsibilities will become part of the employee's consciousness and communication at work. Details such as childhood development, choices of preschools and babysitters, and the ubiquitousness of minor illnesses will be absent from the boss's talk. Instead, the boss's talk will contain many other references that may seem foreign (or at least nostalgic) to the employee. What the two can share will be limited by the differences in their personal contexts for meaning. The same could be said for other differences—for example, in religion, ethnicity, cultural background, gender, and affluence. The key point is that who we are as individuals—our so-called personal lives—strongly affects who we are and how we communicate with others at work. Chapters 8 to 11 continue with this theme, focusing on interpersonal relationships, groups, organizations, and society, each as contexts for interpretation and as bases for dialogue.

Finally, although there are advantages to promoting dialogue in organizations (e.g., greater individual satisfaction and commitment; reduced turnover; greater innovation and flexibility) there is also a downside (see Table 2.3). First, there is the reality of time constraints. While individuals may feel better when they are able to engage in dialogue, it may take too long to make decisions and the company, as a result, suffers. Coping with

TABLE 2.3

SUMMARY OF ADVANTAGES AND LIMITATIONS TO
PROMOTING DIALOGUE IN ORGANIZATIONS

Advantages	Limitations
For the individual Opens possibilities for creativity.	*For the individual* Is difficult to attain and therefore may act as a constraint on relationships.
Enables one to deal productively with instabilities of organizational life through the faculty of forgiveness.	May promote instabilities caused by unilateral risk-taking in relationships.
Enables one to deal productively with miscommunication through making and keeping promises.	May promote miscommunication caused by failure to keep promises or unwillingness to make them.
Values speaking of personal experiences.	Personal experiences may be hard to talk about.
Provides rich contextual details about how interpretations are made.	Information overload.
Individual transformation may lead to organizational transformation.	Seeking transformation may conflict with individual and organizational objectives.
For the organization Greater individual satisfaction with—and commitment to—the organization.	*For the organization* May sacrifice timing for communication and reduce decision-making effectiveness.
Reduced turnover due to enriched job and communication experiences.	May set up expectations that ideas and opinions will be binding or will be implemented.
Greater opportunities for innovation and flexibility.	May lead to a lack of closure or the feeling that there is no "right" answer.

this problem requires some individual or group to take responsibility for screening issues and determining the degree of dialogue that can reasonably be expected. This is risky and vests enormous power in the people deciding which issues can be dealt with, but it is probably necessary in turbulent business environments.

Second, encouraging dialogue may set up expectations among the various communicators that the ideas and opinions that are spoken will necessarily be implemented. At least within the capitalist system, owners and their agents have final veto power. This means that, although there may be an equitable distribution of power and voice in the group, the ultimate power lies with the owners. Recent moves to develop employee-owned companies are beginning to effectively address this concern.

Third, and finally, dialogue may lead to a lack of closure and the feeling that there is no right answer. This problem is part of a larger disillusionment in Western society, which includes public perceptions of science, medicine, and technology. It is our view that all parties involved need to give up the idea of ultimate truths about organizational communication and to focus instead on practical guidelines for action.

Let us conclude this chapter with two big questions. First, is dialogue possible in organizations? Second, what role can the situated individual play in constructing organizational reality through communication?

With regard to the first question, we believe that dialogue is possible in organizations, for we have experienced it. It is also rare. So much communication in organization has to do with convincing other people that their perceptions are wrong—"management shouldn't think that way," "That idea will never fly," "I know my people aren't dissatisfied"—that major barriers to real meeting are commonplace. But there are also instances of dialogue, and much may be gained by expanding the current popular interest in managing diversity to include the coordination of diverse voices in business.

Answering the second question is more difficult. Some would take issue with the whole concept of the "individual" (notably postmodernists; see Chapter 6), arguing that it is just another way of saying that you have a political ideology that favors free will and capitalism (Grossberg, 1991). These people claim that most of our choices are so constrained as to be virtually made for us. What we believe to be free, motivated action is more correctly seen as the forces of the world acting through us, without us having much of a say.

Others, including us, are unwilling to let go of the lived experience of the situated individual (Jackson, 1989). We are born into a society that expects us to act out a balance—however illusory—between individuality and social responsibility. We are expected to make decisions about ourselves and our actions that will influence others and in turn will be influenced by others, but ultimately the responsibility for those actions is our own. If an individual commits a crime, while society may be implicated, it is the individual who goes to jail.

Read yet another way, the individual is a biological system that still functions primarily to maintain that one life, not the whole of the ecosystem. If we choose to destroy our bodies through chemical toxification and hard living, the ecosystem will absorb our loss. However, the individual system that ingested the chemicals and the body that did the hard living will be the one prematurely under the ground.

Finally, our perspective on the situated individual model for organizational communication as dialogue suggests a connection to broader philosophical world-views. Our philosophical world-view is best characterized as existentialism (Sartre, 1957, 1968, 1972,

TABLE 2.4

SUMMARY OF THE PRINCIPLES OF EXISTENTIAL PHILOSOPHY INFORMING THE SITUATED INDIVIDUAL MODEL

1. Our search is for a vocabulary that will serve as the basis for a dialogue across cultures, not a search for universal truths or essences.

2. Human "being" is dispersed into the world in the form of human relationships, intentions, and projects. In seeking to understand that world, we situate ourselves squarely within it rather than taking up a vantage point outside it.

3. We do not privilege any vocabulary as representing the truth or essence of things; instead, we offer a way of interrogating lived experiences from everyday life. To ask questions about lived experiences seems wiser than to make universal claims about which there must always be exceptions to the rule.

4. Existentialism reveals a common preoccupation with our human struggle between yielding to the brute facts of existence—the sense of being abandoned or thrown into a world make by others at other times—and the necessity of appropriating, addressing, and experiencing that world as something for which we are responsible, something we bring into being, something we choose.

5. In sum, existentialism places social facts within an ontological perspective. Accordingly, we neither presume scientific status for our world-views in order to give them authority and legitimacy, nor deign to label the world-views of others "folk" as a sign of their epistemological inadequacy. "Our" world-views are placed on a par with "theirs" and seen not as true accounts of external reality but as ways of helping us cope with life, of making the world make sense.

Adapted from Michael Jackson,
Paths Toward a Clearing,
1989, pp. 49–50.

1982), albeit it has been modified by what we have learned about phenomenology, cultural anthropology, social theories, communication theories, and economics.

Why existentialism? We prefer to pose this as a question here at the end of the chapter. Consider Table 2.4 as the first clue. Read through the five statements and then construct your own account of how the situated individual model of organizations as dialogue derives important premises from existential thinking.

CASE STUDY

The Case of the Many Smiths

JASON, THE JANITOR

Smith is a very tidy man. I pass by his desk at night when I'm in here cleaning up, and his area is the only one that is perfect. Nothing is *ever* out of place. I've made a kind of study out of it. You know, paid lots of attention to it on account of it is so unusual. So you notice things.

I say Smith is a single man. No pictures of family on his desk or on the walls. Most people leave traces of themselves outside the office everywhere—little photographs, stuff they've picked up from vacations, stickers with funny sayings on them. But not Smith. You walk into Smith's area, and there is absolutely no trace of anything except the books and the computer. The books never change positions, which tells me he never has to look things up. So I have come to believe that Smith is a smart man, too.

I have never met him, or if I did, I never knew it. But I see him in my mind as a tall, thin guy with glasses and not much of a smile. He probably is shy. Fastidious people often are shy. Maybe he is an accountant, or perhaps a computer programmer. Hard to say. But Smith is, to me, what makes my job interesting. I watch his desk at night to see if anything changes.

CATHERINE, THE RECEPTIONIST

Smith is okay, a little shy maybe. He says hello to me every morning. Just that, though: "Hello." Nothing more, not even my name. I didn't know his name for months. But then, I didn't really say much to him either.

Then one afternoon he had a visitor. It was a woman, a beautiful woman. She was in her late twenties, early thirties, and asked to speak to Bobby. I said, "Bobby who?" She looked confused, then smiled and said, "Bobby Smith, I thought everyone knew." Well, this was interesting. I mean, Smith has a first name—Robert—but I had never thought of him as anyone's "Bobby." And this woman acted like that is all he could ever be, to anyone. So I paged him, he came downstairs, and when he saw her his face went rigid. It was like he had seen a ghost. Worse. She called his name, he stopped still. I thought he was going to cry or something. Instead, he just stood upright and shook his head, "No." He didn't say it, just shook his head. Then he turned and walked back upstairs, slowly.

The woman watched him but didn't go after him. Then she turned and walked out the door. She was a beautiful woman, and I never saw her again. Girlfriend, sister, friend, I never knew. Smith never said anything about her. It was as if she had never existed.

In this job, you see all kinds of people. I have learned a lot about people working here as a receptionist. But Smith is still a mystery to me. The only three things I know about him are, one, his first name is Robert, but some people call him Bobby; two, he says "hello" to me every morning, regular as clockwork; and three, there was a beautiful woman in his life. Oh yeah, and there is a fourth: He is about 5'7", wears his hair short, has a big handlebar moustache, wears an earring, and obviously works out a lot.

WILSON, HIS BOSS

Smith is a strange one, but a good worker. Never misses a day. Willing to work at night or on weekends to get the job done. His work is always neat and well organized. Personally, I wish he would dump the earring and moustache, but that's just him I guess.

I hired him five years ago in an entry-level accounting position. He was a good worker, quiet, dependable. He got promoted to senior accountant very quickly, as if someone up there in the company was watching out for him. Usually it takes even the best accountant five to seven years to make it to senior status; Smith made it in three. Last fall I asked him to take charge of a major audit, and he has been working on that diligently ever since.

Smith never talks about his life outside of work. And I never ask him. None of my business. He seems to like it that way. The way he is built, I'd say he spends a lot of his time working out, probably in some swanky club. I know he drives a vintage black Porsche, a speedster, and it is always clean. And he leaves it open during the day with a pair of Ray-Bans on the dash. Always in the same position.

I figure he comes from money. He graduated from Stanford. He doesn't talk like a Texan, though. I'd say he is from back East, maybe Pittsburgh. I don't know why I say that.

To tell you the truth, he scares me a little bit. Nobody has a right to be as calm as Smith is. As collected. As perfect. I see a lot of movies and the crazy mass murderer is always like that. Not that I think he is *that* way. But I wouldn't be surprised. I dunno. I wish his damned starched shirts would just one time come back with a rip in them, or something. I know that sounds small. I can't help it. Smith does that to me.

FELICIA, HIS CO-WORKER

Robert is my good friend. He is a warm, sensitive person with a heart of pure gold. He and I have talked a lot over the past couple of years. Mostly about our dreams. We both want to work hard, save a lot of money, and be able to do something else with our lives while we are still young enough to enjoy it.

Robert came from a poor family, grew up moving around from town to town while his mother looked for work in construction. Had two brothers and a sister, all older. He was the baby. His father was killed in the Vietnam War. His older brothers are both in the military and don't have much in common with him, and his sister is a very successful lawyer in Washington. He showed me a picture of her once, and she is a beautiful woman. They had a big argument a while back, he wouldn't say much about it, and he hasn't seen her since. His mother died of lung cancer two years ago.

Robert worked hard in school but won an athletic scholarship to Stanford. He was a gymnast. Or still is, because he spends two or three nights a week working with underprivileged kids downtown teaching them gymnastics. And he is big in Adult Children of Alcoholics, which I took him to. Which is a whole story by itself. He has a lot of hobbies, which, when he does them, aren't exactly hobbies anymore. He is such a perfectionist! Like that car of his, for instance. He built it himself, out of a kit. And you should see his apartment.

JENKINS, THE RETIRED CEO OF THE FIRM

Robert Smith is one of the company's finest employees. And he is an exceptional young man. I recruited him at Stanford when I was teaching there right after I retired. Since then, I've kind of followed his career. I asked him not to say much about our relationship, because a lot of people could get the wrong idea. I want him to make it on his own, which he has. Sure, I put in a good word for him here and there, but never anything too pushy.

I knew his father in Vietnam. He served in my command and was a good soldier. He was due to be shipped home later in the week when he was killed. It was sad. I wrote the letter to his family myself. When I got out of the Army I moved over into the private sector. You can imagine how odd it was for me to walk into that accounting class at Stanford and see Robert Smith, who looks just like his dad except for the moustache and earring, sitting in the front row. I couldn't believe it. Still can't.

In a way I can't articulate clearly, I feel related to Robert. He still comes to visit us on the holidays. I like that.

ASSIGNMENT 1

You are a head-hunter (e.g., an executive recruiter) who has compiled the above information from interviews with Smith's colleagues. You also have his resume and performance appraisal reports to supplement these statements. Your job is to prepare a personality profile of Smith for a firm that seems to be very interested in hiring him. What do you write? How can you explain these different perspectives on Smith? If you were Smith, what would you say about them?

ASSIGNMENT 2

As you have learned from reading this chapter, we live complex (and often contradictory) lives as situated individuals in organizations. In one very important sense, this fact should make us sensitive to the various ways meanings are constructed through talk—whoever is doing the constructing is bringing her or his own situatedness to the verbal portrait given. It is as if we are all, in our own ways, varieties of an organizational Smith. Given this perspective, construct an investigation of yourself using interview statements used by others to describe who—and what—you are. Supplement these statements with your own resume. How many distinctive "yous" appear? What does this tell you about yourself? About your construction of others? About the deeply situatedness of our individual lives in organizations? About the complexities of interpreting meanings?

ASSIGNMENT 3

As a student of communication, you should be interested in finding ways to improve your own—as well as others'—interpretations of meanings. Go back over "The Case of the Many Smiths" and pretend you are working as a communication consultant with the head-hunter. Your job is to help the head-hunter construct better follow-up questions to produce a fuller report. What questions would have helped to resolve the "many Smiths" into a more unified one? Or is a "unified Smith" a false communication goal? What's the best we can humanly do?

FOUNDING PERSPECTIVES ON ORGANIZATION AND COMMUNICATION

"Men [sic] make their history on the basis of real, prior conditions . . . but it is the men who make it and not the prior conditions. Otherwise men would be merely the vehicle of inhuman forces which through them would govern the social world."

—Jean-Paul Sartre

"The recurrent problem in sociology is to conceive of corporate organization, and to study it, in ways that do not anthropomorphize it and do not *reduce* it to the behavior of individuals *or* of human aggregates."

—Guy Swanson

Some forms of communicating and organizing have existed as long as humans have inhabited the planet, and speculation about how we manage to accomplish these things also has a long history. Chapters 3 to 6 attempt to convey the high points along this historical journey, forgoing specific names and dates in favor of identifying critical moments of insight. Specifically, our history focuses on *theories* of organizational communication. The present chapter addresses theories associated with scientific management, bureaucracy, human relations, and human resources.

WHY FOCUS ON THEORY?

Definitions of theory run the gamut from a formal system of axioms and hypotheses that can be expressed mathematically and tested empirically, whose purpose is to explain, predict, and control, to a good idea someone else thought of first. Regardless of the definition we adopt, whether we see theories in their most scientific sense or in a looser, more literary way, or somewhere in between, two observations remain: first, theories are historical and second, theories are metaphorical.

Theories of organizational communication are historical in that they are a product of the times in which they emerge and hold currency. In this sense, theories are history lessons because they become popular in response to specific historical concerns and reflect the interests of the cultures that produce them. Theories are metaphorical in that they suggest, through language, enlightening comparisons between organizational communication and other processes. For example, scientific management theory compares organizations to machines; systems theory compares organizations to complex organisms.

Our approach to the role of theories in the understanding of organizations and communication begins with a practical outlook. As students of organizational communication, we have chosen to participate in a particular discourse community, that is, a collectivity of individuals who share an interest in particular kinds of discourse—in our case, talk and writing about organizations and communication. Alternatively, those interested in computers learn a special language that enables them to talk with other members of the computer-literate discourse community.

The communication theorist Kenneth Burke (1989) has likened participation in a discourse community to entering a room in which conversation is already in progress. We wander around for a while, listen, and occasionally join in the talk. Sooner or later we find ourselves engaged in a conversation that seems important to us at the time. Time passes, and we have many such conversations. Eventually, we notice that the hour is late, and it is time to leave. The conversation continues without us. For each of us, active participation in our discourse community requires detailed attention to the talk that has preceded our entry into the room. Theories are not moments in history to be committed to memory so that they can provide ready answers to test items. They should function as resources to enhance our ability to explain and to act on a wide variety of practical issues, such as where the idea of organization came from; why there are bosses and employees; what motivates people to work; how work should be evaluated; how an employment or appraisal interview should best be conducted; what we should do when we find ourselves engaged in conflict; how we can integrate work and home life; and so forth. The way we talk about a problem directly influences the solutions we can articulate to address the problem. Theories of organizations and communication should enhance our ability to articulate alternative ways of approaching and acting on practical issues.

Theories represent a particular kind of historical narrative: they are goal-oriented stories told for the purpose of explanation. The explanation may be a creative integration of a wide variety of disparate issues—for example, how organizations can be both pro-profit and pro-people, or perhaps why communication and efficiency are linked. Or a theory may provide a complete explication of a very narrow topic—for example, how to lead an effective decision-making group or how to relieve stress on the job. Either way, theories reflect unique historical circumstances and diverse cultural and political interests.

The study of organizational communication theories should treat these accounts as evolving episodes in an ongoing historical narrative. Thus, we should not strive to choose one theory over another, but instead we should learn to see each theory as a participant in a larger and longer conversation. We are interested, then, in more than what theories help us to explain. Like participants in a great conversation we are also interested in the position of the theories in the general stream of events, their relationship to other theories, their unique properties, their strengths and limitations, the participation of the individual theories in the overall story, the interests they represent and the interests they neglect, and, finally, the effect of the telling and retelling of these stories on our conversation and on the world. These are not just academic issues: how we learn to answer these questions becomes part and parcel not only of what we know, but also of who we are.

ORGANIZATION AND COMMUNICATION THEORIES AS HISTORICAL NARRATIVES: THE THREE P'S

We will begin this section with a brief explication of what we call the three P's of historical writing: partiality, partisanship, and problematic.

Partiality

An argument could be made that any attempt to write the history of organizational communication is necessarily misleading because what is absent may be as important as what is present. Obviously, we have chosen to write this chapter anyway. Our primary condition is partiality; our account will contain only part of the story. However, the inability to fully articulate a complete account of the history of organizational communication is neither unique to our field nor disabling. As the French philosopher Jacques Derrida (1972) has demonstrated, all thought is inscribed in language and language is rooted in an inescapable paradox: There is no Archimedian point of absolute meaning outside of language from which to view—or to prescribe—the truth of the world. Because all language is partial, there can be no absolute history, no full account, no one story of organizational communication. Therefore, from the perspective of language our account is necessarily partial.

Partisanship

We write under the limitation of a second condition: partisanship. The story we tell is one that we favor. The historical story of organizational communication largely favors the interpretations of a dominant, male, white, Western culture. What such accounts leave out is how members of oppressed, marginalized, or subjugated groups such as women and minorities would tell the story. Consider, for example, how a Native American might interpret the nineteenth-century expansion of railroads, mining, and manufacturing interests across the Great Plains in terms of what the expansion meant for his or her people. Depending on one's interests—one's partisanship—this story can either be one of great tragedy or of great opportunity.

As our example illustrates, to reinterpret any account assumes familiarity with what has come before it. This means that although scholars and practitioners may disagree about how the story gets told as well as who should be telling it, they will likely agree about at least some of the events and characters comprising that story. In our illustration everyone agrees that the Native Americans considered the Great Plains their natural hunting grounds and that westward expansion by the white man did, in fact, take place.

Without agreement on factual occurrences, a productive conversation would not be possible. Partisanship, then, is not about changing the facts but about what the facts might be interpreted to mean.

All thought is partisan. Our knowledge is shaped by the theories and interpretations we use to make sense of the world, what we call a world view. If a theory is seen as a kind of mini-world-view—a way of making sense out of the world—then clearly not just one theory can explain everything. No one partisan view could ever comprehend all the interests of all the people for all time.

When we read about theories, then, we should think of each theory as telling a particular story. Each story represents the interests of the storyteller and is, therefore, a partisan perspective on the wide, broader stories capable of being told about that world. As we will see, it takes many theories—many perspectives, many ways of revealing partisanship—to tell the complex story of organizational communication.

Problematic

Our third condition for writing this story is that the story itself will be problematic. The term *problematic* means that our account will ask more questions than it answers. It also means that the answers provided here will be based on what is currently known rather than on all that could be known. To admit to being problematic in our narrative is to invite dialogue—to ask the readers to bring to our account their own experiences and understandings.

Taken together, the three P's of our historical narrative provide us with an important perspective on communication and the limitations of any historical account: All talk is partial, partisan, and problematic. The kinds of questions we raise about our reading add to our understanding of organizational communication.

THE CLASSICAL APPROACH

Most contemporary histories of organizations and communication begin with the advent of the Industrial Revolution in England and America. This is not to suggest that organizations and communication did not exist prior to the steamboat, the railroad, or the cotton gin. Instead, their point is to offer an interpretation of modern organizations based on the advent of modern machinery and methods of production, and the accompanying rise of factory bureaucracy (Perrow, 1986). The underlying metaphor of the classical school of management is that organizations should be modeled after efficient machines (Ginsberg, 1982; Morgan, 1986).

Historical and Cultural Background

We begin with the Industrial Revolution for two reasons. First, Michel Foucault (1972, 1979) has pointed out that the rise of the modern factory during this time period must be understood as an extension of a far more complex social (and racial) class structure that sought to stabilize relations among persons through the overt control of the means of production and consumption in society. Before the Industrial Revolution, only rarely would an individual work for someone else in exchange for wages. Compare this situation to today, where "we give it no thought at all. Only about 15 percent of our working population is able to get by without working for someone else. High schools, colleges, and universities train us to accept wage slavery" (Perrow, 1986, p. 50). But it was the Industrial Revolution that marked the beginning of this important shift.

The newly emerging concepts of division of labor and hierarchy would heavily influence the organization of work and communication in the modern factory. Division of labor refers to the separation of tasks into discrete units, whereas hierarchy refers to the vertical arrangement of power and authority that defines important differences between managers and employees. These foundations of the modern organization had their origins in an affluent, paranoid (the rise of the middle class made the upper class fearful), class-conscious view of social control. The rationale was that the organization of work institutions should represent the organization of an ideal form of society (but "whose ideal?" is an appropriate question). Perhaps this is one reason why prisons and factories were modeled on the same architectural principles, and why the behavior of inmates and workers was so carefully monitored and tightly controlled (Sennett, 1978).

A second clue as to why organization and order were linked to hierarchy may be found in the work of Kenneth Burke on language. Burke stated that humans are symbol-users (and abusers) who are "goaded by the spirit of hierarchy [or moved to a sense of order]" (1989, p. 69). From this perspective, language is a symbolic construction of order based on hierarchies used to perfect nature. In our construction of these language-based realities, we create rules for organizing sentences (grammar), rules for organizing arguments (logic), and cooperation based on identification of speakers with audiences through symbols (rhetoric) as the foundation of human activities. It is no wonder that forms of organization mirror our language habits.

These relationships among class consciousness, purposive language, and social control developed concomitantly with the rise of science. Science is more than a highly ordered method of explaining phenomena. From explanation emerges the ability to predict, and from the ability to predict comes the potential to control. The underlying theme of classical approaches to organization is the rationalization of the world. From the classical perspective, organizations are the primary vehicle by which our lives are rationalized—"planned, articulated, scientized, made more efficient and orderly, and managed by experts" (Scott, 1981, p. 5).

From Empire to Hierarchy

During the eighteenth, nineteenth, and early twentieth centuries, organizations were closely linked to the concept of empire. Corporations were extensions of governments in the sense that they expanded the base of capital, provided employment for the masses, and contributed to the economic and social development of a nation (Rose, 1989).

Cities in the New World were mapped according to the appropriation of territories by organizations. In older regions of these cities, we can still see the close relationship between homes and factories, as well as how the accumulation of wealth and status tends to allow a family to move further away from the industry that produces it. The closer a dwelling is to a factory, the less material power and social status the family living in that dwelling tends to have. Thus, social control is effectively produced in part by the relationship between the location of industry to neighborhoods.

It is perhaps no surprise that Eli Whitney's first effective demonstration of the utility of mass production in 1801 was based on standardized parts and divisions of labor aimed at the production of guns—guns also tend to keep order and extend the power of empires. During the mid-eighteenth century, Benjamin Franklin popularized the ideal of early American notions of empire and pragmatism through his publication of *Poor Richard's Almanac.* This work is primarily a collection of parables and quotable lines that elevate hard work (called industry), independence (associated with the accumulation of wealth on individual, corporate, and national levels), and the virtues of planning, organizing, and ultimately controlling one's life through work. It contains such words of wisdom as these, from *The Improved Poor Richard* (1970):

> "Industry need not wish—There are no Gains without Pains."
> "God gives all things to industry."
> "God helps them that help themselves."
> "Sloth makes all things difficult, but industry all easy."
> "Early to Bed, early to rise, makes a Man healthy, wealthy, and wise."

Franklin was not the first writer to make powerful use of these ideas: Similar sentiments can be found in Japanese and Chinese proverbs as well as in the Old Testament and the Talmud. However, he was the first American to popularize them as foundational for our national work culture. In fact, these proverbs were influential precisely because they fit neatly into the wisdom of older narratives that were used in churches, schools, and among businesspeople.

Franklin's nationalistic pragmatism also contained a deeply embedded sexism: "Women and wine, game and deceit, make the wealth small, and the wants great." His work also contained a strong belief in the separation of labor by gender: "many estates are spent in the getting, since women for tea forsook spinning and knitting, and men for punch forsook hewing and splitting" (1758).

During this same period, Frederick the Great (1740–1786) organized his armies based on the principles of mechanics: ranks, uniforms, regulations, task specialization, standardized equipment, command language, and drill instruction (Morgan, 1986). The success of his armies in the name of the Prussian empire served as a model for organizational efficiency based on division of labor and machinelike efficiency. One often-quoted line provides evidence of how his view of organizational hierarchy was linked to the production of efficient work habits: "Men must be taught to fear their officers more than the enemy."

In 1776 Adam Smith, a philosopher of economics and politics, published *A Wealth of Nations,* in which he praised the divisions of labor evident in factory production. As Karl Marx would demonstrate during the mid-eighteenth century, the idea of division of labor was essential to the foundations of a philosophy of organizing corporations and societies along class lines. By 1832 adherents to this position had a blueprint for precisely such an organizational form. Figure 3.1 on page 58 illustrates a typical organizational chart based on strict divisions of labor and hierarchy advocated by what would later be labeled the scientific principles of management.

Notice that the classical bureaucratic organizational chart privileges a top-down or management-oriented view of the organization. Two things about this perspective are

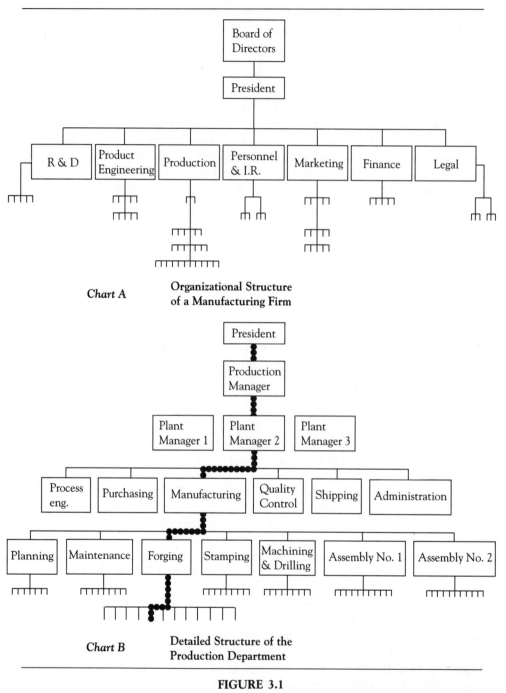

Chart A   **Organizational Structure of a Manufacturing Firm**

Chart B   **Detailed Structure of the Production Department**

FIGURE 3.1
Organization Chart Illustrating the Principles of Classical Management Theory and Bureaucratic
Organization
From Gareth Morgan, *Images of Organization,* 1986. Reprinted by permission of Sage Publications,
Inc.

worth noting. First, the emphasis on developing scientific methods for production was politically and socially linked to providing that information only to managers and supervisors, who would in turn use it to organize and control workers. Second, this model of organizations endorses a passive audience view of human communication in the workplace. By passive audience we mean that workers are silent receptors of management information, incapable of responding, interpreting, arguing, or counteracting this subtle but persuasive form of control. The key to effective communication in the nineteenth century was the giving of orders, a view of communication that gives nearly exclusive emphasis to the downward transmission of information.

The privileging of top-down flows of information in hierarchies also led to the emergence of what we call domination narratives. Within these narratives we can locate the communication values that ascribe a particular reading of how truth, power, and control are constituted in everyday talk. Table 3.1 on page 60 details these communication values; they are described in even greater detail in the next section.

From Hierarchy to Resistance to Domination

During the 1800s, the rapid expansion of industrialism in Northern Europe and North America created the need to organize and manage labor (people) in ways that mirrored the dominant social and political values of the culture. Similarly, the practice of slavery in the Southern states of North America supplied human labor for agricultural work and at the same time mirrored a view of human hierarchies based on racial divisions prevalent among white slaveholders.

One result of these deep divisions between ways of organizing work and the social values that supported them was the U.S. Civil War (1861–1865). The outcome of that war is an interesting and often overlooked part of the history of organizations and communication in North America. When viewed as a struggle between social values that coincided in evaluating organized labor based on hierarchical divisions—but differed in their interpretations of how hierarchies should be determined (i.e., by race or by social class)—the Civil War provides us with a broad societal lens for understanding the role of hierarchically based forms of organizing in the development of U.S. industry.

Where differences exist in the *type* of work people do, differences in how that work is done, evaluated, valued, and compensated will become evident. These differences in value tend to be determined and resolved by those with power. Those in power control the interpretation of differences: the story they tell favors them and their interests. For white slaveholders in the South, the story of slavery was justified on economic and moral grounds. White slaveholders needed a cheap source of labor to farm their lands and felt that God had duly granted whites dominion over darker-skinned humans so that they could accomplish the accumulation of wealth that was at the heart of Calvinist moral advancement (Raban, 1991). From their perspective, slavery was necessary for the productive accomplishment of work that would grant them entry to a Protestant heaven.

Because the white slaveholders had the power to control the daily lives of their slaves, they also controlled the means of resolving conflict based on this partisan view of racial divisions and moral order. Slaveholders considered any slave attempt to challenge white authority as a challenge to the moral order. Although such challenges to authority became legendary in the liberation of American blacks, communication between slaveholder and

TABLE 3.1

SUMMARY OF COMMUNICATION VALUES FOUND IN DOMINATION NARRATIVES

What is Truth?	What is Power?	How is Control Possible
Absolute; Based on dominant ideology, received wisdom, established doctrine, procedural dogma, or consensus account that favors the authority of the power-holders and legitimates the subservience of those defined as subordinates.	Control over vocabulary, including the ability to define key terms for understanding the truth in all situations, strict divisions of all sources of conflict into binary opposites (e.g., black/white, us/them, right/wrong, smart/dumb), and the use of either/or reasoning (e.g., "Either you are with us or against us"); also the ability to exercise discipline or punishment for failure to adhere to the dominant narrative.	Unified (often through causal linkages) integration and presentation of all explanatory narratives.
Communication practices: Use of representative anecdotes that embody the principle; reification of processes into concrete definitions and formulas; evaluation of the *status quo* or the "way things have always been."	*Communication practices:* Use of referent authority (tradition, rules, religion, science, law); simplistic extensions of authority to specific cases; reduction of complex issues into "essences" that can be explained by dominant narratives; use of categorical generalizations and rhetorical syllogisms.	*Communication practices:* Vehement distrust of change; rigid adherence to dominant narratives, definitions, and accounts; dismissal of all competing narratives by relegating them to the status of hearsay, falsity, improbability, or outright absurdity.
Representative story: Great companies have always relied on rational ways of organizing work. That is why bureaucracy is the most rational form of organization. It is the way things have always been—there's no point in questioning it.	*Representative account:* It is a well-known scientific fact that managers are supposed to do the thinking, and workers are supposed to do the working. I am a manager and do the thinking; you are the employee and therefore do what I say, or else!	*Representative explanation:* Flattening the chain of command is crazy and the result will be chaos.

slave was almost exclusively downward and one-sided, and unequivocally favored the interests of the slaveholders.

One feature of societal dialogue that helps us to understand organizational dialogues is the idea of resistance to domination. Thus far, our story about classical approaches to organization and communication has stressed the dominant narratives, such as the account of western expansions of empire, and the influences of science and hierarchy on the development of divisions of labor along class and racial lines. Thus far, ours has been the story told by the powerful.

But in all societies there are other narratives—narratives of resistance to domination—that provide different accounts of what was going on during this time as well as what meanings the events had for those who participated in them (Friere, 1968). Unless the domination is eventually overturned, these stories may be well known but rarely make it into textbooks. These are the stories of the less powerful and the powerless, of those individuals who have either a minor or no voice in the organizational or societal dialogue. An example during this historical period is evident in the stories of slaves.

James Scott (1990) examines how the accounts of the powerless function as hidden transcripts of the other side(s) of the story. A hidden transcript provided otherwise powerless slaves with ways to act out their outrage among peers who share their station in life. The stories they told reversed the order of things by placing the slaveholders in inferior intellectual, moral, and performative positions. This is "a world turned upside down" (Scott, 1990; Stallybrass & White, 1986) in which those without power take control of the narrative and use speech to provide a "performative space for the full-throated acting out of everything that must be choked back in public" (Conquergood, 1992, p. 91). Placing the dominant, powerful narrative alongside the slave account gives a sense of the potential dialogue between the two groups. Unfortunately, such a dialogue remained mostly implicit because the dominant group's narrative is often the only public one, whereas the powerless group's narrative is performed off-stage, in private.

Slave stories were not the only form of resistance to domination. This period also witnessed the rise of slave songs, ditties, and dirges that would later become known as the blues and would set the stage for the advent in our time of rock and roll music, and later rap music, as a major form of resistance to domination (Goodall, 1991). Similarly, we have accounts of resistance to domination from those who were once among the dominant and the powerful, slave traders and slaveholders who "saw the light" and renounced their former practices. Perhaps the best known of these accounts is the gospel hymn "Amazing Grace," which combines the rhythms and sensibilities of a slave song with words penned by a former slave trader turned English minister, John Newton (1791):

> Amazing Grace, how sweet the sound,
> That saved a wretch like me.
> I once was lost, but now I'm found,
> Was blind, but now I see.

Newton's diaries (Moyers, 1989) also contain evidence of the values of hierarchy, empire, and what would become known as scientific management in the operation of slave ships. Perhaps the most dramatic testimony is found in Newton's drawings of how chained slaves were "scientifically organized" for their long sea voyages between Africa and the New World (see Figure 3.2, page 62).

The slaves were kept in tight, straight lines that provided maximum efficiency of space utilization and were treated as no better than cattle or dry goods. The idea was to fit as many slaves as possible into the hulls of the ships. Meager food and water were dispensed according to a rigid schedule, as were opportunities for slaves to relieve themselves. In this case, management was a form of absolute tyranny making judicious (for the slaveholders) use of scientific principles of cost efficiency and production.

Although many of the great economic and technical advances of decades to follow

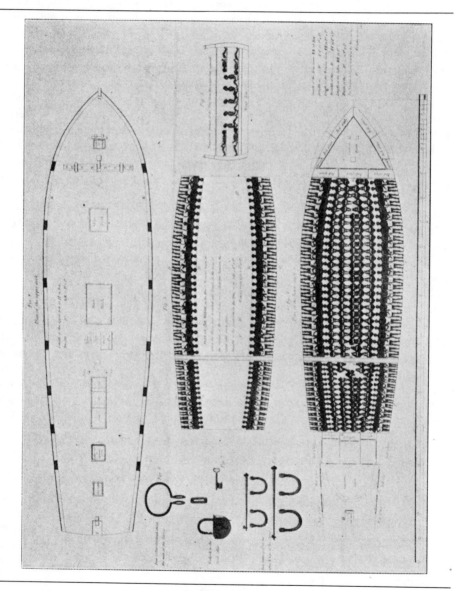

FIGURE 3.2
Diagram showing how slaves were stowed on ships
Reproduced from *Slave Ships and Slaving*, 1969, p. 159

attest to the benefits of rational approaches to organization, the description of scientific management as applied to slave ships shows how principles of scientific rationality are abused by those with absolute power. Moreover, we cannot comfortably relegate this example to the distant past. Similar practices remain in evidence in many places and in many businesses throughout the world. Under severe political and military occupation (Lavie, 1990), hierarchically ordered systems of domination and abuses of power persist, as they do in illegal sweatshops whose workers are immigrant laborers in many major world cities today (Scott, 1990). Table 3.2 on page 64 summarizes the value of resistance narratives to our view of organizations.

These narratives reveal that, even under extreme conditions of servitude or denial of basic human rights, dominated groups find ways to engage in conflict with power-holders. They challenge the elite's interpretations of reality through voices that are spoken but carefully and rarely in public. Rumors, gossip, songs, private jokes, gestures, and stories can express the interests of workers in ways that organizational power holders would never endorse. As we will see in Chapter 5, these nineteenth-century historical developments have broad applications to contemporary organizational cultures, subcultures, countercultures, and present-day resistance to domination.

The end of the Civil War brought with it the end of slavery, but not of hierarchies in society or in organizations. By some accounts, it represented the triumph of one region's values regarding division of labor over another's, with social class rather than race serving as the primary organizing principle. By other accounts, the end of the war marked the birth of a democracy in which social class, race, religion, or creed simply did not matter; a person could advance according to his or her abilities. By still other accounts, nothing much had changed. Slavery based on race may have officially vanished, but racial prejudice was still widespread. The economically disadvantaged blacks who had overcome one form of injustice in the South would merely encounter it again in their migrations to Northern cities and factories, disguised this time as ethnic prejudice and fear of competition for jobs.

Scientific Management

The years from 1880 to 1920 were characterized not only by significant racial and class prejudice but also by unprecedented economic expansion in the United States. Massive industrialization was accompanied by ruthless treatment of workers, and owners subscribed to a survival of the fittest mentality regarding their employees. Those who succeeded were deemed to be morally strong; those who failed deserved to fail, because they were unworthy (Bendix, 1956).

Born in this era was a middle-class white man named Frederick Taylor (1856–1915). Trained as an engineer and possessing a prodigious (some would say self-abusive) capacity for work, he was a pioneer in the development of scientific management. He made many contributions, but he is best remembered for his now classic book, *Principles of Scientific Management*, published in 1913. Taylor's basic assumption was that the best management is a true science, resting upon clearly defined laws, rules, and principles. He developed time and motion studies that led to improved organizational efficiency based on the mechanization of labor and the authority of the clock. Work was divided into discrete units, which were measured according to how long it took a competent worker to

TABLE 3.2
SUMMARY OF COMMUNICATION VALUES FOUND IN RESISTANCE NARRATIVES

What is Truth?	Where is Power?	How is Transcendence Possible?
Depends on the relationship of the story to the position of power held by the storyteller.	In the resistance tactic of countering a dominant strategy; in the performance of "a world turned upside down"; in the performance (telling) retelling of the resistance account.	Off-stage performances of resistance narratives organize and inform opposition to power-holders.
Communication practices: Saving face, indirect confrontation, disguise, artful misinterpretation of instructions, use of secrets, portrayal of dominant elites as immoral, unethical, stupid, or fallible; appearing to comply with domination while actively pursuing tactics of insubordination.	*Communication practices:* Resistance narratives, songs, humor, gossip, theatrical performances, dramatic gestures, and asides.	*Communication practices:* Occupy territory controlled by the dominant interests and use it to stage resistance narratives.
Representative story: "There is an Indian story . . . about an Englishman who, having been told that the world rested on a platform which rested on the back of an elephant which rested in turn on the back of a turtle, asked . . . what did the turtle rest on? [The Indian's response:] Another turtle. [The Indian:] Ah, Sahib, after that it is turtles all the way down" (From Geertz, 1973, pp. 28–29).	*Representative explanation:* "[A] tactic is a calculated action . . . a maneuver 'within the enemy's field of vision,' . . . and within enemy territory. . . . It operates in isolated actions, blow by blow. It takes advantage of opportunities and depends on them. . . . It must vigilantly make use of the cracks that particular conjunctions open in the surveillance of proprietary powers. It poaches in them. It creates surprise in them. . . . It is a guileful ruse" (de Certeau, 1984, p. 37).	*Representative explanation:* Power-holders legitimate their stories of truth, justice, and rationality through control of territory and property and use surveillance (from the idea of surveying one's property) to keep tabs on how "their" places are being used. By contrast, the powerless "appropriate" or "poach" space within the power-holder's place, and use these spaces for performances of resistance that demonstrate what they "know" as well as their hope for the future (see de Certeau, 1984).

Adapted from Dwight Conquergood, "Ethnography, Rhetoric, and Performance," *Quarterly Journal of Speech*, 78 (1992), pp. 80–97.

accomplish them. This principle was then used to plan for factory outcomes, to evaluate the efficiency of other workers, and to train the less skillful. Keeping such a production system operating required divisions of labor, carefully developed chains of command, and a general devaluing of communication other than orders and instructions.

Taylor's goal was to transform the nature of work and of management. He hoped that cooperation between managers and employees in determining the scientific facts would bring a new era of industrial peace and eliminate disputes about how hard one should work or how much money a given job was worth. "Under scientific management arbitrary power, arbitrary dictation, ceases; and every single subject, large and small, becomes the question for scientific investigation, for reduction to law" (Taylor, 1947, p. 211). But things didn't quite work out that way; it is a great irony that Taylor believed he was developing his ideas to help the working person, and yet by the end of his life he was cursed by labor unions as "the enemy of the working man" (Morgan, 1986). Despite the obvious drawbacks and contradictions, Taylor did change the emphasis of much thinking about organizations, focusing for the first time on the relationship between managers and employees as one key to organizational productivity.

Scientific management, then, is a management-oriented, production-centered view of organizations and communication. The ideal of this approach is the efficient machine in which humans are smoothly functioning components or parts. Furthermore, this perspective assumes a fundamental distinction between managers and employees: managers think, workers work (Morgan, 1986). Both the ideal and this assumption have limited utility. In task situations that are straightforward, require no flexibility in responding to contingencies, and offer no opportunities for creative initiative, the machine is an appropriate metaphor, and employees can simply follow orders. But this description of an organization leaves out a great deal. It does not take into account human motivations for working, personal relationships on the job, or the turbulent nature of organizational environments that require extra effort and flexible responses. Moreover, efforts to improve efficiency by raising production quantities alienate workers. Henry Ford's automobile plant, for example, maintained an average 280 percent turnover under scientific management (Morgan, 1986).

Bureaucracy

The early 1900s were a brutal time for most workers, many of whom were young children paid meager wages. Working conditions were often extremely harsh, and job security nonexistent. People were hired and fired (and assigned to better and worse jobs) based on their race, religion, sex, attitude, and relationships to the boss. This approach toward managing employees, called *particularism,* was expedient for owners and managers but often had dire consequences for employees. Particularism and the poor treatment of workers presented a problem of ideology for the United States. "On the one hand, democracy stressed liberty and equality for all. On the other hand, large masses of workers and nonsalaried personnel had to submit to apparently arbitrary authority, backed up by local and national police forces and legal powers, for ten to twelve hours a day, six days a week" (Perrow, 1986, p. 53). It was in light of this conflict between ideology and practice that we must understand the rise of bureaucracy. According to Scott (1981, p. 68), bureaucracy has the following characteristics:

1. A fixed division of labor among participants.
2. A hierarchy of offices.
3. A set of general rules that govern performances.
4. A separation of personal from official property and rights.
5. Selection of personnel on the basis of technical qualifications; equal treatment of all employees.
6. Employment viewed as a career by participants; tenure protects against unfair arbitrary dismissal.

The well-known German scholar, Max Weber (1946), was not a blind advocate of bureaucracy. Rather, he was an extremely intelligent observer of society whose cultural pessimism led him to conclude that the bureaucratization of the world was unstoppable and inescapable (Clegg, 1990). Simply put, although Weber was skeptical of bureaucracy, he believed that it would triumph owing to its technical superiority over other forms of organization. Table 3.3 provides a detailed summary of Weber's principles of bureaucratic organizations.

Today most people associate bureaucracy with red tape and with huge, inflexible companies and public agencies that are totally ineffective. However, this state of affairs may not be a necessary result of a bureaucratic approach. Charles Perrow (1986), in his famous defense of bureaucracy, places its difficulties squarely in the laps of the individuals behind the organizations. Bureaucracy is an efficient machine, he argues, and cannot be blamed for the ends of the people who choose to use it as their tool.

In any case, it is helpful to examine bureaucracy against the background of what came before—particularism—and to understand that one of Weber's key goals was to introduce *universalism*, or standards of fair treatment, into the workplace. Even today, managers struggle to hold on to their ability to hire, fire, promote, and discipline at will. One machine shop foreman we know longs for the "bad old days" when a difficult employee could be assigned a particularly undesirable job until his attitude improved. Prebureaucratic decision making was easier and more expedient for the one who held the power. Bureaucracy makes capricious decisions harder to implement at the same time that it protects employees from abuse. If society and its organizations need to err on one side or the other, which is the better choice? Should some flexibility be traded to ensure fair treatment of employees, or should flexibility and productivity be more important?

The ideal bureaucracy is never fully realized, for three reasons. First, it is impossible to rid organizations of all extraorganizational influences on member behavior; second, bureaucracy does not deal well with nonroutine tasks; and third, people vary in their rationality (Perrow, 1986). Each of these important inadequacies of bureaucracy became the basis for other theories. Later studies of bureaucracy conducted by sociologists reveal that Weber's pessimism about the inevitability of bureaucracy was misplaced (Clegg 1990; Hage & Aiken, 1970). Instead, alternative forms of organizing, which loosen the iron cage of bureaucracy, are in many circumstances more effective and efficient. This loosening of the traditional assumptions of classical organization theory paved the way for a new metaphor for conceiving of human organization.

TABLE 3.3
MAX WEBER'S PRINCIPLES OF BUREAUCRATIC ORGANIZATIONS

Structure and Function of Organization	Means of Rewarding Effort in Organizations	Protections for the Individuals Who Do the Work
Business must be conducted continuously.	Officials had to consider their offices as their sole or primary occupation for which they received fixed salaries, graded by rank.	It is necessary to protect the rights of individuals to ensure a source of personnel and to prevent arbitrary use of power in the service of nonorganizational or anti-organizational goals.
Hierarchy of offices with each office under the control of a higher one.	Officials did not own the means of production or administration.	Officials serve voluntarily and are appointed.
Systematic division of labor based on training and expertise; specific areas of responsibility and action clearly understood.	Officials could not appropriate their offices and had to render an accounting of their use of organizational property.	Service constitutes a career with promotions according to seniority or achievement.
Performance of duties governed by written rules and records of actions and decisions already taken.	Officials had to separate their private affairs and property from their organization's affairs and property.	Obedience is owed the officeholder, not the person.
Benefits: (1) Provided mechanisms for control over performance of individuals and (2) provided means for specialization and expertise and means of coordinating roles to prevent them from interfering with each other.	*Benefits:* (1) Salary rather than other forms of compensation or reward limit potential for abuse; (2) legitimate rather than charismatic leadership (although charismatic still exists in bureaucracies).	*Benefits:* (1) Officials are subject to authority only with respect to their duties; (2) there is the right to appeal of decisions and grievances.

From Charles Perrow, "*Why Bureaucracy?*" *Complex Organizations: A Critical Essay*, 3rd ed. (New York: Random House, 1986).

Implications for Organizational Communication

Classical organizational theorists did not see communication as problematic; they viewed it primarily as a tool for issuing orders, coordinating work, and gaining worker compliance. In a rationalized, hierarchical world, the only kind of communication that matters carries the right information through the proper channels. This approach also poses some important questions about ethics. (See Ethics Box 3.1 on page 68, which provides a narrative account of growing up in the military bureaucracy.)

ETHICS BOX 3.1

"RANK HAS ITS PRIVILEGES": THE INFLUENCES OF ORGANIZATIONAL STRUCTURE ON HOME AND FAMILY LIFE

One of the largest bureaucracies on planet Earth is the U.S. military. Characterized by principles of scientific rationality, the military is organized by pervasive hierarchies (ranks) and relies on standardized procedures for behavioral control. Viewed from the perspective of classical scientific management, the U.S. military operates as a (mostly) efficient machine.

However, one often neglected feature of bureaucracies concerns their influences on home and family life. Put simply, where does the tightly controlled world of work stop and the more loosely organized world of home begin? For persons who work in bureaucracies, do ways of knowing, working, valuing, and doing at work become the principles through which home and family management also take place?

In the following selection from Mary Truscott's *Brats: Children of the American Military Speak Out* (1989), the organizing principle of hierarchy (rank) is associated with how children learn other lessons.

> I learned to snap off a salute before I learned to ride a bike. There were plenty of role models for me to imitate; people who were always saluting my father. It didn't seem unusual. Some men saluted, and others were saluted.
>
> The military jargon that was so pervasive on the post and in our household included many rank-related qualifiers. The size and location of our houses were based on rank. We lived on "colonel's row" in stately three-story duplexes with full maid's quarters in the basement, but we had done our time in apartments before my father made colonel.
>
> My father had "his men," the men under his command. My mother came home from the Officers' Wives Club functions and frequently told my father about the "little captain's wife" or "little major's wife" she had met. Too young to remember when my father had been a lowly major, I developed a mental image of a community of Lilliputian people, captains and majors and their families, inhabiting the smaller and, I knew, inferior housing on the other side of the post.
>
> The ascending rank was always part of a family name. I answered the telephone with "Colonel Truscott's quarters, Mary speaking." I addressed all adults with their surname and current rank. I never knew many men who were "mister," with the exception of school principals.
>
> We lived on the post for the most part, only minutes away from my father's office, but I had no idea of what my father did at work. My dad was in the Army; other men were businessmen, doctors, lawyers, Indian chiefs. In his study at home he had a framed poster from a lecture he had given that had his picture on it and the caption THE NATION'S FOREMOST EXPERT ON RADIOACTIVE FALLOUT. Whatever it was that my dad did at work, I felt certain that if we were bombed and fallout came raining out of the sky, my father would lead us to the designated fallout shelters on the post and we would survive, no matter how awful the blast, because he was "The Nation's Foremost Expert."
>
> We visited my father's office a few times, and it was remarkably devoid of any sign or indication of his work. The walls in his office were pale green, with perhaps a flag and a strictly functional map or two to break the monotony. His desk was typical Army issue, either wood or metal, and the chairs had convex seats covered with slippery green vinyl that made it impossible to sit still. The Army seemed to be a serious, boring place to work.
>
> Rank truly had its privileges. The written and unwritten rules that established the chain of command for the men in uniform also applied to their families. Rank created a virtual caste

system, and life on a military post had no uncertainties. There were stripes and insignia on uniforms, stickers on cars, and name-plates on houses. Families were segregated, by rank, in separate and not necessarily equal enclaves, and there were separate club facilities for officers and enlisted men. Post housing was the most obvious indicator of rank.

The privileges accorded by rank were highly visible, but the social taboos on post were often not apparent or even official. The officers' children tended to cross the lines of rank without compunction, but the children of enlisted men were conscious of the rules that forbade their fathers from fraternizing with officers and kept to themselves for the most part.

Regardless of who the father was and what he did, rank was either a source of pride and status or an embarrassing label that put the military brat on the wrong side of the tracks. And all military brats, no matter where their father had fit in the hierarchy of rank, emphasized, over and over, that rank was pervasive and clearly defined.

Ethical questions can be thought of as sources of creativity or constraint. Using the above example, how would you respond to these questions?

1. What ethical issues come with the notion that "rank has its privileges"? Do those privileges extend beyond the duties and responsibilities of work?
2. How did hierarchical thinking influence Truscott's view of the world? Does this kind of categorical, rank-ordered thinking contribute to our understanding of other similar divisions in society, such as social class, race, age, and gender?
3. Is the kind of total integration of home and work revealed by Truscott's example necessary to the maintenance of bureaucracies? Or is the military a special case? Why or why not?

THE HUMAN RELATIONS APPROACH

Kenneth Burke was once asked why he got interested in the study of human communication. Burke replied: "People weren't treating each other very well. I wanted to help find a way to make relationships better" (cited in Goodall, 1984, p. 134). Burke was referring to the 1930s, one of the world's worst periods of economic depression. It is no coincidence that also during this time old models of bureaucracy began to be questioned and the first theories of human relations appeared.

In this section we discuss the historical and cultural background that contributed to these theories. Then we focus on the major players and events within the human relations movement. Finally, we discuss the legacies of this approach for current thinking about organizations and communication.

Historical and Cultural Background

The Great Depression (1929–1940) created economic and social hardship for millions of Americans. It contributed to major changes in government policies—social security, welfare, government funding of public improvement projects—that had long-lasting effects. The Depression also contributed to a major migration of workers from the drought-ridden central farming states to the West Coast and from the impoverished rural South to the Northern cities. These individuals and families were seeking work, and through work, an improved life for themselves and for their children. The surplus of available workers created by the lack of employment opportunities led to keen competition for jobs. It also led to widespread abuses of workers by unscrupulous managers. It is not surprising, then, that this historical period was also marked by the expansion of powerful labor unions—organizations that advocated human rights for the labor force, fair wages, and improved working conditions.

Important divisions between managers and workers had always existed. During times of economic hardship and strong competition for jobs, these divisions became more intense. The demands for improved working conditions, for example, would be met only if such improvements spelled larger profits through increased productivity. "Fair" wages were determined largely by factory output; increasing the output to improve wages tended to bring with it greater incidence of work-related injury, illness, and death. Human rights often meant, simply, having to work *only* twelve hours a day, six days a week, with one 30-minute break for a meal. Indeed, these difficult economic times contributed to strained relationships between workers and managers.

World War II led to an enormous expansion of new jobs, in both the military and in private industry. It also contributed to the human relations movement by accidentally placing academic researchers, managers, and military personnel in direct communication with each other. W. Charles Redding, an organizational communication pioneer and now one of its leading historians, refers to this accidental grouping as "the Triple Alliance" (1985). He argues that, because of this alliance, managers and military officers benefited from new ideas about organizing work and about the importance of developing trust among workers. Academics benefited from access to industrial plants, where their task was both to study and to train workers, military personnel, and managers. The effects of this war-formed alliance would have lasting impact, particularly for the subdiscipline that was largely created out of that alliance—organizational communication (Redding, 1985).

Another development of this historical period involved primarily academic institutions. Researchers constructed an alternative perspective on human relationships that was not based on the simplistic conditioned response form of behaviorism. Herbert Blumer (1905–1989) would later coin the term *symbolic interactionism* (1969) to represent this new approach to human behavior. Symbolic interactionism draws on the American pragmatism of Charles Pierce, William James, and John Dewey; the social philosophy of George Herbert Mead; and the Freudian interpretation of the symbolic realms of experience. Taken together, Blumer (1969) advanced a deceptively simple but revolutionary alternative to behaviorism: that humans respond to the meanings they have for things. A meaning-centered rather than behavior-centered approach to understanding human action was born. Figure 3.3 shows the fundamental difference between this approach and behaviorism.

These three major occurrences—the Great Depression, World War II, and a new way of understanding human behavior—came at a time when the perceived limitations of scientific management were at their peak.

What Is Human Relations?

Although Taylor tried to emphasize the importance of cooperative relationships between managers and employees, the cold rationality of his scientific methods did little to contribute to the quality of these interactions in the early twentieth century. It was not

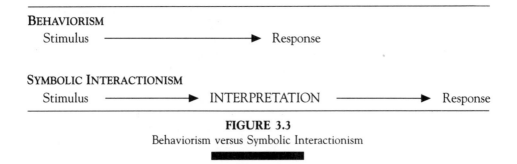

FIGURE 3.3
Behaviorism versus Symbolic Interactionism

until the 1930s that two individuals, Elton Mayo and Chester Barnard, were to conceive of relationships at work in an entirely new way. Their work was both foundational for the human relations movement and a precursor for much modern-day thinking about management. Their perspective marked a clean break from earlier points of view: "People are tractable, docile, gullible, uncritical—and want to be led. But far more than this is deeply true of them. They want to feel united, tied, bound to something, some cause, bigger than they, commanding them yet worthy of them, *summoning them to significance in living*" (Bendix, 1956, p. 296).

Elton Mayo (1880–1949) was a Harvard professor who set out to critique and extend scientific management. Unlike Taylor, Mayo did not see organizations as comprised of wage-maximizing individuals. Instead, he stressed the limits of individual rationality and the importance of interpersonal relations. In contrast to scientific management, Mayo (1945) believed that

1. Society is comprised of groups, not isolated individuals.
2. Individuals are swayed by group norms and do not act alone in accord with self-interests.
3. Individual decisions are not entirely rational but are influenced by emotions.

This period also saw the publication of Chester Barnard's enormously influential book, *The Functions of the Executive* (1938). At the time Barnard was chief executive at Bell Telephone in New Jersey. He went further than anyone had before in asserting the importance of cooperation in organizations—that "organizations *by their very nature* are cooperative systems and cannot fail to be so" (Perrow, 1986, p. 63). The key to cooperation, he argued, lay in persuading individuals to accept a common purpose, from which all else would follow. This was a major change from Taylor's economic inducements; for Barnard, the role of management was largely communicative and persuasive. Effective managers communicated in ways that encouraged workers to identify with the organization. For the first time management was seen as more interpersonal than economic.

The Hawthorne Studies

While Barnard was busy running New Jersey Bell, a landmark event was taking place at another part of AT&T, at the Hawthorne plant of Western Electric (a subsidiary of AT&T) in Cicero, Illinois. Along with Elton Mayo, another Harvard professor, F. J.

Roethlisberger, was called in to study Hawthorne by the plant managers and by W. J. Dickson, an industrial engineer who was also a manager at the plant. The managers were concerned because of the numerous complaints and high level of dissatisfaction that had led to high turnover and reduced plant efficiency. The other consultants who had been brought in—experts using principles of scientific management—had failed to solve the problem. Perrow (1986) picks up the story:

> The researchers at Western Electric took two groups of workers doing the same kinds of jobs, put them in separate rooms, and kept careful records of their productivity. One group (the test group) had the intensity of its lighting increased. Its productivity went up. For the other group (the control group), there was no change in lighting. But, to the amazement of the researchers, its productivity went up also. Even more puzzling, when the degree of illumination in the test group was gradually lowered back to the original level, it was found that output still continued to go up. Output also continued to increase in the control group. The researchers continued to drop the illumination of the test group, but it was not until the workers were working under conditions of bright moonlight that productivity stopped rising and fell off sharply (pp. 79–80).

Over a period of time Mayo and his colleagues realized that the productivity improvements they had measured had little to do with degree of illumination or any other physical condition in the plant. Instead, it was the increased attention given to the workers by management and researchers—the fact that they were placed in specially controlled rooms and carefully watched—that made the difference. The conclusion that increased attention somehow raised morale and that morale in turn boosted productivity came to be known as the Hawthorne effect.

Additional experiments lent further support to Mayo's critique of scientific management. One prominent finding of the Hawthorne studies was drawn from an experiment in the bank-wiring observation room. Even under poor working conditions, it was discovered, supportive informal group norms could have a positive effect on productivity. For the first time, it was shown that individual workers were complex beings with multiple motives, values, and emotions, and were sensitive to group norms. "At the social psychological level, the Hawthorne Studies pointed to a more complex model of worker motivation based on a social-psychological rather than an economic conception of man [sic]; and at the structural level, the Hawthorne Studies discovered and demonstrated the importance of informal organization" (Scott, 1981, p. 87).

In retrospect, precious little evidence exists for these particular conclusions, especially for the claim that a positive relationship exists between morale and productivity. Nevertheless, it fit well with the romantic ideals of the time and became the basis for much of the research that has been conducted on organizational behavior since. Table 3.4 summarizes the evolution of classical to human relations approaches to organizations and communication.

The Legacy of Human Relations

Mayo and Barnard's foundational work led to three widely different lines of research. The first investigated how managerial and leadership style could impact on worker productivity. Of the three lines of research, these leadership studies are most closely associated with the human relations movement. The second part of the human relations legacy, typically

TABLE 3.4

SUMMARY OF HISTORICAL AND CULTURAL INFLUENCES ON CLASSICAL AND
HUMAN RELATIONS APPROACHES TO ORGANIZATIONS AND COMMUNICATION

Classical Approaches	Human Relations Approaches
Theme: Scientific rationality would lead to improved efficiency and productivity	*Theme:* Improved human relations would lead to improved efficiency and productivity
Enlightenment ideals	Romantic ideals
Industrial Revolution	Development of psychology
Scientific methods	Social scientific methods
Dominant metaphor: Organization as machine	*Dominant metaphor: Organization as the sum of relationships*
Supporting principles:	*Supporting principles:*
Ideal form of society is authoritarian and values hierarchical organization.	Ideal form of society is democratic and values open and honest relationships.
Division of labor/social classes/races/sexes/ nations; if "the rules" were applied equally to everyone, individuals who worked hard and obeyed instructions could better themselves.	Divisions of labor/management honored; negotiation of differences through open communication valued.
Conflict based on divisions; dialectical relationships between management and labor based on power and money.	Conflict based on lack of shared understanding; dialogic model of relationships between management and labor based on trust, openness, honesty, and power.
Application of the principles of mechanics to organizations and communication led to operationalizing the machine metaphor (e.g., this business runs like clockwork).	Application of humanistic and behavioral psychology to organizations and communication led to operationalizing "relational metaphors" (e.g., this business is run like a family).
Communication is top-down and procedurally oriented; following "the rules" is valued, and opposing them calls into question the whole moral order.	Communication is relational and needs-oriented; self-actualization is valued if it occurs through work.
Dominant form of organizing: Bureaucracy	*Dominant form of organizing:* Teams or groups within bureaucracies
Stability is best obtained through adherence to procedural forms of order.	Stability is best obtained through relational and personal happiness.
Limitations: Too constraining; encourages mindless adherence to details and procedures; discourages creativity.	*Limitations:* False openness, abuse of trust and/ or honesty; equation of employee happiness with efficiency or productivity.

associated with Herbert Simon, examined the limitations of decision making in organizations and built on Mayo's critique of Taylor's rational, wage-maximizing model of individuals. The third body of work, the institutional school, extended Chester Barnard's ideas about executives to consider communication between senior managers and the organizational environment.

Leadership Style   From World War II through the 1960s, an overwhelming amount of research was conducted on the relationship between management (or leadership) style and productivity. A fundamental shift had taken place in people's thinking about worker performance. Earlier, poor performance was blamed on a lack of worker motivation or character; now it was being ascribed to poor management. Unlocking worker productivity, then, depended on improved management and supervision, and so the best ways to lead, manage, and supervise people were sought.

No single problem in the history of organizations has proven so difficult to solve. Research on the subject began with a ten-year study of leader characteristics at Ohio State University in 1945. The study attempted to catalogue leader traits that predicted work group productivity. The team isolated two factors that described leaders—initiating structure and consideration. A person who scored high in initiating structure was active in planning, communicating, scheduling, and organizing. A person high in consideration showed concern for the feelings of subordinates, promoted mutual trust, and fostered two-way communication. These were not opposite ends of *one* continuum, however; a leader could be high on *both* dimensions (Perrow, 1986). A major finding of these studies was that traditional management skills—that is, those associated with initiating structure—were equally as important as interpersonal skills in promoting productivity.

Similar research was conducted at the University of Michigan, with similar results. Leaders were classified as being, to varying degrees, employee oriented and production oriented. But no blanket conclusions about the best way to manage emerged. Later work offered more complex models of the different managerial behaviors that would work in a given situation. For example, Frederick Herzberg's (1966) two-factor theory of job satisfaction posited that people have two independent sets of needs—to avoid pain and to grow psychologically—and that management strategies that address one kind of need should not be expected to fulfill another. In other words, improving working conditions or increasing salaries would be expected to reduce *dissatisfaction*, but not necessarily to promote satisfaction. (Herzberg called these hygiene factors.) On the other hand, changing the design of the work to make it more rewarding would most likely increase satisfaction. (He called these factors motivators.) In their attempts to motivate worker performance, Herzberg argued, managers needed to maintain a clear distinction between the two and not to expect changes in hygiene factors to make much of a difference in productivity or morale.

Another research program in this category is Fred Fiedler's (1967) contingency theory of leadership. Fiedler maintains that different leadership styles are appropriate for different situations. Specifically, when a group is either very favorable or very unfavorable toward a leader (in terms of clarity of the task and relationship with followers), a task-oriented style is best. Under these extreme circumstances, focusing on interpersonal relations is either unnecessary or futile. When a group is somewhere in the middle (i.e., moderate in task clarity and relationship with followers), Fiedler recommends an interpersonal style.

Overall, research that applies human relations thinking to the relationship between management and productivity has been inconclusive and disappointing. Furthermore, the underlying ideology of human relations has consistently come under attack. Mayo and his colleagues were accused of being "happy boys," willing to trade profitability for employee well-being. William Whyte's *The Organization Man* severely criticized human relations on the grounds that it had replaced the Protestant Work Ethic with a Social Ethic that required employees to dress well, act nice, and fit in, substituting complacency for entrepreneurial drive (see Table 3.5 on page 76 for a summary). In perhaps the most damning comment of all, human relations was dubbed "cow sociology." "Just as contented cows were alleged to produce more milk, satisfied workers were expected to produce more output" (Scott, 1981, p. 90).

There are some important parallels to organizational communication theory and re-search, which has also labored under an ideology of openness which is out of sync with real organizational life (cf. Eisenberg, 1984; Eisenberg & Witten, 1987; Parks, 1982). Of course, all of us want to believe that openness, self-disclosure, and more supportive relationships in general should have a positive impact on organizational productivity and effectiveness, but research has not provided clear evidence of this belief. Without a doubt, models of employee motivation have become increasingly complex, ever refining what is meant by good leadership and the conditions under which it is desirable to focus on interpersonal relations. However, the applicability of these highly situation-specific contingency models has been limited. The result is a body of research with no clear implications for practice:

> The practitioner who wants to apply the human relations approach has no clear directive as to what to do—and this is true not only of the findings on size of immediate work group, the character of informal work group solidarity, degree of identification with company goals, and type of leadership style as related to productivity; it also applies to the findings on the relation of "morale" (i.e., satisfaction with job and with company) to all of these variables. The evidence is typically inconclusive, the interpretations sometimes contradictory (Wilensky, 1957, p. 34).

The key assumptions, findings, and implications of this line of research are summarized in Table 3.6 on page 78.

Simon's Decision-making Model   As mentioned above, Mayo's suggestion that managerial style should affect employee performance was only one part of the critique of scientific management that launched human relations. Another aspect was a revised view of individual decision makers in organizations, from the image of isolated, wage-maximizing, fully rational beings, to a more social model of individuals who, at best, only *intend* to be rational.

Herbert Simon (1957) developed this new view of individual decision making in organizations. He argued that people are only imperfectly rational. While we may attempt to make the best decision, he maintained, aspects of the situation and our limited processing capacities always prevent anything even approaching complete rationality. People lack knowledge not only of the consequences of their actions, but also of the alternative courses of action available, or of the criteria that would make one choice seem superior to others. Rather than maximizing all factors in decision making, the best we can do, according to Simon, is to *satisfice*. Satisficing means that people tend to "settle for acceptable as opposed to optimal solutions, to attend to problems sequentially rather than simultaneously, and to utilize existing repertoires of action programs rather than develop novel responses for each situation" (Scott, 1981, p. 75).

Communication is critical to Simon's model, for communication establishes the defini-

TABLE 3.5

SUMMARY OF WILLIAM WHYTE'S CRITIQUE OF HUMAN RELATIONS

I. WHO IS THE ORGANIZATION MAN?

The "Organization Man" [*sic*] is a person who not only works for a company, but also belongs to it. Whyte says: "They are the ones of our middle class who have left home, spiritually as well as physically, to take the vows of organizational life, and it is they who are the mind and soul of our great self-perpetuating institutions. . . . It is their values which will set the American temper."

Whyte is not limiting his discussion to typical for-profit organizations; he writes: "Blood brother to the business trainee off to join DuPont is the seminary student who will end up in the church hierarchy, the doctor headed for the corporate clinic, the physics Ph.D. in a government laboratory, the intellectual on the foundation-sponsored team project, the engineering graduate in the huge drafting room at Lockheed, the young apprentice in a Wall Street law factory."

II. WHAT IS THE CONFLICT BETWEEN THE PROTESTANT ETHIC (CREATED BY ENTREPRENEUR-STYLE CAPITALISM) AND THE SOCIAL ETHIC (SPAWNED BY HUMAN RELATIONS APPROACHES TO ORGANIZATIONAL MANAGEMENT)?

The Protestant Ethic is "the pursuit of individual salvation through hard work, thrift, and competitive struggle" which is "the heart of American achievement." It is the "old faith" that produced the American dream.

The Social Ethic "could be called an organization ethic, or a bureaucratic ethic, and more than anything else it rationalizes the organization's demands for fealty and gives those who offer it wholeheartedly a sense of dedication in doing so. . . . [Its imperatives are] technique is more vital than content, managing is an end in itself, and expertise is relatively independent of the content of what is being managed." His definition: "I mean that contemporary body of thought which makes morally legitimate the pressures of society against the individual. Its major propositions are three: a belief in the group as the source of creativity, a belief in "belongingness" as the ultimate need of the individual, and a belief in the application of science to achieve belongingness. . . . Essentially, it is a utopian faith."

III. HOW DID ORGANIZATIONS ADOPT THE SOCIAL ETHIC?

    A. **Scientism**

        1. "Social Engineering": The same techniques that worked in the physical sciences will eventually work in the social sciences. By measuring personality, group dynamics can be applied to business decisions about who to hire, how work should be accomplished, and how to manage conflicts. For a person to "fit in" to a company, she or he must possess the appropriate "characteristics."

        2. Bias against conflict and individualism: The whole is greater than the sum of the parts; it is more important to fit in than to stand out.

    B. **Belongingness**

        1. Individuals and groups are told that they have needs that must be satisfied; in particular, there is a deep emotional need for security that comes from total integration with the organization.

        2. Elton Mayo and the Hawthorne studies: The strongest human characteristic is the desire for feelings of security that come from assured membership in a group. By contrast, "conflict" represents a "communication breakdown." (*Breakdown* is a term borrowed from individual psychology—what threatens to destroy the individual personality may also threaten the social fabric of an organization or society.)

76

C. **Togetherness**

   1. It is not enough for the individual to simply belong to the organization; individuals must learn how to belong together.
   2. Social science has "proved" that the group is superior to the individual. The fallacy here is "false collectivization"; just because a collection of individuals can be called a group, this does not mean they function as a group or that they should.
   3. Morally, the ideal of the human is summed up in the term *democracy*. The superior group-person will become the leader; the leader's task is to seek compromise, reduce conflict, and improve the feel-good aspect of collective activity (group morale).

IV. HOW ARE ORGANIZATION MEN TRAINED?

A. **A Generation of Bureaucrats**

   1. The origins of the bureaucratic mind are found societally in conservative politics, stringent utilitarianism, students who want to "be told," and a concentration of effort in political discussions of ends rather than means.
   2. Education complies with this construction of society; students increasingly want the "good life," which they define as calm and ordered. At work they want personnel jobs so "they can be nice to people on company time." Management is the goal of their careers.

B. **A Practical Curriculum**

   1. Education is not simply compliant with the construction of the Organization Man; it is the culprit because education is increasingly vocational and technical and has the added burden of providing social skills.
   2. To choose a career in the humanities is to choose organizational death, so the rumor goes (although this is not true). Better to go into business or engineering (two technical, vocational schools). Who chooses education as a career? Typically, those who score lowest on standardized tests.

C. **Business Influence on Education**

   1. The employee produced by the system of technical and vocational education is likely to graduate into organizational life, valuing precisely those skills and associations that got him where he is. Mostly, this is summed up by having a "B" average and belonging to a high-profile social fraternity.
   2. Later on in his career, this organizational man will contribute to his old school and designate those funds for more technical and vocational studies, as well as support of fraternities and social activities. Eventually, if he rises high enough in the corporate order, he will oversee corporate fund drives and become a sort of extra trustee to education. Once again, the same values that got him through will guide his decisions.

The remaining chapters of Whyte's book are dedicated to:

1. How the executives of major companies do not fit the current profile for managerial train-ees—they are entrepreneurs, risk-takers, rebels. Work is their major source of self-expression; their hobbies are therapy to restore their energies between rounds of work.
2. How "Personality tests" are designed around principles of conformity to corporate ideals. There is an appendix called "How to Cheat on Personality Tests."
3. How organizations conspire to bureaucratize science and scientists so that potential sources of liberation from the Social Ethic are suppressed.
4. How the home life of the Organization Man values transience (company-sponsored moves on a regular basis), living in well-ordered suburbs, inconspicuous consumption, friendship, being outgoing, seeing the church as an extension of business networks, and managing children as extensions of self.

Adapted from *The Organization Man* (New York: Harper & Row, 1956).

TABLE 3.6
THE LEGACY OF HUMAN RELATIONS:
THREE RESEARCH TRADITIONS

Tradition: Leadership style

Key Assumption: Supportive leader communication positively affects productivity and morale.

Findings and Implications for Organizational Communication

- Leader behavior can be classified as employee-oriented or production-oriented; both are key to effectiveness.
- Effective leadership style varies so much by situation that clear, practical conclusions are rare.
- The desire for open, supportive communication by leaders is motivated more by ideology (what people wish were true) than by research evidence.

Tradition: Simon's decision-making model

Key Assumption: Individual decision making is only intended to be rational.

Findings and Implications for Organizational Communication

- Individuals in organizations satisfice, not maximize.
- Decision making is limited through decision premises, which are constructed largely through communication.
- Organizations can exert unobtrusive control over employees through the control of decision premises.

Tradition: Institutional school

Key Assumption: Organizations are dependent on their social environments for legitimacy and survival.

Findings and Implications for Organizational Communication

- There are important differences among organizations.
- Organizations have a life of their own apart from individual members or groups.
- Organizational statespersons must manage relationship with environment.
- Institutions limit certain kinds of communication to shield their technical core from evaluation.

---

tion of the situation, which in turn guides individual decision making. Perrow (1986) summarizes:

> This definition of the situation . . . is built out of past experience (it includes prejudices and stereotypes) and highly particularized, selective views of present stimuli. Most of the individual's responses are "routine"; they invoke solutions they have used before. Sometimes they must engage in problem-solving. When they do, they conduct a limited search for alternatives along familiar and well-worn paths, selecting the first satisfactory one that comes along. They do not consider all possible alternatives, nor do they keep searching for the optimum one. Rather, they "satisfice" or select the first satisfactory solution. Their very standards for satisfactory solutions are a part of the definition of the situation. . . . *The organization can control these standards, and it defines the situation;* only to a limited extent are they up to individuals (Perrow, 1986, p. 122).

Simon's model was further refined in his collaboration with James G. March (March & Simon, 1958). In their book *Organizations* they describe in more detail the ways in which organizations control individuals by controlling their definition of the situation, by actively shaping their assumptions and decision premises. The more isolated an individual is in an organization the more communication resembles monologue and the more constrained are an individual member's decision premises. (The extreme would be a cult where competing interpretations might be purposefully eliminated.) The more sources of information, the greater the likelihood of divergent opinions and competing voices or definitions of the situation, and the greater the possibility for dialogue.

March and Simon's work, then, reveals that organizations can exert unobtrusive (or unrecognized) control over members by limiting alternatives and shaping decision premises. From one perspective, such controls (which include division of labor, job titles, the formal hierarchy, and key rules and regulations, all of which may be taken for granted) are necessary to accomplish Barnard's ideal of cooperation. Seen from a different perspective, such controls represent the triumph of owners and managers over the working person. Not only do they keep people in line, but the jailers are the people themselves. When decision premises are controlled, individuals voluntarily restrict their own behavior according to what they perceive as possible, given their definition of the situation. This latter definition is the driving force behind critical theory, which is discussed in Chapter 6. (See Table 3.6 for a summary of the decision-making model.)

The Institutional School   A final area that takes its cue from the human relations school is Philip Selznick's institutional approach to organizations. Like Simon's, Selznick's (1948, 1957) view of organizations is counter-rational. The major difference is that whereas Simon focused mainly on individual decision making, Selznick was interested in the total organization, which he felt took on a life of its own apart from any individual member or group. But this total organization is far from predictable:

> If the organization as conceived by Weber operates like a smoothly functioning professional football team, Selznick's image corresponds more closely to Alice's [in Wonderland] efforts at croquet with equipment and competition provided by the Queen of Hearts. Alice swings her flamingo mallet but the bird may duck his head before the hedgehog ball is struck; just so, the manager issues his directives but they may be neither understood nor followed by his [sic] subordinates (Scott, 1964, p. 511).

The institutional perspective:

1. Considers the differences among organizations to be important. Through a case study method, it exposes the ways organizations differ from one another, and captures the individual feel of particular organizations (foreshadowing the organizational culture approach discussed in Chapter 5).
2. Maintains that organizations are not simply the sum of individual actions, but rather take on lives of their own, for which no single individual either is responsible or can control. This both reinforces the idea from Chapter 2 that meanings are co-constructed in dialogue and foreshadows key aspects of systems theory to be discussed in Chapter 4.
3. Takes into account the relationship between an organization and its *environment*. Up to this point, organizational theory had focused almost exclusively on inner workings and paid no attention to external factors, primarily because environments

were relatively placid and stable. As environmental turbulence increased, the institutional approach was one theory that considered specifically the relationship between an organization and its environment as key to its survival.

The institutional approach did not, however, apply to all organizations. Only some organizations become institutionalized, in the sense that society prizes them more for the values they embody than for any particular product or service. Examples include libraries, universities, and medical centers. People identify with them and associate their existence with what it means to live in a good society. Institutions become impregnated with community values, and the managers of institutions must be especially skillful in their communication with the public (Perrow, 1986). This is because an institution's survival depends on public legitimacy, not bottom-line performance, productivity, or effectiveness.

John Meyer and Brian Rowan (1977) describe how the institutionalization process works in practice in hospitals and schools. To protect their legitimacy, they argue, not only must their leaders communicate effectively with the community, but data about technical performance must be shielded or buffered from outside scrutiny. Thus a college or university probably has numerous standards and complex measures for awarding a degree or majoring in a particular department. On the other hand, similar quantification is rarely, if ever, applied to the supposed technical output of the university—student learning. Teachers are not evaluated on the basis of how much their students have learned in their courses. Nor is a hospital systematically scrutinized for its quality of patient care.

Although much of Meyer and Rowan's argument still holds, traditional institutions are hardly the fortresses of legitimacy they were 20 years ago. Schools and hospitals alike are being pressured to emerge from behind their defenses of academic freedom and principles of practice to account for the degree of effectiveness of their technical work. The results will be dramatic. In a study of the California state mental health system, J. Rounds (1984) showed that once the traditional decision premises of the institution were effectively questioned (in this case, state decision rules about who could be categorized as mentally ill), pandemonium ensued. Different groups with differing technical expertise and interests scrambled to participate in an increasingly frustrating dialogue. The collapse of an institution's legitimacy opens both the possibility for positive change and enormously complicates further action by the institution.

The institutional school opens up the area of organization-environment communication and redefines the role of at least some senior managers as akin to that of a political statesperson. It also provides further evidence for the importance of communication, not only in the area of information transfer but also as the source of the definition of a situation, of creating organizational reality. Finally, it emphasizes that limiting communication about certain issues (i.e., technical evaluation) can restrict dialogue and hence preserve legitimacy and the status quo. (See table 3.6 on page 78 for a summary of the institutional approach.)

From Human Relations to Human Resources   From a communication perspective, the contribution of the human relations school was the critique of the rational individual model of organizations and the advancement of an alternative view of individuals situated in social situations that are constituted through communication. But while human relations recognized that individual decision making was limited by organizations, it did little to suggest a solution. How could individual employees find a voice to speak with, especially if their perspective was not popular, and particularly in communicating with those in power, their so-called superiors?

Ironically, in their attempts to be more sensitive to individuals, managers used listening and openness as techniques to handle employees but failed to give them any credit for knowledge of their jobs, the work climate, customers, suppliers, or new ways of doing business. It took a move toward what we now call human resources thinking to value the role of upward communication and the employee's voice in decision making. Human resources incorporates most of the assumptions of human relations, but it is more concerned with the total organizational climate and with how an organization can encourage participation, dialogue, and employee voice.

Two theorists who best capture the spirit of the human resources movement are Chris Argyris and Abraham Maslow. In his now classic *Personality and Organization* (1957), Argyris launched a scathing critique of the classical view of organizing, in which he showed that, by accepted standards, the perfect employee is an idiot. In each and every way, he argued, the bureaucratic form frustrates the interests of the individual (e.g., to grow; to have control). Argyris calls for a revised form of organization, one that better meets the needs of the developing individual.

Maslow was also seriously concerned about the individual's ability to grow, develop, and reach his or her full potential. Maslow is perhaps best known for his hierarchy of needs, which says that for humans to become creative they must first satisfy their basic needs for food, shelter, and belonging. Only then can a person move in the direction of self-actualization, or toward their full human potential (see Figure 3.4, page 82).

Maslow also described the workplace in his book, *Eupsychian Management* (1965). Here, he posed the question: "What kinds of management and what kinds of reward or pay will help human nature to grow healthily into its fuller and fullest stature?" Maslow concluded that conditions that are supportive of the healthy individual are often surprisingly good for the prosperity of the organization. He defined the problem of management as that of setting up social conditions in the organization so that the goals of the individual merge with the goals of the organization. In many ways, Maslow's work also paved the work for current theories of peak experience, including specifically Mihalyi Csikszentmihalyi's (1990) theory of flow, discussed further in Chapter 7.

Another management professor, Douglas McGregor, shared Argyris's critical view of classical organizational theory. Scientific management, McGregor figured, assumed that the average employee disliked work and would avoid responsibility unless closely controlled. McGregor called this controlling bureaucratic style Theory X management (1960). In contrast, Theory Y management saw employees as having a potentially high capacity for autonomy and responsibility and being a rich source for creative innovation. In contrast with Theory X managers, Theory Y managers have a much more participative and facilitative management style and treat employees as valued human resources. McGregor was optimistic about incorporating the individual's desires in an organizational framework. He believed that "the essential task of management is to arrange things so people achieve their own goals by accomplishing those of the organization" (Perrow, 1986, p. 99).

Finally, University of Michigan professor Rensis Likert continued this trend toward employee participation and laid some of the initial foundation for what are presently called high-involvement organizations. Likert divided organizations into four types or "systems" according to degree of participation: exploitative authoritative; benevolent authoritative; consultative; and participative group. (These are sometimes simply called

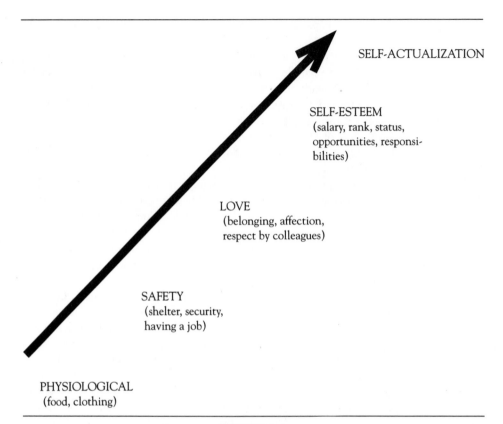

FIGURE 3.4
Abraham Maslow's Hierarchy of Needs

System I, II, III, and IV, respectively.) Likert was a proponent of open communication as one of the most important processes of management. He favored general supervision over close supervision and reiterated the importance of a supportive peer group in fostering productivity. Research on Likert's systems has yielded very mixed results (cf. Perrow, 1986). Many studies show that good classical changes in organizations (e.g., better work procedures and plans) are at least as important as degree of participation in their impact on organizational effectiveness. The human resources approach continues the human relations tendency to treat all organizations as similar or the same, an assumption that is probably unfounded and finds its opponents in the institutional school and the cultural approach (see Chapter 5). And while human resources places more emphasis than before on legitimate participation by lower participants in organizational decision making, neither the pragmatics nor the politics of establishing such a voice for employees is considered directly or in detail. As a result, these prescriptions for participation tend to have limited practical utility.

The ethical dimensions of the human relations/human resources approach are presented in Ethics Box 3.2. Specifically, the box provides an ethical dilemma related to the politics of management common under the influence of human relations/resources approached.

━━━━━━━━━━━━━━━━━━━━━━━ **ETHICS BOX 3.2** ━━━━━━━━━━━━━━━━━━━━━━━

ETHICS AND THE POLITICS OF MIDDLE MANAGEMENT

One of the core assumptions of the human relations approach is that happy employees will be more productive. Whether or not this is true (it often isn't), the ethics of defining other people's happiness is a potential source of tyranny. Consider the following statements about this insidious source of power and control in relation to the role of the middle manager in human relations theory:

1. "The most insidious power is the power to define happiness." Happiness cannot be described, and what cannot be described cannot be attained. So it is that humans create imagined happiness as the opposite of what we can describe—dissatisfaction.
2. All leaders must have the ability to define happiness. In the absence of absolute happiness, we content ourselves with relative happiness.
3. There are three ways in which capitalism and the bureaucratic society conspire to use happiness as a source of fear and reward:
   a. The Merchant offers happiness in the immediate future. Commodity purchases offer material rewards; failure to consume commodities suggests material poverty and, therefore, a lack of relative happiness.
   b. The Manager offers happiness in the future. According to human relations theory, his or her power is largely symbolic (kind words, generous deeds, a pat on the back). But because being in management is a source of symbolic attainment in our society, the manager represents what the rest of us aspire to. As such, the manager is the enforcer of our moral code.
   c. The Despot offers happiness in the historical future. By making prophetic claims about the historical future, he or she is like a secular god and only lacks immortality to be a god. The despot combines displays of material and symbolic happiness, and suggests that others may attain this if only they do as they are commanded to do.
4. When work becomes rationalized and bureaucratized, the resulting order symbolizes levels of happiness. The power of the manager is to define our happiness as the next step above where we are.

The manager's definition of happiness creates the moral system in which white collar workers and some managers live, but the despot's definition, with its ultimate promises and religious demands, has greater effect upon the middle manager's life. In return for historic happiness, the middle manager agrees to the abolition of his freedom, he becomes part of the organization, and he accepts the notion that any sin against the organization may cast him out of heaven and into the limbo of the unemployed. To endure a road to happiness that abolishes his freedom and fills him with unmitigated fear, he allows himself to be deluded about his happiness; and having the credentials of education, wealth, and power, he deludes himself, he expels the meaning of his life from himself and places it in the organization.

SOURCE: Adapted from Earl Shorris, *Scenes from Corporate Life* (New York, Penguin, 1984), pp. 17–34.

Given these thoughts, how would you handle the following incidents:

1. Your boss explains to you that a promotion is in your immediate future if—and only if—you can find a way to cut costs in your department by one-third. You understand this request to

─────────── **ETHICS BOX 3.2** (*continued*) ───────────

mean that personnel will have to be cut, although your boss never directly says so. You are already operating with a reduced staff, stress is high among your co-workers owing to the extra workload, and you fear that even if you could recommend firing someone, morale would suffer and with lower morale would come lower productivity as well as more overall anxiety and frustration. You are heavily in debt and very much need the promotion to make ends meet. Should you gain some happiness at the expense of others? Is the short-term gain of a promotion worth the long-term negative morale and productivity consequences you envision? What should you do?

2. You are a midlevel manager privy to information about your company's intent to restructure and downsize its operation. You know this means that you will be in intense competition with other midlevel managers to keep your job, because downsizing and restructuring typically affect midlevel managers. The vice-president for Personnel, whom you have always considered an ally, has just asked you to keep this information to yourself. She also asks you to prepare an inspirational speech on the topic "Working Your Way Up the Ladder" to be delivered to the supervisory training group, most of whom will lose their jobs too. You are uncertain how you should respond to your boss, as well as uncertain about the ethical dimensions of what you should say in the speech. What should you do? Can this speech be used as an opportunity for more than your own corporate survival? If so, how?

3. What do you think would need to be included in a code of ethics for midlevel managers, using Shorris's concerns as your guide?

SUMMARY

The two founding perspectives—historical narratives—on organization and communication are the classical and human relations approaches. All historical narratives—indeed, all of human storytelling—exhibit the three P's: partiality, partisanship, and problematic.

The classical approach to organizations and communication emerged during the Industrial Revolution, a period characterized by the quest to adapt the lessons of science to technologies capable of making perfect machines. Organizations were built on the model of efficient machines, and management was characterized by machinelike dependence on hierarchy, divisions of labor, strict rules for communication between bosses and workers, and the formal establishment of routines. The concept of bureaucracy is often used to sum up the machinelike precision and quality of organizations structured in this way.

This image of organization does not devote much time or energy to communication. Communication in the image of the ideal machine is what happens before the machine is turned on—when someone (a manager) explains how to operate the machine in the most efficient way to the workers responsible for the labor. When communication occurs during work, production tends to slow down. From this perspective, informal talk is unnecessary and costly.

Gareth Morgan (1986) suggests that the machine metaphor is particularly useful for organizing work under conditions of a straightforward, repetitive task performed in a stable environment, in which precision is at a premium and workers are compliant. He further suggests that the limitations of this approach are a direct outcome of its narrow focus on efficiency: this form of organizing and managing tends to be difficult to adapt to changing circumstances, and has a dehumanizing effect on employees. The repetitive, compliant, noncommunicative nature of this production work often results in mindless work, drug abuse, and illness.

We agree with Morgan. In addition, while the silent obedience encouraged by scientific management may give the appearance of efficiency and rule compliance, it can mask the workers' deep resentment for both the work and management. When opportunities for dialogue and legitimate voice do not exist, resentment can quickly turn into active resistance, such as work slowdowns and sabotage. In Chapter 6 we expand on the concept of domination and resistance. At this point in our narrative, we mention it primarily as a practical consequence of inflexible control and an unwillingness to share power.

In the classical approach, our concern for achieving balance between individual creativity and organizational constraint through dialogue reveals a marked tilt in favor of constraint. The individual needs of workers were largely ignored, communication between managers and laborers was limited to managers giving orders to laborers, and the widespread imposition of rules and routines guaranteed the maintenance of order at all costs. When such strict adherence to structures of hierarchical power are in place and the balance is tilted too much and for too long against individual needs, an underground oppositional or resistance movement that prizes human creativity and liberation is likely to be born. Such was the case during the latter stages of the Industrial Revolution when slavery was legally overturned and labor unions became more widespread.

This new concern for the plight of individual workers led, albeit inadvertently, to the creation of the human relations approach to organizations and communication. Against the cultural and economic background of the Great Depression, studies of attention paid to workers by managers that also improved productivity provided a new way to theorize about communication at work. The balance in the organizational dialogue tipped back toward a concern for individual creativity and the satisfaction of needs.

Perhaps it tipped the balance back too far. Critics of the human relations approach pointed out that making workers happy did not necessarily make them more productive; nor was the new business Social Ethic uniformly endorsed, especially not by those who saw the demise of the Protestant Work Ethic as a loss to individual achievement and entrepreneurship. Refinements of the human relations theory became known as the human resources approach, and with it, advances were made in our understanding of the relationships between individual needs for creativity and organizational structures.

The legacy of human relations, represented in studies of leadership style, decision making, and organizations as institutions, represents a major step forward in redefining the individual in organizations as socially situated and only intendedly rational. This view of the individual also suggests a different role for communication, having to do with the construction of definitions of the situation or decision premises which shape individual behavior. This shift creates a new view of employee motivation and performance. An individual's motives for working are derived from his or her interests, the sum total of which constitutes the individual's definition of the situation. Hence, situations are symbolic constructions of reality that are individualized according to personal needs, desires, and interests. As contrasted with a more scientific approach to understanding employee motives, this view suggests that many employees are motivated by symbolic rewards (e.g., the information they are given, the praise they receive, the quality of their co-workers) at least as much as they are by money.

The human resources movement is a precursor of many of the most common management practices today. Not only have most firms renamed their personnel departments Human Resources, but also an increasing number of companies treat their employees in respectful, valuing, adult ways. This means that employees are being given more leeway to construct organizational reality, through legitimate voice and opportunities for dialogue. This increased involvement does not come without cost, however, and workers are simultaneously being asked to shoulder greater responsibility and accountability for their actions and decisions. Of all the approaches to management that we have witnessed in action, delegation, empowerment, and participative management are perhaps the most difficult and commonly misunderstood. But when these concepts do work, the human resources approach tends to foster more satisfied, committed employees and more productive organizations.

These two schools of thought on organization and management—the demand for formal, tightly controlled bureaucracies and the responsive call for a looser, more empathic give-and-take concern for treating employees as valuable human resources—form a theoretical continuum for understanding organizational communication. At the far right (bureaucracy) is a belief that formal structure and communication that respect the chain of command will ensure productivity and stability; at the far left (human relations/human resources) is a belief that open, honest, thoughtful communication must exist between managers and employees to ensure creativity, change, and the satisfaction of individual needs and motivations on the job. In this chapter, we have seen what happens when the organizational dialogue is tipped too far in favor of either approach. In the following chapters we will see how new theories propose to resolve these problems. Toward that goal, we end this chapter by posing our recurring question: Can organizations be both pro-profit and pro-people?

CASE STUDY

Riverside State Hospital

BACKGROUND

Riverside State Hospital is a 500-bed state-supported mental hospital located along the banks of the scenic Tennessee River. Patients are admitted based on physician or court referrals, and the staff consists of physicians, psychologists, psychiatrists, nurses, dieticians, pharmacists, therapists, technicians, and general housekeeping and groundskeeping personnel, all of whom are state employees. This means, essentially, that the hospital is run primarily as a bureaucracy, with authority and pay based on seniority and rank.

Riverside State Hospital Organizational Chart

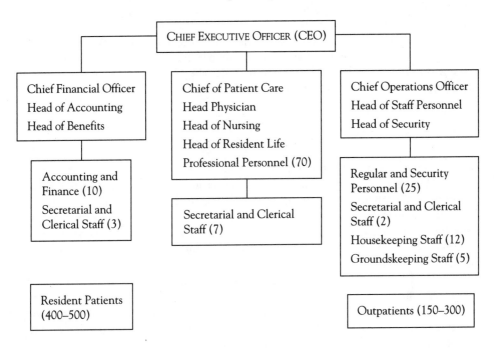

Every employee (including professional staff) holds GS (Government Service) rank; the lowest groundskeeper is a GS-1 (groundskeeping trainee) and the highest administrator (the CEO) is a GS-15. Within each rank are steps that are determined by seniority and achievement; most ranks have seven to ten steps. Performance reviews are conducted annually, at which time promotions in steps or promotions in GS ranks occur. Employees are given annual salary adjustments for inflation and/or cost-of-living. Full state government benefits are provided to all workers.

Every employee is expected to work an 8-hour day, and every employee below the rank of GS-12 (everyone below the rank of Head or Chief) is expected to take a 30-minute lunch break and two 15-minute breaks during his or her day/night. Professional staff (physicians, nurses, pharmacists, etc.) work on a three-shift schedule: 7 A.M.–3 P.M.; 3 P.M.–11 P.M.; 11 P.M.–7 A.M. The hospital operates year-round.

THE PROBLEM

Three days ago a resident patient named Horris James Wilcox, Jr., was killed when the wall next to his bed partially collapsed. Wilcox was 56 years old, had no family, and had been a resident for three years; he suffered from traumatic amnesia and had a borderline IQ score. He was in good health physically, was well liked, and seemed, however slowly, to be responding to treatment.

Hospital administrators explained to state investigators and the news media that this accident was a "tragedy, but that there had been no indication that the wall was weak, or that Wilcox was in any danger."

You are a private investigator retained by Wilcox's insurance company. Your job is to determine if any evidence exists that would make the hospital liable for Wilcox's sudden and tragic death. If such evidence exists, your employer may not be held financially liable to pay Wilcox's death and burial benefits. It is a gruesome job, not one that you anticipated doing when you graduated from college, but here you are and it must be done.

THE INVESTIGATION

You learn from your investigation that Wilcox was a quiet patient who generally kept to himself. He seemed to be preoccupied with his own mental condition, although he did join in with the other patients on his ward for scheduled games and activities. During these times he talked a lot about what was on the news. As it turns out, the news was his major source of entertainment. He watched the cable news channel every chance he got from morning to night; jokes were told among the staff about Wilcox being the most informed person at the hospital.

You also learn that his traumatic amnesia was complicated by his belief that he was directly affected by whatever was on television. News events—particularly family tragedies—affected him deeply. Hospital staff and doctors had tried to reduce his viewing to prevent further complications, but that decision only seemed to further depress him. Instead they reinstituted his television privileges and tried to use the emotions he displayed about news shows in his therapy. Perhaps, they reasoned, some family tragedy had produced the traumatic amnesia.

For the past month, Mr. Wilcox repeatedly complained that "the sky was falling." He made objections most strenuously when confined to his bed at night, or in the mornings upon awakening. He pointed toward the ceiling and walls and maintained that "there is trouble here, trouble from the sky." On several occasions he had to be restrained forcibly with drugs. This all occurred during the month that the Space Shuttle Challenger had exploded in the sky over Cape Canaveral, and videotaped replays of that event had been aired on the news constantly. Given Wilcox's past history of responding emotionally to tragedies, doctors and nurses interpreted his statement "the sky is falling" to reference the Challenger disaster. But perhaps that was not all there was to it. When interpreted alongside his unwillingness to go to bed at night, his complaints about an impending tragedy could have had an altogether different meaning: perhaps the "sky" was a reference to perceived structural defects in the walls and ceiling of his room. Indeed, it could be that Wilcox was trying to direct attention to the actual physical deterioration of his room. That he was a mental patient with a history of placing himself in current news events may only have led those charged with his care to dismiss his allegations as "crazy."

Upon further investigation, you learn that the walls and ceiling in that part of the hospital had been repainted three times during the past 12 months. The cause was a leaking water pipe inside the wall that, you believe, seriously weakened the wall. Certainly, you feel that hospital personnel should have followed up on these signs of trouble. When you press the matter, you discover that state funding for maintenance had been cut back severely during the previous summer, and while there was structural damage to the wall, there was no indication that it was unsafe. From the hospital administrators' perspective, the culprit was an old building combined with a lack of state funding for repairs, and they consistently maintained that the collapse of the wall was still "an unforeseeable accident."

You request copies of the building inspections for the past three years. You see that for the past year the state inspectors noted the continuous deterioration of the wall and ceiling area that eventually collapsed. You see that all these forms are signed by Hillary Hanks, the Head of Resident Life.

In your interview with Hanks, you discover that while her signature was indeed on those state inspection forms, she did not actually sign them. She explains that her secretary, Nancy Ellis, signed her name regularly on state forms to save time. She adds: "There are so many forms to sign that if I signed them all, I wouldn't get any real work done." When you speak to Ellis you find out that Hanks' story is true. Furthermore, Ellis is annoyed because the man who delivered the forms to her was supposed to report any problems that required attention. The problem with the walls and ceiling had not been reported *verbally*, and therefore she didn't say anything to Hanks. Now Hanks was in trouble with her superior and that meant that Ellis would, at the very least, lose her chance at a promotion. Any trouble for Hanks meant big trouble for Ellis, according to Ellis. She admitted that she regularly avoided telling her boss any bad news for exactly that reason. But this time, Ellis claimed, she didn't know there *was* bad news. You conclude your interview with Ellis by asking what she did with the inspection report. She points to the overstuffed filing cabinet behind her. "That's where I put it," she says, "along with all the rest of the paperwork that never gets read around here."

You find out that the report was made out by a state inspector named Blake Barrymore who gave the inspection form to a groundskeeper for delivery to the appropriate hospital administrator. Barrymore tells you that he gave the form to a groundskeeper because "it was raining that day and I was late for another inspection"; he quickly adds that there is nothing in his job description that made it his *official* responsibility to deliver the report himself, or to follow up on it. He tells you that the inspection report was delivered by Jack Handy, a reliable and well-liked groundskeeper. Handy, you discover, is reliable and well liked, but also illiterate. He did not know what the forms contained because he could not read them. He did not report any problems with the walls or ceiling because Barrymore didn't tell him there were any problems. Besides, Handy added, "nobody listens to a groundskeeper anyway. I could tell an administrator that there was a bomb in the hospital and because I'm just a groundskeeper, they'd let it pass." He says he gave up making waves years ago. Now, he just "does what he is told to do"; in this case, he delivered some forms he couldn't read to a secretary who could.

You file your report. The insurance company claims that gross negligence on the part of the hospital indirectly caused the death of Horris James Wilcox, Jr. In a press conference held the following day, the hospital defends itself, placing the blame for the death of Wilcox on a secretary, Nancy Ellis. The spokesperson for the hospital says it was Ellis's responsibility because she had not reported the seriousness of the problem to her superior, Hillary Hanks. The spokesperson adds that Hanks has been "reassigned" to other duties and is unavailable for comment. The spokesperson ends by saying: "The hospital deeply regrets this tragic accident, and reminds the state legislature that until the requested funds for structural repairs are made available, the hospital administration cannot be held accountable for structural defects that are beyond its control."

ASSIGNMENT

Given what you know from reading this chapter, analyze this case and its outcome. Was the problem Nancy Ellis's fault? Why or why not? In what ways was the hospital's organizational structure responsible in the death of Horris James Wilcox, Jr.? What recommendations would you make to help this hospital avoid similar occurrences in the future? How can communication be improved?

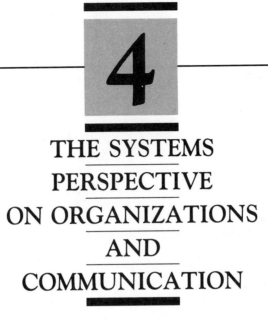

THE SYSTEMS PERSPECTIVE ON ORGANIZATIONS AND COMMUNICATION

While I can know nothing about any individual thing by itself, I can know something about the relations between things. . . . We are learning in fact to deal with the world's tendency to generate wholes made up of units connected by communication. . . . [But] how shall we interpret the responsibility of all those who deal with living systems? The whole tatterdemalion rout of the dedicated and the cynical, the saintly and the greedy, have a responsibility—individually and collectively—to a dream.

The dream is about what sort of thing man [sic] is that he may know and act on living systems—and what sort of thing such systems are that they may be known. The answers to that forked riddle must be woven from mathematics and natural history and aesthetics and also the joy of life and loving—all of these contribute to shape that dream. (pp. 157, 180, 182)

—George Bateson and Mary Catherine Bateson, 1987

This chapter focuses on a powerful explanatory metaphor that dominates both the research literature and organizational practice: systems. The systems approach broadens our way of seeing organizations through the borrowing of concepts from other, seemingly distant areas of study. Contributors to systems theory include engineers, biologists, and information scientists, as well as prominent sociologists such as Herbert Spencer and Talcott Parsons.

We begin the chapter with a general description of the systems approach, followed by a discussion of the historical background for systems thinking. Next, we define the nature of a system, as well as the associated key terms, including interdependence, goals, feedback, environment, and contingency. We also consider reasons why systems theory has such enduring appeal for students of organizational communication. In addition, we summarize the work of Karl Weick, which serves as a bridge between systems and cultural approaches to organizations. Finally, we consider the implications of a systems approach for the situated individual striving to balance creativity and constraint.

THE SYSTEMS APPROACH

A recent ad for BMW automobiles posed the question: "What makes the BMW the *Ultimate Driving Machine?*" Is it the superb handling and braking? The aerodynamic design? The powerful engine? The butter-smooth transmission? According to the ad, none of these things, considered alone, makes the BMW special. What does make the car unique is the way all these qualities work together in a seamless, dependable, high-performance package.

The message behind this advertisement is at the heart of the systems approach. There is an important difference between a collection of parts and a collection of parts that works together to create a functional whole. This functional whole that is more than just a collection of independent parts is called a system. In a system, "the whole is greater than the sum of its parts." Sociologist Walter Buckley (1967) translates this expression: "the 'more than' (in this statement) points to the fact of *organization,* which imparts to the aggregate characteristics that are not only *different from,* but often *not found in* the components alone; and the 'sum of the parts' must be taken to mean, not their numerical addition, but their unorganized aggregation" (p. 42). In other words, organization makes a social system more than its components. In a marriage, family, team, or business, the existence of relationships among the people are what makes the group a system.

HISTORICAL AND CULTURAL BACKGROUND

As we learned in Chapter 3, the classical human relations and human resources perspectives on organization differ significantly from each other. In one respect, however, all these approaches are similar. Each emerged in response to the Industrial Revolution, as differing means for improving productivity and the quality of life of employees. By the late 1950s, however, change was in the wind. A new revolution was taking hold that would have dramatic impact on organizations and communication—the information revolution.

Information Revolution

The information revolution had its roots in new ways of conceptualizing fundamental principles of the universe. Albert Einstein's general and specific theories of relativity provided the initial impetus. Before Einstein, concepts of space and time had been—at least since Sir Isaac Newton—distinct entities operating "in a fixed arena in which events took place, but which was not affected by what happened in it. . . . Bodies moved, forces attracted and repelled, but time and space simply continued, unaffected" (Hawking,

1988, p. 33). Scientific management relied heavily on time and motion studies (whose principles were drawn from Newtonian physics) to provide data to managers about worker productivity.

But what if time and space were not fixed, but were instead relative? What if—as Einstein's general theory suggests—time ran slower nearer the earth due to the influence of its gravitational pull? Did this imply that observations of what appeared to be a fixed reality were skewed by the observer's position? For example, if things happening at the bottom of a mountain (read: organization) appear to take longer to occur from observations made at the top of the mountain (read: upper management), isn't there something fundamentally wrong about a fixed notion of order or reality in the universe? Theories of relativity explain precisely what may be wrong:

> Space and time are now dynamic quantities: when a body moves, or a force acts, it affects the curvature of space and time—and in turn the structure of space-time affects the way in which bodies move and forces act. Space and time not only affect but also are affected by everything that happens in the universe (Hawking, 1988, p. 33).

In other words, everything counts (Goodall, 1989). Rather than conceptualizing time and motion studies within the limited framework of a specific task, the interpretation of the task was expanded to include how it functioned as part of a dynamic interdependent system. Appropriate questions might include: what are the intended and unintended consequences of increased or decreased efficiency? How do pressures to reduce time and eliminate unnecessary motion impact morale, absenteeism, commitment, and turnover? How in turn do these factors affect productivity in important and potentially unexpected ways?

This major shift in our understanding of the laws of the universe did more than simply call into question the rationality of time and motion studies. It brought to the forefront of our understanding the idea of dynamic systems of interacting components whose relationships and interactions pointed to a new kind of order, one based on pattern, not substance of interaction. The ideas of dynamic systems were applied to atomic physics, navigational science, aerospace, and electronics. As we will see, it was not until after World War II that a systems paradigm emerged with applications to organizations. It is not surprising, however, that it took so long for systems theory to be applied outside of the technical realm. Such a radical shift in interpretation from substance to dynamic pattern required a new vocabulary for talking about social collectivities as systems. The development of this complex vocabulary took time, and it took more time for it to gain acceptance.

In addition to the theoretical advances in physics, a second revolution in our understanding occurred in new technologies spawned by industries capitalizing on these scientific advances. Primarily an outgrowth of transistors and, later, the microchip, communications technologies such as television, satellites, and computers contributed to what Marshall McLuhan called the global information society (1964). McLuhan's idea was simple but profound. Instantaneous transfer of information across cultural boundaries meant that our perceptions of reality, cultural differences, political and social events, and ideas of what constituted news ceased being mediated by any fixed notions of space or time. We grew closer as a world because information connected us in ways that these technologies made possible for the first time. The earth became—in McLuhan's term—a "global village."

One application of information technology led to the writing of the present book. We reside in different regions of the country (South Carolina and Los Angeles) and never met face to face in the writing of this book. Instead, we communicate daily and instantaneously through a worldwide computer network called BITNET. This technology allows us to share what we write when we write it, which improves turnaround time for editing. This same network also permits us to communicate with our colleagues worldwide. As a result of all these connections, advances that formerly took years to get into print and to reach colleagues can now be communicated with a keystroke. Consequently, our information environment has become more dynamic and interdependent.

Thus far, we have described the systems approach in generalities. Hence, a more thorough examination of systems vocabulary and concepts is in order. We don't have to look far to see the impact of systems thinking on the field of communication. Consider the terms we now routinely use to describe communication: for example, sender, receiver, feedback, noise, and channel. Prior to a model of communication developed in 1948 by an engineer—Claude Shannon—and a mathematician—Warren Weaver—the vocabulary of communication developed by ancient Greeks was still in use. The older vocabulary was quite different (e.g., speech, speaker, audience, ethos, pathos, logos, and enthymeme). Our language about communication processes was forever transformed by the information revolution. As Stuart Clegg (1990) put it, "Systems ideas are now so much a part of the modernist consciousness that they barely require elaborate iteration" (p. 51). Table 4.1 contrasts the vocabulary and assumptions of systems theory with those of scientific management; the table should be referred to throughout this section.

Biology and General Systems Theory

The information revolution was the broad context and motivation for systems theory; the life sciences, specifically biology, also made important contributions. It is easy to see why. What makes a system alive is not the existence of any particular component or component process (e.g., a respiratory or digestive subsystem) but rather the relationship and interchanges among these processes. Within any system there are subsystems, and it is the connections between these subsystems (e.g., how oxygen gets from the lungs into the blood, then into muscles and synapses) that are the defining characteristics of biological or living organisms. To take an holistic approach means to consider the properties of systems that come out of the relationships among their parts.

Ludwig von Bertalanffy and J. G. Miller advanced the study of living systems. Von Bertalanffy in particular was a force in the creation of general systems theory (1968), an intellectual movement that attempted to apply the properties of living systems, such as input, output, boundaries, homeostasis, and equifinality, to a dazzlingly wide range of social phenomena. Whereas von Bertalanffy's work was inspirational, Miller's was exhaustive: his book *Living Systems* (1978) is a masterpiece of detail. Table 4.2 on page 96 provides an account of the evolution and hierarchy of general systems. Another biologist, Lewis Thomas, writes in his landmark work, *The Lives of a Cell* (1975):

> Although we are by all odds the most social of all social animals—more interdependent, more attached to each other, more inseparable in our behavior than bees—we do not often feel our conjoined intelligence.

TABLE 4.1
EVOLUTION OF SCIENTIFIC MANAGEMENT INTO SYSTEMS

Scientific management did not simply disappear with the advent of human relations/human resources approaches. There was still a strong desire among managers, owners, and academics to apply social science to the problems of organization and communication. Part of the appeal of systems theory was that it capitalized on the complexities of human relationships within a scientific framework that still allowed for description, prediction, and control. This evolution is represented by the following series of advances.

Scientific Management	Systems Theories
Metaphor: Machines	*Metaphor:* Biological organisms
Theme: Efficiency: A machine is the sum of its parts.	*Theme:* Rhizome complexity: A system is greater than the sum of its parts.
Influences: Industrial Revolution, modernity, capitalism, and empire; assembly-line production and management; division of labor, interchangeable parts, coordination of many small, skilled jobs.	*Influences:* Einstein's theory of relativity; McLuhan's global information society; J. G. Miller's biological systems; Ludwig von Bertalanffy's general systems; Shannon and Weaver's telephone model of communication.
Focus of management principles: "The only things that count are the finished product and the bottom line": time and motion studies	*Focus of management principles:* "Everything Counts": Studies of interdependent processes, information flows and feedback, environments and contingencies.
Management of individuals as if they were interchangeable parts	Management of relationships among components; focus on groups and networks
Planning the work, working the plan	Planning the work, using feedback to correct the plan
Motivation by fear and money	Motivation by needs and contingencies
Theory of communication:	*Theory of communication:*
S ——— M ——— C ——— R	
(linear, top-down model)	(Environments)
Theory of leadership: Trait (tall, white males with blonde hair and blue eyes, who come from strong moral backgrounds)	*Theory of leadership:* Adaptive (rhetorical contingency): Anyone can learn the skills of leading by attending to the requirements of behavioral flexibility.
Limitations: Humans are more complex than machines; theory encourages individual boredom and deep divisions between managers and employees, discourages communication, individual needs, job initiative, task innovation, personal responsibility, and empowerment.	*Limitations:* Humans are symbolic as well as biological; theory encourages mathematical complexities that are difficult to put into everyday practices; communication is equated with information.

TABLE 4.2

EVOLUTION OF THE HIERARCHY OF SYSTEMS THINKING

Level	Description and Examples	Theory and Models
Static structures	Atoms, molecules, crystals, biological structures from the electron microscope to the macroscopic level	E.g., structural formulas of chemistry; crystallography; anatomical descriptions
Clockworks	Clocks, conventional machines in general, solar systems	Conventional physics such as the laws of mechanics (Newtonian and Einsteinian) and others
Control mechanisms	Thermostat, servomechanisms, homeostatic mechanism in organisms	Cybernetics; feedback and information theory
Open systems	Flame, cells, and organisms in general	Expansion of physical theory to systems maintaining themselves in flow of matter (metabolism); Information storage in genetic code (DNA)
Lower organisms	Plantlike organisms: Increasing differentiation of system (so-called division of labor in the organism); distinction of reproduction and functional individual ("germ track and soma")	Theory and models most lacking
Animals	Increasing importance of traffic in information (evolution of receptors, nervous systems); learning; beginnings of consciousness	Beginnings in automata theory (S-R relations), feedback (regulatory phenomena), autonomous behavior (relaxation oscillations), etc.
Man (sic)	Symbolism; past and future, self and world, self-awareness, etc., as consequences; communication by language, etc.	Incipient theory of symbolism
Sociocultural systems	Populations of organisms (humans included); symbol-determined communities (cultures) in man (sic) only	Statistical and possibly dynamic laws in population dynamics, sociology, economics, possibly history. Beginnings of a theory of cultural systems.
Symbolic systems	Language, logic, mathematics, sciences, arts, morals, etc.	Algorithms of symbols (e.g., mathematics, grammar); "rules of the game" such as in visual arts, music, etc.

SOURCE: From Ludwig von Bertalanffy, *General Systems Theory: Foundations, Development, Applications* (New York: George Braziller, 1968), pp. 28–29.

Perhaps it is in this respect that language differs most sharply from biological systems for communication. Ambiguity seems to be an essential, indispensable element for the transfer of information from one place to another by words, where matters of real importance are concerned. It is often necessary, for meaning to come through, that there be an almost vague sense of strangeness and askewness. Speechless animals and cells cannot do this. . . . Only the human mind is designed to work this way, programmed to drift away in the presence of locked-on information, straying from each point in the hunt for a better, different point (Thomas, 1975, pp. 89–94).

In other words, the ambiguity of language means that the connections or interdependencies between members of a social system (i.e., among people) are looser than those in biology or those connecting the parts of a car. "Social organizations, in contrast to physical or mechanical structures, are *loosely coupled* systems" (Scott, 1981, p. 103, emphasis in original).

From the advent of relativity to the initiation of analogies between organic systems and human societies, the concept of dynamic systems offers innovative ways of understanding the relationships among functioning components in space–time. But human language—the ability of humans to communicate symbolically and ambiguously—created a powerful new challenge for applying systems theories to systems of human communication in organizations.

From Biology to Organizational Communication

The initial popularity of systems approaches to organizational studies was enormous. In the realm of theory, Daniel Katz and Robert Kahn's (1966) *The Social Psychology of Organizations* was a landmark application of systems theory to organizations. Katz and Kahn argued that organizations were fundamentally open systems in which people were bonded together by psychological constructions and symbolic as well as behavioral responses to their environments. Furthermore, organizations contain a great deal of variety, and therefore uncertainty, owing to the individualistic nature of the humans within them. Variety and uncertainty are in turn balanced by certain control mechanisms (e.g., norms, rules, procedures, hierarchy) that subordinate individual needs to the requirements of effective organization. Creating ways to integrate and coordinate these components—while remaining open to the changing demands of the environment—required systems management by persons sensitive to the dynamic interdependencies at work. The goal was to ensure that the system remained open and hence capable of adaptation. At the same time, care was taken that it wasn't *too* open, in which case it might become overwhelmed by uncertainty.

The analogy between living and social systems is hardly a perfect one; organizations are *not* organisms (Morgan, 1986). Specifically, where the relationships between parts of an organism are physiological, the relationships among parts of an organization are "primarily psychic, involving complex communicative processes of information exchange, and that difference makes all the difference" (Buckley, 1967, p. 43). As mentioned earlier, interdependencies tend to be looser in social than in biological systems.

Academic disciplines whose traditional focus was on complex processes of information exchange embraced systems theory. Albion Small utilized many systems concepts in his influential work in sociology at the University of Chicago. Other prominent social theorists such as Talcott Parsons and George Homans followed suit. The field of organizational communication was equally enthusiastic. Systems theory provided a new, bulletproof connection between communicating and organizing. Enthusiastic about the potential of this approach, Richard Farace, Peter Monge, and Hamish Russell devoted an entire organizational communication textbook to the systems approach (*Communicating and Organizing*, 1977). In doing so, they endorsed the now commonly heard statement that communication *is* the process of organizing. Only through communication do organizations come into being and persist. For Farace et al., communication is not inside, outside, or tangential to the organization: it *is* the organization. Table 4.3 provides a summary of their groundbreaking work.

WHAT IS A SYSTEM?

A system is a complex set of relationships among interdependent parts or components. In this section we define both the nature of these components in organizations and the characteristics of the relationships among them.

Interdependence

Interdependence is the primary quality of a system. It refers, simultaneously, to (1) wholeness, or the total workings of the system and its environment; and (2) the interrelationships of individuals that fall within the system. Relationships vary in their degree of interdependence. For example, a student's refusal to acknowledge one of his or her teachers as a legitimate instructor will have a negative effect on that student (e.g., failing the course) but will most likely have minimal impact on the teacher. This is because the student is dependent on the teacher and is only minimally *inter*dependent. On the other hand, in most marriages, the decision of one partner to withdraw emotionally from the relationship puts the whole system at risk, since most marriages and families are highly interdependent; each individual depends on the others to meet his or her needs. Systems theory posits that precisely these interdependent relationships between people give an organization its character. Furthermore, these relationships are established and maintained through communication.

We recently toured a company that makes high-technology radio transmitters and talked to some of the employees. One of the questions we asked had to do with what kind of jobs their co-workers did, and whether they ever thought about cross-training or switching jobs with people in other departments. We were shocked to discover that employees of this company had no idea what their co-workers did. All they knew was their own work, the processes they directly controlled. They had no sense of either the origin of their materials or the destination of their finished products. Amazingly, even people in the same work group who had daily contact with each other had little awareness of each other's jobs. One person who had been handing over his finished part to a co-worker for 15 years had no idea what the co-worker did with it, only that sometimes it came back when it was faulty.

This company represents a worst-case scenario from a systems perspective. These

TABLE 4.3

SUMMARY OF FARACE, MONGE, AND RUSSELL'S STRUCTURAL-FUNCTIONAL USE OF SYSTEMS THEORY

Theme: Communication processes in organizations include gathering, processing, storing, and disseminating information.		

Organization	Information	Communication
Definition: "Five key elements: (1) two or more individuals (2) who recognize that some of their goals can be more readily achieved through interdependent (cooperative) actions, even though disagreement (conflict) may be present; (3) who take in materials, energy, and information from the environment in which they exist; (4) who develop coordinative and control relationships to capitalize on their interdependence while operating on these inputs; (5) and who return the modified inputs to the environments, in an attempt to accomplish the goals that interdependence was meant to make possible" (1977, p. 16).	*Definition:* "One of the primary ingredients in the concept of information is the discernment of pattern in the matter/energy flows that reach an individual" (p. 22).	*Definition:* "Communication refers to the exchange of symbols that are commonly shared by the individuals involved, and that evoke quite similar symbol-referent relationships in each individual" (p. 26).
Or: Size, interdependence, input, throughput, and output.	Or: pattern discernment that reduces uncertainty in a situation.	Or: shared symbol systems.
Features (1) As size increases, longer time periods are required for messages and materials to move within the organization; therefore, growth poses many problems, including integrating new members into the organization.	*Features*	*Features*
(2) Without interdependence, organization (and hence, larger goal achievement) is impossible.	Einstein showed that matter/ energy are interchangeable; this means that until a pattern is discerned, there is no	Symbols have real-world referents; to the extent that persons use the same symbol systems, effective

continues

TABLE 4.3 (*continued*)

Theme: Communication processes in organizations include gathering, processing, storing, and disseminating information.

Organization	Information	Communication
	information, just matter/energy.	communication is likely. When they differ markedly, communication is impeded if not made impossible.
(3) Organizations have boundaries that separate them from the outside world; inputs originate outside the organization and enter the organization through openings in the boundary.	Discerned patterns *differ* from individual to individual; there is no objective pattern that exists apart from at least one individual recognizing it.	From Ackoff (1957): "We shall say that a communication which changes the probabilities of choice, *informs*; one that changes the value of the outcomes, *motivates*; and one that changes the efficiencies of the course of action, *instructs*."
(4) Throughputs refer to the activities performed by organizational members—the passage of materials, energy, and information from point to point within the organization, to its exit. Control processes are established to govern and regulate throughput activity; coordination refers to a strategy to make every member and every activity operate in harmony.	Patterning and information are *not* synonymous. Patterns may be random; hence, uncertainty refers to how confident you are about something.	*Noise* and *distortion* can interfere with communication; *redundancy* minimizes the negative effects of noise and distortion.
(5) Output activities describe the return to the environment of the materials, energy, and information that have been processed and the rewards or goals sought are reaped.	Uncertainty is a measurement based on (1) the number of alternative patterns identified in the situation, and (2) the probabilities of occurrence for each alternative. The greater the number of patterns, the greater the uncertainty; the more patterns are equally likely to occur, the greater the uncertainty.

The more uncertainty present in a situation, then the more information value a pattern has when it appears. | |

SOURCE: Adapted from Richard V. Farace, Peter R. Monge, and Harmish M. Russell, *Communicating and Organizing* (Reading, Mass.: Addison-Wesley Publishing Co., 1977).

employees don't know where they fit in the "big picture" and fail even to comprehend that they are part of an interdependent system. Whenever division of labor occurs there will likely also be interdependence, and no part of the system can stand alone. Each relies on the rest to effectively do the job. Furthermore, a deviation or difficulty at any point in the system will eventually affect the whole, just as one stalled car on a highway will tie up traffic for miles around.

Goals

One of the most problematic aspects of theories of organization is their treatment of organizational goals. The past century has seen increasingly less agreement on the existence and importance of goals in organizations. From a *scientific management* perspective, goals are critical, and both individual and organizational action is directed at goal-attainment. From an *institutional* perspective, organizations and their members may espouse goals, but rarely do goals actually guide their behavior (Scott, 1981, p. 21). From an open *systems* perspective, goals are negotiated among interdependent factions in the organization, with a heavy influence from the environment.

Michael Keeley (1980) made one of the most important distinctions in the area of goals. Examining the traditional wisdom that says organizations are mobilized around common goals, he distinguished between the goals of individuals and the goals individuals have for their organization. The goals of individuals are personal and highly variable, whereas the goals they have for the organization are more likely to be shared.

The importance of goals varies among different kinds of systems. In self-regulating, cybernetic systems like thermostats, for example, goals are crucial in maintaining critical levels for survival. (These are discussed in the next section on feedback.) Most typically, however, organizations are not tightly connected but are comprised of many loose, shifting coalitions. In these systems, simply staying the course by keeping an eye on a common goal is both rare and impractical.

Finally, goals can differ across systems levels. An example would be a business unit within a large corporation, whose goal is to be as profitable as possible. At the next higher level, the corporation may be under pressure from various stakeholders to raise cash, and because of this corporate goal may try to sell the business unit (a decision that is unfavorable to the unit). At the same time, the business unit goal of increased profitability may conflict with the individual goals of workers or managers within the unit, who may advocate different goals such as raising quality or focusing on certain strategic products at the expense of others. A primary insight of systems theory is that what is good for one level of the system may not be good for other levels. We see this in families when an individual with emotional "problems" causes the family to pull together as a group. For this reason therapy that traditionally treated individuals separately in families is being replaced by therapy that treats the whole family system (Hoffman, 1982). The same is true for organizations (Tichy, 1983).

Feedback

A system is not simply an interdependent set of components; it is also an interdependent collection of processes that interacts over time. In other words, if we sell radio transmitters, we must not only get new orders to engineering or manufacturing, but we must also do so in a timely fashion or risk inefficiency and other workflow-related problems. Engineering must, in turn, deliver timely, accurate drawings to manufacturing, and manufacturing must meet standards of quality and schedule to the customer. A system is indeed an interdependent collection of parts that interact *over time*.

Communication doesn't stop there, however. Suppose the customer is dissatisfied with the transmitter and calls manufacturing directly. Or suppose the customer is pleased with the product but offers some changes in future models that would make her buy even more. These are both examples of feedback, which is another hallmark of the systems perspective. Feedback should be thought of as a system of loops that connect communication and action. Individuals provide messages to other individuals, who then respond to them in some way. Any response closes the loop back to the communicators and provides them with information about how they were received. Another way to think about feedback is as information about the influence of a particular message or action, usually expressed as a deviation from the intended influence.

Feedback serves as a control device on systems of communication, regulating the flow and interpretation of messages. Two types of feedback are commonly referred to in systems theory. The first, corrective or deviation-counteracting feedback, is exemplified by the customer complaint above. The purpose of deviation-counteracting feedback is to reestablish the proper quality levels that were decided on as goals for the product. This self-correcting feedback is typically known as morphostasis or cybernetics, after the Greek word for steersman who uses his paddles to stay on course. The second type of feedback, growth or deviation-amplifying feedback, is exemplified above by the customer who suggests changes to improve the product in the future. Deviation-amplifying feedback is not designed to maintain a steady state or a specific course, but instead to find new avenues of growth and development. This elaborative feedback is often referred to under the general label of second cybernetics (Maruyama, 1963) or morphogenesis.

There are more complex forms of feedback, including causal loops and cause maps, some of which are detailed later in this chapter. For now, it is sufficient to understand deviation-counteracting and deviation-amplifying feedback. As Chris Argyris and Donald Schon (1978) assert in their work on learning organizations, today's businesses need a great deal of both types of feedback if they are to learn how to be successful. They need deviation-countering feedback to ensure adherence to a chosen course or strategy and deviation-amplifying feedback to regularly consider altering that course of action and changing the goal. Argyris's term for this latter practice is double-loop learning, or the ability to "learn how to learn" by stepping back and examining taken-for-granted assumptions and decision premises.

Environment

From a systems perspective, organizations do not exist as entities isolated from the rest of the world. They are located in environments, rich fields of resources that provide inputs to the organization and receive outputs in the form of the organization's products and services. In this area, too, our radio transmitter company fell short. Not only was the company unaware of its internal connections and workflow, but it also didn't know much about where its materials came from (inputs) or what its customers did with its products (outputs). Furthermore, they had no information about their competitors. The analogy to living organisms works particularly well here. Organisms are open systems in that they rely on exchange with their environment to survive. Humans, for example, need food, air, and sunlight to live. In the same way, an organization's communication with its environment is necessary and not just nice. Walter Buckley (1967) states: "That a system is *open* means, not simply that it engages in interchanges with the environment, but that this interchange is an *essential factor* underlying the system's viability, its reproductive ability or continuity, and its ability to change" (p. 50, emphasis in original).

Without interaction with the environment, organizations run down, or approach entropy (see Ethics Box 4.1 on page 104 for an example). An open system that interacts regularly with its environment might be called negentropic, in that it tends to create structure or, more simply, to *organize*.

Openness, Order, and Contingency

Systems theory evokes the image of a complex, interdependent organization operating within a dynamic environment, ever engaged in a struggle to create order in the face of unpredictability (Clegg, 1990; Thompson, 1967). In retrospect, it is amazing that classical theories of bureaucracy paid so little attention to an organization's environment. In these theories, all organizations were treated equally, and management was directed to conduct careful study of the one best way to do the work within the boundaries of the plant. Beyond the factory doors, the world did not exist except as a source of labor, capital, and resources to be exploited. Any interest in the worker's life outside of the organization, the larger interorganizational field, or the global economic or natural environment was neglected.

Open systems ended that way of thinking. Today we have an incredibly different world-view, less reassuring and more unpredictable. Environmental openness leads organizations to understand that they are part of a dynamic system of intricate interdependencies and relationships. Here we should recall from Chapter 1 our example of the effect of a failed anchovy crop on the cost of a hospital stay. Further considerations of these organization-environment connections are being explored in deep ecological and eco-feminist movements (Glaser & Bullis, 1992; Spretnak, 1991). These ideas are discussed in more detail in Chapter 11.

Openness in organization-environment relationships also has implications for some of the prescriptive aspects of organizational theory. The diversity of environments that exists across industries, companies, and even geographical regions means that the same organizing principles and solutions are not applicable in all situations, but are instead contingent on varying environmental factors. The systems term for this idea is equifinality, which means that the same end state or goal can be reached in multiple ways. Jay Galbraith (1973) offers a succinct summary of the principles of contingency theory:

1. There is no one best way to organize.
2. Any way of organizing is not equally effective.

These principles are deceptively simple, but what they imply is not only that the forms of organizing that will work best depend on the environment, but also that the match between certain organizational approaches and specific environments should be explored since some will work better than others. For example, organizations that exist in complex,

THE ADDICTIVE ORGANIZATIONAL SYSTEM

Organizational systems are not always open. Nor do they always foster openness. Sometimes they encourage individuals to become dependent on the system and to shut out external influences. When this happens, employees may become addicted to work and as a result perpetuate sickness in the system by overworking, covering up, and pleasing the boss. Anne Wilson Schaef and Diane Fassel (1988) write:

> The addictive system operates from the same characteristics that individual addicts have routinely exhibited. The major defense mechanism of the addictive system is denial, which supports a closed system. If something does not exist, it simply does not have to be considered. Corporations frequently say, "We have a minor problem, but certainly not a major one." "We are having a sales slump, but it is only temporary." The alcoholic says, "I am not an alcoholic. I may have a small drinking problem, and I may overdo it a bit on weekends or under stress, but I do not have a severe problem."

These authors identify additional characteristics of an addictive (closed) organizational system:

1. Confusion: *prevents us from taking responsibility and therefore helps us remain powerless over our addiction.*
2. Self-centeredness: *allows the addict to interpret all actions of others as either "for" or "against" them; also reduces the complexities of living to whatever is necessary to get the "fix."*
3. Dishonesty: *Addicts are master liars and have perfected the "con." Addicts lie to themselves, to people around them, and to the world at large.*
4. Perfectionism: *Addicts are obsessed with not being good enough and compensate by trying to never make mistakes. This gives them the illusion of control.*

The results of addictive organizational systems should concern us. Consider the above characteristics as you deal with the following questions:

1. Your organization prides itself on having a strong culture that fosters an even stronger work ethic. You and your co-workers enjoy the benefits of working for a highly successful company and feel very much a part of the dominant culture, but lately you have had some serious doubts about what this means. For example, you routinely give up your evenings and weekends to participate in work-related activities, for no additional pay or recognition. Your family has become increasingly more distant from you, and for the past two years have vacationed without you while you stayed home and worked. You love your job and the people you work with and for, but feel estranged from persons and events outside of your organization. You feel this may not be healthy. What would you do about it? Is the answer just to quit your job, or to try to redefine your relationship to your company? How would you begin to speak to your co-workers about what you are feeling? What ethical issues do you think are involved in continuing to participate in addictive organizations?
2. You work for a perfectionist, but he denies it. Although you do your job and do it well, lately he has not been satisfied with your output. He constantly finds "small areas that need improvement" in your reports, and has strongly suggested that if you gave up some of your spare time you would improve the quality of your work. You believe this is because he is addicted to the organization and has no other life outside of it. It is also true that he is a highly valued member of the company, and his work habits are often held up as the standard for all employees. You like him, respect his work, but resent his implication that you are not willing to give enough back to the company that employs you. You feel there is an ethical issue involved here—specifically, how many personal sacrifices a company should expect from an employee—but you also know the issue is more complicated than that. What might systems theory suggest as remedies?

turbulent environments require different forms of leadership, interpersonal communication, decision making, and organizational structures than those in relatively placid, predictable environments (Emery & Trist, 1965; Lawrence & Lorsch, 1967).

Much of the research that adopts a systems perspective on organizational communication focuses on the relationships and interdependencies among individuals. The most prevalent approach of this kind operationalizes these interdependencies as linkages within communication networks, the emergent, informal structures of relationships in organizations that are the subject of Chapter 8. However, there is also considerable interest in another application of systems theory to organizational communication, focusing on the relationships among whole organizations. Researchers like Howard Aldrich and Jeffrey Pfeffer (1976) explain two variations on this approach. The first, natural selection, examines an interorganizational field over time to see which kinds of organizations are the fittest to survive. The second, resource dependency, also makes predictions about the types of organizations that will survive in certain environments, but focuses on the proactive ways in which organizations can establish key interdependencies with others in the field as a means of strategic adaptation. We have not described these approaches in much detail because they tend to pay little attention to actual communication.

THE ENDURING APPEAL OF SYSTEMS THEORY FOR ORGANIZATIONAL COMMUNICATION

Systems theory appealed to students of organizational communication because it highlighted the importance of communication processes in organizing. In addition, it was theoretically capable of capturing much of the complexity of these processes. While experience tells us that communication is complex and takes place over time, prior to systems theory the temptation in theory and research was to act as if communication was like a game of catch with one person throwing a message and another throwing one back.

Systems theory was also a source of disappointment, for two reasons. First, it raised expectations that were not easily met. In general, researchers had a tough time translating systems concepts into either real theories or real research. Not only were scholars not creating dynamic systems theories of communication, but most lacked the methodological tools to analyze complex systems of communication and feedback. Ideally, systems theories can only be tested using statistical methods that accommodate multiple factors interacting over time. Since both theory and methods of this kind were rare, systems theory has often been characterized as an appealing, abstract set of concepts with little applicability to actual theory or research (Monge et al., 1984).

The second reason why systems theory fell short relates to two initial approaches to applying systems theory to communication: structural-functionalism and communication network analysis. The potential of both approaches has been underrealized. Although structural-functionalism was undoubtedly richer than many previous models, it was very mechanistic and focused on a step-by-step identification of inputs, outputs, mechanisms, and traits. Popularized in organizational communication by researchers at Michigan State University and the State University of New York at Buffalo, communication network analysis is a method for mapping the connections between parts of the system, which in the case of organizations usually meant people. The results were intricate maps of communication structure and identification of communication roles certain people played—that is, how connected they were, what cliques existed and who were the members, and who was isolated from communication altogether (see Chapter 8). Both structural-functionalism and communication network analysis, though relatively effective means of learning about organizations, failed to focus specifically on issues of communication content and the social construction of meaning. This was in itself not a weakness, but it had a strong impact on the *kinds of questions* to which systems theory was applied. Questions of broad structure and process were fine; questions regarding the nature, meaning, and interpretation of messages were less easily addressed.

THE FUTURE OF SYSTEMS APPROACHES

The components, strengths, and weaknesses of the systems approach are summarized in Table 4.4. The systems perspective will likely continue to exert significant influence in organizational communication because of the extent to which it has become popular in

TABLE 4.4
SUMMARY OF THE SYSTEMS APPROACH

Components	Strengths	Weaknesses
Interdependence	Represented a major conceptual advance that took advantage of Einsteinian physics; as such, it represents an attempt to connect theories of organization to theories of order.	Expectations for what systems theory could do were not easily met owing to difficulties of translating concepts into real theory or real research.
Process and feedback	Enriched the study of communication and organizations through a vocabulary that focused on the complexities and relationships of human structures and functions.	Structural-functionalism is very mechanistic.
Environment and open systems	Created new ways of identifying communication problems as problems in relationships or networks rather than in individuals.	Communication network systems research failed to focus on issues of communication content or social construction of meaning.
Openness, order, and contingency	Led to an appreciation for the contingent and relative nature of organizations and communication.	
	Models of systems were amenable to sophisticated statistical measurements.	

organizations. Most firms that produce a complex product or service talk a great deal about workflow analysis, internal customers, and cross-functional work groups. Also much in evidence in these firms are control charts and process maps, each of which suggests a growing systems sensibility. Finally, businesses are beginning to exhibit a near-reverent respect for their markets and environments, on which they increasingly depend for survival. The practical impact of systems theory on organizations is unquestionable, hence theory and research are likely to follow.

In the academic world, recent work suggests that systems theory may have simply been ahead of its time. The theoretical and empirical methods for studying complex systems are now being developed. For example, Noshir Contractor (1992) has applied chaos theory to the study of organizational communication processes. Some of the principles of chaos theory from physics have parallels in the way organizations grow and develop. Peter Monge has spearheaded the development of empirical methodologies to study complex organizational communication processes such as equity and participation over time (Monge, Cozzens, & Contractor, 1992). Fred Steier borrowed the idea of self-referential feedback from cybernetics to take a new look at the researcher's role as an involved partner in the communication research process (Steier & Smith, 1992). Finally, management theorist/consultant Peter Senge (1991) has applied systems thinking about feedback loops and organization-environment relationships to his work on learning organizations. Table 4.5 on page 108 summarizes Senge's approach.

Despite these developments, the predominant feeling about systems theory in the 1970s and 1980s was one of disappointment and unreached potential. From our perspective, systems theory fell short because it failed to adequately address issues of meaning. In the language of creativity and constraint, systems theory is silent on all the tough issues of power and voice that we raised in Chapters 2 and 3. In practice, however, the way systems theory came to be applied—via structural-functionalism and network analysis—ended up privileging the constraining aspects of social systems over individual creativity. This is not an inherent characteristic of the systems approach, however, as evidenced by recent work on emergent networks and self-organizing systems.

SENSE-MAKING SYSTEMS: THE SOCIAL PSYCHOLOGY OF ORGANIZING

The founding approaches to understanding organizations described in Chapter 3 set the stage for a new model of organizational communication that would give serious attention to the social and symbolic context of individual behavior in organizations. Systems theory provided half of this model. It demonstrated once and for all that individual actions could only be understood within a network of relationships, and that this network comprised what we had come to know as an organization. Systems theory also gave long-overdue recognition to communication between an organization and its environment. What was missing was the direct consideration of communication itself, or the process by which individual decision premises were shaped through evolving definitions of the situation. What was missing was a focus on social interaction per se.

Enter Karl Weick. His book, *The Social Psychology of Organizing*, originally published in 1969 and revised ten years later, had a great impact on the field of organizational behavior and a defining effect on organizational communication. Weick singlehandedly reinvigorated systems theory by connecting it with issues of sense-making, meaning, and

TABLE 4.5
PETER SENGE'S APPLICATION OF SYSTEMS THEORY CONCEPTS TO
ORGANIZATIONAL LEARNING

1. Today's problems come from yesterday's solutions.
2. The harder you push, the harder the system pushes back.
   a. Compensating feedback is necessary to correct.
   b. The more work you do, the more work there is to do.
3. Behavior grows better before it grows worse.
   a. Example: Conceptualize a person surrounded by very large dominoes. She pushes one over, sits down in a comfortable chair thinking her work is done. As she sits there, the first domino knocks over the second domino, and so on. Soon, just as she is falling asleep, all the dominoes have fallen, except the one just next to her head.
   b. Never assume that a job is finished. Just because it is out the door doesn't mean it won't return in some other form.
4. The easiest way out usually leads back in.
5. The cure can be worse than the disease.
6. Faster is slower.
   a. Managers have learned that the optimal rate of production is less than the fastest rate.
   b. Toward the optimal rate is increased stress on the system and less opportunity for quality control.
7. Cause and effect are not closely related in time and space.
   a. The roots of problems tend to be in ourselves rather than in the outcomes of our systems.
   b. There is a need to look for deep structures of situations.
8. Small changes can produce big results.
9. You can have your cake and eat it too, but not at the same time.
   a. Snapshot versus process thinking.
   b. Increasing quality often lowers costs in the long run.
10. Dividing one elephant in half does not produce two small elephants.
11. There is no blame for individuals when the cure lies in relationships.

SOURCE: Adapted from Peter Senge, *The Laws of the Fifth Discipline* (New York: McGraw-Hill, 1991).

communication. In doing so, he provided a bridge for organizational studies from systems perspectives to the idea of organizational culture.

Weick's starting point was that organizations exist in highly complex, uncertain environments. In fact, the job of organizing is precisely to make sense of this uncertainty through interaction. Weick calls this process equivocality-reduction, which means the development of meanings by human beings for a given situation or event. Equivocality is akin to uncertainty, or unpredictability; it means that the same facts can be interpreted in many ways. How the people of a company communicate to make sense out of equivocal situations is the question central to Weick's approach. Weick's model, then, is an adaptation of ecological, evolutionary theories to organizational behavior (see Figure 4.1). The model has three parts: enactment, selection, and retention. Enactment is the process by which organizational members create their environments through their chosen actions and patterns of attention. Enacted environments vary in degree of perceived

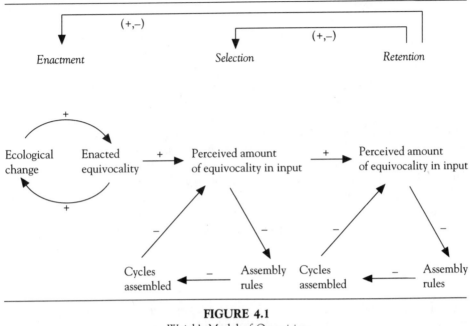

FIGURE 4.1
Weick's Model of Organizing
Karl Weick, *The Social Psychology of Organizing* (Random House, 1979). Reprinted by permission.

equivocality or uncertainty. Once an environment is enacted, organizing requires that participants select from a number of possible alternative explanations of what the environment means. Selection is collective sense-making and is accomplished through communication. Finally, those interpretations that are believed to work, or make sense, are retained for future use. Retained interpretations influence future selection processes, as indicated by the feedback loop in the model.

As the model shows, the system of equivocality reduction is represented as a set of interdependent, interacting processes that provide feedback to each other. In this way, the model connects systems thinking with sense-making. Organizations enact aspects of their environment to attend to, select strategies for reducing the uncertainty of information or equivocality of interpretation in those characteristics, and retain the strategies that work.

Perhaps Weick's most revolutionary concept is the enacted environment. While in theories of *species* evolution, degree of environmental variation is seen as something that can be objectively determined, the same cannot be said of organizational environments. When the people of an organization look to their environment for clues about threats or opportunities, they do not, of course, all see the same thing. As we know, perception is selective. Different people, depending on their physical makeup, interests, motives, background, and behaviors, see different things. A thief walking a suburban street does not notice the same things that a mail carrier or apartment hunter would. Similarly, a company dominated by engineers sees science and technology in the foreground of the environment, whereas an organization made up mainly of accountants would focus on financial markets and global economic trends.

The concept of enacted environment is important because in the business world today, no one can afford to overlook any activity or process. Perhaps the most critical and certainly the most ignored activities necessary for organizational success involve making decisions on which newspapers and journals to buy, who to keep in touch with by phone, and, in general, which issues are important for survival. Many times business people will miss a story that has direct bearing on their company, simply because they haven't seen the publication. The enacted environment is always partial; no one can ever perceive everything out there. But the important questions one should continually ask is, "Am I attending to the right things, at least for now? Are these the factors that either do or potentially could have a major impact on my business?"

Weick's contribution extends beyond his model of organizing. Three concepts in particular—retrospective sense-making, loose-coupling, and partial inclusion—are also critical for communication study. Each is described below.

Retrospective Sense-making

One of Weick's underlying assumptions is that decision making is largely retrospective, not prospective. In other words, people in organizations only *think* that they plan first and then act according to plan. In fact, Weick argues, people act and speak first, and then they examine their actions so that they can later rationalize the possible meaning of what they did. He sums this up in the catchy phrase: "How can I know what I think until I see what I say?" Weick sees behavior as generally coming first.

Weick's idea does not cover all behavior or interpretations. Some people do act first and then interpret, and others strive to act only in accordance to plans. In our view, both processes are always at work; the importance of Weick's argument is that the balance between planned and unplanned behavior may not be as we think it is. This perspective takes Herbert Simon's contention that individuals in organizations are only intendedly rational to its logical extreme.

In any case, this challenge to commonsense beliefs is at the heart of what some call counter-rational approaches to organizational theory and would certainly be counter to the approach of Taylor, Weber, and the like. Weick pushes this position to the limit, even arguing that perhaps random decision processes (like burning caribou bones over a fire and looking for cracks) are superior to rational methods of decision making and planning. Weick's work in this area marks the further unraveling of the scientific approach to management, where communication simply served as a conduit for the one best way of doing things. In Weick's universe, a manager is primarily a manipulator of symbols, an evangelical motivator who helps employees make sense of their work life.

As a result of this shift, interaction is emphasized over reflection and there is an accompanying bias for action. According to Weick, employees do not need common goals to work well together, nor does anyone in an organization need to know what they are doing before they start doing it. The most necessary ingredient is a willingness to engage in coordinated action to reduce equivocality, which in time may lead individuals to figure out (in retrospect) what they have really been doing all along.

Loose Coupling

At the same time that Weick stresses the importance of communication at work, he also points out that, unlike the case in biological systems, the communication connections between people in organizations vary in intensity and are often very loose or weak. Weick's work on loosely coupled systems (1976) has had an enormous impact on our understanding of organizations that are not tightly connected through communication.

Let us consider the typical college or university. Although a great deal of interaction and exchange may exist within departments, few strong ties connect diverse areas. What happens in the History Department probably has little effect on actions or decisions in Engineering. This lack of tight connection usually holds not only among academic units, but also among staff, administration, and faculty. A university is a classic example of a loosely coupled system. Rational approaches would maintain that this lack of connection is a problem. The old way of thinking is as follows: For an organization to be effective, everyone must share a common goal. Lack of connection or communication between parts of the organizational system will deter people from working together and from achieving this common goal.

According to Weick, most organizations do not operate in this fashion. Looser connections between components can even be advantageous for a company. Multiple goals exist in organizations, and coordination is possible without alignment of beliefs (Eisenberg, 1984). Loosely coupled systems are better able to withstand jolts from the environment. For example, if a series of lights on a tree are tightly connected (say, in a series), then damage to any one light knocks out the whole string. If they are wired separately, the group of lights as a whole is relatively resistant to threatening outside forces. While the cost may be greater redundancy and some inefficiency, loosely coupled systems are often most effective. The role of communication in organizations rarely follows the rule of more is better.

Partial Inclusion

Finally, Weick is concerned not only with quality of work life but also with the balance between work and other activities. He utilizes the concept of partial inclusion to explain why certain theories of motivation and employee behavior do not seem to work. All employees are only partially included in the workplace; some of their behaviors, but not all, are there. An employee who is not motivated at work may be a leader in her church or an excellent parent. A top performer at work may have few outside activities. In either case, simple theories of organizational behavior will always be limited if they fail to consider the various groups and organizations in which people are included outside of their main place of work.

At the close of his book, Weick clearly differentiates himself from the profitability-driven, "bottom-line to the exclusion of everything else" point of view. Instead, he argues that organizations are first and foremost communities, social settings in which we choose to spend most of our adult lives. They provide opportunities for storytelling and socializing, and, in the final analysis: "They haven't anything else to give" (Weick, 1979, p. 264).

The door is left open for a closer analysis of organizations as communities, which is the primary goal of the cultural approach, taken up in the next chapter.

SUMMARY

The broad label of *systems approaches* encompasses many different perspectives with varying philosophical assumptions and implications for action. In contrast to previous organizational theories, many of which could be classified according to their underlying view of the goals of organizing and of workers, systems theory is much more open-ended. Adopting a systems approach is mainly an acknowledgment of the complexity of social organizations, and of the critical importance of the processes and relationships among individuals over time.

In practice, however, systems approaches can be either a help or a hindrance to the situated individual. A systems approach can help individuals by giving them the big picture, pointing out critical relationships and networks of contacts that allow groups and organizations to record achievements that are in some way greater than the sum of their parts. Research from a systems perspective can reveal important interdependencies, especially connections with organizational environments, that are key to an organization's survival. But while systems theory highlights communication and relationships, it is mostly silent on the meanings that are constructed through these interactions. Systems theory does an excellent job of pointing out existing and potential participants in a fruitful organizational dialogue, but says little about the nature of the dialogue itself. For these reasons, Weick's work was seen as a significant breakthrough. It augmented systems theory with issues of meaning and sense-making, which are the most important products and processes of organizing.

By the same token, systems theory can be applied in such a way that the whole is elevated far above the individual parts, each of whom may be ignored and dehumanized. Recognition of the role of whole systems must always be accompanied by an understanding of how individuals create, refine, and destroy them. In this way, we not only see the importance of processes and relationships, but also connect these relationships and their higher-order consequences to the tangible actions of individuals.

Anticipating the potential for obliterating the individual in systems theory, one of its founders spoke about the limited applicability of natural systems concepts to the individual in social organizations:

> Man [sic] is not only a political animal, he is, before and above all, an individual. The real
> values of humanity are not those it shares with biological entities, the function of an organism
> or a community of animals, but those which stem from the individual mind. Human society is
> not a community of ants or termites, governed by inherited instinct and controlled by laws of
> the superordinate whole; it is based on the achievements of the individual and is doomed if the
> individual is made a cog in the social machine. This, I believe, is the ultimate precept a theory
> of organization can give: not a manual for dictators of any denomination to more efficiently
> subjugate human beings by the scientific application of iron laws, but a warning that the
> Leviathan of organization must not swallow the individual without sealing its own inevitable
> doom (Von Bertalanffy, 1968, pp. 52–53).

CASE STUDY

The Case of the Engineering Salad

BACKGROUND

Dom Valesquez is head systems engineer for an aerospace design firm. He is also a gourmet cook who has a passion for Southwestern, Cajun, and Italian dishes and has prepared many memorable meals for his friends. For example, he has concocted a blackened catfish enchilada with fresh cilantro and green onion marinated rice that won first prize in a local cook-off. Similarly, his "licorice fish" recipe calling for fresh fennel, garlic, olive oil, and sardines tossed with linguine is a constant flavor reference among local gourmands.

But cooking is not Dom's problem these days. His firm is undergoing a corporate change and transformation process that he has been placed in charge of, mostly against his better judgment. It isn't that he disagrees with the change process. In fact, he is one of its strongest sponsors. Instead, his objection is based on his belief that what is wrong with his company is not something that he is equipped to fix. And what is wrong is *communication;* simply put, it doesn't happen very often, and when it does, it is usually misunderstood.

Ironically, he was placed in charge of the change effort because of his cooking skills. Angela Evans, his CEO, told him: "If you can combine so many different ingredients and come up with an original, wonderful dish, then surely there is something in that head of yours that can help us do the same thing with our company."

"Yeah, right Angela," Dom thought when she told him. "I can cook because when I do it, I only have to talk to myself. But this is a different kind of problem."

THE SITUATION

Dom's company consists of five independent divisions: contracts (responsible for gaining contracts), accounting and finance (responsible for bookkeeping and billing), engineering (responsible for creating designs), technical support (responsible for documentation, graphics, and specifications), and clerical support (responsible for secretarial and office support duties). Each division consists of a head (Dom is head of engineering) and a technical or professional staff. There are 72 employees in the firm, most of whom are engineers.

Their company chart looks like this:

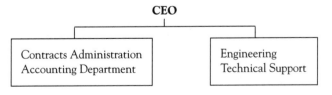

Clerical Staff

From Dom's perspective, even though this chart is relatively flat, it still misrepresents how the information necessary to deliver a design actually works. He sees all the business units as part of a larger, interrelated system: Without Contracts Administration, there is no work to do, but without engineering there is no work, period. Similarly, accounting is to contracts what technical support is to engineering: part of the whole, not a separate unit. Without accounting, nobody would get paid and without technical support, nobody would know what anybody else was doing. For the company to work, as Dom has often pointed out, some mechanism is needed for all the groups to know what each one of them is up to, what the groups' needs are, and a way of providing information and feedback.

Unfortunately, Dom's views are not widely understood. Cody Anders, head of Contracts Administration, believes that if each business unit simply did its job there wouldn't be any problems. Cody, Dom muses, is strictly a meat-and-potatoes kind of guy; he only eats one thing at a time and won't eat anything once it has been touched by another food. Taylor Mims, head of Accounting, more or less agrees with Cody, and this forms a kind of contracts and accounting mentality that the engineers and technical support staff constantly confront. On a more positive note, the head of Technical Support, DeAnna Baker, sides with Dom against Taylor and Cody. In her view, technical support is central to the whole operation, but they need access to everyone in the various business units to do their jobs.

ASSIGNMENT

Dom's task is to find a way to improve communication among the five business units. In his mind he sees this as akin to making a really fine salad out of distinct ingredients. But lately he has come to realize that he is not simply the master chef in this recipe for corporate success; he is also necessarily part of the problem. After all, engineering is the largest business unit, and although he knows the others are valuable, he stubbornly clings to the idea that engineering is what the firm does, and without engineering, there would be no company.

It is at this point in the operation that Dom requests help from a local organizational communication consulting and training firm. You are his contact. What would you recommend? How would you propose Dom and his company adopt a systems perspective for their work? What could be done to help them accomplish better communication? How will what they do affect their change and transformation process?

CULTURAL STUDIES
OF ORGANIZATIONS
AND
COMMUNICATION

"According to convention, there is
a sweet and a sour;
According to convention, there is
a hot and a cold;
And according to convention, there is Order.
In truth, there are atoms and a Void."

—*Demosthenes, 5th century* B.C.

"The value of fiction lies in its consequences."

—*Michael Jackson, 1989*

In this chapter we introduce the idea of organizations as cultures. We explain how the culture metaphor for organizations is a reaction against the mechanics of complex systems. This metaphor provides us with a view of organizing that focuses on the language(s) of the workplace, the routine and dramatic performances of managers and employees, and a wide variety of shared practices that help an organization know its own uniqueness, such as participation in rituals and rites, and the display and meanings attributed to artifacts.

Second, we extend these conceptual frontiers into the everyday practices of persons in organizations. Our concern is with revealing culture as a context for interpretation that influences how individuals and groups make sense out of what they do, and learn to understand that what they do is connected to the overall interests of the organization. To do this we provide an interpretation of cultures through actions, practices, narratives, and dialogue that reveal and construct competing interests, voices, practices, and values within organizations.

Third, we explicate three perspectives on organizational culture, each one providing resources for interpretation. The value of this section lies not in the naming of the perspectives, but in understanding that asking questions about an organization's culture is like directing the passage of light through a three-sided prism: what you see is determined by which way you turn the prism. Turned one way, strong colors dominate; turned another way, there is an interplay of competing colors; turned yet another way, some of the original colors disappear altogether revealing new blends of colors. To capture the many-sidedness of any organization's culture requires being able to ask different questions and to see practices under the influence of differing light.

Fourth, we investigate the idea of organizational sense-making as it is influenced by the cultural dialogue. In this section we provide an insider's approach to organizational cultures by showing how culture creates opportunities for creativity and constraint in individuals and groups and through doing the daily business of the organization.

Finally, we pose the question that has consistently plagued the idea of culture in organizations: Can (and should) a culture be managed? By suggesting ways to approach this question, we use this section to discuss the strengths and limitations of the culture metaphor for describing and analyzing communication in organizations.

THE CULTURAL APPROACH

According to the Wisdom Books of the Talmud, the purpose of life is to discover God's order in all things. One of the things this search produces is culture(s). The primary instrument of this search is the symbol.

Cultures as Meaningful Orders

Marshall Sahlins, a cultural anthropologist, defines culture as "meaningful orders of persons and things" (1976). Each term in his definition is important. "Meaningful orders" refers to the complex processes and relationships evident in all cultures and revealed through each culture's symbols. "Persons and things" are resources for interpreting the meanings of a culture and its symbols. Viewed this way, persons and things are *interdependent.* We learn about cultures not only by what their populations say about them, but also by the tools they use to create them, the values they display in artifacts and in the human development and possession of things.

A culture is like a religion. As T. S. Eliot put it, "no culture has appeared or developed except together with a religion . . . [and] the culture will appear to be the product of the religion, or the religion the product of the culture" (1949, p. 13). Viewed this way, the idea of a culture is accomplished by locating a set of common beliefs and values that prescribes a general view of *order* (e.g., the way things are) as well as *explanation* (why things are like that). This tie between religion and culture is important to organizational studies because it indicates how the search for order and explanation compels beliefs.

Not all members of a culture accept or practice the beliefs in the same ways. Like religions, most cultures include various sects or subcultures, people who share the common order, but whose ways of understanding or carrying out the beliefs differ. This point underscores the importance of approaching differences of perspective on an organization's culture(s) as a dialogue with many voices as well as many points of entry into interpretations of its meaning. Among the participants, the purpose of the culture may be to reduce the ambiguities of meanings used to shape actions; among the observers, that same culture may appear to be *constructing* the symbolic order. Balancing discovery of the culture with the creation of symbolic order—again, balancing creativity with constraint—is the cultural task of employees and the interpretive task of researchers.

Cultures as Symbolic Constructions

The term *culture* is a symbol. Symbol is a word that stands for something else; in the case of culture, the something else includes actions, practices, narratives, and dialogues. To study organizational culture is to study the organization as a symbol (e.g., organized activities that represent a search for meaningful orders) as well as *through* its uses of symbols (e.g., the actions, practices, narratives, and dialogues). Viewed this way, the study of organizational cultures is achieved through interpretations of the meanings of these symbolic constructions.

Viewing organizations as symbols is important for four reasons. First, unlike previous theories of organizations and communication that rely on metaphorical comparisons drawn from *completed* conceptions of machines, organisms, or systems, cultural studies begin with a fundamental appreciation of how our conceptions of everything are formed in language. Language is the organizing locus of human symbolic experience; language therefore creates organizations as well as our understandings of them. Put differently, the search for meaningful orders of persons and things begins with what those persons *say* to each other about the *meanings* of those things.

Second, to understand organizations as symbolic constructions is to recover a perspective on the human being as a symbol-using, symbol-abusing animal (Burke, 1966). Symbols don't simply stand for something else. Rather, they shape our understandings of what something else is, what it means, what it can be used for, and how it should be dealt with. Symbols are instruments of human understanding and human action; we do things with words. In addition, once we have done things with words—built an organization's culture, for instance—those things we have constructed, in turn, do things to *us* (Burke, 1950). The culture of an organization—that thing we have done to ourselves, for ourselves, with words—then induces us to think, act, and behave in particular ways.

Third, symbol-using/abusing is an inherently human activity. As Kenneth Burke once put it: "All animals eat, but we are the only ones who gossip about restaurants or exchange recipes." Similarly, human cultures are inherently human constructions of reality. As such, human symbolic constructions of cultures deserve a foundational place in our understanding. Think of it this way: we make languages out of symbols, and we are the only animals who make cultures out of languages. Therefore, *how* and *why* we make cultures out of the material of symbols and languages say unique and important things about us. To paraphrase the cultural anthropologist Clifford Geertz (1973), the study of cultures tells us what the devil we think we are up to.

Fourth, to view culture as a symbolic construction is to understand symbols in organizations as the material manifestations of culture. This is important because symbols, like cultures, seldom stand alone; they interact; they collide, they provide subtle differences and marked contrasts, they act as motivators and unifiers, as well as reasons not to be motivated and sources of deeply meaningful divisions. As such, symbol-using provides a unique perspective on what it means to be human and what it means to be a human situated among other humans at work.

Burke provides a summary statement of what it means to be a human from the perspective of symbol-using (and, therefore, culture-constructing) in his classic essay "Definition of Man" (1966). See Table 5.1 for the terms of his definition. Burke's view of humans as symbol users helps us to see that symbols not only *represent* (stand for something else), but also *evoke* (bring with them other symbolic powers). For example, the idea of a loss of nature as the root of hierarchy evokes the biblical story of Adam and Eve, the apple, guilt, and redemption. So too is this true with symbols—and narratives—about cultures. This is why we say that to study a culture requires that the researcher/employee provide an interpretation—a reading—of those meaningful orders of persons and things. What is being read are symbols; what is being made out of them is an interpretation of their meanings. How those meanings get coordinated into a representational whole is how—as Burke puts it—humans are "moved by a sense of order."

Let us pause a moment and consider how dramatically distinctive this idea is, particularly when contrasted with earlier scientific management approaches. Two important questions suggest themselves: (1) Why did this happen? and (2) What factors contributed to this development?

HISTORICAL AND CULTURAL BACKGROUND

How did this approach originate? Positioned conceptually among various academic disciplines as an alternative to the systems approach (Pacanowsky and O'Donnell-Trujillo, 1983), a cultural approach to organizations and communication emerged as a result of four major changes in historical narratives about science and society, knowledge and its representation, and the politics of doing research in a contested world. These changes were: (1) resistance to domination, (2) the end of empire, (3) questioning traditional methods of social science, and (4) the development of ethnography as a method to study organizations.

Resistance to Domination

Consider the following passage, written by sociologist Todd Gitlin, about the economic framework in the United States following World War II:

> By 1945, the United States found itself an economic lord set far above the destroyed powers, its once and future competitors among both Allies and Axis powers. Inflation was negligible, so the increase in available dollars was actually buying more goods. Natural resources seemed plentiful, their supplies stable. . . . The Depression was over. And so were the deprivations of World War II, which also brought relative blessings: While European and Japanese factories were being pulverized, new American factories were being built and old ones were back at work, shrinking unemployment to relatively negligible proportions. Once the war was over, consumer demand was a dynamo. Science was mobilized by industry, and capital was channeled by government as never before. The boom

TABLE 5.1

KENNETH BURKE'S DEFINITION OF HUMANS AS SYMBOL USERS

Humans are	
1. Symbol-using (and symbol-abusing) animals	Symbols are shorthand terms for situations (how we talk about an event reveals how we understand it).
	Symbols contain motives for actions (the words we use induce us to behave in particular ways).
2. Inventors of the negative	Thou shalt not (we know what to do, in part, because of what we cannot or should not do).
	Dramatic *action* involves *character* which involves *choice* (choice assumes alternatives that construct opposites).
	To act is to choose.
3. Separated from our natural conditions by instruments of our own making	Language separates us from nature; the Phoenician alphabet was the first technology.
	Culture is made out of the technologies of language, and culture further separates us from nature.
	Progress is the symbol that motivates technologies.
4. Goaded by the spirit of hierarchy (or moved by a sense of Order)	Just as language separates us from nature, it also induces us to separate members of our culture from each other.
	Divisions among social classes, divisions of labor, and divisions of race, age, or gender are first divisions in language and then divisions in how we act toward each other.
	Those "Up" are guilty of not being "Down," and those "Down" are guilty of not being "Up."
	Guilt produces conflict and cooperation, both of which are necessary to maintain hierarchy.
5. Rotten with perfection	We strive toward absolutes: what we name as "right," what we name as "progress," what we name as "good," "beautiful," or "true."
	Perfection is the ultimate symbol of redemption born out of guilt.
	We are rotten in the sense that we inherited the burden of original sin (guilt about eating the forbidden apple), which in turn made us rely on language to make sense out of what had happened and to dedicate our lives to work that would, hopefully, lead us into a more perfect understanding or place.

was on, and the cornucopia seemed all the more impressive because the miseries of the Depression and war were near enough to suffuse the present with a sense of relief (1987, p. 13).

Gitlin points out that these newly found sources of renewal and promise were balanced with an equally powerful image of impending doom: the atomic age is one in which the image of a nuclear holocaust serves as a constant reminder of how fragile our collective hold on life continues to be. The tension created by these opposing influences on the United States and the rest of the world shaped the cultural, political, and economic values of a new generation. But it is important to remember, as Gitlin reminds us, that

> "The Fifties" were multiple, of course, according to whether you lived on Manhattan Island or in Manhattan, Kansas, in Southern California or North Carolina; different too depending on whether you were eight or eighteen or fifty-eight, female or male, black or white, Irish Catholic or Protestant or Jewish, an electrical worker or a salesman of appliances or a housewife with an all-electric kitchen or the president of General Electric; and this is not yet to speak of differences in family style and personality. But one thing we know is that the presumably placid, complacent Fifties were succeeded by the unsettling Sixties (1987, p. 12).

What Gitlin describes are the seeds of various tensions among social, ethnic, racial, political, sexual, and economic divisions that contributed to our evolution, to our conflicts, and to our understandings. The world, which had always been a complex place, grew more so. Important sources of this new complexity came from the relationship of science to society, industry, and ideology.

Science, which at least since the Enlightenment had promised and delivered a progressive and increasingly rational society, suddenly had also demonstrated its ability to produce weapons that could easily destroy all that had been created. Industry, which at least since the Industrial Revolution had promised and delivered newer and better products and services guaranteed to make life easier and more humane, also sanctioned inequalities between women and men and among ethnic and racial groups, and contributed to world tensions through fierce competition for scarce natural resources and commodity markets. Similarly, new information technologies—radios, stereos, televisions, satellites—produced as consumable commodities also contributed to a world in which access to news and entertainment throughout the planet was readily available, and therefore readily open to commentary. And, of course, there were ideological battles between capitalism, socialism, and communism that constantly threatened the peace and produced the Cold War and today's aftermath.

Against this complex background new questions were asked. Although these questions addressed a wide variety of topics, many of them increasingly concerned issues of domination and resistance; work, communication, and management practices in organizations did not long escape critical scrutiny. The enemy of all resistance movements is *control*. Control manifests itself in the power to repress opposition as well as in the power to reproduce the interests and narratives of a dominant group. Consider, for example, the power men exerted over women simply by defining a division of labor according to work/ home locations. Real work was what was done outside of the home and was the special duty of men to perform. Home-work was thus marginalized; it was not given attention or respect; it was not valued for its major contributions to the ideals of family and society. Thus relegated to a lesser status by the narratives of men, home-work brought with it lesser status for the women who by-and-large worked there. The exception to this domi-nant narrative was—and is—found in the stories of traditional farming families, where women and men often work side by side doing chores within the home and in the fields.

When women began asserting their rights to work outside the home, and then assumed positions of responsibility above what was commonly considered women's work—secretar-ial, food preparation, elementary school teaching, and custodial duties—they encoun-tered serious opposition among many men who saw this move as threatening to what they considered to be the way things are. The way things are, of course, was that way because of the dominant stories men had been reared on, stories that valued a separation of the sexes in every sphere of life. These stories were being challenged.

Similarly, members of minority groups were posing challenges to the dominant institu-tions that had long controlled their access to equality in society. People of color, people whose ethnic and religious heritages distinguished them from the dominant Western white majority, people with physical and mental handicaps, people who had served in the armed forces, and elderly people—all, in their own ways, protested what they perceived as unfair social and professional practices. For many of these minority groups, the protests of the 1950s, 1960s, and 1970s were extensions of their long-waged wars against oppression. For other groups, the idea that protests against institutional and social domination could change things was a new and liberating one.

Given that resistance to domination, oppression, and control was so widespread, it was perhaps inevitable that new questions would also be asked about science as the dominant way of knowing and of constructing narratives about knowledge. In relation to studies of organizations and communication, these new questions about science gave rise to alternative approaches to understanding.

The End of Empire

The middle years of the 1960s are commonly referred to among anthropologists, historians, and literary critics as the end of the period of Western colonialism (Greenblatt, 1990; Said, 1978, 1984). By this time, the world had been thoroughly colonized by Western interests. With the end of colonialism came a loss of cultural differentiation, as well as an awareness of how dominant Western interests were accomplices in the political and economic subordination of a Third World (Bhabha, 1990; Clifford & Marcus, 1985; Marcus and Fischer, 1986; Minh-Ha, 1991). Anthropologists, whose discipline is devoted to recording cultures while often being sympathetic to colonizing impulses, were regarded as resources for understanding how cultures were formed, what made them distinctive, and what forces shaped their destinies. These were precisely the sorts of questions important to organizational communication.

One result of asking new questions about cultures was that the language used to analyze organizations and communication changed. As we have seen, the dominant vocabulary of organizational studies had been derived from social scientific measurement techniques developed through applications of statistics to the fields of industrial psychology, sociology, communication, and management. Virtually everything that could be counted was counted: performance, effectiveness of managerial messages given to employees, sources of motivation and reward, functional utility of work units, message flows within hierar-chies, and the outcomes of group problem solving, decision making, and leadership. Our knowledge about organizations and communication was symbolically structured out of the terms provided by the theories, methods, and findings of these disciplines. The dominant language used to describe and analyze communication in organizations was built out of these social science symbols; academic culture was, therefore, dominated by a particular way of knowing and of constructing knowledge. When questions about domination surfaced, one of the principal places where they were raised was in college and universities. Analogies between political and scientific domination were used to suggest that if our society was to embrace multiple perspectives, then perhaps our academic disciplines should learn to do so too. Science—particularly social science—provided terms that controlled our understanding of human behavior. Perhaps it was time to question those terms and, if possible, suggest new ones. With the advent of cultural studies of organizations, the terms changed (see Table 5.2).

As you can see from Table 5.2, this change in vocabulary brought with it changes in what researchers, employees, and managers thought was important and in what they

TABLE 5.2
EVOLUTION OF SOME CULTURAL TERMS APPLIED TO ORGANIZATIONAL
COMMUNICATION STUDIES

Symbols	Language	Metaphors
Words/Actions	Ingroup Speech Technical terms Jargon Jokes Gossip Rumors Gendered usage	Determined by use within the culture
Artifacts Objects Cartoons	Arrangement of the physical work space Personal meanings Humor in the workplace Social/political commentary	Power/status Irony/contrast Resistance to domination
Routines Repetitive behaviors	**Rituals/Rites** Individual performances Group performances New employee Acceptance into group Promotions Annual celebrations Shunning/exclusion Retirement	**Communities** Continuity Acculturation Difference
Use of Objects	**Employee Handbooks** Company brochures Annual reports	**Representation**
Logos Awards	Identification Reward	Symbolic unity Enhancement

examined for meanings. Interpretations of culture broadened the scope of what was considered information about organizations and communication and therefore complicated our thinking about organizational communication processes. For example, feedback was no longer confined to the domain of verbal messages; feedback could be found in artifacts and cartoons, in the arrangement of work space, even in who parked next to whom in the employee parking lot. Put a little differently, the colonization of theories of work brought about by the adoption of social science vocabularies was exposed, questioned, and an alternative arrangement proposed.

The end of the colonial period also marked the beginning of new global economic and political concerns that dramatically influenced critical scrutiny of organizations. The development of multinational firms, the emergence of an interdependent financial system and world economy, and the domination of capitalism—all of which depended heavily on cheap labor in Third World countries—were often exposed in the media and among academics as the sources of global problems. The management of cultural differences gradually became a concern among firms interested in continuing to do business in other lands with people who did not share their language, customs, understandings, or, in many cases, objectives. The model for the management of differences would not be domination but *cooperation*. Finding ways to improve cross-cultural understandings and communication skills was an integral aspect of the cultural approach to organizations and communication.

Questioning Traditional Methods of Social Science

As we have suggested, another ingredient in this resistance to domination and the end of empire occurred within academic disciplines. This change was primarily in the language used to perpetuate the interests of managers over workers. Much of the knowledge generated by social science methods was directed toward providing useful information to managers about the control of workers and their environments. It was not surprising, then, to find that when new questions were raised about the domination of narratives that mainly served the interests of Western, white men, new questions would also arise about the role science played in the creation and maintenance of those narratives.

Thomas Kuhn, in his landmark study of scientific revolutions (1972), suggests that knowledge paradigms (dominant ways of knowing) tend to shift suddenly when old explanations are shown to be inadequate and new ways of knowing are demonstrated to be either more accurate or more properly suited to the politics of an era. The classic example of this notion of a paradigm "shift" in science is Einstein's theory of relativity, a theory (still incomplete) that dramatically altered older conceptions of the universe developed by Newton. Ironically, this example has direct relevance on the use of scientific methods for the study of humans in organizations.

As the new physicists were altering their narratives about the universe based on the relativity theories of Einstein, and later, the uncertainty principle articulated by Heisenberg, social science was still in its infancy, struggling for legitimacy (Smith, 1972). The idea of measuring humans—of scientific accuracy being applied to human behavior—was modeled on a fixed, Newtonian notion of physics and mathematics. But even as physicists were revising their methods to study the universe, social scientists remained steadfast in their loyalty to the model of theoretical physics that had been demonstrated to be deeply flawed (Smith, 1972). Relativity and uncertainty were the cautions of the new physics; but they had yet to be incorporated into the new—interpretive—social sciences (Rabinow & Sullivan, 1986). One way to understand the difference between scientific and interpretive approaches to the study of organizational communication is by conceptualizing research questions about organizations as problems or as mysteries (see Figure 5.1).

Traditional social science research questions are organized on a problem/solution format. We may think about it this way: to name a problem—and then to work systematically to solve it—is to assume that a known Order already exists (that the framework for understanding the issue and making sense of it is already in place). The perception of a problem produces the need for a solution to the problem. To achieve a solution requires manipulating either persons or things within the existing order. These manipulations produce findings about the influences of the manipulations, and, hopefully, solutions to the problem. In turn, solutions to existing problems tend to produce new problems that call for new solutions; while the solutions tend to solve part of the puzzle, they also tend to contribute to new puzzles. For some researchers, this suggests that something is fundamentally wrong with the framework; the order that is being manipulated may not, in fact, be representative of the Order at all.

By contrast, cultural studies of organizations tend to assume that the puzzle is the search for Order, not the destination. That is, symbolic constructions of reality are mysteries that contain clues for reading the meaningful orders as well as the relationship of the meaningful orders to the greater Order, or framework, of understanding. What

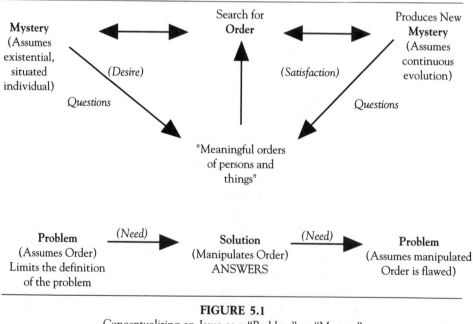

FIGURE 5.1
Conceptualizing an Issue as a "Problem" or "Mystery"

mystery produces is the desire for Order—for the ways in which meaningful orders can be questioned, for the ways stories can be made out of questions, and for the ways the stories can add up to an appreciation for the critical terms of the ongoing dialogue. In turn, cultural studies of organizations tend to produce newer, deeper mysteries about the meanings, the orders, the functions of stories about the orders, and the relationship of an order to a greater Order.

Cultural studies also produce themes, that is, collectivities of symbols that are organized around a central idea. Like their scientific counterparts—findings—these cultural themes act as tentative conclusions or interpretations about meaningful orders in a particular organization during a particular time. Unlike their traditional counterparts—solutions—themes do not seek a level of generalization about other cultures in other organizations. They do not intentionally serve the colonizing interests of managers or researchers. There is a very good reason for this. Cultural studies of organizations are searches for order within a greater mystery—an Order. As such, they produce rich interpretations of pieces of puzzles that are greater than the pieces but at the same time serve as clues to it. Traditional social science studies assume that the puzzle is already known and in place, and the task of the study is to identify and/or correct some perceived flaw or irregularity in the individual piece.

That these differences in perspective occurred within a historical period marked by the exploration of new understandings of the relationships between cultural practices and broader social, political, and ideological meanings is not accidental. The study of cultures provides a unique opportunity to study the everyday practices of humans at work and to see how these practices are shaped and understood as broader reflections of social, political, and ideological meanings. As such, interpretive accounts of cultural performances provide unique resources for understanding relationships between meaningful orders and the Order, or between given interpretations of meaning and an overall world-view or coordinated understanding.

Cultures are performed in everyday practices. By performed we mean that cultural understandings are revealed in the daily interactions of ordinary people. To study the performance of culture from an interpretive posture requires (1) framing those activities with an appropriate metaphor, and (2) using the language of the metaphor chosen to describe and to interpret the meanings associated with the activities. Interpretive studies of cultures develop imaginative, creative insights about the meanings of performances by exploiting the possibilities of the language inspired by a particular metaphor. For example, John Van Maanen (1991) uses the metaphor of a smile factory to describe the cultural performances at Disneyland. The image of smiles (friendly, fun, courteous) being manufactured (e.g., the products of a rigid assembly-line factory) establishes the tensions of a cultural dialogue among Disneyland workers. By using this language, Van Maanen delineates the interplays of a dramatic, staged performance: employees are "members of a cast," who wear "costumes," not uniforms, and who exhibit on-stage, off-stage, and back-stage behaviors. He is also able to use the image of the factory to discuss what goes into the production of smiles: formal, rigid rules about informal behaviors, and the prevalence of supervisory spies who mark every infraction of the rules. The result is an account of a strong culture whose everyday uses of language construct a metaphor that, in turn, becomes its unique sense of place.

The power of interpretations of symbolic actions to provide alternative ways of knowing about and acting in organizations affected our concepts of the language appropriate for organizational analysis. It also influenced the methods through which researchers gain information.

The Development of Ethnography as a Method Useful for Studying Organizations

Dissatisfied with traditional methods of social science, some researchers began to search for new alternatives. Because the cultural approach to organizations and communication was emerging, and because anthropologists had been studying cultures authoritatively for quite some time, it was natural that researchers would attempt to integrate anthropological research methods into the study of organizations and communication (Geertz, 1973; Goodall, 1989, 1991a; Van Maanen, 1979, 1988). Anthropological research methods refer specifically to ethnography, or the writing of culture (Clifford & Marcus, 1985) based primarily on the experiences of the researcher living among the persons researched. For example, in the study of Disneyland cited earlier, Van Maanen relies on his personal recollections of working there while he was a student, as well as his more recent observations and interactions with employees and guests, to write an ethnographic account of Disneyland's culture.

There are important conceptual distinctions between the doing and writing of traditional social sciences and the doing and writing of ethnography. Traditional social science is based on a separation of the researcher from the researched. The classic image of research is drawn from Jeremy Bentham's notion of the Panopticon, a circular platform above and surrounding a research location that would afford the social scientist a full and relatively uninterrupted view of an ongoing scene. The Panopticon is so named because through the creation of distance (and elevation) between the researcher and those researched the social scientist can see everything. It creates a necessary analytical distance from which the researcher may then develop uncontaminated (by actual physical contact with those being researched) objective observations.

In this way, social science attempts to mimic the objectivity of the physical sciences: application of scientific methods to the object of study by a trained, neutral, distanced observer. These scientific methods usually consist of a questionnaire or survey that can be quantitatively assessed; when properly applied, they insure objectivity. The result of this procedure is an account of behavior mediated by the methods of conducting the study. The events of the account, the perspective taken by the researcher, and the meanings of the observed performances belong to or are controlled by the social scientist. The report legitimates the meanings of the social scientist over the meanings of those studied, and the social scientist tends to profit from the publication of results, whereas those studied seldom receive much in return for their contributions. Hence, the report can be read as a colonizing activity. In other words, the social scientist controls the production and meaning of the story; the story, then, can become an additional instrument of domination of the people whose lives and meanings shaped the product.

By contrast, contemporary ethnographic field research is based on closing the distance between the observer (a participant-observer) and the observed (those who are lived with). This kind of research requires immersion rather than distance (Jackson, 1989; Rose, 1989; Stoller, 1989). This is because the culture must be interpreted from an up-close and intensive personal understanding of its language and meanings. Lived experience rather than observed behavior becomes the method of doing the study and, in some cases, of writing the research report (Benson, 1981; Goodall, 1991; Panconowsky, 1988, 1988; Van Maanen, 1988). The account that is reported—the ethnographic story—is, in effect, about a cultural dialogue. That dialogue concerns the competing interests of the researcher and those researched, as well as the various and often conflicting voices of those represented in the study.

An important caveat is in order here. Just because there are important distinctions among competing research methods does not make one right and the other one wrong. Important contributions to cultural understandings have occurred as a result of traditional social science, just as important revisions to the doing of traditional social science have occurred as a result of ethnographic cultural inquiries. In matters of research, just as in all matters of communication emerging from individuals in organizations, it is important to see the issues as an ongoing dialogue constructed by active, competing voices, all of whom seek some balance between creativity (what we are trying to do) and constraint (the problems we confront when we try to do it).

CULTURE AS TEXT

Interpretive, ethnographic approaches to organizations and communication promote the idea of viewing culture as a text (Barthes, 1976; Brown & McMillan, 1991). Here text means that the translation of everyday company events into a written form is accomplished in much the same way as a journalist or novelist constructs the events and characters in a story. Although some researchers criticize text-constructing efforts as producing an account that looks too much like a novel (and therefore less like a scientific study), and other critics wonder whether, as the novelist Flannery O'Connor once put it, "any tale twice-told is a fiction" (as opposed to nonfiction), cultural studies advocates tend to reflect Clifford Geertz's general philosophy:

> The culture of a people is an ensemble of texts, themselves ensembles, which the anthropologist strains to read over the shoulders of those to whom they properly belong. There are enormous difficulties in such an enterprise, methodological pitfalls to make a Freudian quake, and some moral perplexities as well. Nor is it the only way that symbolic forms can be sociologically handled. . . . But whatever the level at which one operates, the guiding principle is the same: societies, like lives, contain their own interpretations. One only has to learn how to gain access to them (1973, 239–240).

Table 5.3 on page 128 displays some of the central ideas in the culture-as-text approach to organizational studies. Notice particularly how the distinctions between viewing organizational culture as a monologue or dialogue shape these issues.

Once organizational scholars more or less accepted the idea of ethnographic studies, it became useful to distinguish among the types of texts that were being written. John Van Maanen, an organizational theorist and cultural ethnographer, identified three types of "tales"—three types of texts—told about organizations: realist, confessional, and impressionist (1988). Table 5.4 on page 129 displays these differences.

One important question about cultural narratives is: how do we know when to trust them? What evaluative standards can be used to determine the merits of scholarly writing that often looks and mostly acts like a novel, or perhaps a piece of investigative journalism?

TABLE 5.3
SUMMARY OF CULTURE AS TEXT:
FROM MONOLOGUES TO DIALOGUES

Culture (Monologue) *Story*	Cultures (Dialogue) *Stories*
Self observes others in contexts, writes the account.	Self is divided into the observer and the one being constructed by those observed; account includes both voices as well as voices of the others.
Presents unified view of a culture usually from the perspective of the dominant group.	Presents diversified view of cultures—sub- and countercultures included.
Problematic: is life the same kind of construction that narratives about it are? Is the story a colonization of the culture?	Problematic: Who owns the text? Who benefits from this writing? Would the narratives agree with what is written about them?

Although responses to these concerns continue to be debated, some basic help can be found by applying the rhetorical critic Walter Fisher's ideas about narrative rationality (1984) to ethnographic texts.

Fisher maintains that any story—any narrative—that is intended for public consumption should be judged according to two principles: narrative probability and narrative fidelity. *Narrative probability* refers to the idea that when we listen to a story we make evaluative judgments based on whether the events as told seem plausible and do not leave anything important out. Similarly, the idea of *narrative fidelity* refers to what happens when, as listeners or readers, we feel that the events in the tale as depicted ring true to our experiences of similar cases. Fisher argues that audiences use these two evaluative standards to determine the relative credibility of any narrative. Conversely, these two standards also form the moral imperative for any storyteller seeking public credibility. Reduced to a simple creed, the advisory to any would-be cultural ethnographer is: Tell the best and truest story you know how to tell, but don't leave anything out that may be important.

Benefits of Ethnographic Texts to Studies of Organizations and Communication

Given these distinctions between types of texts created out of cultural studies of organizations and communication and ways to evaluate their credibility, the incorporation of ethnographic research has significantly broadened our understanding. Three major areas of research have directly benefited from this approach:

1. We have a richer perspective on the actual experience of work. Previous conceptions of work tend to be narrowly focused on the specific attitudes and behaviors that

TABLE 5.4
JOHN VAN MAANEN'S CLASSIFICATION OF ETHNOGRAPHIC
TALES ABOUT ORGANIZATIONS

REALIST TALES "DOCTRINE OF IMMACULATE PERCEPTION" *Conventions*	CONFESSIONAL TALES "SELF-ABSORBED MANDATES" OFTEN WRITTEN AS A RESPONSE TO THE CONSTRAINTS OF REALIST CONVENTIONS AND SCIENTIFIC METHODS *Conventions*	IMPRESSIONIST TALES "PRESENT THE DOING OF THE FIELDWORK RATHER THAN SIMPLY THE DOER (CONFESSIONAL) OR THE DONE (REALIST)"; NOVEL ARTISTRY IN THE TELLING OF THE TALE; INNOVATIVE USE OF MATERIALS, OFTEN DESIGNED TO STARTLE THE AUDIENCE *Conventions*
1. Experimental Authority • Absence of the author from the text • Assumption of good faith ("whatever the fieldworker saw and heard is more or less what any similarly well-placed and well-trained participant/observer would see and hear") • Writer has credentials as a scholar with institutional affiliations	**1. Personal(ized) Authority** • First-person narratives that establish intimacy with the readers • Strive to persuade audience of the human qualities and frailties of the fieldworker • Writer develops the attitude of a student toward members of the culture studied; task is to learn from the culture rather than interpret it according to established Western theories about culture	**1. Textual Identity** • Form of the narrative is dramatic recall • Story stands alone without elaborate theoretical framing • Productive use of maximally evocative language • Show rather than tell about the experience
2. Typical Forms • Documentary style, focused on details of everyday life • Use of the powers of observation to direct the writing and interpretation • Rigid categories of analysis: climate and region, geography, family and work life, social networks, kinship patterns, status systems, beliefs and values	**2. Fieldworker's Point of View** • Inclusion of autobiographical details • Story focuses on the character-building conversion of the writer from an academic who sees things one way to a sympathetic participant who sees things another way • Shifting points of view, depending on the activities engaged in or described	**2. Fragmented Knowledge** • Cultural knowledge is slipped into the story rather than separated by category • Narrative displays the learning process used to acquire knowledge of the culture and people

continues

TABLE 5.4 (*continued*)

• Avoidance of the abstract, focus on the concrete details of everyday life

3. Native's Point of View
• Make continuous use of accounts and explanations by members of the culture about the meanings of events and forces in their lives
• Includes myths and stories indigenous to the culture

4. Interpretive Omnipotence
• Single author, dispassionate, third-person voice
• No-nonsense accounts of "the facts" gotten through observation, interaction, and analysis
• Godlike posture toward those studied

3. Naturalness
• The text provides a sense that the account is reasonably uncontaminated by the author's intrusion into the culture and text
• Writer/fieldworker attempts to normalize her or his presence in the activities of the culture
• A general etiquette of acceptance by the natives
• Displays of empathy and involvement with issues in the member's everyday lives

3. Characterization
• Writer/fieldworker's individuality is expressed as a natural condition of the spirit of inquiry—she or he becomes a character in the story rather than its teller
• Supporting characters are not viewed as representative types but as individuals with names, faces, histories, motives, and things to do
• Use of dialogue; characters have lines to speak

4. Dramatic Control
• Events move back and forth in time to give rise to later understandings
• "You-are-there" feel to the telling of the events; a kind of "organized illusion" of participation in the culture
• Tension is built, then released; the surprise ending is not given away but may later be found in earlier clues
• Standards for text construction and language are literary rather than disciplinary

were related to production efficiency. The cultural approach expanded the concept of work to include the influences of stories (Boje, 1990), sexuality (Hearn et al., 1990), personal style (Hebdige, 1979), and politics (Mumby, 1987).

2. We have revised our conception of leadership and management. Management studies of leadership tended to associate behaviors with outcomes, and offered a

conceptually thin and pragmatically linear view of leadership. A cultural perspective encourages leadership to be defined in coordination with followership—as a kind of dialogue—whose meanings are accessed through stories, jokes, gossip, rumors, and accounts of the performance value of leadership (Trujillo, 1985).

3. Features of organizational life that were previously ignored or neglected are now scrutinized for their influences. For example, how changing metaphors to describe organizations changes organizational practices (Smith & Eisenberg, 1987), passionate rituals and corporate celebrations (Pacanowsky, 1988), coping strategies used to deal with dangerous but routine work (Manning, 1977; Van Maanen, 1988), and relationships between cars in parking lots and organizational personalities (Goodall, 1989) are ripe for study.

The cultural approach offers new ways of conceptualizing organizational communication study and provides sources of critique of other approaches and perspectives. Specifically, a cultural approach incorporates much of what is most engaging but is often left out of organizational communication analyses: the experience of work. In the next section we develop this idea.

THE CULTURAL APPROACH CATCHES ON IN BUSINESS: THE INFLUENCE OF THREE BEST-SELLERS

As with the systems perspective, the vocabulary associated with organizations as cultures first caught on in business. The term *organizational culture* may already be familiar to most students because of three books that enjoyed best-seller status during the 1980s. Let's examine each of these popular texts for their contributions.

William Ouchi's *Theory Z*

The first book to popularize the concept of organizational culture was William Ouchi's *Theory Z* (1981). As noted in Chapter 3, Douglas McGregor introduced the concepts of Theory X and Theory Y to distinguish between scientific management and human resources assumptions about individuals in organizations. Ouchi's *Theory Z* announced that the survival and prosperity of organizations depended heavily on their ability to adapt to their surrounding cultures. Ouchi's use of the term *culture* refers to national standards for organizational performance. He contrasts U.S. standards (called Type A organizations) with Japanese standards (called Type J organizations), and suggests seven major differences between them (see Table 5.5, page 133).

Ouchi proposed a Theory Z type of organization that would integrate individual achievement and advancement but would be dedicated to developing a sense of community in the workplace. A Theory Z organization would be capable of reducing the negative influences of individuals and segmented decision making by incorporating new *cultural* values into the work environment.

ETHICS BOX 5.1

ETHNOGRAPHY AS SILLY PUTTY, SURVEILLANCE, AND COLONIZATION

Although ethnography is a powerful research tool for the study of organizational cultures, it is not without its problems. As with any social science method, in the hands of a trained and competent researcher, ethnography is capable of producing useful, insightful information. However, three major objections to ethnographic methods have been shown to have serious ethical implications. They are:

1. Ethnography is like Silly Putty: Participant-observation methods are akin to Silly Putty (McPhee, 1988) in that the findings are dependent on the intelligence, sensitivities, ideology, and truthfulness of the researcher. The researcher may shape or mold the material of the study into whatever form he or she favors. The findings of an ethnographic account may say more about the qualities of the participant-observer than they do about the company being studied.

2. Ethnography encourages a kind of organizational surveillance: Most ethnographic studies of organizations are carried out by academic researchers or hired consultants. Their data collection depends on careful formal observation and interviews with employees and managers, as well as casual or informal information that comes accidentally through overhead conversations, gossip, rumors, innuendo, and so on. While both formal and informal sources of information are potentially valuable (some would say indispensable) to studies of organizational cultures, for some employees and managers this represents an unwanted intrusion into their daily work and private lives. They fear that ethnography may be little more than a clever disguise for surveillance, particularly when the results of reports are made available to the company's management.

3. Ethnography encourages colonization: A long-standing concern about the ethics of ethnography directs attention to its potential as a vehicle for colonizing the observed and recorded culture. After all, the ethnographer enters a company armed with her or his own political and social interests, theoretical and practical allegiances, and a favored perspective on organizational understanding (e.g., how things ought to be). When the report about the culture is written, the researcher/consultant prospers from it (publication credit that may lead to promotion or tenure for the academic, or a paid fee—and perhaps a training or seminar contract—for the consultant), thus encouraging an unfavorable analogy between ethnographers and colonizers.

With these objections and concerns in mind, how would you address the following issues:

1. Are ethnographers ethically obligated to explain their purposes and procedures to informants? When should they do this?

2. Are ethnographers ethically bound to omit from their written reports material drawn from privileged conversations? What if the privileged conversation contains important truths about the company that could not be revealed any other way?

3. How should an ethnographer handle the pervasive issue of self in the research report? Is it more ethical to use the third-person, omniscient voice or the first-person singular voice? Why? Does the choice of writing tactic involve ethical issues of ownership and responsibility for the report that is produced? What are they?

4. Assume you are a manager interested in hiring a consultant to do a cultural analysis of your firm. Assume the consultant requires complete access to your employees' actions,

conversations, and activities. How would you go about protecting the employees' rights of privacy while not interfering with the consultant's ability to complete the task? What issues would you want to discuss with your consultant?

Terrence Deal and Allan Kennedy's *Corporate Cultures*

The second best-seller to influence U.S. ideas about organizational cultures was Terrence Deal and Allen Kennedy's *Corporate Cultures: The Rites and Rituals of Corporate Life* (1982). Whereas Ouchi was interested in defining the values of a national culture and integrating change based on them, Deal and Kennedy were interested in defining the elements within strong cultures—individual organizations that were good places to work—and using them to help employees do their jobs a little better.

Deal and Kennedy then detailed the five elements of a strong culture:

1. *The business environment:* Deal and Kennedy call this "the single greatest influence in shaping a corporate culture." A large part of the cultural mood of any organization is determined by how well it is doing in the competitive business environment. Success will also determine how well subcultures are integrated into the company and the presence of countercultures that may serve to subvert the organization's goals.

2. *Organizational values:* A strong culture is recognized by the overall dedication to the vision for the organization and for the work that is needed to accomplish that vision. When a vision and the desire to accomplish it are present, values emerge that reinforce and direct work and personal efforts. One problem with strong values is that they tend to limit the ability of organizational members to perceive options, and therefore to limit change and discourage counterintuitive decision making.

TABLE 5.5
WILLIAM OUCHI'S COMPARISON OF JAPANESE AND U.S.
ORGANIZATIONAL CULTURES

U.S. (Type A)	Japanese (Type J)
Short-term employment	Long-term employment
Individual decision making	Consensus (group) decision making
Individual responsibility	Collective responsibility
Expectations of rapid promotion	Slow advancement
Formal organizational control	Informal peer control
Specialized career paths	Generalized career paths
Localized concerns for well-being	Holistic concerns for organization's well-being

3. *Heroes:* A hero is well known for having performed an important deed for the organization. How the hero becomes well known is through stories—sometimes myths—about the individual and the performance. These stories are told and retold throughout the organization, thus contributing to the formation of a role model for other workers.

4. *Rites and rituals:* Celebrations of individual and organizational solidarity such as management meetings and employee award gatherings are important because they serve to integrate the relationship of the individual to the organization. They define what an organization's members believe about themselves and about the organization, therefore reinforcing the core organizational values by publicly inscribing them on the individual.

5. *The cultural network:* This element includes the formal and informal channels of communication—who talks to whom about what? A lot of "about what" will reflect or reveal the culture, and the "who talks to whom" will reflect or reveal the networks within the culture.

Tom Peters and Robert Waterman's *In Search of Excellence*

The third book is Tom Peters and Robert Waterman's *In Search of Excellence* (1982). These researchers studied 62 top performing companies defined by their employees and by external analysts as excellent. Peters and Waterman found eight common themes among these organizations' cultures:

1. *A bias for action:* Top-performing companies are characterized by active decision making; they are not characterized by thinking about decisions for long periods of time or relying on a lot of information to make decisions. If a change occurs in the business environment, they act. This emphasis echoes Karl Weick's work.

2. *Close relations to the customer:* Top-performing companies never forget who makes them successful—their customers. One of the basics of excellence is to remember that service, reliability, innovation, and a constant concern for the customer are vital to any organization.

3. *Autonomy and entrepreneurship:* Top-performing companies empower their employees by encouraging risk-taking, responsibility for the decisions they make and the actions they perform, and innovation. If an organization is too tightly controlled and the worker's performance is too tightly monitored, initiative, creativity, and willingness to take responsibility all tend to decay.

4. *Productivity through people:* A quality product depends on quality workers throughout the organization. Good customer relations depend on valuing service throughout the organization. Top-performing companies recognize these factors and rally against we/them or management/labor divisions.

5. *Hands-on, value-driven:* Top-performing companies are characterized by strong core values that are widely shared among employees and by an overall vision—a management philosophy—that guides everyday practices. Achievement is dependent on performance, and performance is dependent on values.

6. *Stick to the knitting:* Top-performing companies tend to be strictly focused on their

source of product and service excellence. They tend not to diversify by going into other product or service fields. They expand their organization and profits by sticking to what they do best.

7. *Simple form, lean staff:* Top-performing companies are characterized by a lack of complicated hierarchies and divisions of labor. None of the companies surveyed maintained a typical bureaucratic form of organizing. Many of them employed fewer than 100 persons.

8. *Simultaneous loose-tight properties:* Top-performing companies are difficult to categorize. They encourage individual action and responsibility and yet retain strong core values; they encourage individual and group decision making. They are neither centralized nor decentralized in management style because they adapt to new situations with whatever is needed to get the job done.

These three books had an enormous impact on U.S. business and industry. Before their publication, business books had rarely been best-sellers; now they occupy one of the busier spots in most bookstores. Appearing during a time of serious international competition in the marketplace and threats of economic disaster at home, these books helped reorient businesses to new priorities and a new sense of values and leadership that reflect a cultural approach to organizations and communication.

Now that we have discussed the historical and cultural foundations of the cultural approach, it is time to answer the question of how one studies an organization's culture. Here are some ideas that can be pursued in any study of organizational cultures.

1. The study of organizational culture is the study of subcultures, and in some cases, countercultures. Never assume a single culture exists.

2. Organizations do not *have* cultures (or subcultures, or countercultures); they *perform* them.

3. Organizational cultures and their study change over time. Consider, for example, the ways in which Apple Computers—first started by the innovation of a single entrepreneur (Steve Jobs) and then expanded to a major multinational concern that ousted the founder—evolved and changed in the space of less than a decade.

4. The influences of the leader or founder of the organization are often powerful resources for culture. Consider here the impact of Walt Disney on his studios and theme parks, Henry Ford on Ford Motors, Lee Iacocca on Chrysler, or Thomas Watson on IBM.

5. Cultural artifacts and the physical environment (buildings, desks, pictures on the wall, certificates, diplomas, awards, etc.) provide clues to culture, subculture, and counterculture.

6. The language employees use to describe their work, and their working relationships, often contain powerful metaphors about the organization's culture.

7. Regular company gatherings—parties, holiday celebrations, formal meetings, sporting events—are convenient sites for observing the performance of culture.

8. Stories told about the organization's past—including stories that exalt or demonize individuals—are vital resources for the culture.

9. Relationships between or among employees—and especially networks of relationships—provide a human blueprint of influence in the culture.

10. External forms of communication, uses of media, corporate logos and emblems, and patterns of dealing with and defining the organization's audience provide information about the image the organization wants to embody.

THE STUDY OF CULTURES IN ORGANIZATIONS: INTERPRETING ACTIONS, PRACTICES, NARRATIVES, AND DIALOGUES

When we say a company like 3M is committed to innovation, that Northrop is a good place to work but Douglas Aircraft is a cynical place, how do we know? How do organizations develop their own unique identities?

Cultural approaches to organizations and communication seek to describe the "unique sense of place" (Louis, 1980) provided by the physical and symbolic relationships among persons, work, and things. The idea is to find in the symbols, language, rituals, ceremonies, artifacts, and human relationships the meanings that people who work in an organization have for themselves, their work, their artifacts, and each other. A cultural investigation of an organization can provide insightful feedback to organizational members about the ways those meanings are organized in the workplace, and how the organization of those meanings contributes to interpretations of everyday practices.

Stephen Barley, an organizational theorist, suggests that cultural practices show us "how members of organizations symbolically create an ordered world" (1983, p. 83). Cultural studies of organizations then reveal that companies are "speech communities sharing socially constructed systems of meaning that allow members to make sense of their immediate, and perhaps not so immediate, environments" (Barley, 1983, p. 83).

Viewed this way, cultural sense-making is reflected in what organizational members do and say. The symbolically created ordered world of an organization's culture provides members with "a repertoire or 'tool kit' of habits, skills, and styles from which people construct 'strategies for action' " (Swidler, 1986, p. 273) that help them choose what to do and say. A culture's "meaningful orders of persons and things," then, is created in actions and revealed through practices. In this section we explore those actions and practices that organizational members use to construct their symbolically ordered worlds.

Culture as Actions and Practices

It is misleading to think of a culture as something an organization "has." Only rarely, and never for very long, do organizations operate as symbolically ordered monoliths, as single shared interests and practices. In fact, the opposite is usually true: The actions and practices that organization members use to construct cultures are always diverse, and their interests, values, and meanings are seldom widely shared. In this way, it is instructive to consider culture as a collectivity of actions and practices enacted by smaller groups (Hawes, 1974), subcultures and countercultures (Martin & Siehl, 1983), or occupational communities (Van Maanen & Barley, 1984), all of whom are engaged in a constant dialogue. The tensions among these competing interests help reveal the boundaries of the groupings as well as actively construct the dialogic dynamics of the overall culture.

An action is an interpretation of a situation and it sums up the actor's understanding of the culture as well as the actor's place in it. Everything an individual does and says is an action. An action is, therefore, a strategic performance within a culture that has called for or shaped that performance in some way. It is a strategy for dealing with news of the day by using the interpretive tools the culture has provided, and it is a performance enacted within a particular situation or context that is constructed within that culture (Holt, 1989).

A *practice* is a collection of actions that is performed regularly within a culture and whose meanings are commonly shared, although differences for interpreting those meanings are also commonly encountered. Examples include *rituals* such as morning coffee breaks or company-sponsored holiday parties and *rites* such as promotion celebrations and award ceremonies or retirement dinners. Two organizational researchers, Janice Beyer and Harrison Trice (1987), provide a comprehensive list of these organizational cultural practices (see Table 5.6, page 138).

Actions and practices construct and reveal an organization's culture as well as its subcultures and countercultures. The person interested in studying cultures in organizations should view the actions and practices of these groupings as engaged in and/or conforming to ongoing struggles for a dominant construction of the organization's sense of itself. Here again we confront the profound idea of a tension between creative agency and organizational constraint as an active, everyday part of cultural dialogue in organizations.

Culture as Narrative and Dialogue

Actions and practices also serve as the symbolic resources for cultural narratives and dialogues. Stories about the meanings of organizational actions and practices are often interpreted through the telling (and retelling) of organizational narratives. That is, actions and practices—together with their interpretations, are the language of organizational dialogues. According to the anthropologist James Clifford, "a 'culture' is an open-ended, creative dialogue of subcultures, of insiders and outsiders, of diverse factions [and] a 'language' is the interplay and struggle of regional dialects, professional jargons, generic commonplaces, the speech of different age groups, individuals, and so forth" (1983, pp. 136–37).

Culture is what people make or construct when they do what they normally do. Because a culture consists of ongoing dialogues among various subcultures, what is constructed is not—as in the case of systems theory—understandable simply as the sum of its parts. Adding up what goes on inside the various departments of a corporate office does not explain the culture; what must be appreciated and understood are the ways in which individuals and groups within those departments interact with each other. Because those interactions construct alternative meanings and interpretations, they have no final sum (Bakhtin, 1986).

Cultures are composed of ongoing dialogues that are variously complicit or engaged (Conquergood, 1991). A dialogue is complicit when the individuals or groups participating in it go along with the dominant interpretation of meaning. It is engaged when the individuals or groups struggle against a dominant interpretation and try to motivate action based on an alternative explanation. In most organizations most of the time you can find both complicit and engaged resources for dialogues. For this reason, an organizational culture is necessarily a conflicted environment, a site of multiple meanings engaged in a constant struggle for interpretive control (Conquergood, 1991).

Interpretations of actions and practices within any organization's culture are diverse and perspectival (Bakhtin, 1981; Strine & Pacanowsky, 1985). They are diverse because there are always multiple interpretations available; they are perspectival because each interpretation is partial and represents particular interests. In other words, a culture is

TABLE 5.6
A TYPOLOGY OF RITES BY THEIR EVIDENT EXPRESSIVE SOCIAL CONSEQUENCES

Types of Rites	Example	Evident Expressive Consequences	Examples of Possible Hidden Expressive Consequences
Rites of passage	Induction and basic training, U.S. Army	Facilitate transition of persons into social roles and statuses that are new for them.	Minimize changes in ways people carry out social roles. Reestablish equilibrium in ongoing social relations.
Rites of degradation	Firing and replacing top executive	Dissolve social identities and their power.	Publicly acknowledge that problems exist and discuss their details. Defend group boundaries by redefining who belongs and who doesn't. Reaffirm social importance and value of role involved.
Rites of enhancement	Mary Kay cosmetics seminars	Enhance social identities and their power.	Spread good news about the organization. Provide public recognition of individuals for their accomplishments; motivate others to similar efforts. Enable organizations to take some credit for individual accomplishments. Emphasize social value of performance of social roles.
Rites of renewal	Organizational development activities	Refurbish social structures and improve their functioning.	Reassure members that something is being done about problems. Disguise nature of problems. Defer acknowledgment of problems. Focus attention toward some problems and away from others.

continues

TABLE 5.6 (*continued*)

			Legitimize and reinforce existing systems of power and authority.
Rites of conflict reduction	Collective bargaining	Reduce conflict and aggression.	Deflect attention away from solving problems. Compartmentalize conflict and its disruptive effects. Reestablish equilibrium in disturbed social relations.
Rites of integration	Office Christmas party	Encourage and revive common feelings that bind members together and commit them to a social system.	Permit venting of emotion and temporary loosening of various norms. Reassert and reaffirm, by contrast, moral rightness of usual norms.

SOURCE: From Janice M. Beyer and Harrison M. Tricre, "How an Organization's Rites Reveal Its Culture," *Organizational Dynamics*, 76 (Spring 1987), 4–25.

known and enacted through its dialogic practices and exists *in* interpretations of meanings attributed to those practices (Trujillo & Dionisopoulos, 1987).

David Boje, an organizational researcher, suggests that organizations are storytelling systems (1991). Narratives are not simply artifacts of the organization's culture; rather, they contain information about the organization's current state of affairs and serve as the major resources for everyday sense-making (Wilkins, 1984). As discussed in Chapter 4, when an organization is viewed as a system (in this case a storytelling system), the modifications made in the stories represent feedback. Paying attention to the stories that are being told—and to their modifications—is important for employees and managers alike (Mitroff & Kilmann, 1975).

Organizational stories are not just found in speeches or casual conversations but in a wide variety of places, including employee newsletters, company brochures, strategic planning statements, corporate advertisements, fund-raising campaigns, and training videos (Goodall, 1989; Pacanowsky, 1988). Each of these discourses provides opportunities for the organization to talk about itself and to display its values and aspirations. Important differences exist among the stories told about an organization depending on who is doing the telling. The corporate story or the official story produced for outside consumption may be told by advertising agencies in conjunction with high-level managers and stockholders; the inside story is told by employees throughout the organization, who, depending on their view of the ways things are and their vested interests in telling the story, may offer quite different accounts. Recently, these differences were exposed in two separate investigative accounts about the working conditions of fruit pickers and employees in manufacturing plants in the Carolinas. In both stories, the accounts given by the owners and/or managers differed greatly from the accounts of the employees. The owners and managers told the story from the perspective of the number of people they employed and the quality of the products they created at a reasonable cost to consumers. In contrast, the workers told about low wages that were sometimes paid in crack cocaine and alcohol and plants where the average safety inspection occurred once every 75 years. In both cases, federal investigations and congressional hearings resulted.

Clearly, organizational stories represent the interests and values of the tellers. In the above example, there was some coherence in each side's account, and neither side's narrative captured the whole story. There is seldom, if ever, one story (interpretation) of a company's culture; there are many stories. When the organization is viewed as a culture, these competing stories represent different voices. As such, they represent potential dialogues among individuals and groups within the organization. Therefore, it is best to conceptualize an organization's culture as a potential dialogue of subcultures, as a many-sided story.

THREE PERSPECTIVES ON ORGANIZATIONAL CULTURES

Even when a dialogic view of culture is adopted, understanding an organization depends very much on who we talk and listen to, as well as what we choose to observe. As already emphasized, a cultural dialogue consists of many stories, each told from a particular point of view. Recall from our introductory remarks in this chapter the idea that studying organizational culture is like passing light through a three-sided prism: how the prism is turned determines what colors are seen. Two theorists, Joanne Martin and Debra Meyerson (1988), explain this concept by suggesting that there are three major perspectives on organizational culture. While most studies are done using one dominant perspective, most organizations reveal all three. For a summary of these perspectives, see Table 5.7. These

TABLE 5.7
DEFINING CHARACTERISTICS OF THE THREE PERSPECTIVES
ON ORGANIZATIONAL CULTURE

Features	Perspective		
	Integration	*Differentiation*	*Fragmentation*
Orientation to consensus	Organizationwide	Subcultural consensus	Lack of consensus
Relation among manifestations	Consistency	Inconsistency	Not clearly consistent or inconsistent
Orientation to ambiguity	Exclude it	Channel it outside subcultures	Acknowledge it

three defining perspectives are integration, differentiation, and fragmentation. Each of them reveals a different orientation to three key features of cultural study— orientation to consensus, relation among manifestations, and orientation to ambiguity. Let's explore these perspectives in greater detail.

Integration Perspective

The integration perspective

> portrays culture predominantly in terms of consistency (across the various manifestations of culture), organization-wide consensus about the appropriate interpretation of those manifestations, and clarity. From an integration perspective, cultural members agree about what they are to do and why it is worthwhile to do it. In this realm of clarity, there is no room for ambiguity (Frost et al., 1991, p. 8).

From an integration perspective, an organization's culture is portrayed as a monologue, not as a dialogue (May, 1988).

This tradition in cultural studies of organizations can be seen in Peters and Waterman's (1982) descriptions of excellent companies, strong cultures that they portray as adhering to a narrow set of shared values, meanings, and interpretations. Similarly, studies on the influence of an organization's founder (Barley, 1983; Pacanowsky, 1988; Schein, 1991) tend to trace those influences through the organization, sometimes to the neglect of competing values or forces within the company (McDonald, 1988).

The integration perspective typically favors the story held by those in power over other competing stories. As follow-up studies of some of Peters and Waterman's excellent companies have demonstrated, the neglect of competing voices and marginalized groups within these companies eventually led to crises that in turn sometimes produced a reversal in their fortunes. The lesson here is that, although a study may provide useful information about the influence of a founder or a dominant set of values, portraying a culture as the site of one interpretation of meanings is inherently flawed.

Differentiation Perspective

Studies of organizational cultures performed according to the differentiation perspective

> portray cultural manifestations as predominantly inconsistent with each other (as for example when a formal policy is undermined by contradictory informal norms). According to these studies, to the extent that consensus emerges, it does so only within the boundaries of a subculture. At the organizational level of analysis, differentiated subcultures may co-exist in harmony, conflict, or indifference to each other. From a differentiation point of view, subcultures are islands of clarity; ambiguity is channeled outside their boundaries (Frost et al., 1991, p. 8).

The differentiation perspective reveals a preference for a view of organizational cultures as contested political domains—what Martin and Meyerson call a mosaic of inconsistencies (cited in Frost et al., 1991, p. 55)—in which the possibility for genuine dialogue is often seriously impaired. This is because the "islands of clarity" that are the territories of the various subcultures may seldom speak to each other. By reinforcing their own interpretive values and accounts of organizational meanings without seeking external validation or alternative wisdom, these subcultures do not actively participate in the broader interests of the organization.

The differentiation perspective has been used for studies. In the study of Disneyland described earlier, gender, class, and organizational status often conspired to pit one subculture against another (Van Maanen, 1991). In another recent study, a computer software firm created dialogue barriers for its own subcultures when it moved into a new building that physically separated work groups from each other and promoted competition for resources among them (Goodall, 1990a). In yet another study (Rosen, 1985), conflict between managers and employees over a pay freeze was masked at an annual breakfast by a group of speakers hired to create a single, shared story that clearly favored management. This ploy did not work as planned and in the end only deepened the divisions between the groups.

These studies, and many others as well, reveal the many ways in which sources of division among classes of employees often occupy the interests of these subcultures. They also show the nuanced ways in which conflict among subcultures is avoided, masked, or neglected and therefore is never directly addressed. In the absence of productive dialogue among subcultures, these divisions can quickly disable the organization.

Fragmentation Perspective

The fragmentation perspective

> views ambiguity as an inevitable and pervasive aspect of contemporary life. These studies,
> therefore, focus predominantly on the experience and expression of ambiguity within
> organizational cultures. Clear consistencies, like clear inconsistencies, are rare. According to
> this viewpoint, consensus and dissensus co-exist in a constantly fluctuating pattern influenced
> by changes, for example, in events, attention, salience, and cognitive overload. Any cultural
> manifestation can be, and is, interpreted in a myriad of ways. No clear organization-wide or
> subcultural consensus stabilizes when a culture is viewed from a fragmentation point of view
> (Frost et al., 1991, p. 8).

The fragmentation perspective is consistent with postmodern theories of organizations and society (see Chapter 6). One fundamental tenet is that ambiguity replaces certainty as a model for (mis)understanding meanings. Furthermore, ambiguity can be generated or manipulated to support the interests of management (Eisenberg, 1984), as well as to cope with those interests by otherwise disempowered employees (Meyerson, 1991). So pervasive has been the application of ambiguity to organizational communication that it has been used to explain widely divergent accounts given by eyewitnesses to an airline disaster (Weick, 1990), the writing of mostly unread and noninfluential policy statements by analysts with vested interests in writing statements that would be read and influential (Feldman, 1991), and the ways in which marginalized urban dwellers vie for and interpret the meanings of living space in cities and parks (deCerteau, 1984).

The meaning of ambiguity for our concept of organizational cultures as dialogue depends on how we understand dialogue. If dialogue is meant to generate unilateral consensus, then ambiguity makes dialogue unlikely. Conversely, if dialogue is conceptualized as embodying a respect for diversity—and perhaps a deeper form of consensus based on acknowledgment of differences—then ambiguity becomes a natural and even necessary part of how dialogue is accomplished. Furthermore, ambiguity about shared meanings or interpretations of culture is not the same thing as ambiguities about shared practices in which multiple meanings are inevitably found. Recall that an interpretive perspective values shared practices and sponsors multiple interpretations of meanings for those practices. For us, then, ambiguity is necessary to dialogue; in fact, genuine dialogue probably could not exist without ambiguity. If everything was clearly understood, what would there be to talk about?

Perspectives as Frames for Interpretations

As this discussion of perspectives points out, even researchers have reached little agreement about what constitutes an organization's culture or how it should be portrayed. Instead, each perspective offers a framework for interpretation, a way of asking and answering certain questions about an organization's culture and subcultures. No perspective claims absolute status as the one right way; no one perspective dominates the others. All are potentially valuable. Given these important differences in perspective, we can make several statements about an organization's culture. First, the primary mode of understanding a culture is through its actions and practices, as well as through the language in the narrative interpretations of those practices. Second, multiple interpretations of meanings, some more persuasive than others, are always available. To choose among competing interpretations is generally unwise; instead, these competing narratives and practices should be seen as active participants in a dialogue whose subject shifts according to the needs of the participants and whose issues are rarely resolved.

Third, a culture is full of itself. That is, its values (always competing) are performed (Trujillo, 1985) and displayed (Goodall, 1990a) *everywhere*—in symbols, language, stories, work routines, rituals, rites, advertisements, brochures, newsletters, parking lots, memos, cartoons, dress codes, office artifacts, and corporate histories. Thus, culture is not something an organization *has*; it is something an organization *is* (Pacanowsky & O'Donnell-Trujillo, 1983).

Fourth, culture is poetic (Goodall, 1991b). It is seemingly formless, and its outward everyday rhythms reveal deeper structures of knowing and doing. Apparently invisible and intangible, it works to organize what is always seen. Resplendent with ambiguities, paradoxes, and ironies, culture is open to multiple interpretations of even its most dramatic symbols and eloquent signs. Viewed as a dynamic interplay of symbols and meanings straining toward divergent but organized sources of perfection, a culture is playful. The more we try to define and categorize it, the more we realize the vanity of reifying a changing process; the more we try to name it, the infinitely more ineffable it becomes.

Goodall conducted a long-term study of a computer software company, mistakenly trying to find out what the mysterious "it" was that was the secret of this company's culture. An employee summed up the experience of his culture this way:

> *The beauty of the thing is how it changes,*
> *to accommodate new information,*
> *to become the environment,*
> *to meet the total needs of the user.*

It looks like a three-dimensional spider's web,
all of that mysterious calculus,
all of those prize soft numbers,
I don't know.
I made it,
and I don't even know all
of what it is (Goodall, 1989, p. 39).

ORGANIZATIONAL SENSE-MAKING: CREATIVITY AND CONSTRAINT IN THE DIALOGUE OF ORGANIZATIONAL CULTURES

Thus far in this chapter, we have provided an outsider's discussion of organizational cultures. We have talked about cultures, subcultures, and countercultures—and actions, practices, narratives, and dialogues—from the viewpoints of academic researchers and theorists. As a result, we have formulated a language to describe culture and a schematic for understanding how various organizational studies of culture can be interpreted and understood.

In this section, however, we want to provide more of an insider's view. Specifically, we want to explore how individuals situated within the webs of meanings they are constructing make sense of the actions, practices, narratives, and dialogues they partici-pate in. In our view, these webs of meanings are created out of nested contexts: personal experiences of work, relationships with others, groups, committees, and networks, and doing the business of work. As Barbara Czarniawska-Joerges (1988) puts it: "Actors, be they individuals or groups, live in the culture as ostensively defined. Even if they are active, their actions are restricted because they are only part of a larger pattern. . . . [I]t is the actors who in practice define—both for themselves and for others—what culture is, what it contains, what is the whole, and what are the parts" (p. 286).

Individual Sense-making: Naming and Being

Earlier in this chapter, we suggested that a culture can be known by understanding its actions, practices, narratives, and dialogues. This is only partially true, however. From an insider's perspective, it is not knowing and understanding that determine what makes sense, but naming and being. This is because the immediate act of naming or hearing a name fundamentally changes an individual's orientation or being to what has previously simply existed. As the philosopher/novelist Walker Percy states:

> Naming brings about a new orientation toward the world. Prior to naming things, the individual is an organism responding to his [sic] environment; he is never more nor less than what he [sic] is; he [sic] either flourishes or he [sic] does not flourish. . . . But as soon as an individual becomes a name-giver or a hearer of a name, he [sic] no longer coincides with what he [sic] is biologically. Henceforth, he [sic] must exist either authentically or inauthentically (1991, p. 134).

As organizational researcher Meryl Reis Louis (1980) phrases it, the experience of entering an organizational culture for the first time is one of "surprise and sense-making." As the persons and things in the culture are named, they become sensible or meaningful because the individual's orientation toward what was previously unknown has changed with the advent of naming—or the symbolic construction of this new reality.

With this act of naming and sense-making comes the second part of Walker Percy's statement: acting authentically or inauthentically. What does this mean? Consider the following example:

[*Scene: Bob is introducing a new employee—Pam—to the members of her work group. This is Pam's first exposure to this place and to these people.*]

Bob: "Over here we have Jane. We call her "Sweet Jane"—you know that old Lou Reed song? Anyway, she is pretty nice once you get to know her."

Pam [*Shyly*]: "Okay. Jane."

[*Jane stands up from her computer desk and smiles.*]

Jane: "Is Bob showing you around? Be careful, he doesn't know as much as he thinks he does."

Bob [*Laughing*]: "Oh yeah? Well, we'll see about that."

Ellen [*Joining the group*]: "And who is this?"

Bob: "This is Pam, our new writer."

Ellen: "Writer? Oh, is that what we do here?" [*She laughs.*]

Jane: "I thought we were here to dominate Bob. To make him feel inferior. But, of course, that's just because he likes it. Don't you, Bob?" [*She smiles tauntingly.*]

Bob: "Sweet Jane, as I said, is sweet only after you get to know her."

Pam [*Clearly uncomfortable*]: "So this is where we will be working?"

Ellen: "Don't mind them, Pam, they have this love/hate relationship. Just listen to what I tell you and you'll do all right."

Bob and Jane, together: "Oh right."

If you were Pam, what would you think? How would you have made sense out of these cultural clues? How would Bob's, Ellen's, and Jane's statements, laughter, inside jokes, pet names, and obvious collective understandings have made you feel? How would their acts of naming persons (e.g., "Sweet Jane"), relationships (e.g., "I thought we were here to dominate Bob"), and so forth have affected your orientation to this group? How would you have acted in response to these highly situated constructions of meanings? Most important, how would you have acted authentically?

Authentic actions are those that balance the cultural need to fit in with the self's need to act in ways consistent with its being, or who the person is or knows himself or herself to be. Inauthentic actions are those that fail to achieve that delicate balance, either because the person complies in situations he or she opposes or asserts individual agency at the expense or cultural fit. In our example, if Pam had tried too hard to fit in with these people whom she had just met (by joining in jokes and inside statements she didn't understand), she would have been acting inauthentically. By acting as she did—a bit shy, not saying much, trying to go along with their practice of kidding each other—she behaved authentically. Our guess is that this performance worked for her and for her new co-workers. Research on newcomers in organizations consistently reveals a common theme: the process of fitting in takes time. Every new employee is given a series of tryouts or performance trials, and how he or she responds to them determines important rites of passage for the individual with other individuals and with various work groups.

Acculturation describes the process through which a newcomer learns about a culture and learns how to fit into a culture (see Chapter 7). From the new individual's point of view, this process may seem painfully slow. Mistakes are commonly made with people, with the operation of machines, with parking in the employee lot, with choices of lunch companions, with manner of dress and acting in the presence of others. Cruelty may even be exhibited, as when some calculated joke is played on the newcomer and the laughter is purchased at the newcomer's expense. Every day brings surprises, and not all of them are fun.

Remaining authentic is vital! After all, the point of the trials and jokes and testing is to see whether or not a person can fit in, and that means it is important for the employees to know who they are. How they respond to these challenges to their personal identity will construct their organizational identity; they will be known by the actions they perform and the practices they engage in. Usually, when the surprises are far less frequent and the trials seem to be over, most newcomers attain full organizational member status. In some cases, a formal corporate rite of passage may commemorate the event—for example, trainees who are promoted to regular status. In many cases the event will be more subtle and personal, but the newcomer will know.

The tension between individuality and cultural fit is another way of expressing the tension between creativity and constraint. As shown in our description of the complex processes involved in moving from company newcomer to cultural rite of passage to regular employee status, the tension is always there. Too much emphasis on individuality can isolate a new employee from other members of the culture; too little individuality threatens the authenticity of the self and produces organizational groupthink (Janis, 1982).

Group Cultures

Organizational theorist Edgar Schein argues that "culture, in any of its meanings, is a property of a human group" (1991, p. 247). For Schein the formal properties that define a culture are:

1. A pattern of shared basic assumptions,
2. invented, discovered, or developed by a given group,
3. as it learns to cope with its problems of external adaptation and internal integration,
4. that has worked well enough to be considered valid, and, therefore,
5. is to be taught to new members of the group as the
6. correct way to perceive, think, and feel in relation to those problems.

Schein's list and his emphasis on the "groupness" of culture point out that groups are the fundamental analytical and symbolic unit for any organization's culture. We agree.

As we discuss in more detail in Chapter 9, groups are occupational communities. As such, groups represent a dynamic microcosm of the organization's cultural imprint as well as its primary source of creative agency. Groups construct cultures as well as subcultures and countercultures. As a source of tension between creative agency and organizational constraint, the group is alive with actions, practices, narratives, and dialogues that create and constitute a world of interpretative possibilities.

This description may suggest that a group culture is something that "is," or at least that it exists as an already accomplished set of practices and actions, narratives and dialogues that newcomers must somehow simply accept and understand. Actually, the opposite is true. Group structuration theorist Marshall Scott Poole writes:

> As the word structuration suggests, the process in which members structure groups is ongoing and continuous. It happens throughout the life of the group and is never finished. According to this theory, members are always structuring their groups. They do so with every act. . . . Even if the group looks very stable and conservative, it is because members are acting in such a way to create the same group structure over and over, creating an appearance of sameness and stability (1992, p. 148).

The theory of structuration is important to understanding cultures of organizational groups. It emphasizes "the production and reproduction of social systems through members' use of rules and resources in interaction" (Poole, 1992, p. 149). If rules are regarded as equivalent to organizational constraints and resources as equivalent to individual creative agency—and then if these rules and resources are further conceptualized as being informed and shaped by structures that go beyond the boundaries of organizational life (personal, societal, global), we can begin to understand the dynamic tensions that play into the actions and practices of groups.

Structuration affects group cultures in three ways. First, rules and resources are important centering strategies (Bastien & Hostager, 1988) for interpreting group actions, practices, narratives, and dialogues. Every act of communication in organizations takes place in nested contexts, and each of these contexts contains structures of creativity and constraint. To adequately interpret the meaning of any communication requires examining those contexts for the rules and resources structuring them. To begin interpretive activities with the tension between rules and resources that structure a group's culture is to center the interpretive strategy on those tensions.

Second, each group has its own rules and resources, but they are never enough to understand the big picture. Group cultures are structured according to the actions and practices of its members. Some groups may choose to build their culture on the politics of friendship, and others on procedures governing argumentation and debate. The group's choice is up to the group, but it will also be shaped by structures for rules and resources outside of the group culture. For this reason, interpretation of group culture should begin with the group, but it must always take into account sources of agency and constraint beyond the group.

Third, although members make choices about their cultures, they don't totally control the process of structuration. Remember, forces external to the group—such as the demands of the business community or a group member's personal needs for fulfillment and growth—derive power from other nested contexts. Viewed this way, a group's culture is never totally its own; instead, it exists as a tension among various structures.

That, finally, is the message of group cultures. Although participation in it always seems local and somewhat isolated from the broader concerns of business life, it is, in fact, never local or isolated. Everything counts!

The "Business" of Culture

Meanings are the commodities of any culture: Meanings are traded, exchanged, bargained for, shared, argued, bought into, understood, disputed, negotiated, rejected, and sold. Their currency is held in language, style, and artifacts; their power is in their ambiguity.

Fashioned as objects of corporate desire, meanings can be used to advertise, inspire, persuade, seduce, coerce, torture, or manipulate. Fashioned as subjects of business relationships, they can do the same thing.

Business cultures thrive on the continuous construction of social realities. In part, this is because business must continually create new markets for products and services. It must construct new meanings—or at least new interpretations—that can be positively associated with consuming the product or service. And in part it is because in a world context of global hypercapitalism, meanings have currency for shorter and shorter periods of time. One example of these principles can be seen in mall shopping:

> To live in retail America is to purchase more than a product; it is to identify oneself with the environment, to surround the presentation of oneself with images that speak to the worth of the effort of self-display.
>
> On one level it may be seen as a way to participate in the display, to show oneself to be the veritable image of the image itself. On another level it may be to participate in a deep-play narrative dramatization of a more perfect life for people whose lives can no longer be spent enacting the rituals and routines of the merely phenomenal. And on yet another level it may be a way to exercise a sense of self-worth by surrounding that self with symbols of material worth.
>
> Regardless of the reading given to this text, there is one unifying theme, one central statement at the core of our consumer culture. That statement speaks of the need to become one with an appeal that is more appealing, and ultimately more satisfying, than the ordinary reality of just buying a product. The mall, then, is the source of a powerful appeal to our collective middle-class imagination that not only makes possible, but actually markets, the ideal nature of narrative consumer fiction.
>
> To go shopping at the Madison Square Mall is to gain a class-conscious sense of a questing self, a self-searching, ultimately, for that one moment of true feeling that combines the experience of purchase with the ownership of a product, and the ownership of a product with an environmentally induced identity symbolic of imagined, self-actualizing selfhood (Goodall, 1989, p. 105).

The culture of business is dedicated to creating and sustaining a close symbolic relationship between what gets consumed and who a person is as a result of consuming it. This means, in part, that what gets consumed is the appeal of images and meanings that are manipulated for public consumption. The construction of symbolic realities—in advertisements, marketing displays, the image of stores selling the goods and services, the look of the salespersons, the packaging of the product or service, and so forth—is a natural and powerful part of everyday business culture. Put a little differently, business cultures thrive on the risky construction of social realities. Perhaps this is because, as business developer Michael Rosen observes, "culture is built on the edge" (1991, p. 273) of chaos. This is to say that culture represents the symbolic order we construct in an attempt to reduce the ambiguities of meanings we use to shape our lives. These symbolic orders are always, in part, illusions. They exist in symbols; symbols are commodities; commodities get bought into for awhile and then are traded in or exchanged for new products or simply forgotten. Business, as culture, is risk at the edge of chaos.

So what are the influences of a culture of risk on organizational cultures in general? As Peters and Waterman (1982) discovered, one of the influences is a bias for action. Businesses must act; to remain idle or complacent, or even to postpone decision making until more data are in, is to become noncompetitive and to risk failure. In global economic markets, the edges are always being pushed back, redefined, extended, or reframed. If we don't go for it, someone else will!

A second influence is the demand for confidence in the face of ambiguity. Not only must we act now, but we must also act with confidence, for confidence inspires where hesitation makes doubters of us all. This attitude of confidence helps us to interpret the need for corporate advertising, for example, to always accent the new and better, because success, however it is manufactured or sold, must appear to be confident. We must act confidently and appear successful even if we are on the edge of bankruptcy. This demand for confidence is a kind of trickle-down economics of symbolic constructions of reality. This means that the demand for corporate confidence in business ventures filters down from images of business success to successful images for persons employed by the business marketing its success. Businesses don't hire or promote losers, only winners. In studies of selection and appraisal interviewing (see Wilson & Goodall, 1991), the consistent news is that those persons who most closely fit the image of the organization in attitude, appearance, knowledge, and skills are those who get the jobs and the promotions.

The third influence is the blurring of personal and professional aspects of life. Business cultures expect total commitment and involvement from their employees, even if this commitment means sacrificing personal or family goals. As we have consistently pointed out in this book, many employees have responded to this increased incorporation of their private lives by seeking a greater balance between work and family commitments. But the demand is still there. Recently, a friend of ours made plans to spend a weekend with his fiancée, who worked in another state and had made special plans to fly in for the event. His manager called him in and instructed him to fly to South America on Friday night. When he objected on the grounds that he had already made plans for the weekend, he was met with a cold stare. He asked: "Doesn't my personal life mean anything to you?" His manager's answer: "No."

Finally, business cultures value those who produce results. As another friend of ours puts it: "Nobody pays off on effort." While our friend's claim is a little extreme, it nevertheless contains an important symbolic truth: employees cannot expect their company to reward or to retain them if they cannot show how they contribute to the firm's business objectives.

The culture of business is an important (some would say *the* most important) context for interpreting everyday organizational life. Its contribution to an organization's unique sense of place is both overt and subtle. The bias for action, demand for confidence, and results orientation can be easily seen in everyday office interactions. The blurring of the professional and personal aspects of life is not as easily witnessed, but it is just as pervasive. Together, these overt and subtle dimensions of business culture are evident at the surfaces (and beneath the surfaces) of everyday business actions, practices, narratives, and dialogues. Because these dimensions are commodities, they beg an interesting question: Can (or should) an organization's culture be managed?

MANAGEMENT OF AN ORGANIZATION'S CULTURE

In a practical sense, the production and management of commodities *is* the business of business. Whether the commodity is aircraft windshields, the American dollar, or multiple interpretations of organizational cultures, the first principle of business culture is that which can be produced can be sold. The second principle is that which can be sold must be managed.

Culture as Commodity

If we apply these two principles to the concept of organizational culture, we may begin to see an opportunity. During the mid-1980s, organizational culture had become such a powerful buzzword in corporate America that many entrepreneurially minded individuals established consulting practices aimed at helping companies to identify and manage their culture. If these consultants couldn't find a culture, or couldn't find a culture they could manage, they often tried inventing them through company-sponsored programs designed to bring culture into existence. One example is a financial firm in Boston that bought a culture from a vendor—complete with slogan buttons and award plaques and a new policy about casual dress at work—and then made employees comply with it. The results were dismal. Culture became something other than a commodity; it became a comedy of errors, a corporate joke. In the end it was abandoned, but not until after it had seriously damaged the organization through turnover and ill-will among employees toward the managers.

Fortunately, early and widespread failures to sell culture to business have been replaced by a genuine concern for understanding what makes a company unique. This concern is necessarily shared by management and employees, and for good reason: In order for a business to protect its niche in the market as well as its attractiveness to valued employees, it must understand the inner workings of what is already successful. Those inner workings are often approached in the name of culture.

Management's desire to deal with everyday cultural practices is somewhat ironic. What began as a rebel concept positioned as employee empowerment and everyday resistance to the domination of managerial systems thinking quickly became reframed as a management concern: how to manage this thing called culture. Two management theorists, Linda Smircich and Marta Calas (1987), suggest that this co-optation of the culture concept by managers interested in controlling it in their firms spelled the death of its utility. Like the great mystery that divides all social classes from knowledge and understanding of each other (Burke, 1950), once the mystery is gone the capacity to inspire is lost.

A Question Not of Cultural Management, But of Cultural Dialogue

The question we pose at the end of this chapter is whether an organization's culture can or should be managed. This question is intended as yet another reiteration of our central theme—the delicate balance between individual creative agency and organizational constraint. It is also an issue that is squarely at the heart of theories of organization and communication.

Our first response is that the desire to control meanings is a false, impossible organizational or managerial goal. Gareth Morgan suggests that "one of the major strengths of the culture metaphor rests in the fact that it directs attention to the symbolic or even 'magical' significance of even the most rational aspects of organizational life" (1986, p. 135). With this strength arrives an appreciation for the ambiguity inherent to symbol-using (Burke, 1950; Feldman, 1991; Meyerson, 1991), as well as the impossibility of managing meanings that are produced and consumed through ambiguous symbols (Eisenberg, 1984).

Second, organizational cultures are made out of practices. The message here is that shared practices, not shared meanings, should be the concern of managers and employees alike. To foster a business environment in which every person, regardless of status, is encouraged to construct better ways of performing on the job seems far more desirable than trying desperately and futilely to control meanings for those performances.

From an interpretive perspective, multiple meanings can always be attributed to any action, practice, narrative, or dialogue. This tension can be expressed as one that pits employees against managers in a constant struggle to control the workplace, often at the expense of the company's position in the world market. While this description probably fits a number of embattled firms, particularly those characterized by constant disputes between labor and management, our concern here is more general and problematic. From an employee perspective, any attempt to control what "I" think about—the meanings "I" attribute to practices and actions—will likely be met with complaint, if not outright rebellion. From a managerial perspective, however, unless there is some common understanding of what "we" do and who "we" are, there is no organization to manage because there is nothing to decide: I have my own meanings, you have your own meanings, and so what are we supposed to do—just be cool together while the organization falls apart?

Obviously, neither extreme argument is practical or tenable; yet in times of conflict or hardship individuals and groups often retreat to precisely these extreme positions. This is unfortunate because doing so blinds us to alternative solutions. In this case, each argument in the extreme lacks an appreciation for the need for cultural dialogue. As we have shown in this chapter, organizations enact many cultures, not just one. Each one of those cultures should be seen as a resource for an ongoing cultural dialogue about interests, values, and practices. To expect that diverse groups and even more diverse individuals will magically share common meanings is to invite failure. For this reason, the management of cultural dialogue is more practical and certainly more useful than managing an organization's culture, which is something an organization never "had" to begin with.

To manage a cultural dialogue entails equal responsibility for all job levels and functions. All parties to the dialogue need to value diversity, however it is expressed. The basic idea is that multiple meanings will always exist; managers' interests are served by trying to control the production and consumption of everything in their purview; employees will resist those aspects of control they can't agree to or live with. From this assumption emerges the value and valuing of *differences*. The manager's task is to enable employees to make decisions about their work and to provide them with the tools and resources to accomplish that work through whatever actions and practices they choose, within reason. Employees and managers will be held accountable for the results of their actions and practices.

The idea of managing (by which we mean enabling) cultural dialogue rather than the culture is one way in which organizations can promote and integrate the personal, group, organizational, and business aspects of their cultures. The activities that form this cultural practice are shared by employees and managers. The meanings they attribute to those actions and practices (as well as to the resultant narratives and overall dimensions of the dialogues) remain varied and subjective.

Limitations of the Cultural Approach

As appealing as the cultural study of organizations is, this approach has some inherent problems. First, studies of organizational cultures have been used (some would say, abused) by consultants and managers interested in "jumping on the culture bandwagon" (Smircich

& Calas, 1987). Thus, some managers feel, for whatever reason, that if their culture was not strong or if it needed to be changed, all they would need to do would be to apply research about unique and specific other cultures to their own organization. These attempts largely fail. The purpose of doing a cultural analysis of an organization is not to provide a mythical master key to turn the locks in all organizations, but to provide detailed information about an organization's unique culture. It is to study questions of what, how, and why, not how to.

Another difficulty has to do with the widespread belief that an organization's culture consists of the shared attitudes and values of its members. This statement presents two problems. First, culture entails not only attitudes and cognitions, but also activities and practices. Second, nothing about the culture metaphor requires that values be shared (Eisenberg, 1986). In fact, the idea of culture as shared meaning that underlies much of the work on strong cultures was rejected by anthropologists years ago. Instead, *practices* are primary in defining organizational culture—what people do, where they do it, whether they are rewarded or punished for doing it. Attitudes and values sometimes follow from practices, but even if they don't, most cultures show considerably more alignment in practice than they do in the attitudes, opinions, or beliefs of individual members.

The third problem with the cultural approach is that studies of organizational cultures have actually been less prevalent than theories of organizational cultures. Hence, we tend to know a great deal about the concept of cultures and concepts of cultural research, but not very much about specific cultural practices in organizations. One reason for this scarcity of knowledge is that cultural studies require long periods of time to conduct. Another reason may be that researchers feel somewhat overwhelmed by the prospect of studying a "whole" culture. In fact, few studies ever do focus on all three major aspects of organizational culture—how people think, speak, and act. A growing literature on organizational symbolism (see Turner, 1990, but spearheaded initially by Lou Pondy, Peter Frost, and Gareth Morgan) has tended to approach culture from the standpoint of language and other symbols. Others, like Trice and Beyer (1986), have focused almost exclusively on activities (rites and rituals) and generally ignore language, symbols, and their interpretations. Whatever the approach, clearly, much work remains to be done—in the field.

Fourth, the cultural approach may well contain the seeds of its own destruction. Researchers who have done longitudinal studies of organizational cultures often discover that the very complexity that attracts them tends to lead them in directions not encompassed by the culture metaphor. Perhaps other metaphors emerging from field studies capture something beyond culture (McGrath, 1989). In terms of creativity and constraint, we can see that the roots of the culture metaphor were very much in the spirit of creativity, individual self-determination, and symbolic emancipation. But over time, the cultural idea was largely co-opted by management as another method or variable for controlling workers. The balance tipped back toward institutional constraint. (Culture was a commodity; the stronger the culture, the better the commodity.) Still, the idea of culture has not been sold out, and we are witnessing a resurgence of interest by both academics and practitioners who, critical of existing practices, wish to change them. One of your authors, for example, is currently assisting an organization in implementing high-involvement, semiautonomous work teams as part of an overall cultural change. All parties are hopeful that the change will make the company more profitable and also improve the quality of work life.

SUMMARY

The study of organizational cultures developed in response to a wide variety of historical and theoretical issues. Studies of organizational cultures focus on meaningful orders of persons and things and are generally written as ethnographies. How the ethnographies are written, who writes them, what is contained in them, whether or not they are generalizable, or whether they are capable of being translated into practical managerial advisories are all hotly contested themes.

Studies of organizational cultures tend to appropriate the field study methods and vocabulary of cultural anthropologists. Terms such as rituals, rites, cultural performances, symbols, languages, values, and artifacts are used to structure the ethnographies and to construct theories about the meanings of individuals and groups. Researchers tend to portray cultures as being either integrated, differentiated, or fragmented, and they use these distinctions to discuss issues of consensus, values, and conflict. In addition, written accounts of meanings in an organizational culture reflect either an outsider's or an insider's perspective. When the two perspectives are combined, the learning process that produced an insider from a former outsider heightens the drama of presentation.

Although the cultural approach to organizations and communication yields interesting, often entertaining, and highly informative accounts of everyday life at work, it raises important questions about how much trust to place in the accounts and what a reader might profitably do with them. This is not an inherent limitation of the cultural approach; after all, systems, human relations, human resources, scientific management, critical, and postmodern approaches all share the potential for misunderstanding, misapplication, and abuse. But the cultural approach—primarily because it relies on literary narratives about personal experiences and meanings—tends to collect negative criticism from researchers, managers, and employees for whom the dominant social science theories and methods offer the traditional comforts of standardized reliability, prediction, and control.

The most difficult question to answer centers on what should be made of the cultural approach in relation to our guiding concern for achieving a balance between individual creativity and institutional constraints. Although scientific management clearly tipped the scales toward institutional constraints and human relations/human resources tipped it back toward individual creativity, the same sort of equation cannot hold for systems or cultures. Both perspectives complicate our thinking about organizational communication; similarly, they complicate the issues of creativity and constraint.

Conceptually, the systems approach made the image of balance into a kind of spinning orb that determined what was revealed. Perhaps odder still, the cultural approach redefined this spinning orb with a language of symbolic capacities that while we were mastering it posed important challenges to the authority of anyone brave enough to write about it. Certainly, our thinking has improved; it has also become conflicted. Where there was once a singular question about creativity versus constraint, there are now issues about whose creativity or constraint as well as about the ambiguities of symbols used to construct and interpret potential meanings for what constitutes creativity or constraint.

At the end of this chapter, we returned to the idea of interpreting Order as the basic quest. The cultural approach places a value on meaningful orders derived from symbolic constructions. Whether those meanings—those orders—are limited to what appears at the surfaces of culture or whether those surface meanings should be investigated for clues to deeper structures of power, status, personality, or commodities is a clear and persistent question.

It seems appropriate, then, to end this chapter with a meditation that one of us wrote about researching organizational cultures and that both of us have experienced differently.

> A culture—any culture—is like an ocean. There are many wonderful things and creatures in it that we may never understand; they change and so do we, regardless of the depth or perspective of our study. But the ocean is also made up of waves that are as regular as the cycles of the moon, and just as mysteriously musical, powerful, and enchanting. The top millimeter of the ocean is a world unto itself, and a vital one, in which the broader secrets of biological and evolutionary life itself are contained. But even their meanings must be read in a vocabulary that is separate and distant from it. So it is that within that millimeter, among those waves, we find clear and recurring themes. Like the great questions about culture that we pursue, those themes are always with us and not yet fully understood (Goodall, 1990a, p. 97).

CASE STUDY
A Problem of Balance

BACKGROUND

Saint Dollar City is a theme park founded in Death Valley in 1987 as an entertainment/ learning center dedicated to the dual influences of money and religion in U.S. cultural life. The park tries to help patrons achieve balance between monetary and spiritual goals and practices. Patrons accomplish their purpose primarily through creative investment opportunities that produce tensions between making money and planning for the long-term future.

Saint Dollar City is a monument to technical and creative ingenuity. In what was once a barren desert now flourishes a veritable mecca of capitalism and missionary zeal that covers over 40 square miles. Today, Saint Dollar City, Inc. controls enough wealth to rank as the fifth most powerful nation on the planet. Fortunately, it is not a nation, but simply an entertainment/learning center, a theme park for thrill-seeking vacationers interested in combining capitalist and spiritual experiences under one plan and in one fun-filled location.

The downtown area of Saint Dollar City is dominated by the Central Church, the Central Church's shopping mall, and the Central Bank; standing among these cultural icons is a large bronze statue of the pioneer and founder of the city, who also happened to be the founder of the Bank. His back faces the Central Church, and his outstretched hand reaches toward the Central Bank—a source of irony for those investors in Saint Dollar City who are not yet accustomed to seeing the theme of this local culture so predominantly displayed.

Saint Dollar City is divided into two sectors: Commerce Park and the Spiritual Center. The purpose of Commerce Park is "to make money while having fun spending money."

In accord with its purpose, the park is filled with delightful little shops in the central shopping mall and small, enticing investment houses promising high yields on an infinite assortment of opportunities surrounding the Central Bank. Investors (as the guests to the park are called) are encouraged to experience first hand how a business operates by starting their own shop. The admission price covers start-up fees for a small business, a guide to money and power that allows investors to make important business and religious contacts in the community, and a tax guide that essentially encourages investors to give to the Central Church all the money that they do not either deposit in the Central Bank or spend in the Central Church's Shopping Center. Vacation time at the park is spent seeing if your dream idea for making money—and having fun spending money—can come true.

The Spiritual Center is the core of Saint Dollar City, a core some investors lovingly refer to as "Rotten with Perfection." In fact, RWP is a kind of spiritual motto that competes with MMWHFSM (e.g., "making money while having fun spending money") on numbered teeshirts and baseball caps sold by street vendors. For those investors who achieve balance (the purported goal of the park), special gold-lettered AB shirts and caps are awarded.

There is a risk to investment, even in Saint Dollar City. Statistics demonstrate that most of the start-up small businesses fail, mostly because the investors are unable to gain enough money and power in the time they have in the park. Investment consultants (park guides) explain these percentages by saying the same is true nationally, but at Saint Dollar City not only are the percentages somewhat better but there is also the once-in-a-lifetime opportunity to convert your capital into Central Church credits. Thus even if your business goes belly-up, your investment credits will help millions of Saint Dollar City missionaries drum up more business and religion all around the world.

Toward this uplifting end, investors are constantly exposed to "Church Talk," a kind of religious sales pitch that promises everlasting influence instead of immediate monetary gain. Investors must choose between these goals. As their time in the park passes and the end of "making money while having fun spending money" arrives, most investors usually invest the last of their operating capital in the Central Church. Thus, they contribute to the collapse of their business but the enrichment of their influence. Influence credits can earn free trips back to Saint Dollar City or to other "heavenly" theme parks owned and operated by Saint Dollar City, Inc.

There is, of course, a downside to all this available bliss. Although the park advertises that "nobody leaves here broke or alone," some investors inevitably do. In addition, the park advertises that "making money while having fun spending money" provides "a balanced approach to vacationing for the whole family." Some investors go overboard one way or the other, thus failing to achieve balance and ending up either broke or alone. Free sanctuary for the suddenly destitute or anxiety-ridden is always provided by the Central Church, however, where free low-fat meals, bunk beds, and "balance counselors" are available 24 hours a day, 7 days a week, 365 days a year. Free bus fare to your home is also provided, should you fail to achieve balance even with counseling.

THE PROBLEM

At the Central Church there has been a recent turn of events that has the religion managers in turmoil. Some of the younger members of the church hierarchy have formed a secret society dedicated to righting some of the perceived wrongs that the theme park inadvertently promotes. These younger members—nobody knows precisely how many except the members themselves (who are sworn to secrecy)—want to return to the "good old days" when the park attracted families for "good wholesome investment, spending, and spiritual entertainment and learning."

These rebels are now openly threatening the authority of the Central Church and the Central Bank. Whereas Saint Dollar City, Inc. licenses only one brand of soft drink, these rebels now display the competing brand. Whereas Saint Dollar City expects that Sunday is reserved for Central Church services, the rebels now increasingly occupy the Central Amusement Park on Sundays, even sponsoring alternative music festivals in whose lyrics can be found the seeds of discontent and open denial of Central Church and Central Bank values. The rebel leaders, mostly women, have claimed that Saint Dollar City, Inc. discriminates against women, and have made a big deal out of the long-standing Central Church tenet against women serving as balance counselors. Finally, some of the investors in the park—when exposed to subversive rebel messages—have cut short their vacations, often joining the rebels in their public denouncements of greed at the top. And beyond Saint Dollar City, out there in the surrounding territory of Death Valley, there are now upstart rebel counseling centers for investors who have lost everything, funded solely through sympathetic donations.

A preliminary report on the "State of Rebellion" issued by the senior church and bank officials lists the major rebel complaints against the culture and cultural practices of Saint Dollar City, Inc.:

1. Investment counselors have become too greedy: Instead of opting for a 5 to 7 percent ROI in addition to the admission price and the money gained from shopping sprees, the Central Church and the Central Bank now sponsor contests among employees designed to get as much money as they possibly can from the investors. Techniques for getting more money include berating businesses that are succeeding for not contributing more to the church (and thus achieving balance); finding ways to subvert the accumulation of power by investors, thus preventing their businesses from doing well (unless the investment counselor is bought off); and publicizing false or misleading investment information through paid park pawns—persons who have become destitute and don't want to take the bus home in shame and so volunteer to spread rumors, gossip, and innuendo about investment opportunities.

2. Illegal and/or immoral investment opportunities have increased: Gambling, prostitution, and drugs have found their way into the theme park, despite the best intentions of the church and bank hierarchies. Although officials will not admit that these violations occur in Saint Dollar City, everyone knows they do.

3. Money that is invested in the church or bank is being pocketed by some senior officials under the code name "bonuses" for producing particularly high increases in Saint Dollar City, Inc. yields at the expense of many investors: For the members of this rebel band, the whole idea behind achieving balance was a kind of spiritual ideal that would make everyone a better person as a result of their learning experiences operating their own business, making decisions about investments, and so on. But for some senior officials, making money has become an end unto itself.

ASSIGNMENT

Clearly we have a cultural problem in Saint Dollar City, Inc. A subculture—perhaps a counterculture—has appeared in the organization which questions some of the wisdom of the senior officials. The influence of these rebels has already been felt, and competing theme parks are quick to generate rumors that could have a long-term impact on admissions. This is also a delicate issue because it involves deeply felt emotions by persons who are motivated as much by their beliefs as by their work.

You have been retained as a communication consultant by the senior church and bank officials. Your task is to help them understand the cultural tensions at work in their enterprise, and, if possible, to find some way to reduce the negative impact of the subculture/counterculture rebels. What would you suggest? Does the fact that you are being paid by senior church and bank officials influence your determination about what to do? Is there some way to satisfy both the rebels and the senior officials?

6

EMERGING
PERSPECTIVES
ON ORGANIZATIONAL
COMMUNICATION

"Viewing organization as a mode of domination that advances certain interests at the expense of others forces . . . us to appreciate the wisdom of Max Weber's insight that the pursuit of rationality can itself be a mode of domination; . . . we should always be asking the question '*Rational for whom?*'"

—*Gareth Morgan*, Images of Organization, pp. 315–316.

"Postmodernism: Does it exist at all and, if so, what does it mean? Is it a concept or a practice, a matter of local style or a whole new period or economic phase? What are its forms, effects, place? How are we to mark its advent? Are we truly beyond the modern, truly in (say) a postindustrial age?"

—*Hal Foster*, The Anti-Aesthetic, p. ix.

Let us take a last glance over our shoulders at the perspectives we have discussed so far—classical approaches, human relations, human resources, systems, and cultures. We have highlighted the differences among these approaches, but they also share a common characteristic. Whereas each approach offered some direction for changes in organizational theory and/or practice, each pursued these changes slowly and from inside the system. Thus, in time, we witnessed the following developments:

Despite the fact that classical theories of management were resisted on mostly ideological grounds, many of the basic classical principles (hierarchy, due process, division of labor) continued to apply in contemporary organizations. Significant limitations of the classical approach are its narrow view of communication and of the capacity of individual workers for autonomy and empowerment.

The aspect of the human relations movement emphasizing increased productivity through improved morale (e.g., leadership style research) was largely discredited as unrealistic and lacking in hard-headed business sense. The research legacy of human

158

relations, namely, work on decision making and institutional organizations, has continued to influence contemporary theory and practice.

The human resources movement was accepted in theory, with much talk about participative management, but remained a tremendous practical challenge. Personnel departments were renamed departments of Human Resources, but the humans working within them often lack credibility and a clear role in the organization.

Systems concepts became a standard part of management vocabulary, leading to the occasional improvement of workflow processes and big-picture thinking, but were sometimes also used to justify the requirements of the system over the needs of individual members.

The cultural approach delivered on the promise of the institutional school to recognize and value the differences among organizations. At the same time, however, managers and others co-opted the idea of culture as yet another means of controlling employees. Some managers sought to install "new, improved, strong cultures" in hopes of getting people to work harder.

In other words, the approaches we have described thus far posed questions and pursued issues from within the dominant frameworks of capitalism, behavioral science, and modern organizational studies, but did not challenge these dominant frameworks.

More subversive approaches do exist. In fact, each of the perspectives considered in this chapter examines and opposes the taken-for-granted assumptions of these dominant frameworks. Critical organizational theory, which we address first, reveals the often hidden and pervasive power that organizations have over individuals. Next, we examine postmodern approaches which challenge the fundamental assumptions about how we come to know organizations at all. In place of rational, cognitive approaches to studying organizations, postmodern approaches advance counter-rational, reflexive, experiential models for organizational study.

CRITICAL APPROACHES

Whenever we think of people as critical, we imagine them challenging some action or decision they consider inappropriate or unfair. This is precisely what critical approaches to organizations do: they are concerned mainly with the exercise and abuse of power. As we described in detail in Chapter 3, capitalism of the Victorian age was an ugly system: wages were low, working conditions squalid, and the business owners, the so-called captains of industry, were rich (Mead, 1991). Child labor was common, and particularism the rule; employees had no protection from the whim of their employers.

The roots of critical theory can be found in the work of Karl Marx. It is in light of the exploitive capitalism described above that Marx's work should be understood. Marx believed that the division between owners and employees which was at the core of capitalism was misguided and unfair, and that eventually it would lead to the violent overthrow of owners. The world has witnessed many practical and theoretical adaptations of Marx's ideas (the former Soviet Union, for one), too many to consider here. But one particular adaptation merits special attention. A group of professors from the University of Frankfurt, often known as the Frankfurt school, used some of Marx's ideas to develop what is now widely known as critical theory. Critical theory is well known in Europe and gained considerable popularity in the United States during the 1980s (Strine, 1991).

The Rise of Critical Theory in the United States

Practical as well as intellectual reasons account for the current interest in critical theory in the United States. At the turn of the twentieth century, U.S. industrialists broke from traditional capitalism to go in a new direction. For the first time, a clear connection was made between the wages paid to employees and their ability to be active consumers on the other. For example, at the Ford Motor Company, workers were paid the then unbelievably high wage of $5.00 a day. If his workers couldn't buy cars, Ford reasoned, he wouldn't be able to sell them to the masses. This strategy, known as progressive capitalism, dominated U.S. industry from the early days of the Industrial Revolution until approximately 1972, when the average, inflation-corrected weekly wage of Americans reached its peak. Throughout this period of growth, both individuals and corporations experienced enormous increases in economic well-being (Mead, 1991).

And then the bottom fell out. First, as we discussed in Chapter 1, globalization gave U.S. employers the option of paying employees overseas much lower wages to do the same work. In essence, this was a return to the bad old days of early capitalism, but the abuses were far enough away from home to be mostly ignored. Second, as noted earlier, the slack went out of business; worldwide, a movement began to depict the planet itself as a limited resource. Third, the elected leaders of both the United States and England adopted an economic philosophy in opposition to decades of progressive capitalism. In this new approach, more resources were given to big business (e.g., tax exemptions or reduced regulatory fines and controls) in the hope that increased profits would trickle down to the average individual. This sharing of wealth did not occur, however, and the typical employee's wages, benefits, and standard of living declined. Fourth, and finally, U.S. scholarship became more international, and as a result critical studies were discovered in Europe. This new discovery accorded perfectly with the economic climate at the time, thereby creating an interest in critical theory in the United States.

The Centrality of Power in Critical Theory

According to Dwight Conquergood: "Critical theory is not a unitary concept. It resembles a loose coalition of interests more than a unified front. But whatever it is not, one thing seems clear: Critical theory is committed to unveiling the political stakes that anchor cultural practices" (1991, p. 179). Critical theory focuses on the power and control that employers have over employees (Clegg, 1989). Early attempts to define power were based on the assumption that power was something a person or group *had,* and through their actions, power was exercised. French and Raven's (1968) now classic paper offered five bases of social power and followed the assumption that Person A had power over Person B when A had control over some outcome B wanted.

Reward power. A has reward power over B if A can give some formal or informal reward in exchange for B's compliance, such as a bonus or award.

Coercive power. A has coercive power over B if B perceives that certain behaviors on his part will lead to punishments from A, such as poor work assignments, relocation, or demotion.

Referent power. A has referent power over B if B is willing to do what A says because she wants to be like A. Mentors and charismatic leaders often have referent power.

Expert power. A has expert power over B if B is willing to do what A says because he thinks A knows the right thing to do in this situation, that is, has some special technical knowledge.

Legitimate power. A has legitimate power over B if B complies with A's wishes because A has a certain formal position, like division head in the hierarchy.

French and Raven's approach is reflected in much of the research on compliance gaining in business (Kipnis, Schmidt, & Wilkinson, 1980) and in work on behavioral alteration techniques (Richmond, et al., 1984). Examples include how supervisors get subordinates to do undesirable tasks; how employees get bosses and co-workers to give them desired resources; and even how teachers get students to do their homework assignments.

Limits to the Overt Study of Power

This approach to understanding power, however, is seriously incomplete. By focusing solely on the overt or surface exercise of power by individuals, little is revealed about the more covert, deeper structures of power (Conrad, 1983). Although overt power is easy to spot and can in principle be resisted (often at great costs but resisted nonetheless), covert, hidden power is more insidious because it is invisible.

The focus continues to rest on overt power partly because it fits well with traditional, causal models for understanding human behavior. Lukes (1974) and Bacharach and Baratz (1962) were among the first to break from this one-way causal thinking in which power is something one person does to another. In doing so they considered deeper, more hidden types of power. Bacharach and Baratz were concerned not simply with the concrete actions and decisions associated with power, but also with the nondecisions, the things that didn't get done, as instances of power. The idea of defining as power those things that were outside of the usual domain of empirical observation was seen both as a reconceptualization of the power concept and as a further attack on one-way causal thinking in social research (Clegg, 1989).

Power and Ideology

Power is not confined to government or politics, nor is it always overt and easy to spot. According to Michel Foucault (1979), power is a pervasive, intangible network of forces which weaves itself into our slightest gestures and most intimate utterances. Power does not reside in things but "in a network of relationships which are systematically connected" (Burrell, 1988, p. 227). Power exists in the microphysics of daily life. "Since all of us belong to organizations and all organizations are alike and take the prison as their model, we are all imprisoned within a field of bio-power (power over our bodies), even as we sit alone" (Burrell, 1988, p. 228). This power, of course, is never neutral. It is associated with the interests of dominant individuals and groups, and it is often exercised unconsciously. The pervasive powers of a group, at least from the perspective of people outside of the group, are called its ideology.

Apparently, ideology, like an accent, is always something the other person has. According to Jurgen Habermas (1972), most people display the following way of thinking: "I view things as they really are, you squint at them through a tunnel vision imposed by some extraneous system of doctrine." This imposing doctrine is ideology. Terry Eagleton offers further definition of the concept of ideology. Specifically:

1. Ideology refers to the whole complex of signifying practices and symbolic processes in a particular society.
2. Ideology refers to ideas and beliefs (whether true or false) which symbolize the condition and life experiences of a specific, socially significant group or class. It is a kind of collective self-expression.
3. Ideology is about the promotion and legitimation of the interests of such social groups in the face of opposing interests.
4. Ideology confines the promotion and legitimation of the interests to those activities of a dominant social power.
5. Ideology is deceptive because it arises not necessarily from the interests of the dominant group, but from the material structure of society (Eagleton, 1991).

His key point is that ideology is so pervasive as to be hidden and deceptive; power exists in the taken-for-granted social structure of an organization or society.

When Power Is Hidden

In recent decades, this "hidden power" of organizational systems and structures has been the central focus of critical theory. Jurgen Habermas, a major proponent of modern critical theory, did not share Marx's conviction that workers would rise up and revolt against owners for economic reasons. Instead Habermas saw social legitimation as the chief factor holding modern organizations together. To Habermas, capitalist societies are characterized by the *manufacture of consent* in which employees at all levels willingly adopt and enforce the legitimate power of the organization. Only when this legitimate power is challenged might capitalism truly face crisis.

This manufactured consent manifests itself when someone says, "I'm just doing my job" or "It's just business" as a justification for their actions. "Domination involves getting people to organize their behavior around a particular rule system" (Mumby, 1987, p. 115). Any problem or difficulty can then be pinned on the system, but the system is not held accountable for actions taken in its name. There is, of course, some evidence that this situation is changing. A recent law makes the senior management of large corporations personally responsible for criminal actions taken on behalf of the company. Similarly, both Exxon and Union Carbide were held somewhat financially accountable—though some would say not nearly enough—for the environmental disasters, respectively, in Alaska and in Bhopal, India.

The Hidden Power of Communication

The main puzzle to be solved by critical theory lies in the fact that organizational practices that maintain strong controls over employees are "legitimate" and hence not resisted (McPhee, 1985). Conrad has argued persuasively that this kind of legitimation is maintained through symbolic forms, specifically metaphors, myths, and stories. For example, at Ben and Jerry's Ice Cream, the theme of "social consciousness" is used to justify numerous managerial decisions regarding hiring, firing, promotions, and raises. Employees do not as a rule resist these controls because they buy into the overall "story" that distinguishes the organization and its culture. Over time, themes, metaphors, and stories can become shorthand definitions for appropriate behavior that suspend critical thinking on the part of some employees. Ethics Box 6.1 explores this idea.

ETHICS BOX 6.1

METAPHORS CAN SUSPEND CRITICAL THINKING

"Family" is one of the most frequently used metaphors promoted by companies in the United States. For some companies, such as Disney, the metaphor has been very useful. After all, the ideal of a family includes a warm, wholesome, caring, mutually supportive set of interdependent relationships characterized by open and honest communication. Viewed this way, the family is a very positive metaphorical association for any firm.

But are all families like this? Do they conform to the "warm, wholesome, caring, mutually supportive . . . etc." descriptors used above? Or do these terms for describing family ideals sometimes obscure dysfunctional power relationships between parents and children, among siblings, and with relatives? Furthermore, are—or should—our ideal metaphors for successful families be exactly alike? Are all successful businesses exactly alike?

Consider these issues in your response to the following situations:

1. Assume you are an employee in a company where the manager consistently uses the family metaphor to explain behavior (e.g., "Yes, I yelled at you about that report, but you know, even in the best families that sometimes happens"; or "We're all family here. If you've got personal problems, tell me about them just like I was your kind uncle or aunt"). This use of the family metaphor bothers you because you believe your manager uses it to cover irrational behavior as well as to gain unwarranted access to employees' private lives. What should you do?

2. Your company has just announced that during its annual holiday party skits will be performed by individual work teams. Your team has been assigned to write, produce, and perform a skit about how much like a family this company is. You see this as an opportunity to reveal both the positive and negative aspects of the organization's use of power and informal relationships. Two members of your team argue against your proposal, saying that, even though they agree with your ideas, it's best just to portray the positive aspects of this family. They fear that if they "tell it too much like it really is" there may be a high price to pay later. You see their objections as more evidence that a problem exists, and feel that this skit may provide a good opportunity to address it in a fairly nonthreatening manner. How would you argue your case with your team during the next planning meeting?

3. Think about other metaphors used to describe and to organize work relationships you've experienced or heard about. Describe the ethical dimensions of these metaphors.

A story that circulates at a large consulting firm in New York tells of a senior consultant rushing madly to get to a client, ignoring all traffic laws, driving through fences, onto the sidewalk, the wrong way down one-way streets, while all the while a new, junior consultant sits white-knuckled in the passenger seat. They make it to the meeting on time. Afterward, the junior consultant, obviously upset, confronts her boss: "Why did you have to drive like a crazy person! We could have been a few minutes late, and they would have understood!" Later that day, the junior consultant is told to clean out her desk.

The moral of the story is twofold: First, do whatever you have to, even if it means breaking the law, to accommodate a client. Second, don't challenge the judgment of your superiors (or you will be fired). The story reinforces existing power relations in the consulting firm whether it is true or not. The fact that people tell and believe the story to be true is all that is needed to keep people in line.

Hegemony and Communication

Antonio Gramsci (1971) used the word "hegemony" to talk about the all-encompassing power that is hidden and consequently taken for granted by those who are most controlled by it. It is the power of rules, standard operating procedures, and normal routine. When we go swimming, for example, most likely, rules will be posted such as "No running in the pool area." Says who? There is no way of knowing, although if we think about it, the concerned individual is probably whoever holds the insurance policy for the pool. Critical linguists like Robert Fowler call this "agency deletion"—the person exerting the control is deleted and thus made invisible.

This form of power extends beyond the local swim club. Management of organizations works hard to achieve routine. Once employees feel that their behavior is controlled not by other people but by the rules of the game, the game is won. A subtle transformation takes place from "this is how we decided to do things around here" to "this is the way things are done." It is indeed a rare group in which the "way things are done" remains negotiable, and where various members have a significant voice in changing the definition of the situation.

Hegemony is something like the power parents have over young children. Until they reach a certain age, all they know is what the parent says is real, and choices and assumptions are understood only as reality. When a parent gives a young child a choice, the parent has already chosen the options—for example, "You can share your toys or go to your room now." When this kind of strategy works, the child is convinced that these are really her only two choices, and that she is indeed free to choose.

A more familiar example can be drawn from the typical college student's taste in music. Most people would like to believe that everyone has free choice in the matter of music. But we can wonder how free this choice really is. Political processes determine the kinds of people who take up music as a career and who can navigate the politics of the recording industry. The choices we make in enacting our taste in music are already narrowed by larger, sociopolitical forces, such as one's ethnic background, social class, and even gender, all of which affect the sorts of music we hear and will most likely appreciate (Fenster, 1991). And yet, we believe that our taste is freely determined, much as many people believe that the person they choose to marry is "the one right person in the world for me," ignoring the fact that they happen to share the same race, religion, socioeconomic status, college, and hometown.

In his critique of the hegemony concept, Stuart Clegg (1989) specifically implicates communication as the critical factor in maintaining power relationships. Instead of viewing hegemony as a state of mind, Clegg thinks it is better seen as "a set of practices, primarily of a discursive provenance which seeks to foreclose the indefinite possibilities of signifying elements and their relations, in determinate ways" (p. 16). Thus, hegemony resides not so much in what people think, but rather in what they say or do (or don't say, or fail to do) that causes one set of interests to temporarily prevail over another. With the next utterance (or nonutterance!), the power relationship can shift again. The possibilities are infinite, although we may try to "fix" (or stabilize) them through communication.

Example: Feminist Organizational Theory

As we noted earlier, critical theory comes in many shapes and sizes, all concerned with uncovering the uses and abuses of power. Feminist organizational theory focuses on the oppression and exploitation of women in the workplace, and on the ways in which women can gain more power and acquire a voice in organizational dialogue. The progression of research on women in organizations has followed closely the deepening view of power described thus far in this chapter. Early research on women in the workplace centered on the overt strategies and behaviors women needed to engage in if they were to succeed at work. Representative books included *Games Your Mother Never Taught You: Corporate Gamesmanship for Women* (Harrigan, 1977) and *The New Executive Woman: A Guide to Business Success* (Williams, 1977). But these texts failed to challenge the basic status quo of organizations. Instead, they adopted a *deficiency* model of women, claiming in essence that if women would only learn how to behave appropriately, they could make it in organizations. This approach corresponds to the examination of overt power strategies more generally.

Rosabeth Moss Kanter's book *Men and Women of the Corporation* (1977) was a turning point in the history of thinking about women in organizations. In her discussion of tokenism—the promotion of a few women into highly visible positions—Kanter uncovers the double-edged sword of increased publicity and attention. Greater visibility, she finds, increased both pressure to perform and likelihood of failure. Her work shows how the responsibility for change cannot reside simply with the individual, but also with the system; individual-level change without more fundamental organizational change is likely to fail.

More radical feminists have gone further in their critique of the taken-for-granted definition of organization. Focusing on the underlying assumptions and ideology of patriarchy (male-dominated society), they have identified hidden aspects of male-dominated organizations that lead to pervasive discrimination against women and specifically devalue women's voice (e.g., Calvert & Ramsey, 1992; Ferguson, 1984).

Implicit in the feminist approach is the assumption that women have a *distinct way of seeing the world*. Consequently, organizational dialogues would have the potential to be transformed if they were more open to women's voices. Most corporations, according to the feminist critique, are still structured as though there was a full-time wife at home (Freeman, 1990). Even commuter systems—mass transit and ride pools, for example—are designed by men and fail to take into account the realities of women's work lives, especially day care and household errands. Perhaps the most significant difference between women's world-view and male-dominated organizations has to do with hierarchy. While contemporary organizations are almost always hierarchical, women tend to think of organization in terms of a network or web of relationships, with leadership at the center of the web, not on top of a pyramid (Helgeson, 1990). We have more to say about alternatives to hierarchy in our discussion of eco-feminism in Chapter 11.

In contrast to traditional models, women tend to value

1. Fluid boundaries between personal life and work life
2. Relational aspects of work
3. A balanced lifestyle
4. A nurturant approach to co-workers
5. A network of relationships outside the organization
6. Leadership as a web, not a hierarchy
7. A service orientation to clients
8. Work as a means of developing personal identity (Grossman & Chester, 1990; Helgeson, 1990; Lunneborg, 1990).

Valuing women's voice in organizations means opening the dialogue to a different set of assumptions:

> What if we defined competition as "doing excellently" instead of "excelling over" (Calas & Smircich, 1990; Lugones & Spelman, 1987)? What if we defined power as a way to enhance, rather than diminish, the power of everyone (Miller, 1982)? What if we valued and even sought diversity in organizations? What if we saw organizations as having responsibility for social change (Marshall, 1984)? What if hierarchies were abandoned or revisioned as networks (Ferguson, 1984)? (Calvert & Ramsey, 1992, p. 83).

Although admittedly sketchy, our brief description of feminist critical organizational theory illustrates the ways in which disenfranchised, exploited groups can attack the hegemony of the dominant ideology and propose a different set of assumptions and definition of the situation. African-Americans, for example, have always had to deal with both overt and more subtle forms of prejudice in organizations (Jones, 1973). It is hard to overestimate the practical difficulties associated with challenging existing ideology. Until a sufficient level of resistance is reached, the dominant group can simply dismiss such challenges as "crazy" and "unrealistic," stating that they don't make sense within the currently prevailing construction of reality.

Pro-People or Pro-Profit?

The critical approach to understanding organizational communication favors the individual (it is pro-people), and it is often faulted for not taking into account realistic organizational constraints. ("Whose reality?" is an appropriate question.) But if Stan Deetz is right, we have reason to throw our energies behind the defense of individual freedom from corporate domination. In his recent book (1991), Deetz argues that corporate domination in U.S. society runs deeper than most of us recognize, that, in fact, corporations have replaced governments as the controlling force in our lives.

Once again, the key to this control is the fact that it is hidden and that people believe they have freedom of choice when in actuality their options are carefully (and unobtrusively) controlled. According to Deetz, Americans believe that society is democratic because we vote to elect our officials, but there is nothing democratic or participative about most of the daily decisions that most profoundly affect our lives, such as the technologies and products available to us and the working relationships among people (p. 3). These decisions are almost solely under corporate control. Deetz calls this situation the "corporate colonization of the life world."

The most frightening aspect of Deetz's comments is his belief that this corporate domination is leading to the breakdown of other institutions in society, such as families and schools. Former domains of family expertise, such as childbirth, fashion; education, even morality, have been removed from the family and turned into externally purchased goods and services (Lukes, 1989). Where people live, their choices to relocate, and the timing of and decision to have children are all driven by career concerns. This leads to an alienation and loss of identity, which was previously fostered by enduring institutions such as the family or community. Modern education is increasingly concerned with training students for occupations, and the only thing considered to be practical or real is the workplace (Deetz, 1991). In summary:

> With such institutional domination in place, every other institution subsidizes or pays its dues for the integration given by the corporate structure, and by so doing reduces its own institutional role. The state developed for *public good* interprets that as the need for order and economic growth. The family that provided *values and identity* transforms that to emotional support and standard of living. The educational institution fostering *autonomy and critical thought* trains for occupational success (Deetz, 1991, p. 17, emphasis in original).

Critical Theory and Organizational Communication Research

Research from a critical perspective is very similar to the cultural approach outlined in the previous chapter. In order to unearth the deep structures of power the investigator must discover details not only about what happens in the organization, but also why it happens. From a critical theory perspective, the cultural approach moves in the right direction in its focus on meaning and sense-making, but stops short of asking in whose interest certain meanings and interpretations lie. A critical theorist, then, gathers interpretive cultural data about language, motives, and actions, and makes judgments about the power relationships that exist in the organization. It is a very subjective enterprise, with more than a few hazards. Not only can a critical theorist be guilty of all the same things a cultural researcher can (e.g., narrowness of sample, bias in selecting participants and events) but he or she can also be called an elitist.

Critical theorists may be classified elitist since, in practice, the theorist must be willing to argue that certain people or groups are oppressed but don't know it. Imagine a critical theorist visiting a traditional Italian family in South Philadelphia and trying to convince the matriarch of the family that she is oppressed by the male-dominated society. As he was being shown the door, the critical theorist might hear the inevitable question: "Who the hell are you to tell me that I am oppressed? I'm just fine." This is the most serious problem with the concept of hegemony, and the reason why the concept has begun to fall out of favor. In a marked departure from the cultural approach, critical theorists have often maintained that people do not know their own minds (Clegg, 1989).

Let us offer one final example of the personal and professional risks of exposing sources of domination. One of our graduate students was conducting a dissertation study at a nationally known hotel. She had videotaped a general meeting of hotel employees and was showing it back to them, asking them at various points in the tape what was going on and what they were thinking and feeling at that time. In her view, the meeting was insulting and patronizing, but none of the employees saw it that way—they all described it as fun.

Finally, the student lost her patience. After a portion of the tape was shown, she asked an employee (a housekeeper), "What if I were to say that this really isn't so much fun, but just a way to keep you happy so you won't ask for more money? What if I were to say that all the fun and games were created by management to distract you from your real concerns about important pay and working conditions?"

The next day, her dissertation project was terminated. The housekeeper reported our student to the director of Personnel, accusing "that lady from the university" of "trying to put ideas into our heads."

Creativity and Constraint in Critical Approaches

As mentioned earlier, critical theory clearly comes down on the side of the individual, exposing both obvious and subtle constraints on behavior. As should be clear from our discussion of corporate colonization, such an exposé is especially necessary today, when corporations unobtrusively control so much of our lives. Similarly, our discussion of feminism and hegemony reveals the tremendous difficulties associated with opening up the organizational dialogue to diverse voices, as well as the potential gains in new organizing methods that might come from such an inclusive dialogue.

Critical theory is less successful in advancing alternative organizational arrangements that would both liberate employees from domination and allow organizations to survive in our current economic system. While critiques of capitalism have value, critical theory and research often contain no middle ground that would allow people currently living and working in organizations to incrementally improve their lives. Focused on macroeconomic issues, much of this work lacks an appreciation for the contours of organizational life. In this sense, most critical theories of organization lack critical realism.

Despite this limitation, critical theory plays an important role in the overall picture of organizational communication studies in that it reminds us that meaning is always inherently political. The sense that is made of things and the current definition of reality always benefit one individual or group over another. There is no neutral interpretation. Given Deetz's bleak vision of the current situation, we might well be interested in alternative models that promote the participation of diverse voices in a more open dialogue.

WHAT IS POSTMODERN?

The term *postmodern* is the subject of a hotly contested definitional debate. In disciplines ranging from aesthetics and architecture to history, philosophy, and literature, from social theories to film, from theories of organization and communication to politics, marketing, economics, and education, postmodern refers to different historical beginnings, material themes, and theoretical issues (Best & Kellner, 1991; Connor, 1989). Partly because each discipline's interests in the term are articulated differently, and partly because the term itself expresses different perspectives on knowledge and meaning in society, it may best—and ironically—be defined as "a sign that resists a common signifier." Whatever the postmodern is, it has a lot to do with what this debate is all about.

This section explores concepts of the postmodern as they relate to organizational communication. First, we distinguish between postmodernity and postmodernism as the two sources of critique that sum up the postmodern. Second, we discuss three historical narratives on the postmodern, with an emphasis on how these narratives speak to the interests of organizations and communication. Third, we use Stuart Clegg's ideas on Asian ways of organizing work as the embodiment of postmodern theories of organizational communication. Fourth, we ask what postmodern approaches suggest about our central concept of achieving balance between creativity and constraint.

DISTINGUISHING POSTMODERNITY FROM POSTMODERNISM

Stephen Best and Douglas Kellner (1991) provide a conceptual distinction between postmodernity and postmodernism that provides a useful starting point. They write: "the term "postmodernity" [is used] to describe the supposed epoch that follows modernity, and [the term] "postmodernism" [is used] to describe movements and artifacts in the cultural field that can be distinguished from modernist movements, texts, and practices" (1991, p. 5). Three important issues arise from this definition: (1) the idea of a historical break that brought with it (2) important political and aesthetic movements that produced (3) new cultural understandings and practices. Let's examine each of these issues in greater detail.

Historical Break

First, the term *postmodernity* refers to the period in history that follows modernity (Habermas, 1981; Harvey, 1990). When that period in history occurred is much debated. For example, the historians D. C. Somervell and Arnold Toynbee (1947) used the term *post-Modern age* to describe a fourth era in Western civilization: (1) Dark Ages (675–1075), (2) Middle Ages (1075–1475), (3) Modern Age (1475–1875), and (4) post-Modern Age (1875–present). In architecture, Charles Jencks's *The Language of Post-Modern Architecture* (1977) described the demise of an urban housing project in St. Louis in 1972 as the beginning of the postmodern age. In Western literature, postmodern fiction appeared eclectically in the work of a variety of 1960s avant-garde writers (Hassan, 1971, 1987) and reached a pinnacle in practice with the publication of Thomas Pynchon's *Gravity's Rainbow* (1973). And in business, the term *post-modern* was first used by economist and management theorist Peter Drucker in *The Landmarks of Tomorrow* (1957).

What these historical periods delineated, however, was similar from discipline to discipline, and it is summed up in the social, political, and aesthetic movements that are captured by the term *postmodernism*. From historians such as Somervell and Toynbee we gained an appreciation for postmodernism as representing the dramatic break from "the previous modern period as a middle-class bourgeois era marked by social stability, rational-ism, and progress . . . to a 'Time of Troubles' marked by the collapse of rationalism and the ethos of the Enlightenment" (Best & Kellner, 1991, p. 6). These historians claimed that wars, revolutions, economic and social crises, and new ambiguities in cultural values led to a new era of Western civilization.

New Political and Aesthetic Movements

What would that era contain? This is where postmodernity becomes infused with postmod-ernism. Postmodernism refers to social movements characterized by political and aesthetic themes that claim major historical changes have occurred since the advent of postmoder-nity (Foster, 1983). Cultural historian Bernard Rosenberg describes it this way:

> As Toynbee's Great West Wind blows all over the world, which quickly gets urbanized and industrialized, as the birth rate declines and the population soars, a certain sameness develops everywhere. Clement Greenberg can meaningfully speak of a universal mass culture . . . which unites a resident of Johannesburg with his neighbors in San Juan, Hong Kong, Moscow, Paris, Bogota, Sydney and New York. African aborigines, such as those recently described by Richard Wright, leap out of their primitive past—straight into the movie house where, it is feared, they may be mesmerized like the rest of us. First besieged with commodities, postmodern man [sic] himself becomes an interchangeable part in the whole cultural process. When he is momentarily freed from his own kitsch, the Soviet citizen seems to be as titillated as his American counterpart by Tin Pan Alley's products. In our time, the basis for an international solidarity of man at his lowest level, as some would say, appears to have been formed (Rosenberg & White, 1957, p. 4).

In short, "the ambiguity of the new postmodern world, its promising and threatening features . . . offers [us] everything and nothing" (Best & Kellner, 1991, p. 7). One outcome of this mass cultural process of high-speed change and shifting sameness is a view "that reality is unordered and ultimately unknowable" (Best & Kellner, 1991, p. 9). This theme is underscored by the theme in all postmodern movements that social, cultural, and professional life is marked by relativism, populism, and the presence of multiple meanings and images, all vying for vivid but rapidly vanishing attention. Artist Andy Warhol said it best in his famous comment: "In the future everyone will be famous for fifteen minutes." Images—the "nonreflexive" surfaces of persons and things—became the new currency of commodity capitalism; screen replaced scene and networks replaced mirrors as "the smooth operational surface of communication" (Baudrillard, 1983).

Not all visions of postmodern society were as negative or nihilistic. For example, Peter Drucker foresaw "pattern, purpose, and process" as the major themes of postindustrial society (1957). His vision included new technologies that would redefine human power over nature, bringing with it new responsibilities and potential hazards; the increased distribution of education and knowledge that could spell the end of ignorance and poverty; and "the decline of the nation state, the end of ideology, and worldwide process of modernization (Best & Kellner, 1991, p. 8). Similarly, Huston Smith (1982) suggested that the transformation of society from rational modernism to skeptical postmodern-ism "is only a transition to yet another intellectual perspective, one that hopefully will be characterized by a more holistic and spiritual outlook" (cited in Best & Kellner, 1991, p. 9).

Regardless of whether or not the vision of a postmodern society was potentially positive or largely negative, postmodernism movements continue to be characterized by what we will call a political aesthetic. By political we mean that challenges to authority of all kinds—governmental, artistic, scientific, institutional—were associated with attacks on the interests of Enlightenment and Industrial Revolution standards for domination through applications of Western rationality (Featherstone, 1988). The aesthetics of these rebellions were found in various discourses—graffiti, television, street theater, rock and roll (and rap) music, avant-garde novels, new journalism, everyday conversations—that emphasized *pleasure* over rationality, *novelty* over reason (and often just for its own sake), *difference* over consensus, and *speed* (velocity produces change) over static, middle-class sameness. It is, therefore, not at all surprising that the localized site of postmodernism would be located in various cultural understandings and practices. Table 6.1 provides a synopsis.

New Cultural Understandings and Practices

When we combine discourses about postmodernity (as a place in time) with discourses about postmodernism (as movements located within those places), we describe the *cultural territories* claimed by the term *postmodern*. The political aesthetics of these postmodern territories are found in the complex and often contradictory lived experience of everyday life (Jackson, 1989).

TABLE 6.1
SUMMARY OF POSTMODERN THEMES

Postmodernity Theme: *Historical break*	Postmodernism Theme: *Political aesthetics*	Postmodern Theme: *Cultural understandings and practices*
1875–1945	Revolutions, world wars, social and political crises.	Nihilism, class conflicts, loss of history, focus on the present, alienation from—but dependence on—social and political institutions.
1945–1965	Internationalism, new technologies enable increasingly global community, social and political instabilities, end of colonialism and empire.	Skepticism about power and control, questioning of authority and hierarchy, mass culture.
1965–present	Popular culture, expansion of information technologies, global economy and politics, new social instabilities; gender differences; spread of commodity capitalism into all forms of social and political life.	Ambiguity, multiple meanings, trust/distrust of surfaces—images, bodies, messages; velocity, pleasure, novelty, difference; lack of separation between home and work life; greater fragmentation and loss of stable identities.

One of the major sites of that lived experience is represented in popular culture, a place for new poets, novelists, and artists to mediate the modernist distinction between high and low culture through strategic appropriations of materials from both worlds (Lipsitz, 1989). One result of these artistic appropriations is to challenge the authority of all forms of categorical, hierarchical arrangements. Another is to introduce popular audiences to transnational themes, values, and perspectives. As a result, the understandings and practices of lived experience daily confront challenges to authority and hierarchy as well as the news from various international scenes.

A second site of postmodern rebellion in cultural understandings and practices is found in everyday life in organizations (Browning & Hawes, 1991; Goodall, 1989, 1991). This is to be expected because employees who daily confront the challenges of postmodernity and postmodernism in society do not suddenly enter the world of work and see those themes disappear. Instead, as some theorists point out, they see those themes *multiplied*. As we pointed out in Chapter 1, for example, business in the 1990s is characterized by global economic and cultural competition. Increasingly, to remain competitive requires a general flattening of traditional hierarchies associated with bureaucratic forms of organizing as well as the use of new technologies and employee empowerment to distribute information (and, therefore, decision making power) more widely. Furthermore, it is increasingly difficult to find employees at any level who are hired to do one job; instead, they are required to perform flexible roles and carry out multiple responsibilities. Cross-functional training enables employees to define (and protect) themselves as a multiple-use site of organizational information.

In summary, then, the advent of the postmodern era in society brings with it new challenges to the situated individual in organizations, as well as to organizations trying to remain competitive in a global economy. The postmodern also poses intriguing, perplexing challenges to many taken-for-granted ideals of effective communication, and the relationship of communication to organizational survival. Table 6.2 summarizes these concerns. These new challenges can be better understood through an appreciation of three narratives about the postmodern, each of which contributes a major new theme to our understanding of organizations and communication.

THREE NARRATIVES ABOUT THE POSTMODERN

In this section we provide a historical account of three major narratives that construct the central tenets of the postmodern period. Although this choice of narratives leaves out other alternatives (see Best & Kellner, 1991; Harvey, 1990; or Connor, 1989), they provide an organizing focus for applying the postmodern to organizational communication.

Lyotard's Postmodern Condition

First, let us examine the argument provided by the French philosopher Jean-François Lyotard. He begins with the idea that the story a culture tells about itself legitimizes both the storyteller and the right of the storyteller to tell the story (Lyotard, 1984). The product (story) is a "grand narrative" or "metanarrative" that "defines what has the right

TABLE 6.2
SUMMARY OF POSTMODERN CHALLENGES TO TAKEN-FOR-GRANTED ASSUMPTIONS ABOUT ORGANIZATIONS AND COMMUNICATION

Authority and Power	Purposes and Meanings	Effectiveness
Modernist assumption: Divisions of labor and hierarchy lead to increased efficiency.	*Modernist assumption:* Communication should be viewed instrumentally as the means of accomplishing specific tasks and objectives. Meanings should be shared consensually among employees.	*Modernist assumption:* Individual achievement leads to individual rewards; effectiveness is finite and measurable; it is important to separate work and home concerns.
Postmodern challenge: Increased cross-functional training and flattening of hierarchies contribute to greater flexibility and efficiency.	*Postmodern challenge:* Communication is both instrumental and expressive; meanings are situated in contexts of interpretation and are seldom (if ever) fully shared.	*Postmodern challenge:* Group achievement leads to group rewards; effectiveness is determined locally and is only partially measurable; it is impossible to separate work and home concerns.
Application to Communication	**Application to Communication**	**Application to Communication**
Modernist assumption: Speaker and message-centered; passive audience.	*Modernist assumption:* Meanings are in people and can be induced/elicited by choices among symbols.	*Modernist assumption:* Language is symbolic; rhetorical effectiveness is determined by reception of the speaker's meaning by the audience. Power is determined by the ability to shape perceptions of reality through strategic monologue.
Postmodern challenge: Speakers and audiences are problematic categories that reify dynamic processes. Better to think of signifiers who use (and are used by) signs that point to or represent fields of interpretive possibilities. Authority exists through signs of authority; power exists through discourses and practices.	*Postmodern challenge:* Meanings are fluid and changing, locally determined sites of interpretation; they include nested contexts and are generally conflicted or contested. Ambiguity is pervasive, and choice-making is mythic. (E.g., we do not make decisions; we discover them as already existing within our cultures.)	*Postmodern challenge:* Language is poetic and open to multiple interpretations; dialogue is the measure of communication effectiveness; power lies in maintaining a balance between creativity and constraint in the dialogue and in recognizing and responding to the value of difference.

to be said and done in the culture" (p. 23) and results in a dominating language game created by and for those who join in the telling of the story.

In Western cultures, the dominant narrative is derived from two ideas about politics and philosophy that emerged during the Enlightenment. The primary idea is *democratic* politics derived from the American and French revolutions, which has as its goal the liberation of humanity from slavery and class oppression. With a politics of democracy emerges the second idea: *liberal philosophy.* The idea of liberal philosophy derives from the German philosopher Friedrich Hegel's goal of attaining pure self-conscious spirit through the accumulation of knowledge.

For Lyotard, science is the ultimate rational articulation of these two Enlightenment ideas. Science provides a set of procedures (scientific method) that legitimate knowledge. The result is a grand narrative of culture produced and sanctioned by science that subordinates, marginalizes, or represses all other claims of knowledge, all other accounts of culture, history, literature, or philosophy. Hence, the big question which scientific knowledge encourages us to ask about everyday life is: "Can you prove it?" When this question is raised, the appropriate answer is found in scientific principles and findings. The resulting story—the account given about knowledge claims and how they were achieved through science—is "an exact fantasy" (Adorno, 1989).

Examples of Lyotard's claims are easily found in the widespread applications of scientific principles to organizations. From Frederick Taylor's scientism of the workplace through modern uses of computers and robots to speed the performance of work, business consistently invests in scientific rationality. Furthermore, the close relationships between science and business (and government) provide a strong collaboration for the scientism narrative that reduces the ability of alternative forms of explanation to gain a hearing. For example, academic and private-industry research that does not rely on a scientific rationale has far fewer opportunities for tax-supported funding. Furthermore, in many schools of business the operant logic has long been: "If you can't measure it, it doesn't exist." Cultural and critical approaches to organizations suffer.

For Lyotard, then, the modern (read: Enlightenment) project failed when the Grand Narrative legitimated by science moved from its primary cultural role in the service of political and philosophical liberation to a dominating form of narrative authority that sought to marginalize or repress other cultures' explanations and stories. With the end of the colonial period and the extensive media coverage of problems in the Third World, the complicity of science and business in the service of governments became firmly established. Regardless of one's political views, science no longer seemed neutral or particularly liberating. A desire to hear the other side of the story from cultures that had been colonized—Africans, Asians, Indians, Native Americans, Palestinians, women, slaves, punks, street people, the homeless, the nationless—emerged. This request for new stories spread from the most marginalized regions of the earth through the most marginalized regions of academic and professional disciplines. The postmodern was born.

To sum up, for Lyotard postmodern is an idea that "encompasses a multitude of different, incompatible language games, each with its own untransferable principles of self-legitimation. . . . No more Grand Narratives, only splintered micronarratives" (p. 52). The exclusive dominance of modern, Western, scientific narratives is therefore challenged by alternative cultural narratives that neither value science nor share its goals. Ours is a world in which many stories vie for legitimacy and power, each one with its own resources for rationality and its own standards for evaluation. There is no longer "one true story"—one Grand Narrative—to guide our judgments and actions. For Lyotard, the postmodern condition is one in which we inherit a highly ordered, rational, mass-mediated, bureaucratized, and technologized planet on which sense-making is confounded by the omnipresence of alternative constructions of reality and interests. All these interests demand information, speed, flexibility, precision, and performative accomplishment from the individual. The individual's ability to organize and act on interpretations—to make sensible the various bombardments of messages and critiques—is the core of both the postmodern challenge and the postmodern dilemma.

Jameson's "Pastiche" Economics

The second narrative on the postmodern emerges from Fredric Jameson's "pastiche" economics of culture. Here the term *pastiche* is intended in the sense of collage, suggesting what happens when dominant modern narratives collapse as major resources for analytical critique and are replaced by multiple narratives, each one containing its own demands for legitimation and power. The result is that surfaces—represented as styles in fashion and music, as attitude in politics and psychology, and as images on television or computer screens—rule. From this perspective, the postmodern aesthetic is a multiplication of already available styles, attitudes, and images that are often ironically or nostalgically positioned in opposition to one another. This suggests three powerful ideas:

1. Lack of a unified self: Modernist behavioral and cognitive psychology posited the view of self as a unified whole—something inside of us that could be developed, shaped, nurtured. In fully realized (read: rationalized, bureaucratized) form, this self would show outwardly in our taste for conservative clothing, suburban living, and following the socially sanctioned rules for discourse and deportment. The mature self was the whole self, and the whole self was easily recognizable.

   In contrast, the postmodern self exists not as something inside of us to be developed but outside of the body on the surfaces of clothing, makeup, discourse, deportment, the cars we drive, the houses we live in, the furniture we buy, all of which exist primarily as expressions of our desire to be desirable. Jacques Lacan, a postmodern psychoanalyst, furthers this logic by suggesting that language is a replacement for self, not a tool for its development. So, in postmodern society, you are known by your outward appearances rather than by modernist inward tendencies. You are what you wear; you are what you say you are. Life is lived at the surfaces.

2. Individualized linguistic islands: Jameson argues that under conditions of postmodern pastiche, linguistic norms—norms for conversation and writing that served in modernist times as an index for (and the cement of) the rules for society—become fragmented: "each group coming to speak a curious private code or dialect, and finally each individual coming to be a kind of linguistic island, separated from everybody else" (cited in Connor, p. 114). We live our daily lives in a kind of perpetual present in which history, the story a culture tells about itself, fades in relevance and explanatory power.

   The importance of his fragmentation of language codes used to formulate, analyze, and share information cannot be overestimated. One result is that as our economies become more globalized, our communities actually become more localized. Who "we" are is less a nation with its history, or a state with its beliefs, or even a city with its heritage, and more a collectivity of social and professional groups who agree to share a common language and common interests—a discourse community. The second result of language fragmentation is, obviously, a loss of consensus. Under modernist imperatives, every citizen had an equal say and an equal vote (probably more mythic than real) and society was held together by consensus rules—what the majority votes for wins. Under conditions of postmodernity, collectivities do not share the language resources to reach consensus, even if such an idea was important to them, which, given recent low voter turnout records, it is not.

3. Surface signs as commodities: Perhaps the most compelling aspect of Jameson's critique of postmodernism concerns his reformulation of Marxist economic and class struggle values into multinational commodity values. Cultural forms for the economic and social expression of commodity values (such as advertising, marketing, public relations)—once understood by Marxists as the veil that prevented social classes from seeing the true economic face of capitalism—are transformed (principally by mass media) into the principal expressions of global economic activities. Representations of commodities—not the commodities themselves—become primary products. The purpose of the representation is not to induce the buying of products but to serve as a product itself—something capable of creating an audience for its image, for its style of representation.

What we buy when we buy into advertising, marketing, or public relations is far more than a representation of a commodity. We are buying into a cultural function for the sign as a playful, somewhat rebellious, cultural fragment that challenges the modernist scientific ideal of "the proper words for things," or that everything has an appropriate form of expression.

In economic terms, we are buying into an expansion of capitalism's power from chiefly commodity values to values of representation. This move legitimizes what Jameson calls the random play of signifiers in which signs can be made to represent anything and nothing. Equally important, production values are less concerned with making new objects than with reformulating old products. Consider, for example, the nostalgia for 1950s and 1960s fashions. The detachment of signs from their modernist signifiers ceaselessly reshuffles the fragments of preexistent texts, the building blocks of older cultural and social production, in some new and heightened bricolage: metabooks which cannibalize other books, metatexts which collate bits of other texts (Jameson, 1984, p. 92).

One outcome of this new economics of cultural production is that all the resources for identities (signs of meaning for a culture that buys into surface identity) seem to have been used up. Instead of sponsoring innovation through new forms, we reshuffle and reproduce old forms endlessly, like a cultural hall of mirrors. For example, the best new song on the radio is often a remake of a classic; the best new advertisement for clothing, cars, or investment advice is often one that captures some representative nostalgia from the past; the best new look in fashion is often one that combines influences from historical eras. As a female character in a postmodern novel—appropriately titled *Life After Death* (Compo, 1990)—who strives to look and act and live exactly like Marilyn Monroe puts it: "It is as if all the good identities have already been used up."

The postmodern, then, is a kind of free-floating signifier without a centered substance that borrows or derives its meanings from previous associations. Every culture is inscribed as a market in which commodity values replace personal and communal senses of meaning. For example, Figure 6.1, "The Postmodern Turn," captures two competing commodity values vying for space on the same sign.

Baudrillard's Simulacrum

The third leading figure in our postmodern evolution is the French cultural critic Jean Baudrillard, who builds his argument in a similar post-Marxist stance as Jameson and Lyotard. Baudrillard's major contribution is the idea of the *simulacrum* (1983). The simulacrum is simultaneously the conversion of empirical and symbolic reality into empty signs vying for representation in commodity space (endless images and surfaces that bear no resemblance to reality), as well as the replacement of real forms of life by reproductions and mass-manufactured experiences and objects—the hyper-real. In this context, theme parks such as Disneyland or Epcot Center can be viewed as representations of reality, as places where the image of having fun is consumed through a commodity purchase.

FIGURE 6.1
The Postmodern Turn
SOURCE: Courtesy of Lindsley Armstrong.

For Baudrillard the dissociation of signs from their modernist, rational, scientific signifiers also affects our understanding of power and social life. When so many signs are vying for space, when so many competing narratives are competing for our attention, power becomes diffused across narratives, therefore effectively *dis*empowering all of us (Baudrillard, 1988, 1990). All of us are constantly at sea in an ocean of mostly tempting but unsatisfying surface possibilities. The problem here, for Baudrillard, is that we always seem to desire that which we have lost. (Or perhaps that is just a sign of nostalgia for something we can no longer remember.) Hence, we live for the spike in the everyday—danger, crisis, passion, panic—despite the fact that how we deal with these situations is increasingly determined by our association with images of control. How did John Wayne deal with danger? How did Marilyn Monroe deal with passion? Baudrillard puts it this way: "[It is always a question] of proving the real by the imaginary, proving truth by scandal, proving the law by transgression, proving work by strike, proving system by crisis and capital by revolution" (1988).

Social life is similarly targeted. For Baudrillard, social life cannot be said to truly exist anymore because the collectivities that we rely on to prove the social life only serve as images of it. "Are we having fun yet?" How would we know except by recourse to simulacrum? Perhaps if we had a photograph of us smiling, or a home video of our pleasure weekend at the beach, then we would know for sure. Trust the seductive allure of surfaces, the images, the appearances of persons and things (1990). Furthermore, social groups no longer function as textbooks say they should: we resist the logic of society by representing only images of it. This idea is one that is probably enacted on a regular basis. Does one know how to act like a good student in class? Is the student projecting an image of the good student for consumption by professors and peers? Whatever one's look, one has learned to read—and to represent—the surfaces of appeals. Hence, what truths may lie underneath (if anything) dress, discourse, and deportment renders ironic what is represented to be real. Table 6.3 summarizes the major tenets of the postmodern as presented by Lyotard, Jameson, and Baudrillard.

FROM POSTMODERN NARRATIVES TO POSTMODERN ORGANIZATIONS

Thus far in our story about the rise of critical theory and the postmodern we have emphasized how society has changed. In this section we explore the influences of critical theory and the postmodern on organizations and communication. First, we examine two major objections to postmodernism in organizational theories and practices; second, we develop an example of how postmodern principles have been successfully applied to one organization.

Objections to the Idea of the Postmodern in Organizations

Two major objections have been lodged against applying postmodern ideas to organizations and communication: (1) to embrace the postmodern is to give up rationality, and (2) to adopt postmodern ideas requires replacing capitalism with Marxism. Let us examine these criticisms.

TABLE 6.3

SUMMARY OF THREE MAJOR NARRATIVES THAT DEFINE THE POSTMODERN

Jean-François Lyotard	Fredric Jameson	Jean Baudrillard
Basis of critique: Science as Grand Narrative	*Basis of critique:* Pastiche economics	*Basis of critique:* The Simulacrum
Postmodern condition: Knowledge is splintered into many micronarratives, each vying for legitimacy, each with its own standards for evaluation.	*Postmodern condition:* Surface signs (styles and attitudes) act as commodities: (1) Lack of unified self—who we are is at the surfaces of what we wear, drive, live, or enact as the basic attitude in our lifestyle. (2) Individual linguistic islands—our talk is fragmented by a lack of a shared code to interpret meanings. (3) Representation of commodities is the principal expression of economic activity.	*Postmodern condition:* Conversion of the real and symbolic into representational signs and reproductions of mass-manufactured experiences.

One common criticism leveled at the postmodern concerns its basic directive to question the authority of Western rationality (Habermas, 1981). How can business be accomplished without the usual equipment of hierarchy, division of labor, highly specialized tasks, quantitative assessments of performance, and centralized authority? If the idea of the postmodern embraces a counter-rationality—a different way of thinking about organizations and communication—then isn't the postmodern also counterbusiness? The second objection derives from the radical (or far leftist) political aesthetics that characterize the various movements within postmodernism. Because these ideas are historically derived from Marxism and because Marxism offers a strong critique of commodity capitalism, we might ask whether there is a fundamental problem in applying the critical practices of a competing ideology to contemporary, capitalistic businesses.

Our answer to both questions is no. To embrace the postmodern in society it is not necessary to embrace an antibusiness stance, nor is it to give up rationality. In fact, it may even suggest precisely the opposite: the postmodern can provide new energy for business practices by using organizational cultures to provide fluid contexts for deconstructing—and acting on—the strategic ambiguities of signs, thereby redistributing information control and redefining power relations among employees. Let's examine why this is true.

The principal method of postmodernism is deconstruction (Derrida, 1976). *Deconstruction* refers to the critical practice of literally taking apart the meanings that have been socially constructed. It is to ask social, professional, and political questions about what is taken for granted and how things got this way. And as we have seen through the lens of critical theory, it is to expose the interests represented (and marginalized) by the vision and tenets of that construction. In the following section, we examine how deconstruction can be used to take apart an organizational document.

An Example of Postmodern Deconstruction: The Nordstrom Employee Handbook

Figure 6.2, the Nordstrom Employee Handbook, may be considered as an example of a postmodern document, and our discussion of it illustrates how we can deconstruct its meanings and interests.

Let's compare the Handbook with our definition of the new energy in postmodern business practices. First, notice that unlike most employee handbooks, this one is very brief. This is because most employee handbooks are divided into sections that vest

NORDSTROM

EMPLOYEE

HANDBOOK

WELCOME TO
NORDSTROM

We're glad to have you with
our Company.

Our number one goal is to provide
outstanding customer service.

Set both your personal and
professional goals high.
We have great confidence in your
ability to achieve them.

Nordstrom Rules:

Rule #1: **Use your good
judgment in all situations.**

There will be no additional rules.

Please feel free to ask
your department manager,
store manager or division general
manager any question
at any time.

nordstrom

FIGURE 6.2
Nordstrom Employee Handbook
SOURCE: Courtesy of Nordstrom.

authority in the specific, often very precise, language of hierarchy and formal channels of organizational control. By contrast, the Nordstrom document uses strategically ambiguous language to empower the employees at all levels within the organization. Exactly what does "outstanding customer service" mean? Similarly, what does "high" mean in the sentence that reads: "Set both your personal and professional goals high"? For that matter, what is a "goal"? (Notice that the terms *personal* and *professional* are linked with the connective "and" rather than "or," thus emphasizing the interdependence of the two in the total commodity value of the employee.)

In what is the penultimate postmodern move, examine Rule 1: "Use your good judgment in all situations." Then notice: "There will be no additional rules." Rules are part of the unnecessary baggage of a modernist, hierarchical division of labor mentality. Once created, rules tend to act as constraints on individual creativity. In addition, to have rules is also to disempower employees from the responsibility to learn on their own the best ways to accomplish tasks within the immediate contexts in which they occur. By having only one rule—and one rule that empowers one to make decisions within the bounds of what is considered to be responsible and right—the counterbureaucratic logic of the organization is both ambiguously expressed and yet very clear.

Finally, the handbook seems to suggest that should an employee have any questions, he or she should seek assistance. This statement embodies, of course, precisely what anyone using good judgment would do to manifest their personal and professional goals with the Nordstrom culture. It also emphasizes the necessity of interdependence of employees to ensure the overall well-being of the organization. The postmodern logic seems to be: We are all in this business together, and we are all responsible to each other for making sure the business prospers and we all do well. To be a Nordstrom's person means to accept the individual's responsibility for all actions and decisions, and to fit into a postmodern culture that values individual creative effort and initiative. It also means that fitting into this culture requires a willingness to accept ambiguity as a natural condition of work.

This example testifies to the presence of the postmodern condition as an organizing force in what is a highly successful business operation. Rather than acting as a nihilistic, antirational influence, the postmodern seeks to empower employees to accept responsibility and make decisions, engage contexts creatively, and recognize, as well as respond to, the interdependent, fluid, ambiguous nature of a dynamic, commodity-valuing, business culture.

Our deconstruction of the document also reveals the interests represented in its uses of language. For example, the commodity that is most highly valued is not simply the products Nordstrom sells (which are designed to enhance the looks of the purchaser), but the customer service it provides. Customer service is the embodiment of an attitude in what employees say and do, and it is reflected in the styles chosen for the saying and doing. Thus, postmodern business cultures value organizational communication as a commodity whose image is part of what customers consume.

Organizational communication is no longer something extra that functions mainly to give orders down the ranks of the hierarchy. Nor is it, from a human relations/human resources perspective, the feel-good glue that bonds managers and employees. Nor is it, from a systems perspective, the manifestation of information, feedback, or noise. Nor is it, from a cultural perspective, the deep structures of meanings that constitute everyday life through routines, rituals, rites, and communities. From a postmodern vantage, organizational communication is dedicated to sharing power, accepting responsibility, recognizing interdependence, and embodying the unique sense of place as a consumable commodity within fluid contexts of everyday business life.

Postmodern organizational logic offers some intriguing questions to our ongoing historical narrative. These questions direct our deconstructive abilities to issues of power, ambiguity, creativity, and commodity values within (hyper)capitalist frameworks. Postmodernism provides a logic, but it is not a panacea. After all, trusting surfaces and seeing ourselves as consumable commodities can produce a superficial account of what it means to be a human being at work. It can also induce a kind of materialistic high-speed nightmare in which we are required to accept more and more responsibility and power, whether we want it or not.

Pushed a little further, a global postmodern perspective encourages businesses to empower themselves by relying more heavily on part-time or temporary labor in order to reduce costs. With part-time help businesses can forego health insurance, retirement, and corporate benefits packages. Still more intrusions into private life are afforded by providing employees with a flexible work schedule, company-sponsored daycare, and a home computer. These otherwise innocent moves to free up employee time and give choices as to how to accomplish tasks can demonstrate, rather persuasively, how the postmodern blurs traditional distinctions between work and home. It also blurs our understanding of work and leisure (see Carlsson and Lagar, 1990; May, 1988). Whatever its potential for abuse, postmodern logic encourages us to appreciate some fundamental differences in organizations and communication at the end of the twentieth century. In the following section we examine some of the more positive aspects of those differences.

CHARACTERISTICS OF THE POSTMODERN IN ORGANIZATIONS AND COMMUNICATION

Stuart Clegg (1990) argues that postmodern business practices can be found throughout the world but that the deepest imprints are located in Asian organizations. Chinese business organizations (founded on historical relationships between and among families), South Korean business organizations (founded on strong ties to nationalism), and Japanese business organizations (founded on a combination of nationalism and family relationships) all provide excellent examples of how the postmodern emerged and prospers as a major global economic and political force through applications of alternative logics to guide organizations and communication.

Seven Characteristic Distinctions between Modern and Postmodern Organizations

To examine how the postmodern functions in organizations requires delineating seven distinctions between Asian and Western ways of understanding and organizing everyday business practices. Table 6.4 provides a detailed summary of these distinctions. The table positions postmodern organizations as a practical and highly effective response to traditional bureaucratic structures for organizing work. If we begin with the assumption

TABLE 6.4
STUART CLEGG'S DISTINCTIONS BETWEEN MODERN
AND POSTMODERN ORGANIZATIONS

1. Goals, Strategies, and Main Functions

Modern Organizations	Postmodern Organizations
Specialization of tasks	Diffusion of tasks
Rigid structures	Flexible structures
Mass consumption of goods and services (bigger is better)	Market niches (find what you do best and do only that; smaller is wiser)
Technological determinism (use the new machine until it is outdated, then replace with a new machine requiring new skills)	Technological choice (use the same machine and deepen its abilities; develop its applications locally and continuously re-skill)
Highly differentiated jobs (learn one job and one set of skills; employee is a replaceable part in an efficient machine)	Highly integrated jobs (learn all aspects of the enterprise, use multiple skills; employee is a lifetime investment and capable of learning new skills)
Employee relations based on size of the firm; control (own, if possible) all aspects of inventory and supplies	Employment is based on complex and fragmentary sources of interdependence; networks and limited inventory

2. Functional Alignments

Bureaucracy (Top-down information flows and controlled by decision-making input)	Democracy (All employees are valued as information sources and have input on decisions)
Hierarchy determines structure	Market determines structure
Heterogeneous organizational cultures	Homogeneous organizational culture
Employees identify with their occupations and derive status from the image of the company	Employees identify closely with companies that employ them rather than their occupations
Techniques are commodities to be purchased, used, and discarded	Techniques are integrated into cultural contexts of their uses and continuously improved
Individual jobs, limited or no retraining	Overlapping teams and constant retraining
Short-term employment (people change companies and jobs frequently) or employment determined by market conditions	Long-term employment (employees hired for duration of their work life); niche markets limit competition
Autonomous industries with no coordination (collusion is against the law); large inventories insure supplies to market	"Just-in-Time" inventories thorough industry coordination of products and support services
Top-down management	Self-managing teams
Quality assurance programs (judge product quality when it is completed)	Quality circles (product continuously assessed throughout design and production cycle)

3. Coordination and Control

Disempowerment	Empowerment
Manager specialization	Management generalist
Permanent management	Management rotation
Laissez-faire adaptation to business environment	Industrial policies govern adaptation

continues

■■■■■■■■

TABLE 6.4 (*continued*)

Modern Organizations	Postmodern Organizations

4. Accountability and Role Relationships

| Extra-organizational | Intra-organizational |
| Inflexible skill formation | Flexible skill formation and development |

5. Planning and Communication

| Short-term techniques to maximize individual achievement (American managers are "Viking raiders"—they don't plant or harvest—Lester Thurow) | Long-term techniques (Asian managers "plant and harvest"—they see an idea from beginning to ending; they develop and nurture the processes) |

6. Relation of Performance to Reward

| Mistrust of managers by employees, and (often) of employees of each other | Collectivized (whole group is rewarded for performance—no individuals singled out) |
| Power determines ability to make and implement decisions | |

7. Leadership

| Mistrust of managers by employees, and (often) of employees of each other | Trust among managers and employees and between employees |
| Power determines ability to make and implement decisions | Broad-based support before decisions are made or implemented |

that one function of government is to promote the general welfare (see the Constitution of the United States), then one way to accomplish that end is by regulating industrial policies, thereby, limiting unnecessary competition within a given industry. Another interpretation of that assumption, of course, is that free enterprise means totally free—anyone who wants to engage in market competition is licensed to do so. This fundamental difference of interpretation entails two separate, distinctive logics of organizing: a modern and a postmodern. From a modern conception of organizations, characterized by bureaucratic management, scientific rationality, and individualism, tasks should be highly specialized. These tasks are accomplished by increasingly de-skilled workers. (The more limited the job, the more easily it is accomplished and the easier it is to replace the person doing it.) Employees and managers are hired because they can do a particular job or be quickly trained to do it. They are rewarded only insofar as the individual task is accomplished. If they do not like the way they are rewarded, or the people they must work with, they are encouraged to seek employment elsewhere.

The archetypal modern organization is summed up in the term *Fordism* (Clegg, 1990). This term is used to represent the assembly-line production and scientific management philosophy of Henry Ford, although it could just as easily be used to represent any number of successful modern organizations. By contrast, the postmodern conception of organizations encourages a more democratic, diversified, and team-oriented approach to work design, decision making, and work life. Under conditions of postmodernity, an employee is valued as a commodity that can learn, as a voice within a family of interdependent relationships that link everyone from inventory supplier to assembly-line worker to computer network information source. To be hired is to learn to fit in and to acculturate to one's chosen industry, organization and work team. Rewards are based on group performance and productivity, thus reinforcing the idea that "we are all in this together." Furthermore, to not like a co-worker and to think that an individual performance deserves individual reward, signifies personal failure and communal disgrace. They are only rarely used as reasons to seek employment elsewhere, which itself carries a negative social and professional stigma.

An American Example: W. L. Gore and Associates as a Postmodern Organization

One good example of a U.S. firm that began and continues to operate on postmodern organizing principles is W. L. Gore and Associates (see Pacanowsky, 1988, for an extended discussion). Known principally for its development of the fabric "Gore-Tex," the firm was originally started to investigate the uses of Teflon as an insulator of electric wire and, later, electronic devices (such as computer chips) and vascular grafts (used in medicine). From its inception, the company's founder, William Gore, refused to accept bureaucracy and hierarchy as fundamental organizing principles. Instead, people are hired at Gore as associates, and the only other title available is that of sponsor. Any associate can become a sponsor simply by gaining the support of a group of associates, as well as Gore-family financing and approval, for a project that will allow the company to simultaneously "make money and have fun" (Pancanowsky, 1988). Central to Gore-Tex operations is the idea of a lattice organization. The following descriptive passage shows how it works:

> The "lattice organization" is a graphic descriptor much in use at Gore that permits and invites frequent contrasts to the traditional "pyramidal" organization. Where traditional organizations are organized pyramidally, with discrete lines of communication and authority moving upward and downward through a system broad at the base and narrow at the top, the lattice organization looks like a lattice, a regular cross-hatching of lines, representing an unrestricted flow of communication with no lines of authority. As Bill Gore defines it, a lattice organization means "one-on-one communication" with whomever you need to talk to in order to get a job done, no fixed or assigned authority but leadership that evolves over time and that fluctuates with the specific problems at hand that need the most attention, and tasks and functions that are organized through personally-made commitments—not through job descriptions and organization charts (Pacanowsky, 1988, pp. 3–4).

Against this lattice organization backdrop, W. L. Gore and Associates adheres to "The Four Principles":

1. Fairness: Each of us will try to be fair in all our dealings.
2. Freedom: Each of us will allow, help, and encourage (other) Associates to grow in knowledge, skill, the scope of responsibility, and the range of activities.
3. Commitment: Each of us will make (our) own commitments—and keep them.

4. Waterline: Each of us will consult with appropriate Associates who will share the responsibility (for) taking any action that has the potential of serious harm to the reputation, success, or survival of the Enterprise. The analogy is that our Enterprise is like a ship that we are all in together. Boring holes above the waterline is not serious, but below the waterline, holes could sink us (from Pacanowsky, 1988).

Clearly, these directives are characterized by empowerment and ambiguity. But the key question is how successful this method of organizing and empowering employees is. W. L. Gore and Associates is listed in *The 100 Best Companies to Work for in America* (Levering, Moskowitz, & Katz, 1985) but more impressively, it is featured in John Naisbett's *Reinventing the Corporation* (Naisbett & Auberdene, 1985) as "the American corporation that has already gone the farthest to 'reinvent' what organizational life can be" (Pacanowsky, 1988, p. 3). As of this writing, it continues to be highly successful.

Five Principles of Postmodern Organizations

As many observers have pointed out, Asian and Western conceptions of work are closely tied to conceptions of society and the role of the individual in them. But Western organizations cannot simply transfer Asian models of doing business to U.S. locations. Nonetheless, as Clegg's chart demonstrates, certain important principles are inherent to postmodern organizations. These principles can be learned in the West; in fact, many of them are currently in use.

The first principle is that postmodern organizations are characterized by a profound *decentralization of power*. Programs to enhance employee empowerment, decision making, information flows, computer networks, and multicultural language skills in a variety of Western organizations are examples.

Second, postmodern society is characterized by constant, rapid, often contradictory *changes in markets and commodity values*. This, in turn, suggests the wisdom of treating employees at all levels of responsibility as renewable resources capable of learning new skills, rather than as rigid performers of limited skills in tightly monitored occupational or professional categories. Cross-functional training programs, in-house training seminars, and opportunities for employees to go back to school under company-sponsored tuition plans are all good examples of putting into practice some tenets of postmodern theory.

Third, because power is diffused across work groups (a move greatly enhanced by computer technologies) and because employees are becoming increasingly multiskilled and cross-trained, postmodern organizations are characterized by a *flattening of hierarchies*. When viewed as a constraint caused by the sheer velocity of postmodern work and changes in markets, it becomes clear that messages do not have enough time to travel up and down rigid hierarchies. Viewed another way—from the pragmatic insights of systems theory—the more often a message needs to be repeated, the more likely important information will be lost.

With the flattening of hierarchies comes the fourth postmodern innovation: Less hierarchy inspires *a need for cultures of trust built on respect for differences* and mutual cooperation based on interdependence of work tasks among employees and managers. Again, in the present business environment there simply isn't enough time for petty competitiveness, nor is there enough space for mistrust in relationships.

Fifth, postmodern organizations are characterized by the use *of groups:* decision-making and problem-solving groups, work teams, formal, informal, and mediated networks, quality circles, and committees. This is perhaps the most difficult principle to adapt to Western, particularly U.S., organizations. Our romantic obsession with rugged individualism, our cultural preoccupation with individual initiative, achievement, and reward, and our philosophical and moral belief in the value of the individual all mitigate against our willing participation in groups (see Chapter 8). New group initiative programs—generally sponsored by Asian automobile plants located in the United States—have made important contributions to this necessary change. So, too, have many K-12 schools, colleges, universities, and training seminars increased the use of group activities. With such hegemonic forces operating, perhaps Western acceptance (and even joyful acceptance) of groups as the bases of work life may not be far behind.

These five principles are probably not new to the reader. Actually, many of these organizational changes have been underway for the past two decades. In addition, most of us have experienced some of these changes in our places of employment. We recognize them; we just didn't know they were inspired by postmodernism. Here, again, we advise caution. If we have accepted these innovations uncritically, we are living what Lyotard called the postmodern condition by simply trusting the surfaces and living with the velocities of change. It is time to reconsider what we have accepted within the framework of our interpretation of individual creativity and organizational constraints. Ethics Box 6.2 explores this issue.

IMPLICATIONS OF THE POSTMODERN FOR CREATIVITY AND CONSTRAINT

Our discussion of the postmodern has thus far emphasized the complex relationships among organizations, selves, language, capitalism, and societies at the end of the twentieth century. Although postmodern logics of organizing are both rational (admittedly more Eastern than Western) and productive (admittedly more so for Asian than for U.S. companies), we have also tried to show that postmodern theories reframe our conceptions of work in society as well as who we are at work and in society. In this final section we examine what the postmodern contributes to the idea of balance between individual creativity and constraint. First, we investigate how the concept of dialogue is shaped by postmodern forces. Second, we discuss organizational narratives as the localized site of the construction and deconstruction of postmodern meanings. Third, we use the ideas of organizational dialogue and narrative to reframe the concept of work as interpretation.

Postmodern Dialogue

The presence of the postmodern in everyday organizational life draws attention to the emergent, fluid relationships between interpretive practices and communication activities. How we interpret signs and surfaces is both a moment-to-moment attempt at sense-making and an act of creating the conditions of our own organizational cultural understandings. The results of our interpretive efforts and communicative practices are

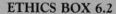

ETHICS BOX 6.2

TRUST THE SURFACES OR SEARCH FOR DEEP STRUCTURES: THE DILEMMA OF POSTMODERN ETHICS

The postmodern is generally associated with a situational ethics perspective: There are no absolute standards for determining right and wrong in all situations. We must interpret ethical choices based on our definition and analysis of the context that produces the need for the choice and our understanding of the potential outcomes of those choices.

While this view of ethics is consistent with our interpretive approach to organizational communication, it suffers from a lack of ethical consistency that troubles many people. Without absolute standards of right and wrong, these critics argue, we are too often left adrift on a sea of relativity. Furthermore, if we agree that contexts shape our interpretations of right and wrong, then it may also be argued that a lack of information about a context can lead to alternative ethical conclusions. Put simply, if we didn't know everything at the time we made the ethical choice, how could we really be held accountable for our actions?

Furthermore, some radical postmodernists, drawing strength from the far left of critical theory, ask: Isn't the whole concept of ethics critically suspect? Viewed this way, ethics refers to and is informed by a Grand Narrative of right and wrong created by and used for the interests of the powerful to suppress the powerless by limiting how right and wrong can be analyzed and understood. For example, employee outrage or anger in response to sexual harassment is justifiable, even though it may be professionally unethical to scream at the offending manager. Whose ethics are we to live by, anyway?

Finally, what are we to make of the irony of ethical determinations in an age marked on the one hand by the postmodernist advisory to trust the surfaces when, on the other hand, it is also intellectually viable to examine a situation for evidence of deep structures of power? Do ethics reside in surfaces or in structures? Or both? Or is there some other formulation?

Consider the complexity of the above issues when you grapple with the following scenarios:

1. You are called into an emergency meeting with your boss, and she informs you that your company needs a press release justifying a recent toxic waste accident that it has claimed was not its fault. "This is damage control," you are told, "and even though all the facts are not yet assembled, we cannot afford to be made to look negligible in the media." What are the ethical dimensions of your decision whatever that decision is? What would you do?

2. You discover that a co-worker has been reading your personal E-mail (i.e., electronic mail delivered over a network computer). Through this medium, he has found out about your secret office romance with another employee. Your company has a strict policy forbidding romantic relationships between co-workers. Your co-worker threatens to tell your boss about the romance if you reveal that he has been reading your as well as other workers' E-mail. What are the ethical dimensions oi this situation? What would you do?

---

themselves commodities. They are bought or not bought, as reasonable accounts of what's going on; they are evaluated as fair representations or unfair representations; they function to create audiences for their appeals.

This view of organizational communication is revolutionary. Combined with an understanding of the commodity capitalism inherent in postmodern culture and the decentralizing of power inherent in postmodern organizations, our view of communication seeks to suggest that meanings have value only insofar as they relate to current market conditions. Hence, in everyday work life the major authority for how things are and what should be done is found in dialogue among empowered employees and managers. There is no authority outside of or beyond what we agree to.

Narratives as Surfaces: The Sites of Postmodern Consciousness

Narratives are a powerful signifying force in our understanding of postmodern organizations and the concept of balance between creativity and constraint. Rather than seeing narratives as something people in organizations do to construct realities (inherent in the cultural approach), postmodern theories endorse the radical idea that narratives are the simulacra of organizational consciousness. Therefore, it becomes important to ask how the stories exchanged by managers and employees act as commodities within markets desiring to consume them. What is the balance of attitudes, styles, or looks that are placed into dialogue with one another as competing or conflicting accounts of creativity and constraint at work? One good example of this principle is the Reagan administration decision not to let Chrysler fold. It wasn't that we really needed their products (after all, there are many car manufacturers) so much as we desired the image of a recovering auto industry to balance against other economic concerns. We wanted to consume a heroic story, a story that included the theme of creative government loans being used to protect the jobs of auto workers. The pastiche image was as media-important as the underlying—and conflicting—economic reality.

A more dismal example is the Savings and Loan crisis during the early years of the Bush administration, a crisis that provides ample narrative evidence of the free-floating signifiers used to represent property values for consumer loans. Here again, the image of prosperity, lending officers were telling each other, was more important than was any empirical reality—at least until the notes came due. Stories of creative financing met broader economic narratives about impending constraints; the balance that had been tipped toward creativity tipped back toward constraint. A new image—one of S&L failures, massive incompetence in lending institutions, and mortgaged properties— replaced older ones. Eventually, a new consciousness emerged in narratives about creative government bailouts. And again, we consumed them eagerly.

In terms of our concern for achieving a balance between creativity and constraint through social interaction, a postmodern view of narratives offers us a metanarrative. This postmodern concept, which itself is a narrative about narratives, tells us that, while narratives in organizations function as representations of consciousness and conflicts, these representations are often nonreflexive. They are stories consumed for their storyness, for that little spike they provide us in the otherwise vast gray everydayness of postmodern simulacra. They are desired and consumed as real surfaces, but is the consumable surface of reality (itself a construction, a set of agreements that are regularly contested) merely a desirable simulation?

For practicing managers and employees, these postmodern views on the role of narratives in organizations are problematic. Although we have long known that good managers are usually good storytellers, the tendency is to resist the idea that organizations are little more than storytelling systems (Boje, 1991). Similarly, although we applaud the ideas of employee empowerment and cross-functional training as postmodern innovations, are we less willing to see these innovations succeed because they threaten to "open up" the workplace to newer, truer, more interesting stories. Or, perhaps, by improving organizational storytelling we teach employees and managers how to live under conditions of shared authority, teamwork, deconstruction of dominant power structures, and respect for differences. Perhaps life as it is represented on the surfaces is where and how the meaningful truths vie for listeners.

Work Reframed as Interpretation

The postmodern view of communication requires a reformulation of our conception of work as interpretation. The idea of work under conditions of postmodernity functions as a commodity whose value is determined by signs of doing one's job. Doing one's job means, then, providing sensible representations of employment against a broader simulacrum of cultural representations. Hence, what one accomplishes is joined in importance by how it is accomplished, and who one is or represents oneself to be must "work" within the interpretive community that is being asked to sponsor that individual identity.

In terms of the question of balance between creativity and constraint, a postmodern view of work reframed as interpretation seems entirely appropriate. To work is to interpret signs within fields of possibilities. At one end, the possibilities are represented by pure individual creativity; at the other end, the possibilities are represented by pure organizational constraint. Somewhere between these two extremes lies the everyday negotiation of meanings with others through dialogues.

Consider this example. We have a mutual friend who has never quite understood why he lost his last academic job. His story was that his teaching and publication record exceeded the departmental average; therefore, he deserved tenure. The alternative narrative, provided by members of his tenure evaluation committee, was that his teaching was uninspired and that his publications looked like the work of a man who knew only that he needed to publish in order to keep his job. Even though this person obviously did his job, his representation of being a college faculty member did not work as a meaningful sign for his colleagues. His failure lay not in failing to do his job, but in failing to create an appreciative audience for it. From a modernist construction of work as empirical performance, this decision wreaks of subjectivity and prejudice. After all, he was doing his job as long as his job was operationalized as teaching classes and publishing research. But from a postmodern construction of work as the interpretation of signs and the creation of a commodity value for those signs within a particular discourse community, it is perfectly understandable. He did not live up to desirable commodity expectations; the stories he told were not highly valued; he failed to engage in dialogue because he walked around believing he was right. In postmodern logic, he acted but failed to communicate.

Finally, we offer this interpretation of what critical and postmodern theories do to the concept of balance: Sometimes creativity and constraint enter the dialogue as interpretive frameworks, and sometimes, in the course of dialogue, they are recognized as signs of other stories that are striving to be represented.

SUMMARY

This chapter presented two faces of opposition and change. Up to this point, organizations (as rational structures) and communication (as the rational instrument) have been understood to work together to improve and refine what those in power thought to be a progressive, liberal, well-ordered society. These modernist assumptions about the need for control of social order and nature, the ultimate victory of rationality over chaos, political power vested in a cultural elite, and widespread dedication of material and human resources to fund and fuel technological progress were all challenged by newer, more critical, and decidedly postmodern approaches to understanding the political, social, and moral implications of organizations and communication.

The two voices of opposition to this dominant narrative teach us to ask different questions. Critical approaches teach us to ask new questions about power, whereas postmodern approaches teach us to ask new questions about order. Together these two intellectual forces have produced alternative ways of understanding organizing and communicating as political and moral processes that can be used or represented as sources of constraint or liberation. Our challenge now is to find new ways to productively organize work by empowering individuals to take more responsibility and initiative while preserving those organizational practices that respect and advocate the delicate interdependence of our environment, our families, our work, and the ever-present need to fulfill the dreams of our creative human spirit.

This chapter concludes our historical narrative about the evolution of theoretical perspectives on organizational communication. The remainder of this text concentrates on applications of these theoretical understandings.

CASE STUDY

Developing a Critical Theory/ Postmodern Code of Ethics

BACKGROUND

WestWear, Inc. is a chain of fashion retail stores located primarily in the U.S. Midwest and specializes in casual sportswear for women and men. Their chief competitors are The Gap and Banana Republic. Dedicated to providing stylish clothing at affordable prices, WestWear also embraces a "customer first" policy that places a premium on high-quality, customer-specific service. In addition, returns are gladly accepted, regardless of condition or origin of sale.

The management of WestWear, Inc. prides itself on being a socially conscious retail operation. Toward this end, they donate 2 percent of their annual profits to various charitable organizations worldwide, the names of which are provided by customers. Donations are made in their customers' names. They also sponsor plastic-free packaging for all sales, use only recycled paper for all gift-wrapping, note pads, sales slips, and correspondence, and sponsor a semiannual glad-rags donation drive to collect old clothes for free distribution to homeless shelters.

WestWear, Inc. is also quite profitable. In a highly competitive and somewhat fickle market, they attribute their success to their socially conscious efforts as well as to their customer first program. To maintain their competitive edge, they have pledged to be the industry leader in earth-preserving and customer service. None of their business decisions is made without taking both aspects of their pledge into account.

THE PROBLEM

Recently, the management of WestWear, Inc. has decided to develop a "WestWear Code of Ethics" that would serve both as an advertisement and as a management plan. Realizing from their own research that business codes of ethics need to encourage individual decision making within a range of desirable options, and having last year sponsored corporatewide empowerment programs, the task at hand seems both admirable and difficult. Their code must be both flexible and comprehensive; it must work within the boundaries of employee empowerment and customer service; and it must respect their pledge to save the earth as well as do high-volume business.

Further research has demonstrated that simply developing a code of ethics based on good deeds is generally not helpful. Instead, WestWear has bought into the idea of Critical Incident Technique (CIT) as a method for generating the ethical parameters of business decisions. Accomplishing CIT requires the development of *typical business scenarios* that are used to generate as many possible ethical and unethical frameworks as the context suggests. The ethical principles are derived from a discussion of the ethics of specific interpretations of contexts. From this step should emerge the statements that may then be refined into a WestWear Code of Ethics.

· ASSIGNMENT

You have been retained as a communication consultant to WestWear, Inc. Your task is to develop a series of Critical Incident Technique scenarios taken from ordinary business contexts in retail. Using your experience with retail outlets as well as your studies of employee-management communication, develop three or four scenarios that can be used to guide a group discussion of ethical issues.

Lead a focus-group discussion to ferret out the ethical principles WestWear employees and managers confront in their daily business practices. Investigate as many possibilities as your group can generate.

The results of your consulting efforts should be a postmodern, critical theory Code of Ethics for WestWear, Inc. that is capable of maximizing empowerment, and initiative in customer service, employee-managerial relations, and public relations while contributing to the earth-preserving aspect of their business pledge.

PART TWO

CONTEXTS

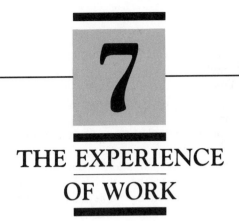

THE EXPERIENCE
OF WORK

The most important step in emancipating oneself from social controls is the ability to find rewards in the events of each moment. If a person learns to enjoy and find meaning in the ongoing stream of experience, in the process of living itself, the burden of social controls automatically falls from one's shoulders.

—*Mihalyi Csikszentmihalyi, 1990*

Our lives are spent in the shadow of one organization or another, and each organization has a potentially different set of rules or expectations for our attitudes and behaviors. While organizations (and the people who own and run them) may seek to control us, at the same time they provide us with resources that help us make sense of life experiences. A high-powered job as a lawyer, for example, can place serious limitations on where we might live and on the time we spend with our family, but it also offers us aspects of an identity, complete with broadly specified attitudes, values, ethics, and social status.

Earlier we noted that it has become increasingly difficult for an individual to survive financially without working for someone else. In exchange for wages, most of us place at least some of our lives under the control of an organization. From the standpoint of the organization, the challenge of the employment relationship is to elicit *cooperation*—to convince people to work together toward organizational goals. From the individual's point of view, the challenge is twofold. It is a quest both for *individuality*—a personal sense of significance at work, a legitimate voice, a way of being more than just a number in a faceless bureaucracy—and for *identification*—a sense of participation in a common dialogue, of commitment to a larger community that further defines who we are (Burke, 1969; Cheney, 1983).

Communication is central to the accomplishment of this cooperation, individuality, and identification because individuals in organizations use communication to symbolically induce cooperation in people who by their nature respond strongly to symbols (Burke 1969; Tompkins, 1987).

Even a cursory look at the corporate landscape reveals the enormous power organizations have over the lives of individuals. Some of this power is overt, but much of it is quite subtle (see Chapter 6). Competitive pressures make matters worse; even among the gainfully employed, job stress is high and job security low. Yet many people manage to survive and even thrive in the face of this pressure, finding ways of coping and otherwise "making a life" for themselves. Put in the best light, economic challenge has created an opportunity for rethinking the nature of occupation, with the hope that new approaches to organization might improve both corporate survivability *and* the individual experience of work (Milbrath, 1989).

This chapter focuses on the individual's experience of work. As such, it examines the insights and implications that follow from seeing work in terms of individual quality of life. We begin with a discussion of organizational assimilation, detailing how people come to organizations in the first place and how they learn to incorporate the organization's definition of reality into their personal behaviors and belief systems. From a communication perspective, the concern here is how new employees enter the organizational dialogue and find (or fail to find) a legitimate voice.

The chapter also addresses so-called indicators of cooperation—employee attitudes and behaviors that imply a positive alignment between individual and organizational goals. These indicators include job satisfaction, job involvement, organizational identification, organizational commitment, and individual productivity. The discussion of productivity pays special attention to the increasing use of communication technology to get work done today. Conversely, the indicators of resistance—negative employee attitudes and behaviors that suggest individual motives and goals are not in line with the organization—are covered. These include stress, burnout, absenteeism, and turnover. Finally, some attention is given to those aspects of individuals, jobs, and organizations that are most likely to lead to either cooperation or resistance. New directions for the organization of work that are currently being considered are explored.

ENTERING THE DIALOGUE: ORGANIZATIONAL ASSIMILATION

Assimilation is the process by which a person unfamiliar with the rules, norms, and expectations of a culture becomes a member of that culture. Everyone is to some extent assimilated into a national and local culture. From birth, parents and others teach children what it means to be a "member"—of a family, community, religion, or country. Assimilation means learning the rules or "ropes" underlying what members think, do, and say. Recent studies reveal the close relationship between learning a culture and learning a language, and specifically how everyday practices like dinnertime conversations teach American children the ways of American culture (e.g., Ochs, Smith, & Taylor, 1989).

The idea of assimilation has also been applied to understanding the process by which an individual employee learns about an organization's culture (cf. Jablin, 1987). According to Fred Jablin, the assimilation process has three broad stages: anticipatory socialization, organizational assimilation, and organizational exit.

Anticipatory Socialization

There are two types of anticipatory socialization: vocational and organizational. Both involve learning about work through communication. The vocational type begins in childhood, and is the process of learning about *work in general—and about specific careers in particular*—from family members, schools, part-time jobs, friends, and the media. While children and adolescents do not likely learn much about the detailed tasks associated with specific jobs or careers, they do acquire knowledge of general attitudes toward work. For example, early on adolescents become aware that power and status are important in organizations (Jablin, 1985) and that, despite formal rules and structures, work can be a source of meaningful personal relationships (Atwood, 1990).

The organizational type of anticipatory socialization refers to the process of learning about specific jobs and organizations. This learning takes place *before* the first day of work and is typically conveyed through organizational literature (e.g., brochures and personnel manuals) and through interactions with other job applicants, interviewers, and employees (Jablin, 1987). Individuals develop a more focused idea of what their prospective job and organization will be like, but their expectations tend to be inflated and unrealistic inasmuch as recruiters and interviewers tend to communicate only the most positive aspects of the job (Wanous, 1980).

Organizational Assimilation

Meryl Reis Louis (1980) has described organizational entry as alternating between surprise and sense-making. As initial expectations are violated, newcomers try to make sense of what is going on. During this initial encounter phase, "the newcomer learns the requirements of his or her role and what the organization and its members consider to be 'normal' patterns of behavior and thought" (Jablin, 1987, p. 695).

Vernon Miller and Fred Jablin (1991) describe the ways newcomers seek to learn about unfamiliar organizations. This search carries with it a sense of urgency. Until they reach a level of familiarity, new employees have difficulty performing their jobs and getting along with others. Potential sources of useful information for these newcomers include: (1) official messages from management, including orientation programs and manuals; (2) co-workers and peers; (3) one's supervisor; (4) other organizational members (e.g., secretaries, security guards, and acquaintances in other departments); (5) sources outside the organization (e.g., customers); and (6) the task itself (Miller & Jablin, 1991, p. 97). In terms of our framework set out in Chapter 2, newcomers attempt to "situate" themselves in an unfamiliar organizational context, and in order to do so, they must first learn a great deal about how existing members define their organization's reality.

Newcomers tend to solicit only some of the information they require through direct questions, for substantial risks may be associated with asking "stupid" questions. Some of the alternative ways newcomers solicit information are summarized in Table 7.1 on page 198. These various tactics are not used in isolation; rather, newcomers may use any and all of them in order to get a feel for the organization's culture.

No one remains a newcomer forever. Over time, individuals who stay undergo a metamorphosis phase through which they evolve from newcomer status into full-fledged membership (Jablin, 1987). The time this transition takes varies across organizations and industries. In organizations such as hotels and restaurants, for example, the new employee can feel like an old-timer after only six months. In others, notably certain universities, hospitals, and professional associations, individuals may feel and be treated like newcomers even after ten years.

During the metamorphosis phase, employees begin to differentiate among organizational rules and norms and to decide which must be followed and which can be ignored.

TABLE 7.1
NEWCOMERS' INFORMATION-SEEKING TACTICS

Tactic	Example
Overt question	"Who has the authority to cancel purchase orders?"
Indirect question	"I guess I won't plan to take a vacation this year." (Implied: "Do we work through the holidays if we don't finish the project?")
Third parties	To a co-worker: "I'm making a presentation to the president. Does he like it if you open with a joke?"
Testing limits	Arriving late to work or wearing casual clothes. (Observe reaction.)
Disguising conversations	"That safety memo was sure a riot. Can you believe the gall of those guys?" (Wait for reaction to see whether they also think it was funny.)
Observing	Watch which employees get praised in meetings and emulate those who do. (Pay attention to specific individuals.)
Surveillance	Eavesdropping on peer conversations; paying careful attention at office parties. (Generally monitor the environment for cues.)

SOURCE: Miller & Jablin, 1991.

Metamorphosis also marks the beginnings of creativity and individuation. Feeling more comfortable with the rules of the game, individuals begin to put their own personal stamp on the job, developing their own unique voice and behaving in ways which while in general may be in conformance with the rules may also reflect some transformation of the rules. For example, a new supervisor may begin to make small changes in the way work is delegated that distinguish his or her department from others in the organization. Whereas newcomer behavior focuses mainly on the discovery of constraints, metamorphosis marks the beginnings of a greater balance between creativity and constraint. The degree of balance—and of an individual's satisfaction with his or her role as a member of the organization—largely determines patterns of cooperation, resistance, and exit.

INDICATORS OF COOPERATION:
DIALOGUE QUALITY

When sufficiently positive, certain factors indicate positive outcomes for both the individual and the organization. Although each of these indicators carries some inherent risks (e.g., too much commitment can lead to blind loyalty), as a rule they are desirable for all parties involved.

Job Satisfaction

The most common measure of the quality of work experience—job satisfaction—is a concern of both researchers and of managers wishing to understand the working climate of a company. Recall from Chapter 3 that concern for employee satisfaction is relatively new in organizational theory, originating with the human relations school. Not surprisingly, protagonists of the human relations and human resources schools were leaders in developing theories of job satisfaction. People like Douglas McGregor, Frederick Herzberg, and Abraham Maslow have all argued, in differing but related ways, that a satisfied employee is one whose needs are being met. Generally, there are three levels of need; failure to satisfy any one of them would be expected to lead to reduced job satisfaction.

Level One needs involve basic working conditions and rewards: sufficient pay, equipment, and a safe workplace. The first prerequisite for job satisfaction is an adequate level of safety. This issue was partially addressed in the United States in 1970 by the passage of the Occupational Safety and Health Act (OSHA), designed to regulate safe working conditions.

Level Two needs are for supportive interpersonal relationships—durable, positive connections with co-workers and bosses. These contribute to employee morale (Richmond & McCroskey, 1979) and to motivation. (The role of interpersonal relationships at work is discussed in detail in Chapter 8.)

Level Three needs are opportunities for growth including challenge, variety, autonomy, authority, personal development, and a clear career path for the future. If needs at all three levels are met, it is a good bet that individuals will report high levels of job satisfaction.

In some companies, basic safety has the greatest impact on employee well-being. Pressures for greater productivity and efficiency have led to rising injury rates in the United States (Baker, 1991). In September 1991, a fire in the Imperial Food Products poultry processing plant in North Carolina killed 25 people. The deaths were caused by locked exit doors; the company had never had a thorough safety inspection. To avoid further tragedies of this kind, a revised OSHA bill is currently being prepared which will

1. Give employees the right to refuse a supervisor's order if they feel it will result in injury.
2. Require all companies of a certain size or larger to form safety committees to review and continuously improve working conditions.
3. Require all companies to report all work-related accidents leading to hospitalization to OSHA within 24 hours.
4. Provide OSHA with the power to fine businesses up to $50,000 per day for serious safety hazards that remain unaddressed.

In summary, a satisfied worker is one who is paid fairly and works in a safe, pleasant environment; who has supportive relationships at work; and who feels challenged and has significant control over his or her job tasks. Accomplishing each of these goals, or meeting all three kinds of needs, is costly for business. But there is little disagreement in theory about the factors that lead to job satisfaction.

Disagreement does exist, however, about what activities individuals find challenging and about the likely consequences of a satisfied workforce. With regard to differences in perceptions of challenge, research shows that an individual's expectations and desire for meeting "growth needs" at work affect the strength of the relationship between the nature of the work and the resulting level of satisfaction (Loher et al., 1985). The degree of challenge in a job is a precursor of job satisfaction only for those people who seek challenge at work. For those with different expectations, meeting these needs is of less importance to their morale.

As we discussed in Chapter 3, considerable disagreement also exists over the direct consequences of a satisfied workforce. Since the 1930s, the enduring hope of researchers and managers alike has been that a satisfied workforce will also be a productive one. Research does not bear out this simple relationship (Loher et al., 1985). If anything, the converse is true: good performers who are acknowledged by the company tend to become happier when their good work is rewarded. It is as likely that an organization with high morale will be *un*productive as it will be highly productive. Job satisfaction does not seem to be, *by itself*, the key factor affecting motivation or organizational productivity.

At the same time, researchers have shown significant evidence for an indirect relationship between job satisfaction and productivity, mainly through absenteeism and turnover (Downs, Clampitt, & Pfeiffer, 1988; Futrell & Parasuraman, 1984). In other words, while a happy worker may not be a productive one, an unhappy worker is more likely to be absent and quit. The factors described below, job involvement and organizational identification and commitment, have been shown to have a more direct connection to performance and productivity.

Job Involvement

Job involvement is the degree to which employees "live their work" and get their personal needs met on the job. The history of the Industrial Revolution can in part be understood as a continuing struggle over appropriate levels of job involvement. On the one hand, the Protestant Work Ethic and its descendant, workaholism, suggest that work should play a central role in a person's physical, emotional, and spiritual life. At this extreme, many people either consciously or unconsciously "live to work"—they eat, sleep, and breathe their jobs.

Conversely, many employees "work to live" and toil mainly to pay the bills and support the part of life that is of greater importance to them, their (family) life outside of work. For this group, work is a means to an end and is not expected to fulfill personal needs.

Surprisingly, extreme variations in job involvement are found in today's workforce, even among high-ranking managers. Some seem completely involved in their work, to the neglect of their families and the outside world; others have more of a time-clock mentality. As an engineer executive put it, "I come to work, put in my eight hours, get my paycheck, and go home to the things that really matter." This same engineer gleefully relays the story of his father, who when asked by his former employer to do some consulting two weeks after retirement, told him to get lost. "He told his ex-employer to go to hell, which is exactly what I would do. He was done with work, and it was time to get on with life."

This tension between making a living and making a life is especially ironic in view of the recent discovery by Mihalyi Csikszentmihalyi (1990) that people's quality of experience tends to be *better* at work than it is at home. In other words, people are most enervated, challenged, involved, and generally more "functional" at work. At home, there is often a lot of unstructured, unchallenging leisure time (often involving alcohol use) that is not used for "re-creation" at all. And yet despite this qualitative difference in experience, most people still say that they would rather *not* be working (Csikszentmihalyi, 1990).

Organizational Identification

George Cheney (1983) and Philip Tompkins (Tompkins & Cheney, 1985) have applied Kenneth Burke's (1969) notion of identification to organizations. Tompkins and Cheney define identification as the natural overlap that develops between an individual's values and those of the group. "As members identify more strongly with the organization and its values, the organization becomes as much a part of the member as the member is a part of the organization" (Bullis & Tompkins, 1989, p. 289). In this way, identification is the internalization of organizational values and assumptions by individuals.

Identification also has a darker side, having mainly to do with the way it operates to control individual decision making. Specifically, identification guides us to "see certain problems and alternatives," and biases our choices "toward alternatives tied to the most salient identifications . . . identifying operates to narrow the decision makers' span of attention" (Tompkins & Cheney, 1985, p. 194). That is, the degree of identification employees have with an organization affects their definitions of what is real or taken for granted in any situation—identification strongly shapes interpretation. In a more positive light, identification provides a sense of community; employees feel a strong urge to identify with their organizations (Bullis & Tompkins, 1989). From a critical perspective, however, identification operates as a kind of unobtrusive control over employees through the control of decision premises (see Chapter 6).

Organizational Commitment

Organizational commitment, like identification, reflects the degree of overlap between individual and organizational goals and values. A critical difference, however, is that commitment refers more to explicit committing behaviors—the extent to which the individual talks up the organization in public as a good place to work, as well as the individual's intentions either to stay with or to leave the organization (Kiesler, 1971; Steers, 1977). Organizational commitment includes both attitudinal identification and behavioral commitment.

Although identification and commitment go hand in hand, people need not be involved in their jobs to be committed to their companies. Many factors have been identified as leading to increased organizational commitment. Some factors, such as generous compensation packages and well-timed promotions, are obvious. Others are strategic and are sponsored by management (such as the intensive orientation/training programs at Disney) with the explicit purpose of creating loyalty to the corporation. Still others operate outside of the formal management structure: employees can be committed to an organization within which they have many friends while still disliking the management and their work (Eisenberg, Monge, & Miller, 1983).

Commitment, Identification, and Empowerment In recent years, many of the old "company loyalties" have been breaking down along with the dominating, paternalistic companies themselves. Taking their place are leaner, more competitively oriented firms that encourage commitment by demonstrating how the individual's contribution makes a difference in the survival or success of the company. This trend is sometimes called high-involvement management (Lawler, 1986).

The idea behind high-involvement management is that people work best when they feel ownership over their work processes and their decision making. Empowerment is the process by which employees come to have control over significant aspects of their work. There are many levels of empowerment, from one-time involvement of employees on a specific project to self-directed work teams. According to Orsburn, et al. (1990), there are six levels of employee involvement:

1. Managers make decisions on their own, announce them, and then respond to employee questions.
2. Managers make decisions, but only after seeking employees' views.
3. Managers create temporary employee groups to recommend solutions to particular problems.
4. Managers meet with groups of employees on a regular basis to identify problems and recommend solutions.
5. Managers establish and participate in cross-functional problem-solving teams.
6. Ongoing work groups assume expanded responsibility for a particular issue, like cost reduction.

In some cases, empowerment, identification, and commitment are achieved through compensation schemes that afford employees ownership in the company. A popular example is the Scanlon Plan, which encourages innovation and gives all employees a share in company profits (cf. Monge, Cozzens, & Contractor, 1991). This trend toward employee involvement is an extension of the initial human resources position—that each employee's input must be valued by the organization. It also suggests a modification of capitalist thinking in that it provides workers with greater control over the means of production which Marx felt was so essential. When high-involvement management works, the result is a highly committed, deeply involved workforce that takes things seriously because it feels responsible for the company's success or failure. The "us versus them" attitude ingrained in most thinking about organizations is replaced by a "we are in this together" attitude.

Naturally, something this powerful is not easy to implement. As we will discuss in Chapter 8, the supervisory behaviors associated with involvement and empowerment are materially different from those of traditional management. Furthermore, even if the new behaviors are learned, employees may resist empowerment for a variety of reasons, including unfamiliarity with the new role, lack of trust in management, or apprehensions about the increased accountability. Clearly, it takes two to empower, for empowerment is not something one person can "do to" another person. Nonetheless, misconceptions abound. For example, a job interviewer in a fast-food restaurant was overheard telling a prospective supervisor that her job would require her to "empower two people," as if it were something she could do to her employees the first day on the job. While organizations and supervisors can help create conditions for empowerment (e.g., through reward systems, opportunities for cooperation, and a chance for personal growth) it is ultimately up to the individual employees whether they choose to be "empowered."

The benefits of a committed workforce, especially in a competitive business environment, cannot be overstated. Not only does commitment cause people to work harder, but also committed employees are more likely to suggest new ideas that can make a substantial difference in cost, quality, profitability, or schedule. Under conditions of high involvement, employees will more likely feel that their voices are heard and valued by management and that work has significance in their lives.

Individual Productivity

From the standpoint of the organization, the most important indicator of employee cooperation is not satisfaction or commitment, but productivity. Productivity is generally defined as the relation between the outputs generated by a system and the inputs required to create those outputs (Campbell, Campbell, & Associates, 1988). While individual productivity is often linked to efficiency (e.g., an individual's ability to convert input into output with minimal cost in a given time frame [Sink, 1983]), there has been a great deal of emphasis recently on broadening the definition of productivity to include effectiveness, which is usually measured in terms of the *quality* of the final product or service. For example, insurance claims adjusters may be measured by the total number of claims they process per day *as well as* by the accuracy of those claims; telephone operators by the number of calls they take in an hour *as well as* by how well they handle the calls; and manufacturing assemblers by the amount of time it takes to make a specific product *as well as* the amount of rework required to make the product acceptable to the customer.

Most organizations do a poor job of measuring individual productivity, except in the simplest of jobs. Moreover, when measuring the quality of a product or service, or when the nature of a product or service is poorly defined (as is often the case for teachers or judges), productivity measures are at best ambiguous and in many cases nonexistent (Jacobson, 1992). Without doubt, the recent emphasis on "total quality," "continuous measurable improvement" and "statistical process control" has improved this state of affairs by encouraging all employees, regardless of their task, to develop and track quantitative measures of their productivity. But these measures are still rare for most white-collar jobs, where evaluation of productivity remains very subjective.

With regard to the relationship of productivity to communication, some studies show a positive association between the two and others either negative or nonexistent associations (cf. Papa, 1989). Annalee Luhmann and Terrance Albrecht (1990) conclude that "the nature of the communication-performance relationship has yet to be demonstrated unequivocally" (p. 2). Results of studies in this area have been inconsistent because a wide range of phenomena can count as either communication or productivity. Certainly, some kinds of communication, such as clear direction from supervisors or improved teamwork across related functions, should have a positive impact on productivity. Alternatively, other kinds of interaction, such as supportive leadership, have been shown to positively affect morale but have little impact on productivity (Scott, 1981). Still other kinds of communication (like the boss throwing a screaming fit) can raise productivity in the short term but have a negative effect over time.

Based on this research, we conclude that two general approaches may be used to link communication and productivity. The first approach, the *monologic,* ties communication to productivity by promoting a work environment in which simple tasks and clear performance measures permit continuous measurable improvement. All the communication comes from the supervisor. Though reminiscent of scientific management, this approach is frequently used today, especially in manufacturing organizations struggling to remain competitive.

The second approach, the *dialogic,* emphasizes mutual, two-way communication between managers and employees working to accomplish complex tasks (see Figure 7.1, page 204). In this approach, the relationship between communication and productivity is mediated by a sense of urgency in attitudes. Sharing business information, inviting employees to participate in decision making, and providing employees with feedback

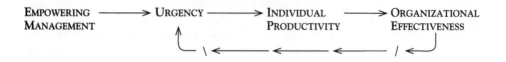

EMPOWERING ——→ URGENCY ——→ INDIVIDUAL ——→ ORGANIZATIONAL
MANAGEMENT   PRODUCTIVITY   EFFECTIVENESS

FEEDBACK ABOUT RESULTS

Empowering Management

- Shares business information at all levels
- Eliminates status consciousness
- Solicits and uses employee input
- Supports teamwork
- Provides clear vision and direction
- Provides clear standards of accountability
- Makes decisions based on data
- Trusts employees

FIGURE 7.1
A Closed-Loop Model of Communication, Empowerment, and Performance
SOURCE: Eisenberg & Riley, 1992.

about the successes and failures of their efforts leads to increased identification, commitment, and involvement, which in turn produce greater productivity.

Individual Performance and Communication Technology   In the 1950s and 1960s, organizational research emphasized face-to-face interaction between supervisors and employees and informal conversations among peers (see Chapter 3). Today face-to-face interaction continues to be important but accomplishing work today requires the use of communication technology, from computer networks to facsimile (FAX) to voice and electronic mail. This section explores the different types of communication technology in the contemporary workplace and the impact of such technologies on individual productivity and quality of work life.

Communication technology developed as a response to the limitations of interpersonal interaction, especially the limits associated with speed, geographical distance, and processing capacity. Most organizations can no longer function without some form of communication technology (e.g., advanced telephone systems, electronic mail, and manufacturing information systems). But the decision to use any new technology is always an emotional one, for adoption usually involves making major changes in the way people do their jobs. They may not only have to learn a new machine, but may also have to negotiate new interpersonal and power relationships (e.g., Aydin & Rice, 1992).

Two broad types of communication technology are currently available to organizations (Huber, 1990).

1. *Computer-assisted communication technologies.* These include all kinds of image transmission (e.g., facsimile, image modems, video conferencing), electronic and voice mail, and computer networks.

2. *Computer-assisted decision-aiding technologies.* These include on-line management information systems (which store, integrate, and make available key business information from throughout the organization), group decision support systems, external information retrieval systems (databases like DRI-FACS and NEXUS, which allow managers and employees to search thousands of sources for information on specified topics), and expert systems (programs that contain technical knowledge on how to accomplish a task that may be queried by managers or employees).

Computer-assisted communication technologies are designed to bring people together more quickly and across long distances. For example, the primary method of communication between the authors of this book was electronic mail, which saved money on plane tickets, postage, and phone bills. Of all the communication technologies available today, electronic mail has perhaps the greatest potential to improve productivity. Being able to receive asynchronous messages without constant phone and personal interruptions presents a clear advantage (Turnage, 1990). By contrast, videoconferences have had the least impact, because they are not regarded as reasonable alternatives to face-to-face meetings (Long, 1987).

Computer-assisted decision-aiding technologies are designed primarily to provide easy access to hard-to-find information needed to make a decision, rather than to link people. For example, a company trying to decide whether to introduce a risky new product may access an external database to obtain timely, up-to-date marketing information. Internal to an organization, a national automobile sales manager might "pull up on the screen" the last quarter's sales figures by dealership and make decisions allocating sales training based on these data. In theory, these technologies allow quick retrieval from complex fields of both internal and external information. In practice, those systems that "truly support decision-making while leaving final decisions up to the user are successful, whereas systems that substitute machine decisions for human decisions or significantly curtail the user's freedom of action are troublesome, and loss of productivity often results" (Turnage, 1990, p. 172).

The effects of these new technologies on individuals at work are not clear-cut. There are at least two sides to the story, one optimistic, the other pessimistic:

> The optimists view technology as increasing both productivity and employee quality of work life. They see the computer as freeing employees to work on more challenging tasks by taking over the routine aspects of jobs, thus increasing productivity and competition and creating more employment in the long run. The pessimists (e.g., Braverman, 1974; Cohen, 1984) associate automation with loss of employment, deskilling (i.e., lowering the skill requirements for job incumbents), physical and mental problems, and a tightly controlled work environment (Turnage, 1990, p. 171–172).

Research has not given us a clear verdict supporting either position. For example, concern has arisen over the health hazards of working with video display terminals (VDTs), including radiation, headaches, eyestrain, sleeplessness, anxiety, and repetitive motion disorders, but actual research findings have been mixed. While some negative health impact no doubt exists, their appearance can have more to with the way the organization uses the technology (e.g., long working hours without breaks; poor ergonomic design of work stations) than with the technology itself (Smith et al., 1981; Steelman & Klitzman, 1985).

Another instructive example is the use of computers for automatic monitoring of employee work. These systems check and measure the frequency and speed of the work being done, and then store this information for review by management. Approximately six million workers are now under some form of electronic supervision in the United States (Turnage, 1990). Monitoring is in widespread use in the telephone industry and among airline reservation agencies to track productivity. Employee reactions to this technology have been surprising. Although some see electronic surveillance as an invasion of privacy, many others are in favor of monitoring because it affords good performers greater visibility and permits the clear and fair discipline of poor performers (Bell-Detienne, 1992).

Communication technologies are rarely used as they were designed; instead they are "appropriated" (Poole & Desanctis, 1990) to meet individual needs. For example, the phone answering machine was originally designed to receive incoming calls in the recipient's absence but has become a tool for selective communication through call screening. Similarly, medical information systems, designed to ensure the tracking of patient prescriptions, tests, and treatments, have become a way for pharmacists to exert greater power and control over the health care process (Aydin & Rice, 1992). There is no neutral technology, and the so-called objective features of any technology are important only in how employees interpret and use them. In Table 7.2, Jan Mouritsen and Niels Bjorn-Andersen (1991) offer six important concerns that should be considered in the analysis of communication technology.

TABLE 7.2
SIX CONCERNS FOR THE ANALYSIS OF COMMUNICATION TECHNOLOGY

1. *Humans are agents.* Accept the fact that "humans are reflexively monitoring what goes on in a particular social system, that they are motivated by wants and aspirations, and that they have the power not to perform the prescription laid down by systems designers" (p. 312).

2. *Tacit knowledge should be respected.* "People know more about their lives than they can put into words. People do know how to handle practical affairs without being able to explain fully what they are really doing" (p. 312).

3. *Understanding is partial.* "There are always unacknowledged conditions for and unintended consequences of people's behavior" (p. 313).

4. *Technology is politically ambiguous.* While on the one hand it can be used to promote dialogue and improve individual quality of life, the same technology can also be used to constrain, limit, and control.

5. *Informal communication needs to be acknowledged.* "Informal informing is an organizational fact . . . it is necessary to understand how formal information is mediated through various more or less structured patterns of informing" (p. 313).

6. *Counter-rational decision making should be acknowledged.* "The rational model is not a viable way of understanding the intricacies of modern business management. On the one hand it is questionable that decision-makers cognitively are able to cope with the complexity and amount of information needed to make rational decisions, and on the other hand, it is probable that all sorts of political and social pressures are called upon in everyday management" (pp. 313–314).

SOURCE: Mouritsen & Bjorn-Andersen, 1991.

Most technologies fail not for technical reasons, but because the system designers or implementers do not take into account the social and political environment in which the technology is to be used. The "rational" use of communication technology is "subjective, retrospective, and influenced by information provided by others" (Fulk, Schmitz, & Steinfeld, 1990, p. 123). According to Noshir Contractor and Eric Eisenberg (1990):

> There is no such thing as pure technology. To understand technology, one must first understand social relationships. . . . Everything about the adoption and uses of media is social. . . . Logical expectations for the adoption and use of the new media are rarely met. The pragmatics of technological communication must always be understood in the context of motives, paradoxes, and contradictions of everyday life (p. 143).

INDICATORS OF RESISTANCE: STRESS AND BURNOUT

Employee stress is on the rise. While the term *stress* itself is general and ambiguous, the costs of increased stress for individuals are concrete and severe. Typical stress symptoms include chest pains, peptic ulcers, anxiety and depression, back pain, stomach problems, headaches, high blood pressure, and fatigue (Ray, 1987). These individual health problems have serious organizational consequences, such as increased absenteeism, tardiness, sabotage, poor quality, turnover, and dysfunctional conflict (Cooper, 1984; Hall & Savery, 1987; Quick & Quick, 1984). Lost working days due to heart disease alone account for over 15 billion dollars in lost wages annually (Ivancevich & Matteson, 1980). And as if this isn't enough, in the 1980s murders in the workplace doubled.

When we speak of stress, we generally mean heightened feelings of anxiety, tension, or pressure. More generally, we can define job stress as a psychologically disturbed state in response to work demands. Over time, a chronically stressed individual may become susceptible to burnout. Extensive studies of burnout in the lives of health professionals show that it has three dimensions: emotional exhaustion, depersonalization (or a negative attitude toward others, especially clients), and a lessened sense of personal accomplishment as a result of work pressures (Maslach, 1982).

What factors will likely increase job stress, and what will lessen it? How does communication contribute to varying levels of stress at work? Four levels of stressors are discussed here: (1) environmental; (2) organizational; (3) job/role; and (4) individual. Research clearly shows that differences at any and all of the various levels of stressors can impact stress (e.g., Israel et al., 1989). In each case, we will highlight the specific role of communication, even when the existing research does not.

Environmental Stressors

Individuals in organizations have the least control over environmental stressors, especially those associated with national culture and norms, customers and the marketplace, and the physical characteristics of the workplace.

National Culture   A nation's prevailing beliefs and expectations about the nature of work, leisure, and employment have a significant effect on on-the-job stress. An obvious example are countries with few safety laws that allow organizational sweatshops that pay very low wages and have intolerable working conditions. Less obvious but equally important are attitudes toward work in more industrialized countries. For all of their positive economic gains, Japanese society has of late been criticized for overworking employees, so much so that they even have a name—Karoshi—for the not uncommon "death by overwork." The United States is similar to Japan in at least one regard: the two countries rank lowest in the world in the average number of vacation days per year. After one year of service, U.S., Japanese, and Canadian workers get ten days off; by contrast, in Austria, Brazil, Denmark, and Sweden, employees get thirty vacation days after one year (Staimer, 1992). In Europe, a six-week vacation is the norm, and often the law (Rider, 1992). In summary, differences between countries in their values about the nature of work can be expected to show up in policy statements and informal norms for behavior, which in turn translate into differences in employee stress.

Customers and the Marketplace   As noted in Chapter 1, in the United States uncertainties about business survival and a weakening competitive position, coupled with a rising demand for quality and customer service, have given rise to feelings of insecurity and hopelessness about the future. The result has been marked increases in stress among salaried and hourly employees. Managers are not helpless to counteract this stress. For example, they can communicate honestly with employees about the changing conditions and the ways they can make a difference in the future success of the company. Unfortunately, however, much of what happens in the marketplace is outside of the organization's control. Perhaps the individual or organization's best recourse is to obtain good information about the market and customers; communicate with customers about new ways of meeting their requirements; and help employees shape interpretations of marketplace conditions in ways that are psychologically positive both for them and for the organization.

Physical Characteristics of the Workplace   Certain rooms and buildings make us feel calm and comfortable, whereas others agitate us. Similarly, some organizations are physically more likely to cause stress than others. Some of the most common environmental causes of employee stress include improper lighting, too much noise, excessively hot or cold temperatures, overcrowding, lack of privacy, and the improper design of tools and equipment (Altman, Valenzi, and Hodgetts, 1985). In their study of female clerical workers at a university, Greg Oldham and Nancy Rotchford (1983) reported on some of these negative reactions and offer an explanation:

1. Employees have poor interpersonal experiences in offices that facilitate excessive contact among employees.
2. Employees in dense, dark, nonprivate offices feel they have less control over their work and find their jobs to be less significant.
3. Employees in dense, dark, nonprivate offices experience low privacy and inability to concentrate.
4. These poor interpersonal experiences, feelings of less control and significance, and inability to concentrate are directly related to work satisfaction and to job stress.

Interestingly, many of the negative reactions uncovered in these studies are related to how certain physical designs affect opportunities for interpersonal communication.

Specifically, workplaces that do not permit both normal informal interaction and some degree of privacy and control over a work area are most likely to lead to employee stress.

Organizational Stressors

As observed in Chapter 5, an organization's culture is the unique sense of place provided by the physical and symbolic relationships between and among persons, work, and things. Accordingly, different types of actions, practices, symbols, and relationships—different organizational cultures—affect individuals in varying ways. Steven Altman and his colleagues (1985) apply Deal and Kennedy's (1982) typology of organizational cultures to their analysis of stress at work:

> A high-feedback, high risk-taking environment is one in which we are likely to find macho-type people who walk fast, talk fast, dress in modern-style clothing, compete with each other for promotion and salary, and live what can be thought of as a very fast life. Conversely, in a low feedback, low risk-taking environment, we are likely to find people who follow the rules, do not make waves, write lots of memos to cover and explain their actions, and tend to live a very structured type of existence. Stress is an organizational culture problem for two reasons: (a) an individual who is mild-mannered may find him or herself in a very stress-creating environment, and; (b) regardless of the characteristics of the environment, even the most successful individuals may find the pressures of the situation to be extremely difficult (p. 433).

Other, more clearly communicative dimensions that have been shown to affect individual experience of work include norms and expectations concerning social support; participation in decision making; diversity; and expression of emotion.

Social Support   Organizations and occupations differ in their expectations regarding social support. According to Eileen Berlin Ray (1987), "supportive interactions are those in which coworkers are able to vent feelings, clarify perceptions, and mutually define the work environment" (p. 188). This type of communication occurs most frequently in stable social relationships at work. Thus, regular opportunities to communicate with others facing similar levels of uncertainty in an organization can be especially helpful in establishing a sense of control. Access to a network of support is critical. Organizations that isolate employees from one another, through incompatible schedules, physical layout, or normative expectations about the inappropriateness of informal interaction, also show the least social support and the greatest likelihood of creating debilitating job stress (Ray, 1987).

Terence Albrecht and Mara Adelman (1987) have developed a theoretical model of social support and job stress. In their model, employees who lack social support are less able to make sense of their uncertain work environment because they lack access to interpretive resources. This disability in sense-making or uncertainty reduction leads to diminished feelings of personal control over the work situation. According to Albrecht and Adelman, it is this reduced personal control that ultimately impacts stress:

> Supportive communication helps people when the process functions to decrease the anxiety and stress caused by the experience of the unknown. . . . The significance of supportive communication that reduces one's perceptions of uncertainty is that it helps the receiver in developing a sense of perceived control over stressful circumstances (Albrecht & Adelman, 1987, p. 24).

This research indicates that "support," in an organizational context, does not refer simply to emotional assistance or a shoulder to cry on. In this way, current studies of social support deviate considerably from the original human relations ideas about supportive communication or leadership. Instead, there is a strong emphasis on the *informational* functions of supportive communication, on the role close co-workers can play in assisting individuals in defining and making sense of their work environment. Just as communication technology has no "objective" characteristics and is instead open to interpretation, so too are organizational characteristics largely constructed through communication (Miller & Monge, 1985; Salancik & Pfeffer, 1978). Social support provides interpretive resources to individuals situated in organizations.

Participation in Decision Making   Organizations differ in their treatment of employees, specifically in the degree to which they trust employees to make important decisions. At one extreme (reminiscent of scientific management), employees are seen as unthinking extensions of managerial direction. At the other, management recognizes that the individual performing the job knows it best, and consequently is best qualified to improve it. Participation in decision making can help reduce stress and improve employee quality of life by giving workers a greater feeling of control and effectiveness (cf. Miller et al., 1990). More specifically, greater participation in decision making gives employees a clearer idea of what is expected of them, and of what is to be rewarded. This should lead to decreased uncertainty and reduced stress (Schuler & Jackson, 1986).

A good example of the relationship between participation and job stress comes from an automobile parts manufacturing company. Two years ago, the company decided to institute a new corporate strategy, namely, to become the lowest cost parts supplier in the industry. Senior management made this strategic decision without consulting lower levels of management or the workers. The results have been disastrous. Because of their nonparticipation, no one in the company feels any ownership or commitment to becoming lowest cost, and workers take the attitude that "nobody asked me, so I'll just do my job (and not a thing more)." Workers are apathetic, stressed, and burned out. Today the company is on the verge of bankruptcy.

Certain organizations are unpleasant and stressful places because they don't value employees as resources, but treat them instead as replaceable cogs in some giant machine. Evidence of mistrust and the replaceability of employees can be found throughout an organization in its surveillance systems (e.g., time clocks, style of supervision), compensation policies, working conditions, parking lot, and even the layout and condition of the building. Each of these elements sends a message of caring or uncaring about personnel. They send more explicit messages as well, evident in the stories people tell about what happened when an employee tried to provide input to management. If a complaint is met with "don't let the door hit you on the way out," the message is clear. At the other extreme, Domino's Pizza's motto, "It is better to ask forgiveness than to ask permission," sends a strong message about attitudes toward individuals and the extent of employee involvement in important decisions.

In sum, organizations affect the quality of their employees' work lives by the way they value them as human beings, and consequently are able to balance profits with people. This is not an easy feat. Organizations usually tend toward overcontrol, but, as happens when a plane is being tossed in a storm, this approach tends to hurt rather than help. It is necessary to let go of the wheel precisely when the risks for doing so are the greatest.

THE ETHICS OF REWARDS

In "for-profit" hospitals, bonuses are typically awarded to senior management based on their ability to lower operating costs, thereby increasing revenues for the company and profitability for the shareholders. These bonuses are often spread out and down the hospital hierarchy to reward various department heads, chiefs, and managers, but the big money bonuses generally are allotted only to the CEO (chief executive officer), the CFO (chief financial officer), and senior VP levels. Bonuses at these levels can equal or exceed annual salaries.

In a regional for-profit hospital, impressive bonuses were awarded to three VPs and to the CEO and CFO. The VPs each received approximately $95,000, and the CFO and CEO each received checks for $250,000. It had been a very good year. The problem, however, was that the changes in operations that produced the lower costs were attributable to the work of one dedicated female VP, the only woman in the upper echelons of the company. The other two VPs had done very little to lower costs, the CFO had been mostly invisible, and the CEO had taken the year off to attend various leadership conferences, notably those located near prime golf courses. When the bonuses were handed out, the CEO told the dedicated VP: "We owe it all to you. Keep up the excellent work."

The VP requested a private conference with the CEO. He agreed and a time was selected. On the morning of the meeting, the VP told the CEO that she didn't understand how the distribution of bonuses could be equal among the VPs, despite the obvious fact that she had been the only one who had actually lowered costs.

"Susan, I'm surprised at you," he admonished. "How could I ensure an esprit de corps if you were the only one to receive a bonus?"

"I thought I was being rewarded for the work I did, not just my title," she retorted.

"You are," responded the CEO. "In fact, I was considering asking you if you would be interested in Ted's job. How would you like to be the new CFO (chief financial officer) of the hospital?"

"I didn't know Ted was leaving," Susan answered. "I'm flattered, of course."

"Neither does Ted," replied the CEO. "Nor should he, at least not right away. Let me handle that." He smiled. "Your performance last year clearly indicates to me your superiority for the job. Ted's bonus was a kind of severance pay, anyway. And of course there would be an appropriate—shall we say substantial—monetary increase for you involved in this promotion."

Susan left the CEO's office feeling a little giddy and very guilty. Ted had been her friend and mentor and had "brought her along" in management of the hospital. Now she was being asked to replace him in what she considered to be a callous way. She felt she deserved the promotion but did not want to accept it at Ted's expense. She would have to think about it.

Questions:

1. Does Susan have an obligation to Ted to let him know about her conversation with the CEO? Is this decision complicated by the issue of money? Status? Friendship? How do these complications lead us to address the theme of creativity and constraint in ethical dilemmas?

2. Does the CEO have an ethical obligation to rethink the bonuses for next year? Should a whole group be rewarded for the work of a single individual? Conversely, should individual rewards be given for a whole hospital effort to reduce costs? What about employees at lower levels in the hospital?

3. Review the conversation the CEO had with Susan. What are the ethical themes in evidence in the talk? In our American culture, does the capitalist ideal of monetary/status rewards for hard work conflict with the personal experience of friendship? Mentor relations? Where do trust and honesty in personal relationships conflict with hierarchical demands for privilege and privileged conversations?

4. Given your ethical stance, should there be "privileged" conversations in business?

To remain competitive, companies must seek to create a culture in which honest dialogue is encouraged in all directions and negative information is shared without fear of reprisal.

Diversity: Differences in Voice   An organization's handling of differences among employees can contribute to employee stress, particularly for minority employees. Not only women, blacks, and the physically challenged, but also other groups are the subject of an increased sensitivity to diversity issues at work. This research attention is well justified. According to Ann Morrison and Mary Ann Von Glinow (1990):

> The number of women, Blacks, and Hispanics in management has quadrupled since 1970, and the number of Asians has increased eightfold. However, the rate of upward movement of women and minority managers provides "clear evidence of nothing less than the abiding racism and sexism of the corporation" [Bradshaw, 1988, p. 1] (p. 200).

Imagine a physically challenged, black, female middle manager in a high-tech electronics firm. What factors would be expected to have the greatest impact on her day-to-day quality of life? Her demographic and background information (i.e., female, black, physically challenged) already tells us a lot about what to expect about her work life. All three of these categories are targets of social discrimination, and so she can expect to be ignored, not taken seriously, patronized, and/or scrutinized and singled out for opportunities that she may not be sure she yet deserves (i.e., she may be made a "token"). In speaking with others at work, she will very likely find people uncomfortable in speaking with her, going out of their way to finish her sentences, to interrupt, avoid, and find countless ways to discount what she has to say. The discrimination will most likely be subtle, though not always so, and she will face a formidable challenge in trying to overcome it. In every case, the challenge of working with a minority status is an issue of voice—of finding a way to speak with authority, to be heard.

The popular press refers to this suppression of minority voice as the "glass ceiling"—an invisible barrier to managerial and executive positions faced by minorities and specifically by women. A recent report by the U.S. Labor Department (August 1991) finds that women and minorities face numerous barriers to career development, some of which are as follows:

1. *Recruiting and hiring.* When recruiting managers, many companies fail to inform search professionals of equal opportunity requirements or of their desire to promote diversity.
2. *Succession and promotion.* Managers usually choose their successors, following a "similar-to-me" bias. All else being equal, managers "clone themselves," and since most are white men, their clones tend to look much the same.
3. *Affirmative action.* Usually these legal guidelines and restrictions are well known in the human resources department but less well known or ignored by the managers who are most directly responsible for hiring, firing, and promotion. This is worst at the executive level, where offers are made within a close informal network and records of hiring patterns are rarely kept.
4. *Performance standards.* Managers use different criteria evaluating men, women, and minorities. Minorities are especially susceptible to "tokenism," being set up for an excessive amount of scrutiny and then collapsing under the pressure. Women tend to be evaluated using emotional standards—their cheeriness and friendliness are considered as important as their job performance.

5. *Exclusion from line management.* Women and minorities who do make it into management usually end up in support or staff functions like human resources and facilities,
not in line management (e.g., production, engineering). (Hawkins, 1991).

Sabbaticals are especially costly for women: "taking a break from work to raise children
or to pursue other noncareer interests does permanent damage to a woman's earning
power" (Silverstien, 1992, p. 1). In many corporate cultures, women who take time off
are thought to be less dedicated and more likely to leave again; consequently, they are
given less responsible jobs. These factors taken together result in greater job stress for
women and minorities receiving similar treatment.

Lack of tolerance for diversity can be either overt or subtle. One of your authors
encountered an overt example at a public utility where he was asked to conduct a training
session. When management discovered that the course was to be taught by a woman
(with a Ph.D.), the general manager balked and said, "our guys don't like being told
things by women." Discrimination is not usually so obvious. For example, Edward Jones,
Jr., (1973) describes personally what it is like to be a black manager. Rather than overt
harassment or prejudice, he encountered naivete and a failure to acknowledge the real
differences between him and his white colleagues, and how these differences made him
feel constantly tense and ill at ease.

Other attitudes about diversity are expressed in organizational policy statements and
in practices that are taken for granted. For example, although many gay and lesbian
couples live comparable lives to heterosexual married couples, organizations generally
deny them dependent health benefits. The Lotus Corporation's recent move to recognize
gay and lesbian "spousal equivalents" in their benefit packages is symbolic of a culture
that supports a certain kind of diversity. Nonetheless, sexual preference is not as a rule
treated this way. Instead, gays and lesbians are seen as unprofessional or offensive (Woods,
1991).

In summary, one determinant of employee stress is organizational expectations about
the relative treatment of different groups of employees, and in particular the degree of
voice afforded to diverse groups. Members of groups who are not allowed to speak up will
be more likely to experience stress and a reduced quality of work life.

Expression of Emotion   One line of research (Rafaeli & Sutton, 1987) has shown that
certain industries and organizations require employees to hide their true feelings and to
display only emotions that are part of their work role. For example, flight attendants are
expected to be cheery, bill collectors hostile, funeral directors sad. Organizations reinforce
these emotional expectations through their recruitment practices, their socialization
efforts, and their offers of rewards and punishments (Hochschild, 1979). As pressure for
improved customer service increases (see Chapter 1), more companies are following the
lead of Disney and Nordstrom's in training their employees to communicate good cheer
to customers.

The organization can reap benefits from these canned emotional displays in the form
of greater customer satisfaction, increased sales, and repeat business. The effect on
individuals is less clear, however. At one extreme, Arlie Hochschild (1979) has argued
that emotional labor is detrimental to psychic health, and she uses flight attendants as
an example:

A young businessman said to a flight attendant, "Why aren't you smiling?" She put her
tray back on the food cart, looked him in the eye, and said, "I'll tell you what. You

smile first, then I'll smile." The businessman smiled at her. "Good," she replied. Now freeze and hold that smile for fifteen hours" (Hochschild, 1983, p. 127).

Others have argued that simulating and disguising one's real emotions at work is both necessary and at times advantageous. For a food server, for example, the payoff in tips is often worth the feigned goodwill. Among physicians, the ability to retain some emotional detachment is one of the first aspects of socialization and key to personal well-being and professional success (cf., Rafaeli & Sutton, 1987).

Katherine Miller, Jim Stiff, and Beth Ellis (1988) provide one of the more sophisticated analyses of the relationship between the expression of emotions and employee stress and burnout among human services workers. They maintain that because of the lopsided nature of the caregiver-patient relationship, the caregiver (e.g., nurse, physician, social worker) must be careful to distinguish between two different ways of communicating emotional support, namely, emotional contagion and empathic concern. When caregivers communicate empathic concern, they are showing concern for the other person, but they do not themselves experience the same feelings as the patient. Emotional contagion, or the vicarious experience of the patient's emotional turmoil, is very different, and is much more likely to lead to stress and burnout (Maslach, 1982). Research by Miller, Stiff, and Ellis (1988) supports the idea that to remain effective, caregivers must develop "a stance in which concern for another can be held independent of emotional involvement" (p. 262).

In summary, while certain organizations have specific expectations for employee displays of emotions that may be different from an employee's real feelings, the research findings on the importance of this practice are mixed. Some have shown a negative personal impact, whereas others have shown neutral or even positive consequences for the employee.

Job Stressors

In one respect, the kinds of jobs that lead to stress flow directly from the characteristics of organizations and their environments. For example, a restaurant chain that goes out of its way to meet customers' special needs but doesn't value employee participation in decisions is likely to design jobs that are hard to take. Nevertheless, at least three relatively independent dimensions of jobs make a difference in employee quality of work life: work load, role stress, and job characteristics.

Work Load   Work load can be regarded in several different ways. Quantitatively, it can refer to the number of projects or processes an employee is responsible for over a given period of time. Qualitatively, while the amount of work might not be overwhelming, a newcomer in an organization might balk at the complexity of a task and feel that he or she doesn't yet have the training or experience to complete it successfully. Work load, then, refers to either "too much" or "too difficult," and it has been linked to a number of symptoms of stress (cf. Miller et al., 1990).

In the final analysis, work load is a highly subjective concept and depends on an employee's capacity (Farace, Monge, & Russell, 1977). For example, a waiter in a busy restaurant most likely faces overload, especially on Saturday night—but the actual level of overload is relative to his or her serving ability. For a physically coordinated person with a good memory and decent interpersonal skills, waiting tables can be rewarding and even "easy." For a person lacking this capacity, the job can be nearly impossible.

Work overload can be addressed in numerous ways and can potentially be altered. One method is to do a manpower analysis as a means of determining how many hours it takes to do a specific job and then staffing to reduce the load to a manageable point. Another approach is to conduct a work flow analysis that identifies which operations within a total work process are redundant. This analysis can also be used to "level the load" or "balance the line" in a company. For example, if it takes longer to cook food than it does to take orders, hostesses in restaurants may decide to slow down the rate at which people are seated to even out the load in the kitchen. Alternatively, the inflow of customers can be kept constant, but waiters can assist in food preparation as a way of leveling the load between them and the cooks.

Finally, an individual's capacity does not necessarily stay constant. A primary purpose of college and professional school is to expand the individual's capacity for handling workload in order to enhance abilities to deal with higher levels of rate, volume, and complexity.

Role Stress   Employees can often cope with overload as long as they have a clear idea of what they are supposed to be doing. Without clear direction, however, even simple jobs become stressful. Role stress can be defined as the tension that results from unclear or conflicting expectations about job duties. It has many causes, including a supervisor who is unable to clearly spell out the employee's responsibilities; a supervisor who himself has not received clear expectations from his or her boss; or conflicting directions from two different people, each of whom has a different idea of what his or her subordinate's job is (e.g., two bosses in a matrix organization). Research has linked conclusively role stress to work-related stress in general (cf. Miller et al., 1990).

Job Characteristics   Human experience with work activities can be placed on a continuum from boredom to anxiety (Csikszentmihalyi, 1990). At one extreme, the individual is bored when a job is insufficiently challenging. At the other pole, too much variety or too many challenges make the employee anxious and fearful of failure. According to psychologist Mihalyi Csikszentmihalyi, the best jobs fall midway between these two extremes, and are various and challenging enough to require close attention. But they are not so demanding as to greatly exceed an employee's ability to perform. When a balance between boredom and anxiety is reached, the individual may experience "flow" or "jamming"—a loss of self-consciousness in the joy of performance (Eisenberg, 1990).

Much of the research on improving employee quality of work life has focused on the specific design of jobs (cf. Altman, Valenzi, and Hodgetts, 1985, pp. 384–424). The overriding conclusion of this research has been that simply expanding an individual's responsibility (i.e., job enlargement) is not sufficient to improve quality of work life and reduce stress. Instead, a total set of job characteristics—variety, task identity, task significance, autonomy, and feedback—should be altered to achieve job *enrichment* (Hackman & Suttle, 1977).

The job characteristics model is presented in Figure 7.2 on page 216. *Variety* refers to the degree to which the job requires the employee to use different talents and skills. *Identity of the task* is the extent to which the job allows an employee to complete a whole piece of work (as opposed to a part or component). *Significance of the task* is the degree

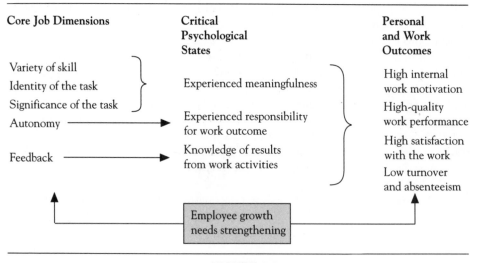

FIGURE 7.2

The Job Characteristics Model of Work Motivation

SOURCE: Adapted from J. Richard Hackman and J. Lloyd Suttle, eds., *Improving Life At Work: Behavioral Science Approaches to Organizational Change* (Santa Monica, Calif.: Goodyear Publishing Co., 1977), p. 129.

to which the job has an impact on other people's lives. *Autonomy* is the degree of freedom or control an employee has in deciding how to schedule and perform the work. Finally, *feedback* is the degree of communication provided to the employee about the results of his or her work activities.

Taken together, a focus on these core job characteristics reflects a view of human behavior that values the individual's need and desire for a sense of meaningful, responsible involvement in organizational dialogue. To the extent that jobs are designed with these factors in mind, we can expect certain critical psychological states to be attained—a greater sense of meaningfulness and responsibility, which in turn should lead to greater work satisfaction, motivation, and performance (Hackman & Oldham, 1975). To the extent that they are not achieved, increased stress, burnout, absenteeism, and turnover can be expected.

Altman, Valenzi, and Hodgetts (1985) offer five specific suggestions for the enrichment of jobs, namely:

1. *Combine tasks.* For example, if a car salesperson makes the initial sale and then someone else in the office follows up to check satisfaction, the two jobs could be combined so that the salesperson handles the whole transaction. This improves perceptions of task identify and variety.

2. *Form natural work groups.* Instead of placing typists in a separate work pool, each one can be assigned to a specific department so that they can be part of a task team that routinely works together. This provides both greater task identity and improved visibility to the results of one's work and one's impact on others.

3. *Establish customer contact.* Wherever possible, employees should have a direct rela-

tionship with the customer, which improves autonomy and provides direct and often dramatic feedback.

4. *Delegate decision making.* Information should be pushed down to the lowest level of the organization, restoring to the job greater discretion over schedules, work methods, training, and so on. Additional authority should be granted, and individuals should be provided with detailed financial information about the "big picture" and the effects of their decisions. One food manufacturer provides computer terminals that employees can check each day for a report on their productivity.

5. *Open feedback channels.* All the natural forms of feedback—between work groups, from the customer, and from the work processes themselves—should be allowed to flow unimpeded. At the same time, performance feedback should be provided continuously, and not be limited to annual performance appraisals.

Notice that most of these suggestions emphasize changes in communication, with the overriding goal being that of increased personal control or autonomy over work processes. Of all the job characteristics, autonomy is perhaps the most important contributor to reduced stress and improved quality of work life. Seeing oneself as effective, resourceful, responsible, and trusted by others is a key way to inhibit job stress (Jackson, 1983; Karasek, 1979; Luhmann & Albrecht, 1990).

RAA Delegation   From a managerial viewpoint, autonomy may be encouraged through RAA delegation; that is, employees should be encouraged to assume Responsibility, Authority, and Accountability. When a supervisor asks a junior engineer to design a new product, she should also give him the responsibility and authority to accomplish that task; the junior employee should not have to fight with others for resources and information or keep running back to her for approval. If he doesn't have the authority, he will feel a lack of autonomy. By the same token, the supervisor's responsibility is to provide the big picture—detailing specific objectives and accountabilities. For example, however he designs the product, it needs to meet certain standards (e.g., it must be done by next month; it must be designed to a fixed cost).

RAA delegation gives people the authority and autonomy to do a job their way, and at the same time holds them accountable for specific performance goals. It represents one secret of contemporary management, and it is what Peters and Waterman (1982) called "managing the loose-tight paradox." Indeed, it is one way in which we can achieve autonomy within a capitalist system. The forces of creativity and coordination, of creativity and constraint, are always at odds with one another, and no company can give employees so much autonomy that the big picture and performance requirements are lost. At the same time, continued obsession with the opposite extreme (i.e., don't trust employees, "I'm not paying you to think") will be similarly fatal. Instead, "just enough" autonomy is required both to promote positive work experience and to improve productivity through high involvement.

Having said all this, we should recognize that competitive pressures often work against empowerment and job enrichment. Specifically, some manufacturing organizations have reverted to scientific management as a way of coping with pressures to deliver higher quality at lower costs. Fierce global competition has caused many organizations to simplify jobs into the smallest possible functional activities, which in turn can be done by just about anyone, regardless of skill or training. One manufacturing manager boasts that it takes only three days to train someone to do any assembly job in his factory. Consequently, he can hire the least skilled employees and pay them the lowest possible wage. In California, in addition to a dramatic reduction in the total number of manufacturing jobs, the nature of the jobs has changed as well, from complex, $14 an hour assembly work to $7 an hour repetitive, simple work. This may make sense as a short-term business strategy (it is pro-profits, for sure), but what does it do to the people whose jobs are now routine, devoid of variety, and lacking in task identity, autonomy, and significance? In the long run the almost inevitable outcome will be increased stress and decreased motivation and productivity.

Individual Stressors

The causes of stress on the job sometimes have more to do with an individual's personality, life events, and communication abilities than with the organization or job itself.

Personality   Workaholics are people who never stop working—not to eat, vacation, or socialize. Even when the absolute amount of work in an organization decreases, workaholics can be counted on to volunteer for new assignments. Workaholism may be an attempt to avoid other parts of life that are stressful (e.g., family), but it can also reflect the hard-driving, competitive, and continually active personality—commonly called the Type A personality.

Comparisons of Type A and Type B personalities show that Type B personalities are less driven than Type A. In the long term, Type A behavior is dangerous because individuals with this orientation tend to sacrifice all other life pursuits to their goals. "In addition to competing with others, they constantly compete with themselves, setting high standards of productivity that they seem driven to maintain. They tend to feel frustrated in the work situation, irritable with the work efforts of subordinates, and misunderstood by superiors" (Burke, Weir, & Duwors, 1979, p. 57).

Some researchers, rather than focus on the negative personality characteristics that lead to stress, are more interested in how to stay healthy under stress and have developed the idea of hardiness (Kobasa, Maddi, & Kahn, 1982). The hardy individual is more likely to see bad news and negative events as opportunities or challenges. This research suggests that hardy individuals (who feel committed and in control of their lives and welcome change) will fare better under stress than will their less hardy counterparts.

Most dysfunctional personality patterns are related in some way to low self-esteem. Personality differences at work may be thought of in many ways, but we have found sense of self—the extent to which a person knows their strengths and weaknesses, likes and dislikes, is the clearest predictor of quality of work experience, both for the individual and for others around them. As Warren Bennis found in his study of the great leaders, they above all knew themselves and they resisted being seduced by what others felt they ought to be doing.

A final aspect of personality that affects quality of work life is the management of attention (Larkey, 1980; March & Olsen, 1976). People come to organizations with different attention habits, which in turn have an impact on their experience of work. In contrast to other animals, humans are drawn by the nature of language and consciousness to focus on the past and the future, often to the exclusion of the present. At work, this may mean holding a grudge, regretting a business decision, hoping or planning for a certain level of sales, anticipating catastrophic changes in the marketplace—none of which may be happening at the moment.

While there is no doubt a place for ruminations and speculations about past and future, perhaps more critical to success today is the ability to adapt, cope, react to and enjoy the moment. In the past employees knew there were calmer, cushier times ahead if they were successful; in postmodern organizations there is no corner office or "back to normal," no pot of gold at the end of the rainbow, only learning to enjoy driving in the rain.

The implication of all this is that the most functional attitude toward work—whether it be window-cleaning or running a midsized company—must include a capacity to inhabit and appreciate the moment, to pay attention to what is going on *right now*. Work that is most involving reduces self-consciousness and approximates optimal experience (Csikszentmihalyi, 1990; Eisenberg, 1990). Yet this kind of involvement is exceedingly difficult to obtain. The difficulty causes many managers to live in an environment of "avoided tests" (Weick, 1979) wherein they fail to seek out critical feedback about ongoing progress and operations. Attention and feedback on a moment-to-moment basis are central to both sanity and success in a turbulent world.

Life Events   Some causes of stress at work have little to do with work at all, but can be traced instead to events in an individual's personal life. This set of concerns is becoming more salient given the changes in values regarding work discussed in Chapter 1. For example, family problems—especially marital separation or divorce and a sick child—can significantly increase an employee's stress. A second source of stress is relocation, which commonly affects managers on the way up the organizational ladder. A third is financial problems, especially during tight economic times. Overextended credit, increasing bills, costs of a child's education, or a laid-off spouse can all increase stress. In general, these extraorganizational factors underscore the humanness of the human beings who work and emphasizes that the boundaries between work and nonwork are permeable. Rather than being "contained" in any one organization, all people are only "partially included" in any single organization or group (Weick, 1979).

Communication Style and Skill   A person's willingness and ability to communicate can also affect his or her degree of stress and overall quality of life. People who are shy and afraid to communicate with others are also most stressed and least likely to do well in many organizational settings (Phillips, 1991). Similarly, people who are rated as competent communicators and who are predisposed to communicate are also evaluated more positively and are in general more successful at work (Monge et al., 1982).

Certain communication skills help an employee to cope with work. An interesting parallel to the work on Type A personality discussed earlier is the recent research contrasting assertive with argumentative style (Infante et al., 1984). Assertiveness, the ability to clearly state a position without either hedging or attacking the other person, is associated with positive impressions and overall quality of work experience. Argumentative people, on the other hand, are more aggressive, insecure, and less likely to be well regarded or to be happy at work.

Finally, another specific communication skill that inhibits stress at work is the ability to exhibit empathic concern (Miller et al., 1990). As discussed earlier, inherent in many jobs is a fine line between showing concern for a client's problems and getting caught up in the client's emotional state—that is, emotional contagion. The ability to be empathic and at the same time retain emotional distance is both a learnable skill and a key to quality of work life in jobs that make high emotional demands on employees.

NEW DIRECTIONS FOR WORK ORGANIZATION

The challenge of improving the quality of work life and of organizational dialogue is complex and is not easily met. Nonetheless, there are myriad approaches to this problem, each one contingent on how the problem is defined, that is, on the questions that get asked.

For example, the current problem can be defined in terms of the individual's lack of coping skills. From this perspective, the employees' resistance to cooperation, along with job stress and its associated disorders, stems either from their lack of knowledge of how to cooperate or their lack of desire to do so. These people can learn coping strategies. (For a list of coping strategies, see Table 7.3). Although most of these strategies are to some degree effective for the individual, they are only one way of telling the story.

A second way to approach the problems of arrested dialogue and negative quality of work life is to redesign jobs and organizations. As we discussed earlier, a tremendous amount of effort is expended today on job enrichment, teamwork, and constructing the empowering organization. These approaches all focus on redesigning work and shaping organizational culture in ways that are more favorable to employees.

Yet a third approach is to tackle these issues at the societal level. In a capitalist society any individual or organization has only limited means at hand to buffer its employees from the effects of the marketplace. Although they are often viewed as malicious and unfeeling, most senior managers who make decisions that hurt employees do so at the urging of shareholders, without whose approval they themselves would be unemployed. In many cases, the employee's misery is due not to any individual or organization, but rather to the rules of the game. Perhaps the best way to make lasting changes in the employee's quality of work life is to review some of the underlying assumptions of capitalist society.

Peak Performance

But work *can* be more than an endless source of stress. Taking a highly optimistic view, writers such as Mihalyi Csikszentmihalyi and Charles Garfield have made extensive studies of what makes peak performance possible at work. For them, simply meeting needs is not enough; to feel fully alive at work, certain social and psychological conditions must be met. Furthermore, these conditions may not necessarily be at the expense of profits; that is, peak performance for individuals may not be inconsistent with peak organizational performance.

A similar line of research and practice deals with the creation of self-directed work teams (Willens et al., 1991). The idea behind these teams is to remove away as many obstacles as possible from a team's ability to make the decisions necessary to do a superior job. The concept is gaining acceptance slowly because of management's fears and, in

TABLE 7.3
STRATEGIES DESIGNED TO COPE
WITH STRESS

Physical maintenance strategies
  Attention to diet and nutrition
  Required amounts of sleep
  Exercise
  Participation in leisure and recreational
    activities

Internal assistance strategies
  Relaxation response
  Biofeedback
  Meditation

Personal organization strategies
  Stress planning
  Delegate responsibility
  Choose or alter the work environment
  Engage in creative problem solving and
    decision making
  Set goals
  Manage time
  Manage conflict
  Restructure jobs
  Use self-assessment measures

Outside assistance strategies
  Psychoanalysis
  Stress counseling
  Employee development programs
  Behavior-modification techniques

Situational and support group strategies
  Assertiveness training and role playing
  Development of supportive relationships
  Avoidance of substance abuse

SOURCE: Sailer, Schacter, & Edwards, 1982.

some cases, justifiable concerns about what decisions teams of workers can and should make. The Toyota/General Motors joint venture in Fremont, California, New United Motors Manufacturing, Inc., (NUMMI) is often cited as a good example of self-directed work teams. Even at NUMMI, however, employees cannot cross certain boundaries pertaining to accountabilities, safety rules, and personnel.

Finally, Eisenberg (1990) devoted a paper to the preconditions and characteristics of "jamming" experiences—which are moments of fluid behavioral coordination that reflect both peak experience for participants and peak performance for the group. Two critical implications for practice have to do with *staffing* and *risk*. Jamming requires that team members be of comparable skill. One's quality of work life is directly affected by the relative abilities of the people with whom one works most closely. The more comparable the skill levels, the more positive the experience. With regard to risk, jamming cannot be engineered. Rather, it requires a combination of practice and surrender—a willingness to get ready to perform, but then to release control to fate and the group process.

SUMMARY

This chapter is a call for understanding the individual experience of work. We began with an exploration of the process of organizational acculturation. We next examined cooperation and resistance, and the attitudes and conditions that lead to the development of these reactions. Finally, we identified alternatives to the current system, new directions that organizations might take to improve the employee's quality of work life. In each case, communication figured prominently in the creation of an organizational environment in which individuals feel supported and valued, and whose jobs afford a good measure of variety, significance, freedom, and control. If there is one overarching trend, it is one leading to greater employee voice, which should not only improve quality of life but should also help organizations become more productive.

CASE STUDY
The Case of the Secretive Fisherman

Tom Douglas lacked one course in his degree program in business administration, so he didn't graduate from the local college. This fact did not bother him.

Tom Douglas also turned down four offers in the past five years for promotion to supervisor, promotions that would have taken him out of his Sunshine Snacks delivery van and put him into a nice office making more money working a regular 9 to 5 job. With a secretary. And an expense account. These facts also did not bother him.

But they do bother his regional manager, Renee Brown. In fact, these facts bother Renee Brown primarily because she cannot understand it. She asks him about it, regularly. All Tom says is, "I like my job. I do it well. Don't ask me to give up what I like to do for something I know I won't like. Please." This is as far as the conversation ever goes. Renee doesn't push it; Tom doesn't volunteer any other information. Viewed one way, she tells you, she should be glad to have someone as dedicated and reliable as Tom working for her in the delivery van. But, she adds, Tom is almost a college graduate and is very bright; his talents could be put to better use in the office. At least this is how she sees it. It is also true that Renee doesn't understand how a guy like Tom, with a wife at home and two small children, could turn down the money.

You are a friend of Renee's, and a friend of a friend of Tom's. The irony is that even though you don't know Tom, you know why Tom won't accept the promotion. It has nothing to do with money. Or a secretary and an expense account. It has a lot to do, however, with the reason he didn't graduate from college. And that reason is simple: fishing. Specifically, bass fishing.

Your friend who is Tom's friend told you all about it. It is the best kept secret in town, and one that you wouldn't have found out about, except by accident. Which is how it happened.

The truth is, Tom Douglas is a trophy bass fisherman. He enters tournaments all over the South and has won his share of prizes, including $25,000 last year in cash. The amazing thing is that Tom can enter tournaments precisely *because* he drives a Sunshine Snacks delivery van, and can map his own routes and schedules and deliveries at his own pace. A lot of his customers know that he will come out early in the morning or late at night to keep them well stocked, as long as he can fish during the daylight hours on tournament weeks. Tom's personal dream is to win enough tournaments to gain a corporate sponsorship: with the sponsorship, he could quit his job and fish full-time.

What does fishing have to do with his not graduating from college? As it turns out, the only course he lacks is only taught during the Spring semester at the local college, and it meets only on Thursday evenings. Thursday evenings are registration times for bass tournaments, and many tournaments begin on Thursday nights. Besides, if he missed class because of a conflict with a bass fishing tournament, well, as you might imagine, his professor would not accept his reason as a legitimate excuse. So, rather than give up what is most important to him, he chose not to graduate. He used to hope that eventually the business administration department would change the course time so he could graduate, but now he realizes that if he graduated Renee would just lean on him even more to take the supervisory job.

You don't fish much, and never seriously. At first Tom's situation seemed somewhat odd, if not downright absurd. But you have come to realize that this attitude is largely unfair. After all, who are you to pass judgment on the quality or meaning of another person's personal experiences? If Tom loves fishing, so be it. But you are an organizational consultant, and it seems to you that there might be another solution to this problem, one that could work to everyone's advantage.

Corporate sponsorship. That is what Tom wants. With it, he could enter the big money tournaments, play in the big bass fishing game he dreams about. And what fisherman have you ever seen who didn't eat Sunshine Snacks? What if you could convince Renee to offer Tom a corporate sponsorship for his fishing talents?

Your task, as you see it, is to find the right arguments to convince Renee to do precisely that. Given what you have learned about personal experience and the need to balance creativity with constraint in organizations, what might your argument be?

8

RELATIONAL
CONTEXTS FOR
ORGANIZATIONAL
COMMUNICATION

Influential managers are ones who have developed and maintained a balanced web of relationships with the boss, subordinates, peers, and other key players; influence in each of these directions is banked for leverage to accomplish goals in the other directions. If knowledge alone and positional authority alone will not accomplish the manager's job, those who would be influential must fill power gaps with webs of influence.

—*Keys & Case, 1990, p. 49*

Cathy Bryson has been director of marketing for Ajax Advertising, Inc. for two years. Before that, she worked 15 years at Astro Toys. When Astro went bankrupt, she decided to try advertising. Because of the speed with which she had to change jobs, Cathy took a large pay cut to come to Ajax. Management at the agency had high hopes for her future with the company.

Two years later, Cathy is depressed because she doesn't "fit in" at Ajax. She feels that everything takes more effort than it should. It's hard for her to imagine herself on any kind of career path, or even to envision the next job after her current one. Still, she doesn't want to leave Ajax. She feels it will be hard to get a comparable position elsewhere, and she won't be fully vested in the company's stock ownership program for three more years. So she's decided to stick it out but wants some advice on how to make her work life better.

Her adviser starts by asking questions about her performance as a marketer, company sales figures since she arrived, and so on. The answers she gives speak well for her technical effectiveness. Her most recent ad campaigns are also excellent. So what's the problem? Offhandedly, she admits to having "a little problem" in getting along with people: they see her as cold, aloof, and uncaring, even snobby. Her subordinates, peers, boss, and even customers share this perception. But if her job performance is superior, why should these interpersonal problems matter?

This chapter explores the role and functions of interpersonal relationships at work, and in doing so addresses the question posed by Cathy's situation. Why do relationships at work matter? The answers depend on one's perspective. Recall from Chapter 3 that classical theorists were concerned mainly with formal reporting relationships, and saw informal communication as dysfunctional and an obstacle to work. In contrast, the human relations and human resources schools defended the importance of the informal organization, and viewed relationships as crucial to employee well-being and productivity, as well as to organizational innovation and adaptation. While the predictions of the human relations school linking informal relationships and productivity were not supported by research, the subject of informal work relationships has remained on the research agenda since the Hawthorne studies. Advocates of institutional, systems, and cultural perspectives all see interpersonal relationships as critical both to the character and success of organizations.

THE CHANGING ROLE OF RELATIONSHIPS AT WORK

Recent changes in organizations and their environments (detailed in Chapter 1) have made interpersonal relationships more crucial than ever. To remain competitive, organizations must be flexible; strict rules and procedures are a hindrance in turbulent times. Achieving this flexibility requires responsive informal systems for sharing information and getting work done. Without the time to formalize these relationships, their effectiveness depends on the trust that develops over time between people.

Put simply, good interpersonal relationships at work are no longer a luxury but a *bona fide* qualification for effective job performance. From the organization's perspective, then, one answer to the question of the importance of relationships at work is that without relationships, work will simply not get done, or will be done slowly and poorly. From the employee's perspective, positive work relationships provide social support and a sense of identification with and participation in the organizational dialogue (see Chapter 7). People who are socially isolated at work often feel voiceless, which over time has negative consequences both for them and for the organization.

In all these ways, relationships matter. Management theorists are clear in their declaration of the new centrality of interpersonal relationships in organizations. Rosabeth Moss Kanter (1989), for example, wrote that the nature of managerial work changed fundamentally in the 1980s—from an emphasis on planning, organizing, and coordinating to a focus on communication. Specifically, successful managers today put less emphasis on formal position power and more on establishing informal influence through networks of relationships.

Taking a similar approach, Bernard Keys and Thomas Case (1990) argue that "influence must replace the use of formal authority in relationships with subordinates, peers, outside contacts, and others on whom the job makes one dependent" (p. 38). Since positional authority is no longer sufficient to get the job done, a web of influence or a balanced web of relationships must be developed. "Recently managers have begun to view leadership as the orchestration of *relationships* between several different interest groups—superiors, peers, and outsiders, as well as subordinates. Effectiveness at leadership requires balance in terms of efforts spent in building relationships in these four directions" (Keys & Case, 1990, p. 39).

Finally, building on Kanter and on Keys and Case, Patricia Riley and Eric Eisenberg (1992) have developed the ACE Model of Management Competencies, which they have used in consultation to organizations. According to this model, effective managers excel in three areas, each of which is explicitly communicative: Advocacy, or making winning arguments to the boss; Cross-functional communication, forging connections across departmental and professional boundaries; and Empowerment of subordinates. (These types of communication are discussed in detail later in this chapter.)

In summary, the role of relationships in organizations has moved from a perspective that viewed them solely as a conduit for information (or as unnecessary "socializing") to a position that they are an important strategic resource for amassing influence, achieving goals, and obtaining social support. Furthermore, no single type of relationship is most critical, but a variety of different kinds of contacts (i.e., with subordinates, co-workers, customers) are understood to contribute to an individual and organization's effectiveness.

COMMUNICATING WITH SUPERIORS

Attitudes concerning how to communicate with the boss have changed drastically over the years. In this section, we first discuss the concept of semantic-information distance, or the inherent differences in perceptions between superiors and subordinates in an organizational hierarchy. Second, we explain the most common communication problem associated with upward communication, upward distortion of information. Third, we explore the idea of "managing your boss," of how subordinates can communicate strategically with their supervisors. Finally, we discuss *mystery and transgression*, the process by which individuals both define and resist taking their "proper" place in the status hierarchy.

Semantic-information Distance

The superior-subordinate relationship is one of the most researched in organizational communication. This research reveals that supervisors spend from one-third to two-thirds of their time communicating with subordinates, and most of this communication is verbal and in person (cf. Dansereau & Markham, 1987). Given all of this communication, we might expect supervisors and subordinates to think similarly about a number of much-talked about issues.

Quite the contrary: supervisors and subordinates hold dramatically different perceptions of relevant organizational issues—so much so that they sometimes seem to exist in different worlds (cf. Jablin, 1979). This gap in understanding between superiors and subordinates is called semantic-information distance. Issues on which there is often disagreement (and hence high semantic-information distance) include degree of participation in decision making (Harrison, 1985) and the subordinate's basic job duties (Jablin, 1979). In addition, superiors and subordinates may have differing perceptions of communication itself. Fred Jablin's (1979) review of this research comes to the following conclusions:

1. Superiors believe they communicate with subordinates more frequently than they actually do.

2. Superiors believe they communicate with subordinates more effectively than they actually do.
3. Subordinates believe that superiors are more open to communication than they actually are.
4. Subordinates believe that they have more persuasive ability than superiors believe they do.

Some degree of semantic-information distance between superiors and subordinates is a natural result of hierarchy. What is disturbing, however, is not the distance itself but the widespread lack of awareness of these differences or gaps. In other words, not only do supervisors and subordinates have different perceptions of key issues, but they are most likely not even aware of these differences. Consequently, miscommunication is rampant. The boss assumes that an employee "understood" what she said, so she never tests this assumption. The gap isn't discovered until much later, once costly damage may have already been done.

The realization that managers and employees are not always aware of the degree of their differences has led to research on *meta-perceptions* (e.g., the supervisor's perception of the subordinate's perception) and *co-orientation* (Farace, Monge, & Russell, 1977). Co-orientation refers to the degree of alignment of perceptions in a dyad, and includes not only agreement (e.g., how similar are our perceptions of our product), but also accuracy (e.g., how well do I *know* how *you feel* about our product?) and perceived agreement (e.g., how similar do I *think we feel* about our product?). Of these three kinds of co-orientation, perceived agreement has proven most important to superior-subordinate relationships. While a superior and subordinate may agree or disagree on an issue, and be more or less accurate in predicting what the other believes, the internal *perception* that employee and boss think alike leads to more positive evaluations of the relationships overall (cf. Eisenberg, Monge, & Farace, 1984).

Although shared understanding is crucial in some situations—as in high-risk operations such as air-traffic control—in general it is more important that the individuals in the relationship perceive themselves as being in relative agreement. From the organization's perspective, low levels of agreement and accuracy can be disastrous, and leave important misunderstandings unrecognized and unaddressed.

Upward Distortion

Semantic-information distance is a natural outgrowth of different job responsibilities and positions in the hierarchy. A more purposeful attempt to create gaps in understanding is upward distortion (Roberts & O'Reilly, 1974). People in positions of low power frequently distort the information they send upward, particularly when it reflects negatively on themselves (cf. Dansereau & Markham, 1987). At least four common types of distortion have been identified (Fulk & Mani, 1986):

1. Gatekeeping, when not all of the information that has been received is passed upward.
2. Summarization, or changing the emphasis given to various parts of the message.
3. Withholding, or keeping things from superiors by being selective.
4. General distortion, or wholesale changing of the message to suit one's own motives or agenda.

Some of these types of distortion are not necessarily a problem and can be seen as part of a supervisor's job. For example, in traditional hierarchies managers expect their subordinates to communicate selectively those issues that are deserving of attention at that next higher level. The assumption is that the individual in the lower position can routinely address the issues that are not raised. Other kinds of distortion, however, can be very dangerous. Withholding and general distortion, though potentially innocuous (e.g., in the communication of personal information unrelated to your job) can also be quite devastating. Examples include the failure to report a safety hazard (as occurred in the launch of the space shuttle *Challenger*) or the selective reporting of negative financial information to superiors.

Subordinates who are ambitious and have high security needs are more likely to distort the information they give to their bosses. Obviously, distortion is more prevalent with messages that make the subordinate look bad. But the motivation to distort derives largely from the subordinate's perception of his or her relationship with the boss. Subordinates withhold information from supervisors whom they do not trust (cf. Jablin, 1985) or when they see their supervisors themselves actively withholding information (Fulk & Mani, 1986). Paul Krivonos (1982) summarizes this body of research:

1. Subordinates tend to distort information upward in a manner that pleases their superiors.
2. Subordinates tend to tell their superiors what they want them to know.
3. Subordinates tend to tell their superiors what they think they want to hear.
4. Subordinates tend to give their superiors information that reflects favorably on themselves and/or does not reflect negatively on themselves.

That issues and events are filtered and distorted as they are passed "up the ladder" is really not a surprising finding. What senior management finally hears is much attenuated and often very different from the original message. A management team may encourage its employees to "share bad news" about work processes, but generally employees remain reluctant to take the chance. Reducing upward distortion requires that upper management be willing to hear alternative versions and interpretations of reality, versions that may differ markedly from their own. The ability of managers to do their jobs depends almost entirely on the quality of the information they receive from others, and in particular from their subordinates.

One way senior management can fight upward distortion is MBWA—management by wandering around (Peters & Waterman, 1982). In this way, the manager can learn what is really happening in his or her organization. Better upward communication is also fostered by organizations that reward questions, suggestions, and innovations. The challenge in making such programs work is overcoming the employees' initial distrust that management will "shoot the messenger" for identifying a problem or giving bad news. Once trust is established, the benefits of reliable upward communication are immeasurable.

In companies where managers are authoritative and not communication-minded, employees quickly learn to filter the information they share with superiors. Fearing repercussions if they bring bad news, people who work in unsupportive climates fail to pass negative information upward. We spoke to a general manager at a hotel about reports from low-level employees that information they were sending up the chain of command was getting distorted or filtered. He looked us in the eye and said: "That's impossible. All my managers know if they ever did that they would be fired on the spot." What he considered to be his insurance against distortion was actually more of a guarantee that he would *never* be told the truth.

Managing Your Boss

Subordinates can use a variety of influence tactics to secure resources and maintain a positive relationship with the boss. A recent study of public sector supervisors revealed that quality superior-subordinate relations were also characterized by a high degree of upward influence (Waldera, 1988). But how is this informal influence accomplished?

David Kipnis and Stuart Schmidt's (1982) *Profile of Organizational Influence Strategies* identifies six dimensions of influence employees may use with their superiors: reason, friendliness, assertiveness, coalition building, appeal to higher authority, and bargaining. One early study revealed that friendly ingratiation (making the superior feel important) and developing rational plans (reason) were the two most frequently used tactics for influencing superiors (Kipnis, Schmidt, & Wilkinson, 1980). More recent work reinforces this basic finding but takes a closer look at the mixture of influence attempts used by employees on their managers (Kipnis, Schmidt, & Braxton-Brown, 1990). Employees use four very different approaches to get something from the boss:

1. Shotgun—The employee uses all available approaches.
2. Ingratiation—The employee is friendly and warm.
3. Tactician—The employee uses reason.
4. Bystander—The employee avoids all approaches in general.

Research by Keys and Case (1990) has further confirmed that rational explanation is the most frequently used type of upward influence. As a rule, rational explanations include some sort of formal presentation, analysis, or proposal. A host of other tactics, such as arguing without support, using persistence and repetition, threatening, and manipulation, were not found to be effective. In fact, subordinates who used these tactics with their bosses usually failed miserably (Keys & Case, 1990).

One final tactic linked with positive upward influence is personal communication. Vincent Waldron (1991) found that "by encouraging discussion of non-work issues, subordinates solidify friendship ties with supervisors while presumably adding stability and predictability to the formal authority relationship. . . . A history of such contacts may work to the advantage of the subordinate, by reducing the perceived 'riskiness' of upward influence attempts and other potentially threatening messages (e.g., complaints, protests)" (p. 300). Nevertheless, not all supervisors will respond positively to these informal advances. No one influence tactic will be superior in all situations; instead, the subordinate must learn to tailor his or her approach to the individual influence target and objective that is sought (Keys & Case, 1990).

Some writers envision the whole process of relating to one's boss as a sustained, strategic program for "managing up." In this view, the subordinate role can be perceived as a kind of performance. James Thompson (1967), an adherent of the institutional school, speaks of subordinate "dramaturgy," which involves, above all, making the boss look good. More specifically, John Gabarro and John Kotter (1980) provide a series of questions that subordinates must answer if they are to be successful in "managing up." At a minimum, these questions include knowing the boss's chief professional goals and objectives; personal goals; strengths and weaknesses; preferred style of working; and attitudes toward conflict. Gabarro and Kotter also maintain that subordinates should know their own answers to these questions, and try to foster a relationship that accommodates both individual needs and styles.

According to Riley and Eisenberg (1992), the primary skill individuals must cultivate in managing their boss is advocacy—the process of championing ideas, proposals, actions, or people to those above you in the organization. Advocacy requires learning how to read your superior's needs and preferences, and designing persuasive arguments that are most likely to accomplish your goals. The advocacy approach differs sharply from traditional views of superior-subordinate communication, which emphasize the importance of subordinate compliance and dramaturgy, of playing the good underling, and making your boss look good.

A number of factors are involved in becoming a successful advocate.

1. *Plan.* Impromptu appeals for resources or decisions tend to result in awkward silences, outbursts, or whining. You need to think through a strategy that will work.
2. *Determine why your boss should care to listen.* Even captive audiences have been known to zone out. Connect your argument to something that matters to your boss, like a key objective or personal value.
3. *Tailor your arguments to the boss's style and characteristics.* Your boss may find statistics to be persuasive or may respond well to a particularly poignant story; she may need to see detailed evidence or prefer to rely on you and the big picture. Adapt your evidence and appeal to those things that are persuasive to the boss, not those things that are persuasive to you.
4. *Assess prior technical knowledge.* Be careful not to assume too much about your boss's level of knowledge and vocabulary or jargon. If she does not understand your technical arguments, she will be put in an awkward position of having to ask an embarrassing question.
5. *Build coalitions.* Your arguments need the support of others in the organization. Your good reasons alone will rarely carry the day, but if you have the support of others, you will be more likely to prevail.
6. *Hone your communication skills.* An articulate, well-prepared presentation is critical when you are requesting support from your boss. Even the best ideas may not carry the day if they are presented in an unconvincing fashion.

Underlying each principle is one fundamental idea: that effective communication is always tailored to an audience. Too often employees are frustrated about their boss's unwillingness to go along with their ideas and requests, but fail to give even a thought to what it would really take to persuade him or her.

Mystery and Transgression

The superior-subordinate relationship is highly symbolic of the hierarchical distribution of power and status in most organizations. Hierarchy is inevitable in social relations and can be constructed out of a broad array of symbolic resources: age, gender, fashion, family background, kind of car driven, or school attended.

Hierarchies are created to make distinctions by those whose interests are served by the maintenance of those distinctions. For subordinates, the usual strategy is to satisfy superiors in order to symbolically move closer to them and in time to take their place. Many of the tactics and strategies described above are aimed at doing that. For superiors, keeping a distance from subordinates is valuable, since too much intimacy threatens to dissolve any legitimate sense of difference between the two parties. Kenneth Burke (1969) talked about this sense of difference between superiors and subordinates as a kind of mystery:

> Mystery arises at that point where different kinds of beings are in communication. In mystery there must be strangeness; but the estranged must also be thought of as in some way capable of communion. . . . The conditions of mystery are set up by any pronounced social distinctions, as between nobility and commoners, courtiers and kings, leader and people, rich and poor, judge and prisoner at the bar, superior race and underprivileged races or minorities. Thus even the story between the petty clerk and the office manager, however realistically told, draws upon the wells of mystery for its appeal (p. 115).

The traditional hierarchy works when subordinates buy into the mystery and pursue it up the organizational ladder. But as corporate executive/critical theorist Earl Shorris (1981) has pointed out, the secret is that there is no secret. Nevertheless, subordinates continue to believe that happiness is located at the next level of the hierarchy, despite considerable evidence to the contrary.

Sometimes, however, if only briefly, the fixed organizational hierarchy is turned upside down through transgression. Transgression occurs when a subordinate behaves like a superior and fails to acknowledge his or her proper place in the organization. Traditionally, transgression occurs under relatively safe conditions in organizations such as in comic skits or at office parties (Bakhtin, 1984). A major hotel in California has a monthly general meeting at which employees put on a humorous play. In the play, employees are cast as managers and satirize them mercilessly. This "controlled" transgression is tolerated, even encouraged, because if offers no real threat and may in some ways even serve to reinforce the status quo.

On the other hand, the movement toward empowerment and the general flattening of organizations reveals instances of transgression that are more serious and threatening to the status quo. As employees strive to forge a new, more equal partnership with management, many managers react with alarm, fearing a loss of authority, status, and, ultimately, identity. When the boss loses the ability to say "I am the one in charge here," what direction can he or she now take?

COMMUNICATING WITH SUBORDINATES

The question of the best way to communicate with subordinates is as old as the idea of hierarchy. A number of possible answers have been discussed in our review of the history of organizational theory. From the standpoint of classical theory, downward communication was to be formal, clear, and work-related. Human relations stressed supportive communication, while human resources emphasized the need for superiors to involve subordinates in decision making and innovation. And while systems and culture theories made no specific prescriptions about communicating with subordinates, critical and postmodern approaches have moved even further toward a general leveling of power and authority. So-called "subordinates" are afforded the resources and opportunities to construct legitimate identities that are as important to the organization as are those of their so-called "superiors."

This section focuses on five related aspects of communication with subordinates: openness, supportiveness, motivation, empowerment, and leadership.

Openness

Openness in superior-subordinate communication refers at a minimum to openness in message-sending and in message-receiving (Redding, 1972). According to Fred Jablin (1979), in an open communication relationship, "both parties perceive the other inter-actant as a willing and receptive listener and refrain from responses that might be perceived as providing negative relational or disconfirming feedback" (p. 1204). Openness has both a verbal and nonverbal dimension, in the form of facial expression, eye gaze, tone, and the like (Tjosvold, 1984). Numerous studies conducted by W. Charles Redding (1972) and his students at Purdue University revealed a positive relationship between supervisor openness and subordinate satisfaction with the relationship. Specific findings include:

1. The better supervisors tend to be more communication-minded. For example, they enjoy talking and speaking in meetings; they are able to explain instructions and policies; and they enjoy conversing with subordinates.
2. The better supervisors tend to be willing, empathic listeners; they respond under-standingly to so-called silly questions from employees; they are approachable; and they will listen to suggestions and complaints, with an attitude of fair consideration and willingness to take appropriate action.
3. The better supervisors tend (with some notable exceptions) to "ask" or "persuade" in preference to "telling" or "demanding."
4. The better supervisors tend to be sensitive to feelings. For example, they are careful to reprimand in private rather than in public.
5. The better supervisors tend to be more open in their passing along of information; they favor giving advance notice of impending changes and explaining the reasons behind policies and regulations (p. 433).

Many of these conclusions, drawn from work done in the 1960s, still apply. But later researchers have suggested that the concept of openness is more complex—there is, for example, a difference between disclosing feelings and talking candidly about work-related matters. Furthermore, the specific outcomes of openness are not easy to predict and can be counter to what might be expected. Eric Eisenberg and Marsha Witten (1987) identified three distinctly different types of openness: supportive listening; personal and nonpersonal disclosure; and relative degree of ambiguity of communication. Depending on the context in which a supervisor decides to be open, results can vary dramatically. Supervisors can be indiscreet, or insincere, or may make open disclosure a club they hold over subordinates, using it as a kind of public embarrassment or intimidation. Eisenberg and Witten argue that the role of openness in organizational communication needs to be reconsidered in light of these multiple definitions and contingent uses, and that the effectiveness of open communication depends on the intricacies of the communicative situation. Should supervisors be open in their communication with subordinates? As a general rule, probably yes, but this preferred bias toward openness should not override other concerns such as confidentiality, ethics, and tact.

The problem with the concept of open communication is that to some people it implies full disclosure and total honesty rather than a sensitivity to the nature of the context and the appropriate communication for any given situation. Open communication of the full disclosure kind is desired more for ideological reasons than for any significant evidence revealing its effectiveness (Bochner, 1982; Eisenberg, 1984). In contrast, the notion of supportive supervisory communication can be more useful in the actual practice of supervision.

Supportiveness

The main program of research dealing with supportive supervisory communication was presented by George Graen (1976). According to his theory of leader-member exchange (abbreviated LMX), supervisors discriminate in their supervisory behavior—different subordinates get different resources from supervisors—and leader-member roles are negotiated through communication in each superior-subordinate dyad. The two generic types of relationships between supervisors and subordinates are in-group and out-group. In-group relationships are "characterized by high trust, mutual influence, support, and formal/informal rewards" (Fairhurst & Chandler, 1989, p. 215). In contrast, out-group relationships are "characterized by the use of formal authority, low trust, support, and rewards" (Fairhurst & Chandler, 1989, p. 216).

Overall, in-group relationships are preferable for both individuals and organizations. In contrast to out-group exchanges, in-group exchanges are associated with greater member satisfaction, lower turnover, better member performance, and greater agreement about the severity and nature of job problems and involvement in decision making (Graen, Liden, & Hoel, 1982; Liden & Graen, 1980; Scandura, Graen, & Novak, 1986).

Graen's distinction focuses broadly on issues of trust and support, but does not prescribe open communication as the sole means for attaining this kind of relationship. Instead, supervisory communication is seen as an ongoing attempt to balance among multiple, competing relational, identity, and task goals (Dillard, Segrin, & Harden, 1989; Eisenberg, 1984). In other words, while certain types of communication might ensure subordinate compliance in performing a task (e.g., "Do it *my way* or else"), these same tactics might demoralize subordinates to the point that they lose involvement and commitment, or are overcome by stress. Effective supervisors strive to communicate in ways that simultaneously promote task accomplishment, show concern for the relationship, and demonstrate respect for the individual.

Nevertheless, little data exist on the specific ways this complex balance is achieved in real superior-subordinate communication. An exception is work by Gail Fairhurst and Theresa Chandler (1989), which extends LMX theory to examine specific conversations that constitute in- and out-group exchanges. In their analysis of a supervisor's interactions with three subordinates in a warehouse, Fairhurst and Chandler found consistency in the communication resources deployed within each type of relationship. In the in-group relationship, there was more influence by mutual persuasion—both parties challenged and disagreed with each other frequently. In addition, the subordinate in the in-group exchange was given greater freedom of choice than was available to other subordinates. In the out-group relationship, authority was imposed and suggestions from the subordinate were ignored. At the same time, a traditional chain-of-command reporting relationship was maintained.

Motivation

Motivation refers to "the degree to which an individual is personally committed to expending effort in the accomplishment of a specified activity or goal" (Kreps, 1991, p. 154). As explained in Chapter 7, a host of factors contribute to an employee's motivation to cooperate, only some of which relate to supervisory communication. This section focuses specifically on the role of supervisory communication in encouraging employee motivation. Communication functions in two ways to motivate employees. First, managers can provide information and feedback regarding tasks, goals, performance, and future directions. Second, managers can communicate consideration, encouragement, empathy, and concern. In both cases, the motivating effect comes from the manager's ability to endorse particular interpretations of reality through communication (Sullivan, 1988).

Three traditional process theories of employee motivation have been proposed: goal-setting, expectancy, and equity theory.

Goal-setting Theory   This theory, championed in the organizational behavior literature by Edwin Locke and Gary Latham (1979), maintains that an employee's conscious objectives are most likely to influence his or her performance. As a result, the theory suggests that supervisors assist subordinates in developing goals that are motivating. Some of the most important research findings in this area are as follows:

1. Setting clear and specific goals has a greater positive impact on performance improvement than does "do the best you can" goal setting.
2. Employee goals that are seen as difficult but attainable lead to higher performance than do easy goals, as long as the worker accepts the particular goals.
3. Support has been reported for the superiority, in terms of performance improvement, of participative goal setting over the use of assigned goals.
4. The use of frequent feedback in the goal-setting process brings about higher individual performance than when such feedback sessions are not employed.

Note that of these four conclusions, three deal squarely with issues of communication. To be motivating, goals must be clear and specific; they must be arrived at through a dialogue with employees; and feedback on performance against these goals must be frequent. The need for feedback (a concept from systems theory) is especially important and is well documented. It is nearly impossible for employees to feel motivated when they don't know what happens to their work when they are done with it, or how their efforts contribute to the success or failure of the company. Feedback is defined as "messages conveyed to a subordinate about his or her task performance" (Cusella, 1987). Subordinates who receive feedback from their superiors on progress toward goals tend to be more satisfied, perform better (Jablin, 1979), and are less likely to leave (Parsons, Herald, & Leatherwood, 1985).

A recent field experiment provides support for the importance of goal setting and feedback in shaping performance (Pritchard et al., 1988). Eighty Air Force employees who repaired electronic equipment and stored and distributed materials and supplies took part in the study. Productivity measures for the nine months prior to the study were compiled. For five months, employees were provided with monthly feedback on their productivity. For the next five months, employees working in groups set difficult but attainable goals for themselves. During this five-month feedback period, productivity improved, on average, 50 percent over the initial nine-month baseline. Improvements in morale were also recorded. These results support the positive motivational effects of setting measurable goals coupled with specific, immediate feedback about performance against these goals (Katzell & Thompson, 1990, p. 149).

Feedback on goals can take many forms; what is clear is that, to be effective, the feedback must be frequent and specific. Annual performance reviews, even when they are done conscientiously (and they almost never are) are inadequate for making a difference in employee behavior (Ilgen & Knowlton, 1980). Feedback about performance should be provided on an ongoing basis, but most managers tend to store up all their negative comments and talk about them only once a year (if at all). One manager we know leaves annual performance appraisal forms in his employees' desks after hours with an attached note: "See me if you have any questions." This is both cowardly and ineffective. The best time to receive corrective information about performance is in person and as soon as possible. The longer the wait, the less likely the feedback will impact behavior. Needless to say, a manager's ability to provide constructive feedback is highly dependent on the existence of clear goals to begin with. Without clear goals, the feedback is likely to come more as an unwelcome surprise than as useful information.

Not all feedback need be negative. Peters and Waterman (1982) have argued that the best managers "catch people doing things right." The degree to which people get formal or informal recognition and receive positive reinforcement for a job well done is an extremely important determinant of their work experience. Simply put, positive feedback makes people feel valued, and engenders job satisfaction, identification, and commitment to the company (cf. Larson, 1989).

Recently, some companies have begun building feedback into certain kinds of jobs through management information systems. At Frito-Lay's Cheetos and Doritos factory in California, for example, computer terminals in the packaging areas allow machine operators to receive instantaneous feedback about their day's performance. Available information includes the number of pounds of raw material used, how long the assembly line was out of commission for repair, and how many person hours were employed. According to one operator: "I think that people have more pride in their work now. We go to the computer at the end of the day and see how much we made or lost. If the numbers are good, we feel proud because we know we did it. If the numbers aren't good, we get with our team members and figure out what went wrong. Before, we seldom even saw the numbers. It's no wonder we weren't very interested in the business" (Grant, 1992, p. D7). This example highlights both the importance of clear goals and immediate feedback, and the increasingly popular tendency to shift the source of feedback from interpersonal communication to data coming out of the process itself through the use of computers.

Finally, because motivated subordinates hunger for feedback, and because most supervisors don't provide enough of it, subordinates will sometimes actively seek feedback rather than wait for it to be provided to them (Ashford & Cummings, 1983). The feedback-seeking process is not unlike the newcomer stage of assimilation discussed in Chapter 7, and especially in one respect—not wanting to look stupid or uninformed. "Feedback seekers may be faced with a conflict between the need to obtain useful information and the need to present a favorable image . . . impression management plays a key role in the feedback-seeking process" (Morrison & Bies, 1991, p. 523). Perhaps because both parties face the risk of embarrassment, a "silent conspiracy" exists between supervisors and subordinates. That is, supervisors are generally reluctant to give negative feedback, and subordinates generally avoid seeking it out (Larson, 1989).

Expectancy Theory   Initially developed by Victor Vroom (1964), expectancy theory makes three assumptions about human behavior. First, employees perceive a relationship between a specific work behavior and some kind of payoff. This relationship is called an *instrumentality*: behaving in a certain way is instrumental to getting the reward. Second, each reward or positive outcome has a *valence* associated with it, which refers to how much the individual wants to attain it. Third, employees perceive how likely it is that they will be able to succeed in performing the desired behavior. This degree of likelihood is called an *expectancy*.

Analysis of these factors shows that employees are most motivated when outcome valences are high (e.g., the payoff is a big raise, and they really need the money); expectancies are high (i.e., the employees feel they *can* perform the desired behavior); and instrumentalities are clear (i.e., employees understand what outcomes or rewards will follow from their performance).

When the expectancy model has been applied in real organizations, it has often led to improved situations for employees (Steers, 1981). From a communication perspective, the key to expectancy theory is the clear communication of instrumentalities to employees. Motivated employees are those individuals who know what the payoff for hard work will be.

A variation on expectancy theory is Robert House's (1971) popular path-goal theory. Whereas expectancy theory focuses on the performance-reward relationship, path-goal theory emphasizes the role managers can play in identifying relevant rewards and specifying the most likely path employees might take to attain them. A popular management tool based on path-goal theory is Management By Objectives (MBO) (Kreps, 1991). In MBO, supervisors and subordinates negotiate individual goals that are connected to agreed-upon rewards.

Equity Theory   Equity theory takes a different approach to employee motivation, focusing on the discrepancy employees may feel between the rewards they are receiving for their efforts when compared to their co-workers' level of work and level of rewards (Altman, Valenzi, and Hodgetts, 1985). When an employee feels that his reward-to-work ratio is less favorable than that of a co-worker (e.g., he receives fewer rewards but does more work), he may slow down and do less work, or at the very least experience dissatisfaction. Judgments of equity involve personal perceptions of fairness, which are largely shaped by communication. Communication by supervisors can affect perceptions of equity. For example, a manager may feel she is underpaid relative to her co-workers, but is incorrect (and doesn't know it) because of pay secrecy. Alternatively, a supervisor might explain why certain individuals don't make good comparisons for determining equity, because of their differing levels of education or skill.

Equity theory highlights the fact that the bottom line of employee performance and cooperation is ultimately highly subjective. A supervisor may strive to establish a supportive relationship with a subordinate, and the job and organization may be structured in ways that maximize the likelihood of identification and cooperation. However, individuals may still feel dissatisfied and unmotivated if they believe they are underrewarded relative to their level of effort. This conclusion recalls Elton Mayo's and Herbert Simon's initial reconceptualization of employee decision making. Far from being a rational calculation, the judgments and decisions that lead to variations in employee attitudes and performance are subjectively determined and heavily influenced by social information.

Finally, supervisors often attempt to motivate employees to perform through informal compliance-gaining tactics. Supervisors who accept and encourage subordinates with positive feedback are most likely to achieve both task compliance and subordinate satisfaction (cf. Daniels & Spiker, 1991). Recent work has investigated the choices of strategies used by superiors to influence subordinate behavior (Keys & Case, 1990). Rather than giving orders, managers

> often use the tactic of explaining (policies, tasks, benefits) or delegating assignments when attempting to influence subordinates. Frequently they showed confidence, encouragement, or support when trying to win subordinates over. The use of reason or facts often came in the form of a suggestion of a superior procedure or an example. Managers often counseled with subordinates or solicited their ideas to influence them (Keys & Case, 1990, pp. 41–42).

In dealing with chronically poor performers, these "friendlier" types of influence attempts may be avoided, or tried briefly and then discarded. In a study of bank managers' compliance-gaining choices (Fairhurst, Green, & Snavely, 1984), a discrepancy was found between how administrators said they dealt with problem employees, and what they actually did:

> Branch and personnel administrators in the banks we studied advocated the use of the punitive approach [direct criticism and reprimand] only after the problem-solving approach [reliance on questions to discover the source of the problem] repeatedly failed. Yet, in the field, we find that the punitive approach predominates from the start for many, [while] the problem-solving approach is used by some but is quickly abandoned (Fairhurst, Green, and Snavely, 1984, p. 289).

The overriding conclusion of research on supervisory compliance-gaining tactics is similar to our earlier conclusion about upward influence: that is, it is no longer sufficient for either superiors or subordinates to rely on traditional, formal lines of authority. Instead, successful supervisors use a combination of influence tactics tailored to the needs and personalities of individual subordinates, and to the specific goals to be accomplished.

In summary, research on motivation can be placed in a compliance-gaining context. Setting clear goals, articulating instrumentalities, providing immediate feedback—all of these become part of a supervisor's repertoire, alongside questioning, joking, and cajoling. From a communication perspective, it is finding the right combination of these messages—and conveying them successfully–that will help motivate employees.

Empowerment

The history of superior-subordinate relations is characterized by a trend toward democratization and empowerment (Burke, 1986). Nevertheless, definitions of the term have been confusing. Some define empowerment as the process by which a manager shares power with subordinates, usually through delegation or participative decision making. Still others take a broader view of empowerment as enabling and motivating employees, mainly by removing roadblocks and building feelings of personal effectiveness or self-efficacy. We subscribe to the second view and define empowerment as "a process of enhancing feelings of self-efficacy among organizational members through the identification of conditions that foster powerlessness and through their removal by both formal organizational practices and informal techniques of providing efficacy information" (Conger & Kanugo, 1988, p. 474).

Empowerment requires managers to be more like coaches and less like supervisors; to manage more by wandering around, which involves getting out to hear employees' real concerns; and to place less emphasis on close supervision and more on trusting employees to work hard within a framework of clear direction. A manager who helps subordinates become empowered must be responsive to employee critiques of the current system and expect employees to come up with new and better ways of doing things.

An empowering organization encourages employees to take on ever increasing responsibilities and to make use of what they know and learn. Michael Pacanowsky (1988) conducted a study of the company W. L. Gore and Associates and uncovered the following six rules of empowering organizations:

1. Distribute power and opportunity widely.
2. Maintain a full, open, and decentralized communication system.
3. Use integrative problem solving involving diverse groups and individuals.
4. Practice challenge in an environment of trust.
5. Reward and recognize people so as to encourage a high-performance ethic and self-responsibility.
6. Become wise by living through, and learning from, organizational ambiguity, inconsistency, contradiction, and paradox.

None of these rules "forces" decision making downward; rather they all allow empowerment to occur by providing the resources and opportunity. As the saying about the effectiveness of empowering another person goes: "You can't make a dog happy by wagging his tail *for* him." The supervisor who values empowerment can at best create an environment that will encourage subordinates to take greater responsibility for their work.

A pattern can be discerned as to how most organizations achieve this equalization of power. Figure 8.1 and the accompanying box provide two different representations of the empowerment process. The figure describes five stages in the process of empowerment, from the use of techniques to remove feelings of powerlessness to the kinds of communication that encourage self-efficacy. Box 8.1, page 240, presents the empowerment philosophy of the police chief of Los Angeles, Willie Williams. Note in his point of view not only a bias toward empowerment, but also RAA delegation and a willingness to manage the loose-tight paradox (Peters & Waterman, 1982). Also note the close relationship between empowerment and the notion of dialogue as described in Chapter 2.

In the final analysis, promoting empowerment is both pragmatic and paradoxical. It is pragmatic because, as a practical matter, organizations are more successful and individuals more satisfied and productive when they have real authority and control over their work. Empowerment is paradoxical because there is something contradictory about supervisors "requiring" empowerment, since this stance reinforces existing power differentials. The point is that empowerment is neither easily orchestrated nor does it originate in manage-

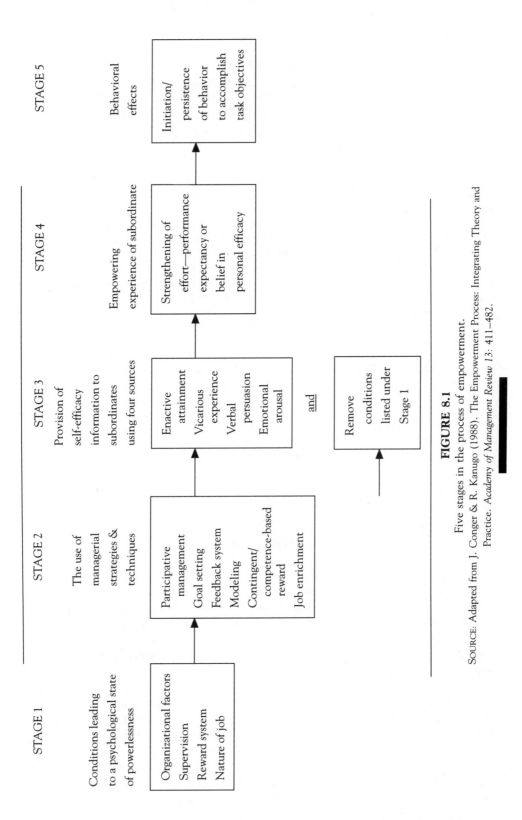

FIGURE 8.1

Five stages in the process of empowerment.

SOURCE: Adapted from J. Conger & R. Kanugo (1988). The Empowerment Process: Integrating Theory and Practice. *Academy of Management Review 13*: 411–482.

BOX 8.1

LOS ANGELES POLICE CHIEF WILLIE WILLIAMS'S PHILOSOPHY OF EMPOWERMENT

"In general, we try to customize the service within reason to the particular neighborhoods, and the way you do that is you talk *with* people. You don't talk *to* them. We used to come into a neighborhood and say: this is how many officers you are going to get, this is the kind of service you are going to get, and we'll tell you when you are going to get it.

"The police commissioner, the chief of police, has to be a person who is willing to share responsibilities, power, and authority. And you have to share it on two levels. You have to share it with people at your level in the community. I have a chief's advisory board that is made up of CEOs from major businesses and corporations, universities and religious communities. They sit and advise me in areas of strategic planning, training, budget, and things of that nature, looking at it from a corporate perspective, because I have the largest operating budget in the city. You also have to share responsibility with your own police officers. The best-managed police departments are those that move toward decentralized authority and accountability.

"A recent concern [of an investigative commission] was that the authority to make certain decisions was given to lower levels in the LAPD, but the responsibility and accountability for those decisions weren't. People were given points and so forth for promotions and transfers and assignments, but the commanders had no responsibility or accountability to review the disciplinary files, to look at the training. As chief, you have to be willing to push down decision-making to lower levels, but hold those commanders accountable for the actions that they take and [be] responsible for those [actions]" (Domanick, 1992, p. 14).

---

ment. Instead, managers can only provide a context in which individuals who seek empowerment can take it.

Leadership

Leadership is perhaps the most studied phenomenon in organizational behavior. Recent research discusses many of the same issues we have covered in this section, including supportiveness, motivation, and empowerment. Contemporary views of leadership view it as a system of relationships through which individuals motivate followers to desired values and behaviors (Hollander & Offerman, 1990). The history of thinking about leadership reveals a developing awareness of the importance of interpersonal relationships and communication.

Historically, the earliest, so-called trait conception of leadership held that certain individuals were born with leadership characteristics. This approach emphasized genetics and minimized the importance of interaction and the social context. By the late 1940s, trait approaches gave way to situational approaches, the thrust of which was that "situations varied in the qualities demanded of leaders, so those qualities were appropriate to a particular task and interpersonal context" (Hollander & Offerman, 1990, p. 180). For example, the type of leader who would be effective in the start-up phase of a high-tech company would differ dramatically from the type who could preside successfully over a mature government agency.

This basic insight spawned a variety of contingency theories of leadership, most notably Fred Fiedler's (1967) least preferred co-worker (LPC) model. Though highly controversial, this model distinguished between two types of leader styles: task oriented and relationship oriented. Fiedler maintained that the effectiveness of the different styles is contingent on aspects of the situation, including the nature of the task and the relationship with followers. For Fiedler, a good match between leadership style and situation is most likely to lead to high performance.

In the past 20 years, the research focus has shifted gradually from leader to follower, and to the leader-follower relationship. Specifically, it is the followers' perceptions of the leader that are most critical to success or failure (e.g., Calder, 1977). These perceptions evolve in leader-follower communicative transactions. Hence, this general orientation has sometimes been called the transactional approach. Graen's (1976) leader-member exchange (LMX) model discussed earlier in this chapter is a good example of the transactional approach. Individuals are leaders only in the eyes of those followers with whom they have an in-group relationship, with whom they exchange resources such as support for employee performance. Transactional approaches were the first to explicitly consider the importance of communication in the development of leadership. Their emphasis, however, was on the ability of individuals to tap into the needs and desires of followers, which are assumed to be relatively fixed.

In contrast, yet another approach views the leader as a transforming agent who attempts to change the fundamental outlook and behavior of followers—the transformational leader. Transformational leaders seek to transcend the bounds of routine follower behavior to offer the possibility of a new vision for the organization. Transformational leadership suggests a much expanded role for communication in leadership: it recasts leadership as the management of meaning (Bennis & Nanus, 1985). In other words, apart from setting goals and focusing on tasks, leaders help followers interpret organizational events and to make sense out of what is happening in the work world. Toward this end, Karl Weick (1980) has said that contemporary leadership skills are more akin to evangelism than to accounting; effective leaders are expert in the symbolic framing of situations for employees.

As already noted, many organizations today face increased competition, decreased market share, and a steady stream of layoffs. While many companies fail under the weight of these pressures, some survive—and those that do usually have effective communicators in leadership roles. When faced with bad news, the skillful communicator can be honest, critical, and optimistic, and look toward the future all at once. The leader's own enthusiasm and confidence can inspire employees to see the glass as half full, not half empty, and turn potential cynicism and resignation into increased urgency for success. The difference is not in the objective business data—data cannot speak for themselves—but rather in the prevailing interpretations of these data. Effective leaders shape these interpretations.

COMMUNICATING WITH PEERS

Peers provide social support, and informal work group norms can enhance or inhibit morale and commitment. Managerial success increasingly depends on the ability to extend a web of influence, not just up and down the hierarchy, but with co-workers and peers.

Three types of peer communication are common in organizations: *within group, cross-functional,* and *unstructured.*

Within-group Communication

Until recently, most research on peer communication has addressed contact within an intact work group or team. For example, studies (e.g., Boland & Hoffman, 1983; Roy, 1960) have shown how the use of humor in manufacturing work boosts morale and helps employees pass the time. Much of the legacy of the human relations school focused on the importance of informal group norms. (In Chapter 9, we describe recent research on work teams in detail.)

Cross-functional Communication

Lately, cross-functional peer communication has become a significant concern of most organizations. An example taken from automobile manufacturing helps show why cross-functional communication is presently receiving more attention. In the traditional American automobile company bureaucracy, clear roles and the division of labor led to the establishment of isolated departments and vertical lines of communication that were rarely crossed. Departments of engineering, manufacturing, sales, and administration all kept largely to themselves, creating what is often called a silo effect. Each department's communication and commitment were for the most part internal, and little communication took place across departmental (or professional) boundaries. A story heard in practically any car company in the United States is that the engineers designed the product, then "threw it over the wall" to manufacturing, who then tried to make it; they in turn passed it to sales, who tried to sell it. The problems that result from this approach, which effectively isolates each function or specialty, are legion—designs that are impossible to build, and products that when finally built are impossible to sell. While it remains an expensive struggle, recent attempts by Ford (notably with the Taurus) and General Motors (with Saturn) have shown some success in breaking down the walls that have traditionally obstructed cross-functional communication. For example, concurrent engineering—which involves assembly workers up front in the design process—has been shown to dramatically cut the time and costs required for assembly.

Cross-functional communication among peers is important primarily because the actual flow of work does not respect departmental boundaries. Typically, it has little to do with the formal relationships drawn in the organizational chart. For example, when a person has to go into a hospital for surgery, the majority of that person's experience consists of being passed from department to department—from admitting to anesthesiology to surgery to nursing and to finance and accounting. Most complaints about hospitals have to do with the way customers (patients) are treated "in-between" departments, waiting to be transferred, tested, examined, or discharged. Patients come to feel that they have somehow "slipped through the cracks" between the functions of the formal organizational chart.

Cross-functional communication is essential to the success of every company, regardless of industry. The need for more and better cross-functional communication is driven by a competitive marketplace and by rising customer expectations. When we call a store for service or repair, it is no longer enough to be told that "some other department" screwed up. Instead, we want the person speaking to us to *take responsibility* for communicating with that other department and to fix our problem. Increasingly, the people who build products or process information sit on cross-functional teams with the people who design products or systems, and give input about how the process works in real life. Similarly, sales and marketing professionals are joining such teams, contributing their perceptions about what will or won't sell.

For most organizations, cultivating productive connections between co-workers is difficult. Individuals may feel such interaction is unimportant, as long as they do their assigned job. Or they may try to cooperate but experience unresolvable conflicts as a result of personality clashes or differences in professional training. (Conflicts between engineering and manufacturing, for example, are typical.) And yet customers don't care about these internal breakdowns; all they're interested in is getting what they paid for. So contemporary organizations are challenged to cultivate excellent cross-functional or interdepartmental relationships. Just as a chain is only as strong as its weakest link, so too is an organization's work processes only as effective as the weakest handoff in its workflow. These handoffs occur almost exclusively between departments or functions.

Peer interaction across functions may be cultivated in many ways. Informal gatherings, like picnics and sports leagues, allow accountants to get to know assemblers, engineers, and maintenance workers. Organizational orientations or tours help people see where their task fits into the overall workflow, and how they are in some way part of a larger system. Two effective methods for promoting horizontal communication are managing the white space and cultivating "internal" customers.

Managing the White Space   The motive behind most cross-functional communication is a realization that the old way of protecting one's own turf is obsolete. In its place, employees are encouraged to identify with the total organization as a processing system or workflow process. Each individual and each function is responsible for a subprocess that contributes to the total work of the organization. An organizational chart only shows the functions and reporting relationships, but most of the work actually takes place between functions, in the "white spaces." Management must learn to manage the white space in the organizational chart, the horizontal workflow processes that will make or break them (Rummler & Brache, 1991). A focus on improving workflow process is a natural outgrowth of the systems perspective in that it emphasizes the informal relationships that are key to the work of the organization.

Internal Customers   Everyone in business understands the idea of an external customer—the man, woman, or company that purchases the products or services. Less well understood is the fact that to deliver a quality product or service to its end user, there are many "internal customers," people within the organization who depend on other's work as input to their job or task. The traditional bureaucracy encouraged workers to see these co-workers as independent entities and even as competitors for resources. As a result, workers didn't always pass on work of the highest quality, because they had little idea or concern for where it went when they were finished with it. Today the internal customer idea is transforming workflow processes. If a worker sees the people down the hall from him who receive the output of his work as his customers, he is much more inclined to talk with them about their requirements and to try to satisfy them by passing on only high-quality work. The same logic can be viewed in reverse: everyone in an organization is not only an internal customer, but also an internal *supplier* of whatever work they pass on to the next step in the workflow. A human resources manager, for example, supplies data on workers' compensation claims and compliance with Equal Employment Opportunity (EEO) laws to management, who are one of their customers.

Hewlett-Packard is one of many companies that have widely adopted the internal customer philosophy. The company's departments of maintenance and facilities see operations as their customer; human resources and accounting see most of the other departments as their customers as well. The result is a radical change in horizontal working relationships—from ignorance of each other's duties, competitiveness, and neglect, to frequent communication, understanding, concern, and commitment to a common goal of satisfying the external customer through effective communication among internal customers.

Unstructured Peer Communication

One final type of peer communication important to organizations is unstructured and occurs neither with members of one's own work group nor with internal customers or suppliers. Unstructured communication takes place outside of formal work expectations,

---

ETHICS BOX 8.1

YOU CAN'T ALWAYS HEAR WHAT YOU WANT

Major Ramone Martinez had just returned from a management workshop on empowerment. One of the best things to come out of the experience was a fresh perspective on his role as an active listener. Ramone had always felt that he was a "naturally" good listener owing to his empathtic nature, but this workshop had sharpened his skills and he was anxious to try them out.

Captain Eileen Davis worked for Ramone in the procurement department of the United States Army. She had always had a close professional relationship with him, but lately he seemed more eager to engage her in conversations, during which times he would appear totally wrapped up in whatever she was saying. His new attitude made her feel even closer to him, and with this feeling came an overwhelming desire on Eileen's part to share everything with him.

So it was that one day she decided to tell him the one secret she had kept from everyone at work, the one thing, in fact, that could mean her job if it became public knowledge. She told Ramone that she was a lesbian. Homosexuals were still not allowed in the military, but she felt that if just one person knew—someone who was her friend and her confidante—even if that person was her supervisor, well, she would feel much better.

When Eileen told Ramone her secret, he was surprised but more important, he suddenly realized that he was now in a precarious position. As her supervisor he had a duty to report her; that was part of the Military Code of Conduct he had sworn to uphold. On the other hand, he had encouraged her frankness by being an active listener, and encouraging her to share information with him about herself that a more distanced approach to management surely would not have exposed. In his mind, he was complicit in her situation.

What should Ramone do?

in the mailroom, the car pool, or over lunch. Unstructured peer communication can be a source of social support and of identification; it can also lead to innovations that would otherwise have gone unrecognized. Recently, some progressive companies (like 3M) have required employees to spend up to 30 percent of their time *not* working in their areas of responsibility, in the hopes of promoting new ideas.

Perhaps the greatest limitation to unstructured peer communication is that people tend to communicate most with similar others, where they feel the greatest degree of comfort. In practice, this also means that unstructured peer communication often breaks down along typical gender and racial lines—white males talk to white males, female secretaries to other female secretaries, Latinos to Latinos, Vietnamese to Vietnamese. Sometimes these cliques form because of language barriers, but more often they are the result of people self-selecting others of their same general background. The recent emphasis on managing diversity in organizations is valuable, but until individuals of diverse backgrounds participate in unstructured peer communication, real dialogue in these organizations will not occur.

COMMUNICATING WITH CUSTOMERS AND SUPPLIERS

Quality and customer satisfaction are accomplished mainly through effective work relationships. This section focuses exclusively on *external* relationships with customers and suppliers that span the organization's boundaries. In doing so, we observe that the actual workflow doesn't stop or start at the doors of most companies, but rather is reflected in a network or chain of internal and external customers and suppliers.

Communicating with Customers

The growing demand for quality customer service is undeniable, but little research has been done on customer communication and none in the field of communication. In the absence of such systematic research, we will focus on what work does exist to guide service practice. The primary spokespersons for the service revolution in the United States have been Karl Albrecht (1992) and Tom Peters (1987). Both advocate a customer service revolution in which getting close to the customer—listening to and understanding customers' needs and requirements—is the only thing that really matters. According to Albrecht (1992), managing the customer's "experience" is key:

> The outstanding companies approach the service challenge from the point of view of managing the customer's experience, not from the point of view of doing things. This "doing things" mindset seems to express an unconscious view of the customer as a nuisance. There is a powerful, unconscious tendency in most organizations to depersonalize and dehumanize the conception, discussion, and operation of the service delivery. Things are easier to deal with than humans, so we prefer to think of the people—both customers and employees—as just interchangeable elements of a big impersonal blueprint (p. 35).

Peters' Customer Revolution   Peters' approach is more detailed and communication-focused than Albrecht's approach. According to Peters (1987), an organization must emphasize ten activities to achieve total customer responsiveness.

1. *Specialize/create niches/differentiate.* From a communication perspective, specialization is a question of rhetorical strategy, of tailoring the product or service (and messages about the product or service) to a clearly defined audience or public. Products and services that appeal to a broad customer base are being replaced by those targeted to the needs of a narrowly defined niche market.

2. *Provide top quality, as perceived by the customer.* The only perceptions that matter are the customer's, and it really doesn't matter if you disagree. Customer perceptions *are* reality for organizations, and a company that is responsive to customers listens carefully and takes action based on customer perceptions of the quality of their product or service.

3. *Provide superior service/Emphasize the intangibles.* This guideline calls attention to the importance of relationships with customers and to the positive or negative impact of their encounter with an organization. Research has consistently shown that the intangibles—such as accuracy, dependability, and the interpersonal relationship with the service provider—outweigh other factors in determining customer satisfaction (Zeithmal, Parasuraman, & Berry, 1990). A customer's problems or complaints should be handled in such a way that they become customers for life. A frequently cited example of superior service in the United States is Nordstrom, where gift wrapping is done on the spot, all merchandise can be returned "no questions asked," and salespeople are encouraged to use their good judgment in achieving their only goal—outstanding customer service.

   One software company we know has gone so far as to pay for an annual user's convention of everyone who has bought their product in the past. At this convention, their assembled customers discuss ways in which the software ought to be improved, after which the sponsoring organization then makes the changes suggested. In this and related cases, the customers are so close they literally become product designers.

   The most progressive companies value and train those employees who have the most customer contact, to both ensure that they say the right things and that they have the necessary communication skills to make a good impression. As customers, it is obvious when an employee has been told to care about customers *and* is taught the needed skills to do so. Where this orientation exists, it serves as a strong competitive advantage. Even in the realm of high-tech products, services, and technology, the quality of interpersonal relationships (with internal or external customers) will make or break a company.

4. *Achieve extraordinary responsiveness.* Time is often a customer's most precious commodity. An increasingly common way to achieve superior responsiveness is through the use of communication technology that allows constant contact between all aspects of an operation. Companies like Frito-Lay and Federal Express have been leaders in electronic connectivity; each of their trucks is equipped with an onboard computer terminal. Through a combination of process improvement and communication technology, Motorola has reduced the time between when a customer ordered a pager to when it was shipped from the factory from 45 days to just under two hours.

5. *Be an internationalist.* This emphasis means not limiting the definition of the customer to domestic markets, but cultivating relationships globally. This effort requires patience, empathy, and the communication skills needed to get along

with people of other cultures. It requires people to learn the culture of their non-native customers and to adapt their product, service, and communication to that culture.

6. *Create uniqueness.* To survive in the competitive commercial marketplace, an organization's product or service must stand out. Organizations should have as a goal a unique strategy or market niche ("they're always the cheapest," "they make the highest quality components in the world"), and make sure that everyone in the organization can articulate this uniqueness.

7. *Become obsessed with listening.* Peters says that listening to customers must become everyone's business. There is no place for explaining to customers why they are wrong in their needs or requirements—they will just go somewhere else. Good listening means avoiding distractions, paying close attention to the main point, and taking action on what is heard.

8. *Turn manufacturing into a marketing weapon.* The point here is that the source of most of the improvements customers care about is in the core of the company's operations, which for many firms is the factory. This emphasis is closely aligned with empowerment and the need for cross-functional communication described above. If employees are treated as responsible adults and are working on issues that matter to customers, they are most likely to achieve customer satisfaction.

9. *Make sales and service people into heroes.* This means reversing the current trend toward undervaluing those individuals who deal most with customers. To the customer, the temporary employee answering the telephone *is* the company—even more so than the sales or service representative. Peters suggests "overinvesting" in these people as an indication of the top priority placed on customer responsiveness.

10. *Launch a customer revolution.* Become obsessed with the customer. From a communication perspective, this means a change in what people talk about on a daily basis. In one organization, the manager calls the employees together at the end of the day and asks each one of them—"what have you done for the customer today?" and gives an award for the best deed.

Customer Service as Emotional Work   Peters' guidelines are offered in the spirit of businesses taking advantage of the current economic climate. But what impact does a fanatic customer focus have on the well-being of the individual employee? For example, when the president of Pepperdine University recently suggested "customer satisfaction" as a way of thinking about college students, many faculty and staff were outraged at the possible implication that students were "always right," and that faculty and staff were to do their bidding.

Anat Rafaeli and Robert Sutton (1991) have conducted an impressive program of research that investigates the actual behavior of servers and the reasons behind their choices. Most problematic are jobs in which employees must display emotions that differ from their true feelings in the name of superior customer service. Organizations recruit, reward, and punish employees for the appropriate or inappropriate display of emotions (see Chapter 7). Airlines hire flight attendants who are able to maintain smiles over long flights; retail outlets use "secret shoppers" to identify employees who fail to offer a "friendly greeting" to customers entering the store. These emotional displays are enforced because they are felt to have a positive impact on sales and customer satisfaction. "Smiling cocktail waitresses receive larger tips than unsmiling ones . . . and smiling nuns garner larger donations than glum nuns" (Sutton & Rafaeli, 1988, p. 463).

Sutton and Rafaeli's research, however, reveals a number of surprises. Employees do not as a rule submit to the control over their emotional displays, but instead develop a coping repertoire contingent on the situation. For example, while cashiers may smile and make eye contact during slow times, during busy times they will avoid eye contact so as not to prolong a transaction. Interestingly, customers also adapt to different situations and appreciate a no-nonsense approach when the store is busy. By contrast, during slow times both customers and servers may see the encounter as a kind of entertainment (Sutton & Rafaeli, 1988). In addition, customers' expectations for service vary by organization. That is, where superior service is part of the organization's image (e.g., Disneyland, McDonald's), customers are less likely to tolerate poor service.

Finally, Rafaeli and Sutton (1991) acknowledge that not all customer communication is of the friendly variety. Bill collectors, for example, use negative emotions to garner payments from delinquent customers. More generally (and reinforcing the idea that servers use a variety of strategies to accomplish multiple goals), Rafaeli and Sutton find that bill collectors use "emotional contrast strategies" to get compliance. These contrasts involve alternating between positive and negative displays (or alternating between positive and negative bill collectors with the same customer) of emotion to induce fear, relief, and compliance in customers.

Communicating with Suppliers

A machine shop may sell a tool to an engine shop, which in turn sells the engine to a car company, which builds a subassembly for sale by another car company under its name. The finished car may then be sold as part of a fleet to another company, which then charges its customers for using the cars. Nested customers and a chain of requirements is the rule in today's organizations, not the exception. For example, Douglas Aircraft (DAC) is for the most part an assembly company. Most of the parts for the DC-10s and MD-80s are manufactured by other companies and then shipped to DAC to be put together.

In most organizations, responsibility for communicating with customers and suppliers is limited to select individuals, known generally as boundary role occupants or boundary spanners (Adams, 1980). In a bank, for example, tellers and new account representatives are boundary spanners; in a restaurant, hosts and waiters play this role. In large manufacturing firms, an entire department may be devoted to supplier management, purchasing, or procurement. The responsibility of this function is to establish good, accountable working relationships with everyone who supplies the company with parts or services.

Recent research on supplier relationships suggests that, up to a point, the closer the relationship the better. An increasingly popular model today is the partnership arrangement, whereby the company works with its suppliers to identify areas needing improvement. Some organizations even insist that their standards of cost, service, or efficiency be applied to the supplier's organization, or they will cease buying from the supplier. In any case, suppliers are increasingly being asked to be "part of the team" and consequently are being held increasingly accountable if they fail to be team players. Competition is too stiff, and the need for flexibility and quick response time is too great to do it any other way.

INTIMACY IN WORK RELATIONSHIPS

"Sex is like paperclips in the office: Commonplace, useful, underestimated, ubiquitous. Hardly appreciated until it goes wrong. It is the cement in every working relationship. It has little to do with sweating bosses cuddling their secretaries behind closed doors . . . it is more adult, more complicated, more of a weapon" (Jones, 1972, p. 12).

The ideal of most organizations is to foster interpersonal relationships that are "close but not too close" (Pacanowsky & O'Donnell-Trujillo, 1983). Yet as long as human beings reside in organizations, there will inevitably be close couplings and potential problems with romantic and sexual relationships. Some of these relationships may be welcome, providing mutual interest to the involved employees; others may be one-sided advances and harassments. Some may be harmlessly flirtatious; others may be consummated. Whereas classical theories of organization discouraged fraternizing among workers for fear of inefficiency, over the years organizations have become more tolerant. Most have no formal policy against such pairings, and the typical organizational response to knowledge of a relationship is to do nothing (Dillard & Miller, 1988).

Organizational Romance

Robert Quinn (1977) conducted the first study of why employees seek romance with co-workers. He isolated three motives underlying such relationships: love, ego, and job. Persons motivated by love have a sincere desire to find a long-term companion or spouse. Those motivated by ego are looking for sexual excitement and adventure. Finally, those with job-related motives may hope the romance will make their job more secure or bring them more power in the organization.

Recent research using Quinn's categories (cf. Dillard & Miller, 1988) reveals that some of society's stereotypes about why people form relationships at work may be overly simplistic. For example, in one study of organizational romance (Dillard & Segrin, 1987), only 14 percent of the relationships included a female high in job motives paired with a more powerful male. On the contrary, passionate love (high in love and ego motives) and companionate love (high only in sincere love motives) comprised 59 percent of the relationships studied.

Dillard and Miller (1988) conclude that organizational romance is motivationally complex: people seek more than one thing from their partners. Their findings about the consequences of such relationships are also surprising. Although we have all heard stories about (or had first-hand experience with) office affairs that destroy people's productivity and careers and poison the office climate, these are apparently not the rule. Most often there are no changes at all, and in some cases employee performance improves, perhaps in an attempt to overcompensate for others' negative expectations. No research has been done comparing heterosexual and homosexual relationships along these lines, but we would expect the findings to be similar.

There is no single interpretation of any organizational behavior, not least something as charged as office romance. Whatever the "facts" of the case, others' negative perceptions and interpretations can do significant damage to individuals. Along with the gossip often comes a changed perception about the motives, character, or performance of the involved parties. Unfortunately for the involved partners, "no matter how the relationship has or has not affected the work of partners, the perception of coworkers will be that behaviors have changed, and perceptions are very real" (Butler, 1986, p. 32).

Sexual Harassment

As we described in Chapter 6, organizations may be viewed in terms of an ongoing struggle for power. Furthermore, such struggles are often not obvious on the surface, and those with less power may be complicit in their domination because they accept the current state of affairs as "just the way things are." Romance and sexuality in organizations are predictable sites for the use and abuse of power. "Women as a group have less formal and informal power than men in organizations, confront more obstacles on their path to developing organizational power, and have fewer opportunities to acquire organizational power through activities and alliances" (Bingham, 1991, p. 92). A well-known manifestation of this lopsided power relationship is sexual harassment.

The term *sexual harassment* was coined by feminists "to refer to behavior of men which humiliates women and treats them as objects for men's use" (Bingham, 1991, p. 88). While sexual harassment is commonplace in organizations, the definition of what constitutes harassment is somewhat cloudy, partly because those who have grown up in a male-dominated society are unwilling to consider changes in what they have always believed to be harmless, acceptable behavior. Recent attempts to further define sexual harassment inevitably challenge traditional assumptions about what constitutes the organizational status quo.

Some judgment will always be involved, but according to Julie Tamaki (1991), the following behaviors, *if unwelcome,* constitute sexual harassment:

Verbal comments, even those sometimes defended as compliments (e.g., "I wish my wife were as pretty as you").

Nonverbal gestures, such as outlining body parts or elevator eyes (looking someone up and down).

Visual objects, such as revealing posters, girlie (and male beefcake) calendars, or nude dancers at office-related parties.

Terms of endearment (e.g., sweetie, dear, babydoll).

Physical acts, such as patting, fondling, or stroking; standing in the doorway and not letting an employee pass.

Requiring submission to sexual advancement as the basis for an employment decision.

Actual or threatened retaliation against a person who complains or intends to plead sexual harassment.

Tamaki believes that the first response of individuals who feel they have been sexually harassed should be to confront the harasser with their displeasure. If the behavior continues, then they should resort to increasingly more formal responses, such as telling the boss or the human resources department; keeping a written record of the offenses; finding and confiding in supportive colleagues; filing a formal complaint with the Department of Fair Employment and Housing or with the Federal Equal Employment Opportunity Commission (EEOC), which will launch an investigation; or filing a lawsuit. While the Anita Hill/Clarence Thomas hearings made clear how difficult it is to prove harassment in a "my word against yours" kind of situation, legal awards for victims of sexual harassment and discrimination are increasingly common.

Finally, Shereen Bingham (1991) offers an explicitly communicative approach to managing sexual harassment at work. According to Bingham, simply "confronting" one's harasser is difficult because the person being harassed (typically a woman) has multiple goals in the situation:

> To make a decision women must weigh in the balance economic necessity, prospects for other jobs, a good recommendation rather than a poor one, the chances of being fired, attitudes of husbands, friends, lovers or parents, interest in the job and rate of pay, the number of times the abuse has been experienced, and countless other factors (Farley, 1978, p. 23).

Because of the complicated nature of this situation, Bingham suggests that there is no one best way to respond to harassment. At varying times, and under various circumstances, assertive, nonassertive, and even aggressive responses may be appropriate. Most authors on the subject advise assertiveness as the best response (i.e., standing up for your beliefs in a direct, honest, and nonattacking way). However, assertiveness has a potential downside if it is seen as rejecting the other person. In dealing with sexual harassment, Bingham suggests that there may be practical value in tempering assertiveness with empathy in responding to a sexual proposition. Consider these two alternatives:

Assertive: "No I will not have sex with you, and I think your behavior is completely inappropriate. This is a workplace and I expect to be treated accordingly."

Assertive-emphatic: "I don't mean to hurt your feelings, but no, I won't sleep with you. I enjoy working with you and I want to keep our relationship strictly professional."

Bingham suggests that organizations design educational programs for employees that will assist people in analyzing sexual harassment situations in terms of multiple goals and obstacles, and in deciding which strategy will work best in each situation. The ability to respond effectively to harassment bears close relationship to one's general ability to communicate at work, which is the final topic we consider in this chapter.

INTERPERSONAL COMPETENCE AT WORK

People underestimate the importance of interpersonal relations at work to their quality of life. Upon retirement or unemployment, many are surprised to discover how much the people at work really meant to them and to their self-concepts. Three factors influence the ability to forge the relationships people need so very much: valuing relationships, assertiveness, and active listening.

Valuing Relationships

The first step in building interpersonal relationships at work is learning to see the importance of relationships in business. As noted in Chapter 1, although power bases have shifted toward relationships, not many people recognize this change as yet. Technical workers in particular may still regard anything other than technical work as "unproduc-

tive," or "goofing off." On the contrary, for many individuals interpersonal communication is the work of the 1990s, particularly among managers. In this sense, the commonly
heard complaint about "too many meetings" is typically off the mark. While many
nonproductive meetings could certainly be shortened or eliminated, meetings themselves
are good. In many organizations, talk *is* the work, although people may not yet realize it
(Gronn, 1983).

A company with whom we work has agonized over the past 20 years over the fate of
one of its senior managers, a brilliant man seriously lacking in interpersonal skills.
Although he currently holds a high-ranking position, he got there by upsetting just about
everyone in the 10,000-person firm. Business has fallen off significantly, and now the
question is: What to do with him? After numerous failed consultations and training
courses designed to boost his skills, the general manager decided to lay him off, and the
rest of management was shocked. How could someone with such good ideas be fired? The
answer is simply this: In management today, relational skills are not a desirable add-on
to the job; they are a big part of the job. Valuing relationships is central.

Assertiveness

The ability to be assertive is the extension of authenticity into the realm of communication. When and if an individual has developed a voice, a strong sense of strengths and
weaknesses, likes and dislikes, he must then learn to assert himself, to stick up for his
needs in a direct, nonaggressive fashion.

The importance of assertiveness to developing relationships becomes obvious when we
consider the alternatives. On one hand, the avoiding, or *passive-aggressive*, individual
whines, complains, and frets privately about problems at work, but if asked directly about
what is wrong admits nothing. The result is a consistent inability to raise and resolve
problems, needs, issues, and concerns. At the other extreme, *aggressive* individuals sabotage their ability to meet needs (and to establish supportive relationships) by creating
defensiveness and alienating others. In the first case, needs won't be met because people
don't know them; in the second, they won't be met because people are too angry to care
about them.

Assertiveness means clearly articulating what a person wants from others in terms of
behavior, not presumed motives. It is direct, centered, and nonattacking. It allows the
individual to sleep well at night, avoiding constant regret over what they "should have
said."

Consider this example. A co-worker promises to get you some financial information
you need to close the books for the month. He doesn't get it to you. Do you:

1. Avoid him altogether and make up some numbers?
2. Tell everyone you see what a jerk he is (just not to his face)?
3. Call him and tell him what an irresponsible jerk he is?
4. Call him and ask nicely again for the figures?
5. Call and say: "When you're late with these numbers, I get frustrated because it
   keeps me from doing my job of closing the books"?

Obviously alternative 5 is the assertive response and the one most likely to get the co-
worker to change, since it is least likely to put him on the defensive. Nevertheless, all of

us have had the experience of making the other choices, and by avoiding being assertive about the truth, have compromised our own ability to meet our needs in our relationships with others at work. Over time, relationships can fall into dysfunctional patterns that get increasingly hard to break. Thus, the best advice is to be assertive from the beginning.

Active Listening

The other critical factor in building supportive relationships at work is active listening. Like assertiveness, listening is a learned skill and one that very few individuals ever master. Talking to someone who really knows how to listen actively makes you feel valued, important, and free to speak your mind. In an ideal organizational communication situation, assertiveness and active listening go hand in hand as people are able to express their own perceptions and desires and at the same time attend to the perceptions and desires of others.

There are many ways to become an active listener. The first is to create a supportive listening environment. This means minimizing, to the extent possible, physical and psychological "noise" that might interfere with an individual's perception that his or her words have really been heard. Note that it is the individual's *perception* of listening that is critical. The desired outcome is not attained if you contend that "I'm listening, even if I don't look like it." The focus has to be on the other person's perception of you as a good listener.

Managers who create a supportive listening environment do a few simple things. They clear their desks when talking with people, so as not to be distracted by papers in front of them. They avoid phone calls during conversations. If they are distracted by physical noise or psychological pressures, they say something like this: "I really want to listen to what you are saying but this isn't the right place. Can we get together later at (specified time) when I can give you my full attention?" Active listeners understand that listening takes concentration and demands to be taken seriously. They also understand that in business (as in life!) listening is a sure route to power.

A second way to become an active listener is to keep the focus of the conversation on the other person. Our tendency in making conversation is to relate what someone else says to something in our experience, which steals or "takes away" the conversation from them. This tendency is especially marked when we comfort people or give advice. When someone reports that they are seriously ill, for example, a typical response is to tell stories about all the people we know who had that same disease and what happened to them. (This is not really comforting!) When someone is agonizing over a decision, what is called advice usually means, "how *I* did it when I had to make a similar decision." This is even the case when someone isn't asking for advice but just wants us to listen. Good listeners ask for details, clarify, and react, but they rarely interrupt, and they keep the focus on the other person.

A commonly taught skill for maintaining focus on the person who is speaking is paraphrasing, which is sometimes called a listening perception check. Paraphrasing involves periodically repeating the substance of what has been said to show interest and be sure that the listener is getting the point. Thus, if a student says that she is "sick of this school and everything in it," a fair paraphrase might be: "so you're fed up with your teachers and your friends?" To which she might clarify: "No, the teachers are all right, and I have some good friends. I just can't stand the bureaucracy you have to go through to take classes. They treat you like a number!" It is amazing how often paraphrasing reveals a misunderstanding of what someone meant and provides the needed clarification.

A word of caution: like assertiveness, paraphrasing feels awkward at first. Learning a new skill always is; compare it to learning gymnastics or tennis. Over time, you will be able to be assertive and paraphrase others in ways that don't stick out so much. In the meantime, you might suffer under the brand of an effective, concerned communicator.

A third key to active listening is supportive nonverbal behavior which requires consciousness of eye contact. Look at someone when you are listening to them. Nod appropriately to show interest and approval. For too long the typical business "look" of interest has been an expressionless mask. Looking interested both keeps you involved in the conversation and brings out the best in the speaker.

A fourth and final way to learn active listening skills is to value alternative experiences. Possibly the greatest resource an organization has is its employees' diversity of experiences. We remember a brochure from a ten-member training company that boasted "over 200 years combined training experience." The question is: How well do most companies utilize the experience of their employees? The answer is, not very well, and the reason lies in a specific type of poor listening habit.

The habit we mean is the tendency of managers and employees to deny the validity of their co-workers' experience of reality. For example, a supervisor in a paint manufacturing company is invited to a management meeting to give input about morale in the plant. After some vague discussion, the supervisor gets up the nerve to tell the truth, as he sees it: "Morale stinks. My people don't trust management ever since OSHA came here and gave all those safety violations for working conditions. The people keep making suggestions, but none ever get acted upon. They're cynical and fed up." What happens next? Most often others in the group will attack the supervisor's experience as if it were up for debate. For example: "They *couldn't* be that unhappy. Who did you talk to?" "Things have gotten a lot better in recent months, though, haven't they?" "How do you know they are telling you the truth?" Or more to the point: "You're wrong! Our people are nothing like that! How could you even feel that way!"

Whereas most people recognize that it is fruitless to disagree about experience, say, with regard to a movie (if you hated it and I loved it, is there any way we can decide how good it "really" was?), we lose this perspective in the world of relationships. Active listening means respecting the validity of other people's experience, especially if it doesn't coincide with yours. Just as assertiveness requires the belief that everyone has an inalienable right to speak the voice of their experience, active listening adds the insight that others' voices are equally valid.

So rather than saying "I disagree!" or "You're wrong!" the responsible communicator is more likely to say "I take an alternative view" or "I see it differently" or, even better, "I understand that you feel that way, but my experience has been different." The consequences of *not* denying others' experience are tremendous in organizations. Suddenly, new ideas emerge from unexpected places. Moreover, the fact that each idea does not have to "beat out" other versions of reality leads to better joint decision making and problem solving.

A useful exercise for getting some distance on our own relationships is to look at how we are already listening to others even before they open their mouths to speak (Hyde,

1991). In other words, each of us has a general orientation to relationships that appears in how we approach listening. For example, some people approach listening with this thought in mind: "How can I help you fix this problem?" Others listen with a thought like this: "I know this already. Get to the point." Or: "Yeah sure. I don't believe it." Or even: "How can I get you to like me?"

Reflecting even briefly on your general listening orientation can be a liberating experience. Understanding your implicit framework for approaching other people is the first step in developing alternative approaches that might be more appropriate to a given situation.

CREATIVITY AND CONSTRAINT IN RELATIONSHIPS

This chapter presents two themes about relationships. The first is utilitarian—good relationships are good business, because they minimize problems with internal work processes and convince customers to keep coming back. The second theme is more individual and creative—good relationships make a difference in life, not just work, and the ability to develop supportive working relationships makes an important difference in a person's quality of life.

The relationship between these two themes returns us to issues of creativity and constraint. The nature of this dialectic is quickly revealed when we consider how the various relationships discussed in this chapter are formed. For example, a cross-functional team may be convened by management, but in all likelihood close relationships already exist among some members of the team. Similarly, groups of people may band together informally over a long period of time, and these relationships at work may be of critical importance to them. What is most interesting is that relationships are hard to control, and dialogue is hard to manage. We connect with people for many reasons; things happen that change patterns of power and status and bring us closer together or farther apart. At the same time, constraints of the system ensure us that regardless of the variations in patterns of relationships that do exist, the outcome will most likely be limited—by what is reasonable or even possible within a "rational," hierarchical organization.

SUMMARY

Good organizations are places where authentic people listen well, respect the validity of others' experiences, feel free to be assertive, have a clear sense of direction and control, get good feedback about their performance, and feel valued as intelligent human beings. Good organizations provide multiple opportunities for employee voice, which leads to higher rates of employee retention (Spencer, 1986). Good organizations encourage good conversations and are sites of authentic dialogue, which is simultaneously supportive and critical, loose and tight. Good organizations both promote a positive experience of work and are able to remain profitable in a competitive marketplace. It is hard to imagine anything quite so difficult.

CASE STUDY

THE FIRST YEAR OF LIFE

THE SCENE

The First Year of Life is a venture-capital specialty store located in a medium-sized southeastern city. The store is dedicated to acquiring, marketing, and selling a wide variety of products designed for children in their first year of life. Some of the goods and services include:

Clothing designed for "preemies" (prematurely born infants), newborns (1 to 3 months), and infants (4 to 12 months).

Accessories for children (and their parents) for home care, travel, and emergencies. These include diaper bags, traveling cribs, strollers, high chairs, thermometers, medicine, formula, bottles (reusable and disposable), nipples, cleaning supplies for bottles and nipples, receiving blankets, sheets, blankets, comforters, and the like.

Specialty toys for the first year of life, particularly those that focus on "learning." (Note: This store is NOT trying to compete with Toys'Я'Us or discount stores; the toys carried by The First Year of Life are not likely to be found in other outlets.)

Information products, including books about the first year of life, "mood" music to help soothe, comfort, or accustom the newborn to various sounds, voice cassettes providing various advisories about child-rearing and care that parents can listen to as they commute to work and so on, and an on-staff registered nurse who will answer questions from parents. (Note: A special feature of this store is that any child in the first year of life can be weighed and measured, and a "Growth Chart" will be provided and updated free of charge.)

The marketing prospectus is particularly strong. Americans are spending more money on children than ever before. Americans in the middle class spend approximately 30 percent of their disposable income on a first child during the first year of life. The primary marketing target for this store is "Yuppie Parents," a segment of the overall First Year of Life market that has a relatively high level of disposable income and desires high-quality information and products that combine substance with style. A secondary—but important—market comprises friends, family, and work acquaintances of parents who have children in their first year of life.

The store is located across the street from a major shopping mall in a strip mall with ample parking and lighting. The appearance of the store is clean, inviting, and bright. Inventory is kept in the warehouse in the rear of the store; products are purchased by taking a bar-coded slip to the cash register, and delivery is made after the purchase.

THE PLAYERS

The owner of the store is a retired couple in their mid-fifties who have reared three children and (so far) two grandchildren. The man (Clarence) is an ex-military security specialist with a strong preference for operating the store as what he calls "a well-run machine." The wife (Martha) is the real information specialist on the first year of life, both from practical experience and from two years spent researching this venture and available products. She says she wants "everyone who comes into the store to feel at home, and to develop good relations with the sales staff, the owners, and other customers." The owners do not plan to be on the premises everyday or even year-round. "We did not retire to go to work," both of them agree. (It should be noted here that a substantial part of their venture capital was acquired by winnings in the state lottery; their savings have not been put into the business.)

Because they do not plan to be on the premises everyday during working hours, they have hired a seasoned retail manager (Catherine) to run the operation. Her background is in retail clothing, and she has worked for fifteen years for a major fashion chain. Her educational background includes a bachelor's degree in nursing and a master's degree in business administration. (She spent four years as a registered nurse after graduating from college and made a career change when she entered graduate school.) She says that her management philosophy is based on the work of Karl Weick and the systems approach to organizing. "Everything counts," she says with a smile, "but you can't count everything." By this last statement, she apparently means that the bottom line is not necessarily the only measure of business success.

There are four full-time sales associates. Three of them are women in their mid-fifties with experience rearing children; one of them is a young male college student pursuing a career in marketing. Their primary responsibility is to make the customer feel "at home," and to answer questions about the goods and services available. Their secondary responsibility is to make sure the store is always clean and neat, and that all the items are properly displayed and marked. The male marketing student (Ricardo) sees this new store as a rare opportunity to "get in on the ground floor of a store with great potential" and hopes one day to move into management, preferably as the person who determines marketing campaigns for the store. The three other sales associates are as different as their fingerprints. One of them (Clarice) is an ex-elementary school teacher who believes she will make better money and experience less stress here; another is a former homemaker (Fern) who has never worked outside of the home before; the third is a young grandmother (Jan) from a farming family who believes in hard work and Jesus Christ.

There are two inventory/warehouse workers (Bill and Ben) whose job is to process the orders once they are received and to keep up with the inventory. These workers were acquired from Toys'Я'Us. Both of them have about ten years' experience in stockroom and inventory control, although the Toys 'Я' Us system was computer-controlled and ordering was handled by the managers. Here they have new responsibilities, and all the orders come from a phone link to the cash register. They get along well together and on the side operate a custom car painting shop (Bill and Ben's Kustom Kar Kapers).

There are two registered nurses on staff (Ella and Anne). They occupy a prime space in the center of the store and have the necessary weighing and measuring devices on display, as well as a good stock of helpful books and cassettes giving advice to parents. Both of the nurses have extensive experience with children; both were hired from the staff of a private local physician after he retired. They know and like each other, and seem to work well together, but clearly miss working with the kindly old physician whom both of them loved and respected. One problem is that they don't always recommend products to parents, preferring instead to give free advice.

After the store opened, it enjoyed almost unheard-of business success. For the first quarter of operation, sales were exceptional; for the second quarter they were good. Now the store is in its third quarter, and sales have slacked off. Relations among personnel have similarly suffered. Because of the unprecedented success of this store, a local group of businesspeople have decided to open their own operation across town. Clearly, things are getting more complicated.

TESTIMONY ABOUT THE PROBLEM(S)

Here is what the players say:

Clarence: "Sales are down because things aren't running smoothly. Stock is down and doesn't get reported so orders are made and we don't always have what we advertise or what is on display. (Note: display items cannot be sold.) We need tighter control of employees and stock, more uniformity in how we deal with customers. I don't like Bill and Ben parking their race cars out in front of the store either. It's the wrong image. I'm a little worried about the new store across town, too. Not much we can do about it right now, but unless we get our act together, and fast, well, I dunno. But it won't be good."

Martha: "Sales are down because the newness has worn off and because we didn't take enough time with each customer. I think we need more emphasis on human relationships and caring, more of a sense of warmth in the store. Busy, busy, busy—that's been the problem. We need to realize that what people get here is more than products—they get feelings of security and friendship. We need to work on that."

Catherine: "We've had some problems communicating due to the unforseen traffic in the store. I had no idea we would become so popular! In retrospect, there are things we should have done differently. For example, I should have encouraged the nurses to understand their role in sales support; they still think of themselves as primarily nurses working a doctor's office. The inventory is a real problem because there is no daily record kept of what we sell, so we don't know we are out of something until it isn't there in inventory after a sale on the floor has been made. And I'm not sure we shouldn't sell display items, either. But these problems are only symptomatic of a larger systems problem. We aren't coordinating our activities, working as an integrated team."

Bill: "Man, the problem is simple. At Toys'Я'Us the computers keep up with stock and sales. When the inventory is low, a flag comes up and that signals the managers that it's like, ordering time. Do we do that here? Hell no! Me and my partner have to do it all. Ben, he can't even balance his own checkbook. And me, I didn't get into this line of work to be a suit, you know? I ain't no manager, I'm a worker. Out at our shop, *there* we manage and work. But here, man, we just make the minimum wage. Let the owners do their job and we will do ours."

Clarice: "At first I made good money, real good money. But I'm not making the money anymore. That's the problem. And the reason is because we don't always have what we are supposed to sell, and because the nurses—both of them are real nice ladies, but . . . —well, they just don't help us. I don't know how many times I've overheard them saying that a customer didn't need to make a purchase, that a home remedy would work just as well. See what I mean? I hear that a new store like this one is opening up soon. Maybe they will need an experienced person on their staff."

Jan: "There really aren't any problems here that hard work and honest prayer can't solve. These days people are just working for themselves, not for the company, not for the customers, and not for each other. And you should hear how those stockroom guys talk!

I don't talk to them anymore. I've heard enough of taking the Lord's name in vain. I didn't come to work to have to put up with that. And how Catherine jokes around with that college boy is a little hard on me—I know, I know—you think I'm just an old fuddy-duddy. Well, maybe. But telling sex jokes and gossiping about what people in the store do for fun on the weekends is not my idea of what's right! And I'll bet he gets the big raises and promotions because of it, too."

Fern: Life used to be so simple. You went to work, you did what you were told, you got paid at the end of the week. But now it's not like that. Work overtime, Fern. Work weekends, Fern. Can you shorten your lunch, Fern? You know what I mean. The store comes first, and we are all supposed to put everything else in second place. I think Clarence has the right idea: we need rules, procedures, boundaries. There is too much asked of us if we don't have rules. That's what I think."

Ella: "I miss working for Dr. Sidney. There I was a nurse, his nurse. I had the right to do my job without interference. I was trusted. I felt needed. Here I don't. I might as well be in sales! Sell, sell, sell, that's all I hear. I'm a nurse! I'm a professional, not like some people I know who work here. If I didn't have to work, I wouldn't. But my husband died last year, right after Dr. Sidney retired. There was a little insurance, but not enough. But even if I do make a little more here than I did in private practice, I'd go back to it in a skinny minute if I could."

Anne: "I don't really think anything is wrong. A business is different than a doctor's office, that's all. I'm still learning what is expected of me here. Oh, I loved working for Dr. Sidney, but this is a lot more fun. The children we see are usually clean and healthy. And everyone is so friendly! In a doctor's office mostly you see people who are hurting, bleeding, or suffering from a life-threatening illness. It's sad, and it's not much fun. Here we don't see that. I don't have as much emotional baggage to carry home with me at night."

YOUR ASSIGNMENT

You have been retained as a consultant to find ways to improve communication at the store. What will you recommend?

COMMUNICATING IN
GROUPS, NETWORKS,
AND TEAMS

A combination of forces—from the rapidly changing business environment to the new work force to astonishing advances in technology—is forging a breakdown of the large, traditional hierarchical organizations that have dominated in the past. We think that this dismantling will result in highly decentralized organizations in which the work of the corporation will be done in *small, autonomous units,* linked to the megacorporation by new telecommunications and computer technologies.

—Deal & Kennedy, 1982

Consider what happens when two friends are talking and are joined by a third person. Chances are good that they will alter their conversation to include the new member. Individually, each may talk less frequently to allow space for the third person in the conversation; or each may talk more frequently if the new person is someone they wish to impress.

Now add fourth and fifth members to the group. Let's say that the group knows one of the new people slightly, but the other person not at all. Now how does communication change? It changes in ways that are influenced by the relationships among all the group members, and in ways that serve to complicate processes of interpretation and communication. Topics of discussion will change to accommodate the new members; coalitions or subgroups may form around specific interests and break away from the larger group. Individuals may withdraw from communication altogether or step forward to dominate the interaction.

As a college student, you have most likely had the occasion to work on a group project. Unless you are extremely fortunate, it probably wasn't a very good experience. Perhaps someone did all of the work and got no credit for it; maybe one of the group members didn't show up until the end, and then refused to take responsibility for his or her absences. When all was said and done, you may have concluded that nothing was accomplished in the group that you couldn't have accomplished better alone.

Why are these negative experiences so typical? Could it be that all people are fundamentally self-centered and refuse to cooperate with others if it inconveniences them? Or is it simply that people lack the communication skills necessary to work in groups? It is our belief that group work is difficult and frustrating because groups are microcosms of society, and consequently are sites for negotiating the toughest social problems—problems of creativity versus constraint, monologue versus dialogue. Effective communication in groups requires the ability to strike a balance among the diverse interests of individual members and the needs of the collectivity. While this has been called the central problem of organizing, it is perhaps easiest to see working (or more often, not working!) at the group level.

Of course, there is a positive side to group membership. Humans are social animals, with needs for affiliation and identification. Of all the threats to health, social isolation is perhaps the most severe, and potentially much more devastating than lack of exercise or a high-fat diet. Despite the frustrations of group work, people are drawn to groups for psychological, social, and biological reasons (Ross, 1989). A positive dynamic can occur when a group of people gets together. This makes something wonderful out of a routine or forgettable day, something that no member could have achieved individually. When the members are "in sync," group work can be extremely satisfying, even transcendent (Eisenberg, 1990).

One way to conceptualize organizations is as collectivities of individuals who work in groups (Hawes, 1972). Groups in organizations take many forms and serve many purposes. This chapter explores three broad kinds of collectivities in organizations: formal groups, networks, and teams. In so doing, it should be observed that organizations are increasingly relying on small, autonomous working groups for many of their activities.

FORMAL GROUPS IN ORGANIZATIONS

A group can be defined as "a collection of more than two persons who perceive themselves as a group, possess a common fate, have organizational structure, and communicate over time to achieve personal and group goals" (Baird, 1977). By this definition, passengers on a plane are decidedly not a group, since they lack organizational structure and most likely do not perceive themselves as a group. On the other hand, the crew most likely is a group, for it meets the above requirements.

Groups in organizations can be seen through each of the various theoretical narratives offered earlier in this text. Most authors approach groups from a systems perspective, defining them as subsystems that are linked to the larger organization. For example, a sales force can be viewed as a relatively self-contained system whose outputs (new orders) become inputs for other groups in the organization. Groups can also be viewed as subcultures that to some extent reflect the larger organizational culture but can also be quite different. Groups in organizations may develop unique norms, stories, and practices. An executive team, for example, often develops its own character separate and different from the rest of the company.

This section addresses aspects of formally convened groups in organizations, including the types of groups that exist; the roles of group members; the communication processes of groups in organizations; and conflict in organizational groups.

Types of Organizational Groups

When an organization is formed, its goals are as a rule clear, and communication among members is relatively simple. (There are, of course, exceptions.) The first real group in an organization is senior management, which consists of the founders of the organization as well as those managers they have entrusted to help run the business. If the organization is successful, more people are hired to perform functions that the original management team can no longer handle themselves. For example, salespeople may be hired to bring in new business; engineers to design new products; assemblers to build them; and accountants to keep track of financial data.

If the time comes when multiple people are performing each function, the organization will most likely form departments housing each of the separate functions. These functional departments are the next formal groups to form in organizations. A distinction is usually made between those departments that directly perform the service or build the product (called the line functions) and those departments that support the line functions (called the staff or support groups).

Over time, if the organization continues to grow, departments may be further divided into subgroups. For example, a customer service department in an electric company might have separate groups that handle commercial and residential customers. These subgroups are sometimes called primary work groups. Neonatal nurses in a hospital, for example, comprise a primary work group within the department of nursing.

As the discussion of cross-functional communication in Chapter 7 showed, these functional groupings can create communication problems if they become too isolated from one another. Interestingly, most of the other kinds of organizational groups that are formed are either attempts to promote greater coordination (among functional departments) or clearer direction (for the total organization).

Groups for Coordination Perhaps the group most commonly used for coordination is the project team (which is discussed in detail later in this chapter in the section on teams). For now, let it suffice to say that project teams are commonly found in high-technology organizations and either design new products or ensure coordination of departments in the delivery of a product. The project team helps "manage the white space" between departments to get the product designed and delivered. (Rummler & Brache, 1991).

Whereas project teams are relatively long-standing, *ad hoc groups* or *task forces* are convened to study and solve a particular problem. Members of these groups can either be from the same or from multiple departments. Frequently, their goal is to increase organizational effectiveness, either by improving product quality or by reducing the time it takes to do something (i.e., cycle-time). In the 1980s, informal problem-solving groups called quality circles were popular. Quality circles are "small groups of organizational members (usually between 5 and 12) from all levels of the organization who voluntarily meet for about one hour weekly to discuss and attempt to solve common job-related problems" (Kreps, 1991, p. 175). Quality circles have now gone out of fashion and have been replaced by groups whose mission is to reduce cycle-time. For example, a hospital might want to decrease the time that elapses from patient check-in to settling in a room; or a computer software firm might want to halve the time it takes to get a new product to market. Ad hoc groups are convened to work toward these goals; they may be dissolved once the goals are reached, or they may be reassigned to take on a new challenge.

Recently, organizations have been taking some rather novel approaches to bring people together to solve sticky problems. For example, the Work-Outs at General Electric were started in 1989 by GE CEO Jack Welch (Stewart, 1991). Work-Outs convene a group of 40 to 100 employees, selected by management to represent multiple levels and functions, at a three-day session at a conference center or hotel. A facilitator breaks the large group into five or six smaller groups, who work the first two days (without their manager present) listing and debating everything that is currently wrong with the company, and preparing a presentation to the boss about what they would like to see changed. On Day 3, the boss, unaware of the details of what has been going on, returns and stands in front of the room. Each group takes turns making its proposals. The boss has three options: agree on the spot, say no, or ask for more information. If he asks for more data, a group must be set up to collect it by an agreed-upon date. One manager described the experience: "I was wringing wet within half an hour. . . . They had 108 proposals, and I had about a minute to say yes or no to each one." Work-Outs are one example of how organizations are using groups to encourage creativity and to open a dialogue between management and employees.

Groups for Direction   A number of groups serve to reinforce the organization's direction. Most powerful of these is the *board of directors* or *board of trustees*. The owners of the organization select the board members to provide oversight to the company. If the company is owned by private individuals, this selection is relatively informal; if it is publicly held, the board is elected by stockholders. (In other not-for-profit organizations, the board may be elected by members of the community.) Typically, board members are highly experienced members of the business, political, or educational community who can see problems before they get out of hand, and communicate with the community at large on behalf of the organization. The board can be very powerful, and usually retains the ability to hire and fire the company's senior management. Many board members serve on multiple boards, which constitutes a powerful interorganizational network (cf. Eisenberg et al., 1985).

A second type of group that gives direction to the organization is the *standing committee*. Standing committees are formally appointed and in place for the long term. An organization might have a standing committee on rewards and recognition, for example, that monitors compensation and benefits policies on an ongoing basis. Universities, in addition to their departments, have numerous standing committees to evaluate curriculum, set admissions standards, and review faculty for tenure and promotion.

Group Member Communication Roles

Earlier we suggested that the challenge of group work is in dealing with diversity, or striking a balance among the individual needs and goals of different group members. Although individual behavior in groups varies widely, research on the subject reveals that members play typical communication roles (Goodall, 1990). A role is an expectation about individual patterns of behavior. Just as family members may take on predictable roles like "the good son" or "the caretaking mother," organizational members also tend to occupy roles that emphasize task behaviors or socio-emotional concerns.

The classic typology of group member roles was developed by Kenneth Benne and Paul Sheats (1948), who identified three broad role types: task roles, maintenance roles, and self-centered roles. Two sample task roles are the *summarizer/evaluator,* who restates ideas and summarizes progress to date; and the *initiator,* who is usually first to offer a new idea or suggestion for doing things. Two typical maintenance roles are the *tension reliever,* who tells jokes or changes the subject when things get sticky; and the *harmonizer,* who seeks to mediate and reconcile differences that come up in the group (Shockley-Zalabak, 1991, pp. 189–190). Finally, two common self-centered roles (both of which are considered to be bad for the group) are the *dominator,* who acts superior and won't let anyone else speak; and the *clown,* who diverts the group's attention and pulls them off track by refusing to take things seriously.

Obviously, such a list of group member roles can never be exhaustive, for there are always new ways of describing people's behavior. For example, H. L. Goodall (1990) added some roles to Benne and Sheats's list, including the *Prince,* who fancies himself a brilliant political strategist and sees the world politically; and the *facilitator,* who focuses entirely on the group process (e.g., sticking to the agenda, consensus decision making), sometimes to the exclusion of important substantive issues.

Crucial to communicating in groups is recognizing that these roles will appear from time to time and figuring out which role one usually plays. Once this is done, it is easier for the employee to modify or "flex" his or her own behavior across situations as needed. For example, while it may be appropriate for individuals to play "facilitator" in groups for which they have little concern about the outcome, the initiator role may be more appropriate for outcomes that are of greater concern. Beginning with the employee's first meeting in a new organization, it helps to be conscious of the roles he or she plays in various groups.

Group Communication Processes

Now that we have explored types of organizational groups and the roles group members play, we turn to the nature of the group communication process itself.

Norms Although formal, written rules about group behavior are relatively rare, all groups have norms. Norms are informal "rules that designate the boundaries of acceptable behavior in the group" (Kreps, 1991, p. 170). For example, group norms may apply to promptness and preparation for meetings; in some organizations, people are expected to be on time and to distribute their prepared meeting agenda ahead of time. Or there may be norms about conflict; some groups don't tolerate open disagreement, while others may encourage it. The success of Motorola, for example, has recently been attributed to its norms about conflict; the company is more than willing to disagree loudly in its group meetings (Browning, 1992). Similarly, 3M's success is sometimes linked to a normative "bias for yes"; when in doubt, it tends to be proactive and do something, rather than to wait.

Group norms are shaped by organizational culture and in turn shape group member roles. For example, one aerospace company manifests a general cultural belief that conflict is bad, which is reflected in most of their practices—from the conduct of staff meetings to the procedures for conducting performance evaluations. Predictably, groups in this organization, whether they be functional, project, or ad hoc groups, tend also to avoid conflict. Consequently, the company is full of harmonizers and tension relievers, but few summarizers/evaluators or energizers to reach closure and prod members to action. Group norms are enforced informally through the disapproval of other members, and like aspects of organizational culture, they are very difficult for any single individual to resist.

Decision Making An increasing number of decisions in organizations are delegated to relatively autonomous small groups. Group decision making has many advantages. First, the more people involved, the greater the absolute pool of information. Second, when people get involved in a decision, they are more likely to understand and support it. Third, when people participate in a decision, they are better able to communicate it to their co-workers. A major weakness of the classical theories of organization was the separation of decision making from implementation. As we saw in Chapter 6, when employees can retain control over decisions that directly affect their jobs, their stress level decreases markedly. "Generally, the more complex and challenging the issues under evaluation, the more powerful the outcomes of decisions, and the greater the number of people affected, the better groups are for making the decisions" (Kreps, 1991, pp. 173–174).

Group decision making is not without drawbacks, however. People may perceive safety in numbers, and as a result groups tend to make riskier decisions than individuals acting alone, who may try to hide behind the group should there be negative consequences. (This is called the "risky shift" phenomenon; see Cartwright, 1977). Group members may dominate interaction, be intimidated by others, or care more about social acceptability than reaching the best solution. Perhaps the best-known problem associated with group decision making is Irving Janis's (1971) "groupthink." Groupthink "refers to the need for individuals in a group to suppress dissent and go along with things" (Gibson & Hodgetts, 1986, p. 149). Janis further describes the concept this way:

> In a cohesive group, the danger is not so much that each individual will fail to reveal his [sic] objections to what the others propose but that he will think the proposal is a good one, without attempting to carry out a careful, critical scrutiny of the pros and cons of the alternatives. When groupthink becomes dominant, there is also considerable suppression of deviant thoughts, but it takes the form of each person deciding that his misgivings are not relevant and should be set aside, that the benefit of the doubt regarding any lingering uncertainties should be given to the group consensus (p. 44).

Half the battle in dealing with groupthink is an awareness that groups tend to go off track in this direction. Jane Gibson and Robert Hodgetts (1986) suggest eight remedies to groupthink that reflect good communication principles and apply to most organizations:

1. The leader should encourage participants to voice objections and critically evaluate ideas.
2. Members should take an impartial stance and not get wrapped up in ego and emotions, affording a more objective view of the decision.
3. More than one group can work a problem, which may lead to radically different recommendations.
4. Each member can be encouraged to discuss the group's deliberations with people outside of the group, and get their feedback.
5. Outside experts can be invited into the group for their input and feedback.
6. One of the group members can be appointed devil's advocate to assure that all sides of each issue are explored.

7. The overall group can be divided into subgroups each of which works the problem separately and then reports back.
8. A "second chance" meeting can be held after a preliminary consensus is reached to allow members to express doubts or concerns that may have come up.

Another reason why group decision making is challenging is that it requires the ability to consider and accommodate multiple interpretive frameworks—multiple versions of reality—and to emerge with a single recommendation or course of action. Those involved in group decision making experience a great deal of impatience, criticism, and exasperation, for individuals have difficulty tolerating perspectives that are too radically different from their own. For this reason, optimal ways to make decisions in groups have been the subject of extensive research.

The majority of research on the group decision-making process attempts to divide the process into discrete, identifiable phases. Through an analysis of group interaction, Robert Bales and Fred Strotdbeck (1960) first specified three phases that described problem-solving groups: orientation, evaluation, and control. Their phase model was later modified by Thomas Scheidel and Laura Crowell (1964), who proposed a "spiral reach-testing" model of group process. In terms of this model, as groups attain agreement in one area, they reach out to test some new ideas and areas. If these also lead to agreement, they spiral forward, and if they do not, they spiral back to their last position and start the cycle again. The main point is that group decisions emerge slowly, without discrete phases, and that progress in groups is made through a back-and-forth building on prior commitments.

Aubrey Fisher's (1980) four-phase model of group decision emergence is one of the most well examined in the research literature. According to Fisher, decisions are the product of four stages: orientation, conflict, emergence, and reinforcement.

Orientation When a group gets together for the first time, two kinds of talk characterize the meeting: (1) talk about the reasons for the group meeting and the nature of the task to be accomplished; and (2) talk about the nature of the group, designed to reduce tensions and uncertainties about "who we are and why we are here." This phase serves two important functions. First, it allows people to get to know each other before accomplishing a task; second, it tends to articulate a level of trust among the group members. This phase may be thought of as a period of adjustment during which members get acquainted and make some preliminary judgments about others' interpretive frameworks and about themselves in relation to these others.

Conflict Once the group has determined (or at least tried to determine) what it is to accomplish, communication about the task surfaces. During this phase, initial arguments are made, countered, extended, and abandoned, new ideas are taken up, and old ideas are rehashed. These verbal exchanges are characterized by conflict, now that individuals begin to reveal their positions, styles, and world-views. If the group manages this stage well, the diversity of perspectives will be a benefit, and a source of greater information and points of view. Also in this stage, initial alliances and coalitions are formed, preliminary evidence is weighed, and there is gradual movement toward a single "group" position.

The biggest mistake some groups make during the conflict stage is premature problem definition. For example, in a board of directors meeting of a large retail store a presentation was being made about customers being late in paying their credit card bills. Without much discussion, the board decided to send out a very aggressive letter after 30 days had passed on a customer's delinquent account. Management and employees almost immediately came to regret this quick decision. Any financial benefits of the change were far offset by customer complaints and a significant loss in customer good-will. Groups are as a rule better off if they take time in the conflict stage to brainstorm a variety of ideas (even seemingly "crazy" ones) and hence avoid a premature decision about "what the problem really is."

Emergence   Out of conflicting positions and arguments (sometimes) emerges the group's position, what "we" believe. Coalitions give way to a working consensus. Emergence is a delicate phase because signing up to a group position requires a great deal of compromise and allowances for people to back off or modify original positions and still save face. If trust is lacking, or if differences are simply too great, the group will disintegrate, or some members will withdraw. As a result, the remaining members will assert the power of their positions over those of the rest of the group.

As difficult as it can be to make a decision, harder still is ensuring the implementation of the decision. Many decision-making groups struggle with getting closure on actions. Until the group develops rules or norms that will ensure that individuals will be held specifically accountable for the actions that come out of the meeting, and these actions will be followed up, many good decisions will go unimplemented.

Reinforcement   Once a group has made a decision, there tends to be a kind of afterglow; an intense spirit of cooperation and unity is expressed by group members. Conflict rarely occurs at this stage, and group members generally share a sense of real accomplishment.

Modifications of the Stage Model   More recent work on group decision-making processes explicitly challenges the normative unitary model. This model, typified by Fisher's four stages, holds that most task groups follow a fairly rigid, linear path of development. Specifically, work by Marshall Scott Poole (1981, 1983; Poole & Roth, 1989) maintains that group decision making is more various and complicated than the unitary models suggest. Poole and Roth (1989) found that groups go through periods of disorganization that are both unpredictable and don't follow unitary phase models. Rather than following a lockstep process, groups tend to go through cycles, sometimes repeating stages two or more times. And rather than following a single process throughout, groups manage multiple threads of activity (e.g., task process, working relationships) that may or may not develop in a coordinated fashion. When the threads match, the resulting group process may look like an emergence phase, but when they don't, Poole and Roth argue, no pattern or phase is discernible.

Although in some ways similar to Poole's work, Connie Gersick's (1991) punctuated equilibrium model suggests an entirely new way of seeing group process. Drawing on similarities across many fields and subject areas (e.g., individuals, groups, organizations, academic disciplines, and species), Gersick offers three concepts as key to understanding group development. The first is *deep structure*, which in the case of a group is the set of assumptions and performance strategies used to approach the problem. The second is the *equilibrium period*, a time in which groups work within the established framework without questioning their fundamental approach to their task. The third is the *revolutionary period*, during which groups examine their operating framework and reframe what they are doing as a basis for moving forward.

Gersick (1988) found that working groups experience revolutionary periods at "half-time," the temporal point halfway between their inception and a deadline. Successful groups approach this revolutionary transition period as an opportunity to examine their basic operating assumptions. Unsuccessful groups tend to ignore calls for self-examination and plow ahead according to the initial deep structure. Identifying the phases of group development has proven to be one of the most difficult problems faced by organizational and group communication researchers. We can safely conclude that there is significant variety in the way groups approach their work and that there is no simple recipe for effective group development.

Randy Hirokawa and Kathryn Rost (1992) have made important contributions to the study of effective group decision making. They begin with the belief that effective groups are more attentive to the group process (the procedure they use to solve problems) than are ineffective groups. This increased attentiveness to group process is formulated as "vigilant interaction theory" (Hirokawa & Rost, 1992), which has four aspects: (1) assessment of the nature of the task; (2) assessment of the standards for evaluating various decision options; (3) assessment of positive qualities of the various possible choices; and (4) assessment of negative qualities of various options. The authors conclude that vigilance has its virtues; "group decision performance is directly related to a group's efforts to analyze its task, assess evaluation criteria, and identify the positive and negative qualities of alternative choices" (p. 284).

Finally, a sustained effort has been made to apply communication technology to group decision making, specifically in the form of group-decision support systems—GDSS (Poole & DeSanctis, 1990). GDSS technology gives decision-making groups access to a number of different tools, including software for creating a common electronic display (which may be projectable on a screen and accepts inputs from all group members); software for problem solving and decision analysis; and even expert systems (cf. Contractor & Seibold, 1992). We can begin to envision how GDSS works by picturing a typical group meeting in which everyone there has a networked terminal in front of them with access to various databases and the capability to send both public and private messages to other group members. Although GDSS is only in its infancy as a technology, in principle it should assist groups in the retrieval and communication of information that should improve decision making. Of course, all the predictable problems and ironies of implementation discussed earlier can be expected with GDSS.

Conflict and Consensus in Groups   As described in Chapters 5 and 6, conflict is inherent in organizations, for they are made up of people pursuing different interests. In this section we take a more pragmatic look at groups as sites of conflict. Although the enormous literature on conflict cannot fit neatly into a chapter on groups (or even in a *book* on organizations, for that matter), the major principles can be illustrated in this context.

Conflict in organizations can occur over many issues. Typically, differences emerge among individuals in different departments, with different professional training, serving on a cross-functional task force or committee. Also common are conflicts between line and staff groups, and between individuals of different status who perceive inequities. Conflicts can occur over personalities, on the one hand, or because of workflow blockages, on the other. Conflict can occur between individuals, in groups or between groups, in public or in private.

Conflict can be defined as "the interaction of interdependent people who perceive opposition of goals, aims, and values, and who see the other party[ies] as potentially interfering with the realization of these goals" (Putnam & Poole, 1987, p. 552). In organizations, these goals usually pertain to the acquisition and use of resources. The key terms in this definition are "interaction" and "interdependent." Conflict is a kind of communication, and as such changes are to be expected as a situation evolves—that is, conflict is unpredictable. Furthermore, conflict takes place in interdependent relationships, where each individual depends on the others for some resource. When no one individual can easily force his or her will on the group, or withdraw completely, he or she is forced to negotiate. Conflict is a fact of life in interdependent relationships; what is more, it only increases as the parties come to know one another better. Lack of conflict over a significant period of time is more likely a sign of group stagnation than of effective communication.

Attitudes toward conflict in organizations have changed over the years and have for the most part mirrored society. In the United States in the 1950s, conflict was seen as something to be avoided at all costs. By the 1970s, people had recognized the potentially many benefits of conflict—for surfacing different points of view, acting as a safety valve, facilitating information sharing, and avoiding groupthink. Different societies have characteristic attitudes toward conflict, with some openly argumentative (e.g., Middle Eastern countries) and others more conflict-averse (e.g., many Asian countries).

Research on conflict in organizations can also be characterized according to the theoretical narratives presented in our early chapters. For example, studies in the classical tradition see conflict as evidence of a communication breakdown and treat hostility between participants as "noise" (Hunger & Stern, 1976). Alternatively, the cultural approach sees conflicts as disputes over definitions of organizational reality. Ruth Smith and Eric Eisenberg's (1987) study of competing root metaphors at Disneyland is one example of this approach. Research on conflict cycles and the escalation of conflict are best characterized by the systems perspective (cf. Putnam & Poole, 1987). Finally, critical theory explains superficial organizational conflicts reflecting deeper imbalances of power in the organization (see Chapter 6).

The main point of this work is that, in working groups, conflict is inevitable. But what is most important is how the group members handle the conflict. Here again as in Chapter 8, the virtues of assertiveness and responsible communication apply. Once conflict has surfaced in a group, however, it quickly becomes difficult to stay calm and to communicate effectively. One indicator of how a person might handle conflict is their conflict style. Individual conflict styles vary along two dimensions: concern for self and concern for others (Kilmann & Thomas, 1975). Figure 9.1 on page 270 shows the five possible combinations of conflict style.

Examining this grid gives a better understanding of individual conflict style; not all styles, however, are equally effective. In general, the two highly assertive styles, *competition* and *collaboration*, are the most effective; one or the other is to be preferred depending on the other party and the overall situation. (But remember the reasons for tempering one's assertiveness in response to sexual harassment in the last chapter.) Contrary to what most people think, *compromise* is not a very good choice for resolving a conflict. Compromise is usually classified as a "lose-lose" solution from which neither person gets

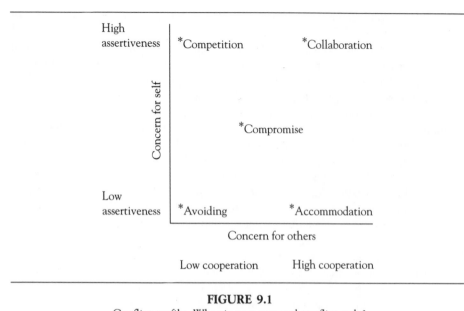

FIGURE 9.1
Conflict profile. What is your personal conflict style?
SOURCE: From R. Kilmann and K. Thomas, "Interpersonal Conflict-handling Behavior as a Reflection of
Jungian Personality Dimensions." *Psychological Reports* 37 [1975] pp. 971–980, fig. 1.

what he or she wants. Collaboration is better, because when it works the parties can come
up with a potentially novel solution that satisfies everybody. And in most cases, although
there may be good reasons to choose *accommodation, avoiding* a situation is typically
counterproductive for it leads to stress for the individual and fails to provide the group
with potentially valuable creative input.

A strategy session at a public hospital illustrates the potential costs of repressed conflict.
Each member of the six-person group wrote his or her own version of the company strategy
and presented it to the group. When they were into the third hour of trying to pull all
these different positions into one statement, it seemed that consensus was finally close at
hand on the final wording. At this point, it became obvious that one of the most vocal
members of the group had fallen silent. When asked directly if he had any problems with
the draft of the statement, he said no—three times—until he was finally pushed into
saying what was on his mind: "I'm not sure what our legal department would think of
some of the words in this latest draft." He then proceeded to make some excellent
suggestions, which led to a much clearer and better conclusion, one that would have
never been reached had he not been pushed into speaking his mind.

Research has not demonstrated clear relationships between an individual's general
conflict style and his or her actual communication in a conflict situation. For example,
while supervisors' conflict styles do seem to be in accord with their initial strategies for
dealing with conflict, subsequent strategies tend to be coercive no matter what their style
(Fairhurst, Green, & Snavely, 1984). This tendency to move toward firmer, compliance-
oriented strategies applies to most supervisors, but takes somewhat longer for women
(Conrad, 1991). The overall conclusion from this research is that multiple situational

factors and multiple goals affect conflict strategy selection. Consequently, conflict style is too simple a predictor of actual communication behavior (Conrad, 1991).

A commitment to collaboration—and to consensus—is a commitment to constant communication. As we will discuss in the section on communication networks, in many organizations democratic consensus-building is too time-consuming to be effective. On the other hand, consensus is an extremely effective way of making important decisions with long-term impact. Unfortunately, few people know what consensus really means. Consensus does *not* mean that everyone in the group agrees with the decision or course of action, but only that people feel that they have been heard. According to Ed Schein, "If there is a clear alternative which *most* members subscribe to, and if those who oppose it feel they have had their chance to influence, *then a consensus exists*" (1969, p. 56). This view of consensus emphasizes the importance of ongoing dialogue in the group, and it assumes that over a period of time, each individual will at some point have to go against personal preferences and go along with the consensus of the group.

In conclusion, good conflict management means accepting the inevitability of differences and making a commitment to dialogue. By dialogue, we mean (see Chapter 2) a willingness to value individuals and their varied world-views, to be open to alternative perspectives (and aware of the limitations of your own), and to strive above all for a communication environment that is both positive for individuals and encourages exceptional, creative decision making.

ORGANIZATIONAL COMMUNICATION NETWORKS

Another enduring concern of researchers has been the structure of organizational groups. The actual pattern of communication among group members is called the group's communication structure. Many factors affect this structure. For example, management may design a group in such a way that communication is purposefully limited. In the absence of such restrictions, people with lower status (e.g., newcomers) within a group may be less willing to speak up than those with higher status. Alternatively, the geographical location of members may cause some people to be more likely to communicate than others. Finally, formal lines of authority and formal rules about communication may restrict information flow in an organizational group.

Small-group Networks

The original work on communication structure was a series of experiments conducted on five-person groups. The term *communication network* was first introduced in these studies. The purpose of the experiments was to determine the effects of centralized versus decentralized communication networks on decision making. Richard Scott (1981) picks up the story:

> In a technique developed by Bavelas (1951), a small number of individuals are placed in cubicles and allowed to communicate only by means of written messages passed through slots in the cubicle walls. The slots connecting each cubicle can be opened or closed by the experimenter, so that different communication patterns can be imposed on the

interacting subjects. . . . A typical task presented to groups of individuals placed in these networks is to provide each individual with a card containing several symbols, only one of which is present on the cards of all subjects. The task is defined as completed when all participants are able to correctly identify the common symbol (Scott, 1981, pp. 148–149).

The four small-group communication networks that were the most frequent focus of study were the circle, wheel, chain, and all-channel networks. The circle and all-channel reflect a relatively high degree of decentralization; the chain and wheel are centralized (see Figure 9.2). Results showed that centralized networks were more efficient than decentralized networks in their performance, as reflected in the speed with which they completed the task (Leavitt, 1951). Further investigations, however, revealed that centralized hierarchies were not superior to the decentralized arrangements in all cases:

as tasks become more complex or ambiguous, decentralized nets are usually superior to centralized structures . . . formal hierarchies aid the performance of tasks requiring

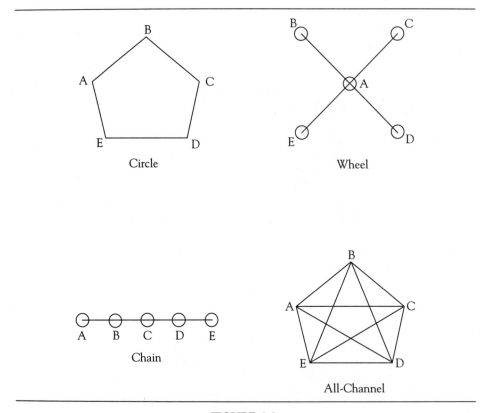

FIGURE 9.2
Examples of communication networks (five-person groups).
SOURCE: W. R. Scott, *Organizations: Rational, Natural, and Open Systems*, Engelwood Cliffs, NJ: Prentice-Hall (1981), p. 8.

the efficient coordination of information and routine decision making whereas they interfere with tasks presenting very complex or ambiguous problems. . . . Specifically, hierarchies impede work on the latter by stifling free interactions that can result in error-correction, by undermining the social support necessary to encourage all participants to propose solutions, and by reducing incentives for participants to search for solutions (Scott, 1981, pp. 149–150).

This early research on small-group communication networks yielded some interesting, if common-sense, contingencies to be considered in decision making. For example, when a group faces a routine, unequivocal task, or a very short deadline, seeking participation and input from all members is probably a waste of time. On the other hand, if the problem is complex, it is a better idea to seek an open dialogue on the issue, which is both more likely to promote member satisfaction and a better quality long-term solution.

The research leading to these claims has not, however, been without significant criticism. Most of the criticism has focused on the artificiality of the experiments and their use of new groups without any work history. The claim was that such experimental groups had little in common with real groups in real organizations (Farace, Monge, & Russell, 1977). This dissatisfaction was the impetus for broadening the focus of communication network research to include not just patterns of interaction in decision-making groups, but also the informal patterns of communication that characterize all organizations.

Emergent Networks

Although formal groups in organizations are important, they don't tell the whole story. The most powerful and important groups in organizations are not appointed by anybody; instead, they emerge from the formal and informal communication in which people engage as a normal part of their work life.

The enduring focus on communication networks in organizations today is due primarily to the widespread philosophical acceptance of the systems perspective. As discussed in Chapter 4, systems theories lead to a focus not on individuals, but on the connections between them, the relationships that constitute organization. The communication network paradigm (Rogers & Kincaid, 1981) looks specifically at those relationships that emerge naturally within organizations, and at the associated patterns, groups, and individual roles that come out of such an emergence. Formal and emergent networks coexist, and each ought to be understood in the context of the other (Monge & Eisenberg, 1987). For example, a new employee may be given a copy of the formal organizational chart, detailing reporting relationships and the structure of functional departments. Over time, he or she will find that the actual communication relationships fail to mirror the organizational chart precisely. Departments may have no formal linkage but need to communicate continually to manage the workflow; secretaries or salespeople from different product lines may have no formal connection but gather in the lunch room to talk about their common experiences. A great deal can be learned about an organization's culture by exploring the discrepancies between the informal emergent network and the formal organizational chart.

Perhaps the earliest work on emergent communication networks investigated the organizational "grapevine" (Davis, 1953). Building on the work of Chester Barnard (see

Chapter 3), Keith Davis made the point that informal communication was critical to the health of an organization. The word "grapevine" is a reference to a communication system used during the Civil War, in which telegraph wires were strung through trees and resembled a grapevine (Daniels & Spiker, 1991). Research shows that the grapevine is oral, fast, and more accurate than the formal dissemination of information (Hellweg, 1987).

Managers and researchers alike have a strong interest in identifying the paths informal communication takes—the structure of the informal network. In this way, they can better understand the spread of rumors and the distribution of informal power in the organization. Toward this end, Davis (1953) developed a technique called ECCO analysis, in which a single message was "placed" in an organization and then "followed" to other areas of the organization. More recently, more complex network analysis techniques have been developed that "map" the total emergent communication network of an organization (cf. Monge & Eisenberg, 1987). The most common mapping technique involves asking each member of the organization to fill out a survey indicating how often they talk to everyone else, and about what topics. A cutoff point must be established to determine whether two individuals are considered to be linked in the network. Although it can vary tremendously, in most organizations contact at least once per week is sufficient to justify a linkage between two people.

In envisioning emergent communication networks, we are concerned mainly with the overall pattern of interaction (especially the existence of cliques or groups); the communication roles individuals play within the network; and the content of communication that flows through the emergent structure.

Overall Network Pattern   Figure 9.3 shows a sample communication network of an organization that has been overlaid on the formal organizational chart. Notice that there are quite a few informal groups, which are comprised of people who literally have the majority of their communication with one another. In network terminology, informal groups that emerge from people's reporting about communication contacts are called cliques. In the figure, some of these cliques cut across functional lines, indicating other bases for these relationships.

Organizational communication networks vary in density. Density is a measure of the total number of linkages or connections among all organizational members, divided by the total number of possible connections. A professional association, for example, is a very low-density network. While there may be many members, and consequently many possible relationships, communication among members is infrequent. On the other hand, the kitchen crew of a restaurant is a highly dense network in that most members have some regular occasion to communicate with everyone else. Along these lines, formal hierarchies structured according to classical theories of management are less dense than more progressive organizations that encourage participation and communication in all directions.

Research on organizational innovation (Albrecht & Hall, 1991) suggests the importance of dense clusters of individuals in organizations that have considerable influence over whether other employees will adopt a new idea or technology. In their study of elementary schools and their administrations, Albrecht and Hall found that personal relationships played a key role in the development of new ideas by creating an identifiable structure of cliques or clusters who focus on the innovation. These close connections help

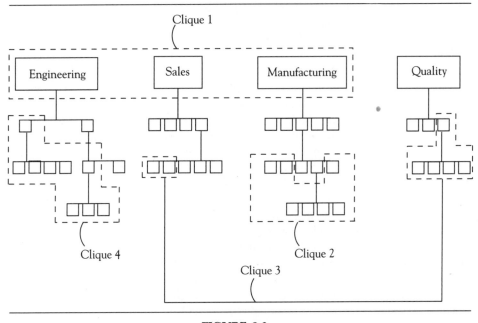

FIGURE 9.3
Sample organizational communication network.

people feel comfortable with the uncertainty of the innovation and consequently make them more likely to adopt it.

The density of an organizational communication network can have some less intuitively obvious implications for organizational effectiveness. Mark Granovetter (1973) has written about the importance of "weak ties" in networks, as sources of new information. When everyone is closely connected, individual knowledge bases begin to converge, and the risks of groupthink may increase. Michael Papa (1990) makes a similar point in his study of employee performance with new technology in an insurance company. Papa measured network diversity, which reflects the number of *different kinds* of people with whom an individual communicates on a regular basis. Papa found that "the more diverse an employee's network was, the more coworkers he or she talked to about the new technology, and the more frequently he or she talked about the new computer, the more productive that employee was likely to be using the new system" (Papa, 1990, p. 361). Finally, Karl Weick (1976) has enumerated the benefits of loosely coupled systems (in which decisions and actions can occur independently and even redundantly) as sources of organizational flexibility, adaptation, creativity, and competitiveness. These writers alert us to the risks of assuming that more dense networks and tighter connections overall necessarily promote organizational effectiveness.

Communication Network Roles   The communication network roles individuals play differ from content roles (such as initiator or clown) in that they specifically refer to a person's structural position in the information flow. Just as informal cliques play a critical role in employee morale, an individual's communication network role is likely to be personally important. One reason why is that well-connected individuals in organizations are also the most personally influential (Brass, 1984). One should think twice before breaking up a clique or changing a person's role in such a way that their informal power base is significantly altered or eroded.

Four roles that are most commonly identified in network analysis are isolate, group member, bridge, and liaison. *Isolates* are those people with no appreciable communication contact in the organization; they either work alone by choice or are in jobs that are structurally or geographically set apart from the rest of the employees. *Group members* are individuals who have the majority of their communication contact within an informal clique, which may roughly coincide with a department, profession, or demographic grouping (e.g., old-timers, nurses, Vietnamese workers). *Bridges* are persons who are both group members and have significant communication contact with at least one individual who belongs to another informal group. Finally, *liaisons* connect two or more cliques without being exclusive members of either one.

Let us say a few more words about the importance of liaisons—they are the keepers of the dominant interpretations, the core of the organization's culture (see Chapter 9). They "run" the grapevine; they know things before anyone else, and they have tremendous influence on the direction of the company. Anyone who seeks to make changes in an organization, whether it be a new supervisor, a CEO, or a consultant, ought first to consult these key communicators. They have the ability to transform any "message" into an interpretation that is consistent with their beliefs and to pass that interpretation quickly throughout the company (and sometimes to customers and the community as well). When organizational improvement efforts succeed or fail, it is almost always a result of the proper or improper mobilization of these key communicators or opinion leaders.

The identification of network roles in an organization is a sensitive subject for two reasons. First, employees do not always *agree* on their degree of communication contact with others. Occasionally, for example, a subordinate will report daily contact with a superior, and the superior will report no communication at all with that subordinate. This is a reciprocation problem and often has to do with either the perceived status of reporting communication with certain people or with an individual's perception of the people with whom they "ought" to be communicating. Second, the results of a network analysis may put certain individuals in a *bad light*. A communication network analysis of a professional association we studied revealed that one of the department heads was an isolate in the eyes of his subordinates; this finding ultimately led to his dismissal from the organization.

Network Content   Unlike a formal group, which is created for specific reasons but may begin with little to talk about, emergent communication networks develop around specific topics or content areas of communication (Farace, Monge, and Russell, 1977). Each content area can be regarded as defining a separate network. A bank, for example, may have a *social* network for communication about personal matters and a *task* network for discussion of work duties. Distinctions are made among types of network content because the emergent structure will likely be different for each content area. In other words, the cliques, bridges, isolates, and liaisons in a task network may differ dramatically from those same roles in a social network in the same organization.

The identification of multiple types of communication content also allows linkages between people to be viewed more precisely. Specifically, if two people communicate only about one topic—say, task issues—their relationship is said to be *uniplex*. Alternatively, when individuals communicate about more than one topic—say, personal, task, and new ideas—their relationship is *multiplex*. Multiplex linkages have been found to be very important in social support and organizational innovation (Albrecht & Hall, 1991; Ray, 1987).

The content of communication networks takes on added significance because we are increasingly concerned not simply with who talks to whom in an organization, but also with the sense-making process that takes place through such networks (Richards, 1985). In an attempt to extend the cultural approach to organizations, Peter Monge and Eric Eisenberg (1987) have advocated applying network analysis methods to the concerns of meaning and interpretation in organizations. Their proposal is to consider something called *semantic networks,* or the connections that exist between people who hold similar interpretations of key organizational symbols or events. Although all the same network measures can be used (e.g., clique, isolate, liaison), here they refer to groups that share similar interpretations, are isolated from mainstream values and beliefs, or connect disparate subcultures. A dense semantic network, for example, is one in which there is shared meaning on major organizational issues. The approach has been successfully applied to the analysis of perceptions of organizational mission statements (Contractor, Eisenberg, & Monge, 1992).

In summary, the communication network approach can be extremely useful in any consideration of the informal, emergent structure of organizations. Above all, network approaches sensitize us to the creative tendency of individuals to forge new linkages, regardless of formal rules or boundaries. It is impossible to "formalize" an organization's communication network; even if one were to revise the organizational chart to match the informal network, it would immediately be obsolete. Informal communication in organizations is fluid and constantly changing. While formal reorganizations may occur only infrequently, the informal organization is in a constant state of reorganization (Monge & Eisenberg, 1987).

Interorganizational Communication Networks

Not all of an employee's work-related communication is with other employees, of course; much of it is with outsiders, some of whom are customers and others of whom are members of other organizations and institutions. Account managers in an advertising agency, for example, interact with many different individuals in the course of their day, including representatives from various media organizations such as newspapers and television stations. In universities, the person responsible for gifts and development may also communicate with a wide range of people, including alumni, accountants, lawyers, and local officials. For this reason, there are clear advantages to seeing organizational communication networks as crossing organizational lines.

Interorganizational relationships "are the relatively enduring transactions, flows, and linkages that occur among or between an organization and one or more organizations in its environment" (Oliver, 1990, p. 241). Interorganizational networks vary in their openness, density, and interdependence; all the same advantages and disadvantages of loose and tight coupling described above apply here as well. Tightly coupled, highly interdependent interorganizational networks are very sensitive to environmental "jolts" that can threaten an entire industry. For example, since the deregulation of the airline industry, even the slightest change on the part of one carrier (say, in offering lower fares) sends shock waves throughout all the others and has resulted in a rash of bankruptcies.

As noted in Chapter 4, open systems theory afforded greater significance to an organization's environment, without which the organization could not survive. For some researchers, "organizational environments can be usefully regarded as consisting mainly of networks of other organizations. The complexity of this network of interorganizational relations is a variable, and higher levels of causal texturing present increasing challenges to organizational adaptation" (Metcalfe, 1981, p. 505). According to Charles Perrow (1986), an organization's environment is a kind of "nested box problem," wherein each network exists within a larger network or system, from department, to division, organization, interorganizational field, industry, region, nation, and the world.

Organizations can participate in an interorganizational network in numerous ways. For example, two organizations are said to be vertically integrated if the first builds parts or provides a service necessary for the second to provide their product or service. (For example, Pratt-Whitney makes aircraft engines for sale to Boeing.) Alternatively, two companies are horizontally integrated if customers can be passed from one to the next in the service cycle. A clinic that does cancer screening, a hospital that treats cancer patients, and an outpatient counseling center that provides support for cancer survivors are horizontally integrated. Finally, a company may form strategic alliances or joint ventures with competitors.

Eisenberg et al. (1985) developed a typology of interorganizational communication that specified three types of linkages—institutional, representative, and personal—for the exchange of materials and information. An institutional linkage occurs when no specific individuals are involved, as in the automatic transfer of data between banks. A representational linkage exists when individuals meet on their organization's behalf, as in contract negotiations or planning for a joint venture. Finally, a personal linkage occurs when members of two organizations communicate in a nonrepresentative or private capacity.

Having explained this typology, let us quickly say that like all category systems, the reality is slightly different. Specifically, the line between personal and representative linkages is a fuzzy one. People can meet without any intentions of discussing business, but business does get discussed, and the results can be significant. The different types of linkages may also be related in time. For example, an engineering firm is planning a joint venture; the first steps involve numerous lunches and dinners designed to make the principals more comfortable with each other personally. If this stage goes well, representatives will be identified to work out the details; later on, data and materials may flow between the two organizations with little or no human involvement.

One interesting and subtle point associated with interorganizational communication is that the most efficient way of sharing information across organizational lines may not be any form of overt communication, but the flow of individuals themselves. Organizations most frequently get new information by hiring new employees. If they have experience, these employees bring with them interpretations from their former organization. Ideas about management, marketing, organizational structure, communication, and the treatment of employees are "imported" in this way, through personnel flows. For this reason, hiring someone with "relevant work experience" is always a double-edged sword. Such persons bring with them a technical ability and an interpretive framework which may inject needed change. For example, when Hughes Aircraft Company hired C. Michael Armstrong from IBM to be its new CEO, he was the first CEO of the company ever to emphasize business and financial management over engineering (and he was the first nonengineer). In other cases, the new employee's experience can be an obstacle to the organization's ability to do things differently.

While personnel flows are routine examples of interorganizational exchange, many organizations today are undertaking more radical arrangements. In an era of economic limits, organizations are more likely to engage in strategic alliances to enhance their own financial and political power (e.g., mergers, acquisitions, industry associations, joint ventures, research and development consortia). Recognizing that no organization can be all things to all customers, most companies are narrowing their scope of services and coordinating with other organizations that provide compatible products and services that they do not. This has been true for some time in health care (particularly in highly technical services such as transplants) and is increasingly the case in higher education, as universities recognize that they can no longer afford to offer the same programs as the school down the road. Similarly, many companies are partnering with foreign organizations in the hope of penetrating international markets. Finally, high-technology organizations are investing in joint research and development consortia in order to cut the costs of development and take advantage of the potential synergy among scientists.

All of these new interorganizational forms are at times awkward to manage. Scientists assigned from their home organization (say, Rockwell International) to a research and development consortium (say, SEMATECH) may feel personally ambivalent about sharing their best ideas with scientists from competitor organizations. More formal interorganizational alliances are also risky in that they require a good deal of trust, a willingness to surrender autonomy, and the juxtaposition of incompatible organizational cultures. In many mergers and acquisitions, the partnering organizations differed in their levels of formality and attitudes toward employees, which led to major problems of integration.

Interorganizational communication networks are interesting because, like multidisciplinary groups, they are potential sites of productive dialogue. Without question, the future holds increased interorganizational cooperation across organizational, industrial, national, and even planetary boundaries. This increased communication will bring even greater challenges of championing dialogue in the face of diversity, and of encouraging communication that both values individuals and promotes organizational effectiveness.

TEAMS

The past ten years have witnessed an explosion in the use of teams in organizations. While the importance of teamwork has been known for some time, this new emphasis on teams is more than simply learning to work together. It is an explicit attempt to involve and empower individuals from all levels of the organization to do "more with less" in an era of shrinking resources and increased competitiveness (see Fig. 9.4, page 280). In this way, a team-based organization is more radical than either the idea of teamwork or any of the formal organizational groups described above.

Teams are most likely to be effective in companies that offer no other choice: either

Our Team Needs One Good Multiskilled Maintenance Associate

Our team is down one good player. Join our group of multiskilled Maintenance Associates who work together to support our assembly teams at American Automotive Manufacturing.

We are looking for a versatile person with skills in one or more of the following ability to set up and operate various welding machinery, knowledge in electric arc and M.I.G. welding, willingness to work on detailed projects for extended time periods, and general overall knowledge of the automobile manufacturing process. Willingness to learn all maintenance skills a must. You must be a real team player, have excellent interpersonal skills, and be motivated to work in a highly participative environment.

Send qualifications to:

AAM

American Automotive Manufacturing
P.O. Box 616
Ft. Wayne, Indiana 48606
Include phone number.
We respond to all applicants.

Maintenance Technician/Welder

Leading automotive manufacturer looking for Maintenance Technician/Welder. Position requires the ability to set up and operate various welding machinery and a general knowledge of the automobile production process. Vocational school graduates or 3-5 years of on-the-job experience required. Competitive salary, full benefits, and tuition reimbursement offered.

Interviews Monday, May 6, at the Holiday Inn South , 3000 Semple Road, 9:00 A.M. to 7:00 P.M. Please bring pay stub as proof of last employment.

National Motors Corporation
5169 Blane Hill Center
Springfield Illinois 62707

FIGURE 9.4
Team employment advertisement and traditional employment advertisement.
SOURCE: Wellins, Byham, and Wilson, 1991, p. 20.

management and employees learn to cooperate, or they are history. Traditional centralized hierarchies are inefficient and not responsive to rapidly changing market conditions. Alternative structures, such as high-involvement management or self-managing work teams, have begun to take the place of the traditional hierarchy (Cummings, 1978; Lawler, 1986). In 1990 there were already over 300 manufacturing plants in the United States using some kind of highly participative team approach.

Despite this widespread enthusiasm for teams, the definition of what constitutes a team has remained ambiguous, particularly in the United States. This may be because Americans have had more experience with the classical, hierarchical organizational structure than with teams. The roots of contemporary interest in work teams are in the findings of the Hawthorne studies (which attested to the importance of informal groups, as described above) and in European experiments with autonomous work groups (Kelly, 1992). Work by Eric Trist (1981) with teams of coal miners in Britain in the 1950s, for example, focused on the communication processes that would simultaneously optimize social and technical systems.

> In the mines, employees worked together, helping each other and often trading jobs. Trist discovered clear indications of higher productivity and job satisfaction among those workers who were given more control of their jobs. Trist's studies also indicated that organizations with workers who were more involved in the operation were better equipped to respond to changing markets and political conditions—something that large and rigid organizations found difficult (Wellins, Byham, & Wilson, 1991, p. 8).

Trist's work—in concert with other European experiments in self-management, such as a Volvo plant in Kalmar, Sweden—was the impetus for what became known as the *sociotechnical* school. The basic tenet of the sociotechnical school is that organizational and job designs should be participative and open-ended with minimal critical specifications and constraints. The overarching goal is to discover workable alternatives to hierarchy (Herbst, 1976).

Because of the misguided tendency to call any working organizational group a team, we take a more narrow perspective. Specifically, we identify two types of teams in organizations: project teams and work teams. To avoid confusion, any other working collection of people is best referred to as a committee, a task force, or an ad hoc group.

Project Teams Project teams have existed for a long time in many organizations. They are standing groups that help coordinate the successful completion of a particular project, product, or service. One type of project team is comprised of people working to design and develop a new product or service. Members might include designers, manufacturers, and salespeople as needed. An example would be "a team of engineers, programmers, and other specialists who design, program, and test prototype computers" (Sundstrom, DeMeuse, & Futrell, 1990, p. 121). A second type of project team might be assigned to a specific issue or problem. For example, a well-known savings and loan recently formed a ten-person business development team whose sole purpose is to come up with ways to bring in new business.

Yet a third type of project team exists within a matrix organization (see Figure 9.5, page 282). According to Scott (1981):

> The hallmark of the matrix is the simultaneous operation of vertical and lateral channels of information and of authority. The vertical lines are typically those of functional departments that operate as "home base" for all participants; the lateral lines represent project groups that combine and coordinate the services of selected functional specialists around particular projects. All participants are responsible to their functional superior and one or more project leaders. . . . Matrix organizations are to be found in the more highly innovative industries such as contract research, electronics, and aerospace (p. 220).

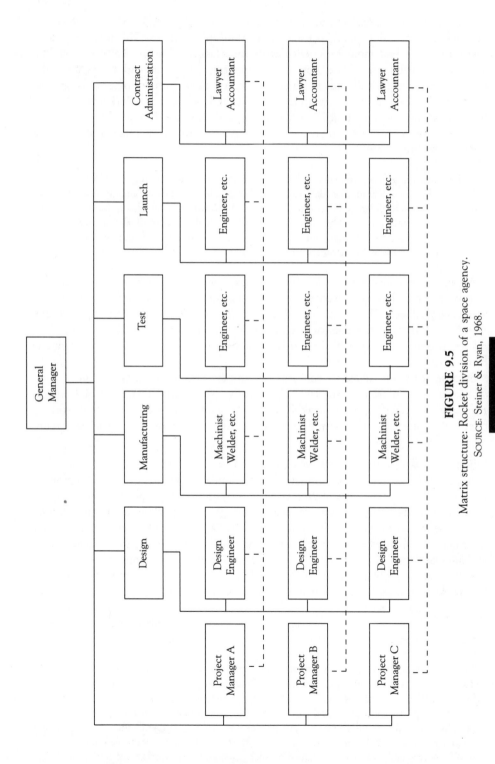

FIGURE 9.5

Matrix structure: Rocket division of a space agency.

SOURCE: Steiner & Ryan, 1968.

While it is difficult to make matrix organizations work (people have trouble answering to two bosses, and there can be redundancy across project teams), the reason for their existence is clear. Without these cross-functional project teams, individuals tend to get isolated in their particular functions and lose attention to customer requirements. Project managers lead project teams whose purpose is to manage the white space between the functions and to ensure that the project gets done properly and that the customer is happy.

Work Teams   Of all the kinds of teams currently popular in organizations, work teams are the most exciting. By work team we mean specifically "an intact group of employees who are responsible for a 'whole' work process or segment that delivers a product or service to an internal or external customer" (Wellins, Byham, & Wilson, 1991, p. 3). For example, an eight-member intact work team at a southern California aerospace company is responsible for all metallizing of components in the company. The team resides together, has mapped its internal workflow (i.e., the steps in applying metal to parts), and is continuously improving its work process (which in this case means making the metal coating as thin as possible). Other well-known companies, such as Federal Express, General Electric, Corning, General Mills, and AT&T, have all recorded significant improvements in productivity through the implementation of work teams (Wellins, Byham, & Wilson, 1991).

Just as it is for individuals, the most important question surrounding the use of work teams is empowerment—how much discretion and autonomy can be delegated to the team? For work teams to be effective, management must make a commitment to empowerment. There is nothing more frustrating than getting a group of people together to work on a problem, who subsequently discover they don't have the authority to implement their proposed solutions. Lyle Sussman (1976) explains why managers should try to empower work teams with as much decision-making authority as possible (i.e., to be relatively self-managing): "a group can more effectively allocate its resources when and where it is required to deal with its total variance in work conditions" (p. 183). In other words, if you give a team sufficient information and the discretion over who performs which tasks on a given day, and how to accomplish a specific job, the members will respond better than if they only see part of the picture.

In practice, work teams can be classified by their degree of empowerment. Figure 9.6 on page 284 shows a team empowerment continuum indicating the responsibilities delegated to the team at four levels of empowerment. Notice that teams begin by doing things like running their own meetings ("housekeeping"), training each other ("cross-training"), and scheduling. As empowerment increases, they may take responsibility for continuous improvement of their processes, selecting new members, electing the team leader, and making decisions about capital expenditures. Finally, at the top right of the chart lies the self-directed or self-managing work team, which in addition to all the above duties is also responsible for performance appraisal, discipline, and even compensation.

Although true self-directed work teams do exist, they are still rare. One problem in creating such teams is that their existence typically calls into question every other system in the organization, including organizational culture, performance appraisal, security, training, compensation, strategic planning, and even the physical layout of the company (Sundstrom, DeMeuse, & Futrell, 1990). Most factors that promote or inhibit a team's performance are external to the team (Donnellon, 1992). Richard Hackman's (1990)

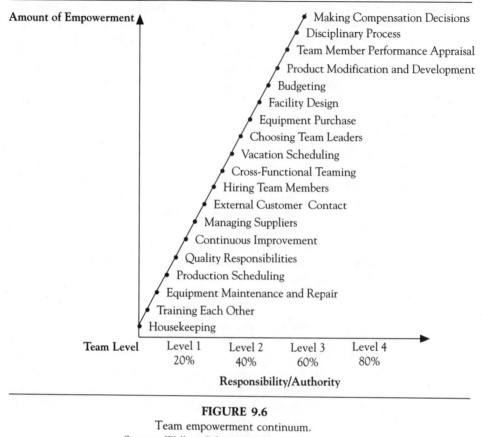

FIGURE 9.6
Team empowerment continuum.
SOURCE: Wellins, Byham, & Wilson, 1991, p. 26.

normative model of group effectiveness provides an excellent illustration of how both individuals and groups are situated with regard to their ability to be effective. According to Hackman, a team's effectiveness is the function of many variables, including the degree of supportiveness of organizational systems, such as rewards; the composition and design of the group; the level of effort and amount of knowledge brought to bear on the task; and the sufficiency of material resources.

A second barrier to the effectiveness of work teams is union agreements that prohibit cross-training or set out rules that conflict with the goals of self-management. These union obstacles can be overcome, however, if management is committed to a true and equal partnership with employees.

A third and final source of resistance to self-managing teams is management itself, most typically first-line supervisors whose roles change drastically in this kind of environment. These supervisors often feel "stuck in the middle" if they are asked to abandon their old management style but do not as yet feel comfortable with what it might mean to "manage" a self-managing team (Tjosvold & Tjosvold, 1991). A manager's ability to oversee an empowered work team is one of the most critical skills for ensured success into the next century. As a result, perhaps the largest growth area in management training is in the "front-line" leadership of semiautonomous work teams. Few of the old supervisory skills apply. Instead, the new supervisor overseeing a team needs to

1. Act like a facilitator, keeping the group on track while respecting a free play of ideas.
2. Be hard on rules, agenda, goals, and accountability, but soft on the means by which the team chooses to organize itself and do its work.
3. Communicate extensively with his or her boss and peers, to keep the team "hooked in" to the big picture of what's going on with other teams and with the organization as a whole.

In other words, managers of project and work teams must above all value, understand, and create a climate for honest yet supportive dialogue. Such a shift requires an enormous transformation in management and nonmanagement roles; the communication skills necessary to perform such roles are formidable. In any case, clearly anyone thinking about

---

ETHICS BOX 9.1

THE ETHICS OF MID-LEVEL MANAGEMENT WITHIN A FRAMEWORK OF EMPOWERMENT

Fred Myerson was troubled. His company was making a strong commitment to change that included the evolution of self-managing work teams through an intensive program of employee empowerment. Fred had been a mid-level manager in the old way of doing things; now he was a "coach" responsible for facilitating work teams.

Fred believed in the change and was dedicated to making it work. But lately he had encountered a problem with empowerment that his training seminars hadn't prepared him for. The problem was how to diplomatically handle unusable ideas from work teams without discouraging the teams from contributing new ideas in the future. Put simply, not all ideas were equal, even though all the ones that reached him were sponsored enthusiastically. The problem was complicated by the fact that Fred didn't want to be seen as a person who was "resisting change," but neither did he want to be left out of the decision-making picture simply to make his work teams feel good. He had been a good manager before this change effort occurred, but he was finding it difficult to remain one.

As he saw it, he had three bad choices. He could pass along what he felt was a bad idea, which would be an ethical violation of his duty to the company but would support the empowerment aspect of the organizational change effort; he could ignore any proposal that he felt was unsound, thus behaving unethically toward the work teams and probably undermining the change effort; or he could argue against a proposal and risk being seen by the work team as simply falling back on his old "command and control" management routine, thus disempowering them and probably reducing their willingness to suggest future changes.

What should Fred do? Given what you have learned about group contexts in organizations, what other alternatives does Fred have?

entering the workplace today and in the future must know more about how to work on teams than almost anything else.

A FINAL CAVEAT: RETREAT FROM TEAMS?

In many respects, the ideal of the self-directed work team is the natural culmination of the two forces described in Chapter 1: that is, increased competitive pressures, and an increased desire for autonomy, responsibility, and an improved quality of life. While in many ways these two forces might be viewed as contradictory, in the effective self-directed team we may see them converge.

But this is still mostly wishful thinking; in real organizations, teaming has a spotty record. Companies like Ford, Procter & Gamble, and Honda have recently undertaken a "retreat" from teams, which in many cases were found to take too long in making decisions (Chandler & Ingrassia, 1991) and shielded people from taking responsibility. Even General Motors's renowned Saturn plants, which began with the model of work teams inhabiting the "factory of the future," have been "steadily moving back to the Detroit-style assembly line" (Drucker, 1992). Finally, the partnership between labor and management which is essential for teaming in a union environment has been strained by recent decisions to downsize and lay off employees.

Why are teams failing? We close this chapter with two related answers to this question. First, teams may fail because they suggest a radical reframing of power relationships in organizations, which few if any members of management are genuinely prepared to examine. Many employees entering the workforce have the expectation that jobs are unpleasant, that organizations are cold and unfeeling, and that bosses are unreasonable and out of touch. They are slow to be convinced otherwise. When teams are originally proposed in an organization, the first reaction is extreme skepticism, but if the conditions are right, the best employees can become the strongest advocates. Then comes the moment of truth, when the new interpretive framework is tested, and the main question is something like: "Do our opinions really matter?" or "Do we really have the power to make critical decisions?" At this moment of truth, many managers falter and fail to offer the degree of empowerment that was promised. Team members then retreat to their old world-views with a vengeance.

Management expert Peter Drucker (1992) makes a similar point in saying that teams fail because management doesn't know what kind of team they want, and in particular how much team members should be expected to know each other's jobs and to cover for one another. An interesting irony associated with teams is that the more empowered, self-managing, and cross-trained a team becomes, the more strong leadership is required from a "coach" or "conductor." A failure to meet employee expectations about either degree of empowerment or type of team contributes to the failure of the team approach. Furthermore, such expectations cannot be communicated gradually. When it comes to implementing teams, slow change cannot work; there has to be a break with the past, however difficult that might be (Drucker, 1992).

CREATIVITY AND CONSTRAINT IN GROUPS, NETWORKS, AND TEAMS

Like interpersonal relationships, groups in organizations are examples par excellence of the challenge of balancing creativity and constraint, of promoting an organized diversity of interpretations. When people first join a team or group, their first reaction is anxiety about who they are in relation to the others; each participant struggles to find a voice that makes sense in the context of that group. This can be a formidable challenge. For example, we were recently involved in setting up a change management team in a large manufacturing organization whose job was to oversee the company's transition to work teams. The elected team leader was an African-American human resources professional. Half of the team members were also African American, and some of these individuals were members of the union. Consider the plight of the team leader as an extreme case of what happens to all of us in groups: he literally didn't know how to speak to the group. He had developed a number of different "voices" for communicating with other African Americans, union members, and upper management, but he had never had to speak to them all at once.

This initial problem of finding a voice might appropriately be assigned to the orientation phase of group development. Seen this way, both the conflict and emergence stages involve individuals articulating their perceptions, which, while often creative, are heavily weighted with elements of constraint (e.g., "we tried that, it didn't work," or "there's no point in even having this discussion, management will never take it seriously anyway" or, finally, unbelievably: "it doesn't matter what the customer says—this is the way we've always done it"). Other constraints, such as meeting places and times, agenda items, action items, or problem-solving procedures can be useful in promoting group or team effectiveness. Overall, however, the ability of a group of people to function together in an organization depends on the skill with which they can balance the creative contributions of each individual member with the overall constraints, concerns, and will of the group.

SUMMARY

Group communication differs from relational communication in more than simply the number of participants engaging in the dialogue. Because language—and the interpretations of its meanings—increases in complexity, so too do the possibilities for miscommunication.

An understanding of groups in organizations begins with the idea of contexts. The three types of organizational groups are formal (senior management, functional departments, and primary work groups), coordination groups (project teams, task forces, and ad hoc groups), and directive groups (board of directors or trustees and standing committees). We identified many of the group member communication roles and group communication processes that characterize group contexts in organizations.

The three network contexts described here are small-group networks (circle, wheel, chain, all-channel), emergent networks (communication networks, grapevines, cliques, loosely coupled systems), and interorganizational networks (institutional, representational, and personal linkages). Communication roles and types of communication within and among networks were defined.

Finally, we described organizational teams. We delineated differences between project teams and work teams, and discussed the essential role of empowerment in moving a team toward self-management.

In summary, then, group contexts in and among organizations create and respond to norms, decision-making processes, and conflict and consensus that reach from the personal experiences of group members through organizational cultures to the broad interorganizational field. Maintaining productive dialogue at every group level is vital to the health of individuals, organizations, and societies.

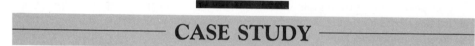

CASE STUDY

The Case of the Lost Camaraderie

General Software (GS) has recently relocated to a new, state-of-the-art corporate building in the city's Research Park. Previously, GS was housed in small, cramped rented office space on the other side of this midsized Midwestern town. The move to luxurious new offices affords the employees many new status perks, as well as improved working conditions.

There is a downside to this move, however. One of the great things about GS is its strong company culture, a culture that was built, in part, by requiring everyone to pull together to get the job done back in their old cramped office quarters. Because people were brought into the company as contracts expanded, no attempt was made to segregate office space based on organizational function. Hence, marketing people were found next to software engineers and technical writers, who were often across the hall from senior management and personnel. This ad hoc method of organizing work space helped produce camaraderie and a sense that everyone was pitching in for the good of the whole company. Informal communication was a primary source of new information.

The new building is neatly segregated into four quadrants, referred to as business units: management (including personnel), marketing, engineering, and documentation. Each business unit has its own budget, staff, and electronic machinery. Numerically, the business units are broken down as follows:

Management: 12

Marketing: 17

Software Engineering: 32

Documentation: 11

One result of the move has been a dropoff in the frequency of informal and formal contact among employees from different business units. Another result has been a kind of "silo" thinking about the individual business units, as if each unit were in competition with the others for resources and rewards. Yet another result has been a kind of separation of management (management, personnel, and marketing employees) from staff (software engineers and documentation specialists) based on the fact that management has offices on the second floor, whereas staff has offices on the ground floor. Recently, some valued employees left the company, complaining that "things aren't like they were."

You have been retained as an organizational communication consultant to improve the operation of GS in its new building. What recommendations would you make?

COMMUNICATION
AND
ORGANIZATIONAL
EFFECTIVENESS

Insofar as man's [sic] ethical ideals are concerned, and however barbaric and cruel the reality may have been, economic relations in ancient times were to some extent conceived of as religious relations. . . . In this lofty sense, despite the slavery, oppression, and warfare . . . money symbolized the loving giving and taking among individuals which gave men the feeling of having emotional roots in their community. The community was a religious congregation, and all members felt themselves to be fellows in a sacred communion. . . . Money originated as a symbol of man's soul.

—Desmonde, 1962, pp. 20–25

Definitions of organizational effectiveness are notoriously ambiguous. Altman et al.'s (1985) approach is typical. They define organizational effectiveness as the degree to which an organization is able to "achieve its formal goals while managing its human resources well" (p. 60). But it is their commentary on the definition that is most revealing: "In the final analysis organizational effectiveness must be the ultimate concern of everyone. After all, if an organization cannot attain its objectives within the necessary time, cost, and quality parameters, *it will eventually cease to exist*" (p. 60, italics added). In other words, although organizational effectiveness ought to mean striving to be both pro-profit and pro-people, for most businesses failure to turn a profit means ending up with *no* people. This is the reality of business organizations in a capitalist society, and one that is all too often ignored by students of communication and other disciplines that emphasize the human side of organizational life. Failing to explore the financial or business side of organizations is a costly mistake, however, especially for those whose primary interest is in people. It is a mistake because it takes us out of the dialogue with precisely those individuals who decide the fates of organizations and their inhabitants based on their financial performance. In so doing, they may relegate us to the margins of organizational life, to the study of things that are nice to know but not directly related to the "bottom line."

A willingness to enter the financial dialogue does not at all mean an uncritical acceptance of profits over people. Unfortunately, some business owners and managers do indeed use the survivability of the organization as a reason to treat their employees poorly. Like most arguments, this one contains a grain of truth (and may be absolutely true in some situations), but it may also mask a much different state of affairs in which money is available and senior management gets a disproportionate share of it. The argument ultimately boils down to a difference in how the current organizational and financial reality is interpreted: How bad is it? What is the source of the current problems? What must change? When we add to this situation a degree of mistrust between the parties, together with the dominance of most managers and owners, the potential for antagonism and dysfunctional conflict is great.

In the end all sides of the argument must be heard. Even in a capitalist society, owners have much to lose by making profits the last word at the expense of competing arguments and interpretations. As a rule, *people* are the means to achieving the highest financial performance. Profits and people go hand in hand, and little is gained by placing them in competition with one another. In most industries, there are no people without profits, and there are no profits without people.

In some respects, most of the topics addressed in this book (e.g., stress, relationships, and teams) concern organizational effectiveness, but they are not the total picture. First, in addition to those topics, we should consider more typical aspects of business, such as financial performance, image, and competitive strategy. Second, we should explore the role of communication in running a business. Third, we should make connections among all these elements—people, communication, and profits—when we describe the nature and importance of organizational communication.

A feature of this chapter that is unique to basic business books is its focus on the symbolic side of organizational finance (Eisenberg & Riley, 1988). What we mean by symbolism here is not that financial indicators like profits and losses aren't "real," but rather that they are always open to multiple interpretations. Money is the ultimate symbol: it has value only to the extent that a group of people give it value. For example, the rise and fall of stock prices is tied heavily to public perceptions, and the economy as a whole reacts to abstract clusters of beliefs such as consumer confidence. Much as is true of other areas of our lives, our perceptions about economic issues often create their own reality. As a classic example of the self-fulfilling prophecy, we can point to the bank runs that set off the great Depression in 1929. The initial rumors that the banks were failing and that depositors' money was at risk were mainly false—at least until the rumors started to spread. Customer fears of an impending disaster led most people to stampede to their local banks and to withdraw all their money at once, which in turn caused many banks to fail.

COMMUNICATING FINANCIAL PERFORMANCE

Most students of organizational communication, as well as many business owners, managers, and employees, have little or no training in accounting. This is unfortunate, for a basic understanding of financial reporting can enhance a company's chances for success, as well as indicate typical signs of trouble. Financial statements provide the owners and managers of organizations with valuable information for making decisions. Moreover, an understanding of financial concepts can help improve communication with supervisors, peers, and employees. For example, in Chapter 8 we discussed theories of motivation that encourage supervisors to share company financial information with employees. Before any such sharing takes place, the supervisor must first have a clear idea about the key financial indicators and what they mean. Four terms basic to any discussion of financial performance are revenues, costs, profits, and cash flow.

Revenues

Sometimes called sales or the top line on an income statement (see Table 10.1), revenues are the monies that a business receives through the sale of a product or service. When you go grocery shopping, for example, the money you pay the cashier becomes revenue for the store; at the end of the day all the money paid to the cashier is added together to calculate total revenues for the day. Other types of products or services may require immediate payment. If you meet with a lawyer, for example, he or she will record the amount billed to you as revenues the day the bill is mailed—even though you may not pay it for some time. In most cases, "the revenue is recorded when the product or service is delivered to the customer, rather than when the payment is actually *received*" (Hume Corporation, 1987, p. 7).

TABLE 10.1
BUDDY'S PAELLA PALACE: SAMPLE INCOME
STATEMENT FOR THE YEAR ENDED DECEMBER 31, 1993

Revenue	
Total restaurant sales	$270,000
Investment income	5,000
Interest income	3,000
Total revenue	$278,000 (top line)
Costs/Expenses	
Employee wages and benefits (chef, manager, food servers, etc.)	$215,000
Rent	10,000
Equipment leases (large oven, freezer)	3,000
Cost of meats, fish, poultry	12,000
Cost of produce (vegetables, fruit)	8,000
Restaurant supplies	8,000
Advertising and promotion	15,000
Insurance and taxes	5,000
Total costs	$276,000
Income/Profit	$ 2,000 (bottom line)

Although the separation of revenues from payments is typical, it creates a problem for organizations—collecting the payments. Large organizations such as colleges, insurance companies, banks, and department stores often have entire departments devoted to collections. Once a sale has been made and recorded as revenue, it becomes a *receivable,* which means that the company expects to receive the payment but doesn't have it yet. Most companies keep a receivables list (sometimes called accounts receivable) of the charges that have been made but not yet collected. One way that lenders and credit agencies rate companies is by the *aging* of their receivables—that is, how long, on average, it takes customers to make payment on what they owe.

The role of communication in the generation of revenues and the collection of receivables is varied and significant. With regard to the generation of revenues, in all but the smallest companies a salesperson or sales force is responsible for communicating with potential customers. This can be accomplished by mail (e.g., magazine subscriptions), phone (e.g., stock offerings from a broker), face to face (e.g., cars), or through print or broadcast advertising (e.g., restaurants), depending on the nature of the product and the desired customer base. Much has been written about the communication skills of successful salespeople. In general, effective sales requires (1) the ability to establish a comfortable rapport with people; (2) a talent for listening and audience analysis (i.e., tuning in to buyers and tailoring one's approach to their individual needs and orientation); as well as (3) an ability to know how and when to "ask for the order," or to "close" the deal. Ineffective salespeople are those who make customers feel uneasy and who don't take the time to understand what potential buyers really need, but all the same may attempt to get them to buy something they don't need or even want.

With regard to the generation of revenues, many companies make a distinction between sales and marketing. As a rule, salespeople have direct contact with customers and are called on to solicit business and to close deals. In contrast, marketing personnel are more focused on medium- to long-term business prospects. They play a key role in researching customer preferences, which can then be used to develop products or services that fit particular niches or markets.

The collection of receivables is also a highly communicative act. Bill collectors usually write or call customers, beginning with a friendly reminder and progressing toward threats of legal action and even repossession of property that has not been paid for. The collector's job is complicated by the fact that the customer's lateness in paying may have to do with some problem with the product or service received, or with the bill or invoice. For example, some years ago a division of Hewlett-Packard was having problems collecting their receivables on a timely basis. The company's assumption was that the problem lay with the customers. However, a study into the reasons for nonpayment revealed that the largest percentage of nonpayments could be traced to incorrect invoices, which were generated at Hewlett-Packard. Once the invoices were fixed, it became easier to collect the money.

Collecting receivables is hard because the collector is asked to balance multiple communicative goals. Except in the most extreme cases, the aim of collection is to get the money in a way that will not alienate the customer. Consequently, bill collectors have developed a sophisticated repertoire of "good-cop/bad-cop" strategies to maintain this balance through communication (Rafaeli & Sutton, 1991).

Costs

Different kinds of businesses incur different types of costs. Returning to Table 10.1, we see that significant costs would include rent for the space, employee salaries and benefits, and inventory, which is the expense of the food and other products kept in stock (but not yet sold). Additional costs include office supplies, phone bills, taxes, and advertising expenses. In contrast, a doctor's office will have fewer expenses in inventory and rent, but more money will go toward malpractice insurance and expensive diagnostic equipment.

Like revenues, costs are recorded when the expense is actually incurred, not when payment is made. For example, if a doctor's office hires a temporary employment agency to provide a receptionist for a day, the expense is recorded when the bill from the agency is received, not when the doctor gets around to paying it. Again, most companies keep a list of all the bills they have received but have not yet paid; these are called *accounts payable.*

The costs associated with doing business are always higher than people expect. Consequently, a major challenge is communicating to employees the full range of costs in the company, as well as how their decisions and behaviors affect these costs. For example, many companies undertake communication campaigns to explain the high cost of employee benefits, especially medical insurance. Organizational effectiveness requires that employees understand both what leads to increased revenues and what drives costs. Left unattended, the costs of running a business will naturally outstrip revenues.

Most companies regularly conduct cost-cutting campaigns to eliminate or reduce reliance on high-cost practices, especially in the areas of temporary services, overtime, subcontractors, office supplies, equipment, and mail. If these reductions are not sufficient, more radical cost-reduction efforts may be implemented such as downsizing (reducing the total number of employees across the board) or downscoping (abandoning less profitable businesses to focus on what the company does best, an effort that also involves laying off employees). The significant challenge of these activities is to cut costs without having a serious negative impact on the people and processes most critical in providing the company's product or service.

Each and every decision an employee makes—whether it involves wasting paper or wasting time—shows up somewhere on the income statement as a revenue or cost. For example, the decision to leave work early on a Friday afternoon might delay completion on a product, which in turn may push back a day the time when the company can deliver and bill for it. This decision, therefore, has a direct impact on revenues and receivables. Enrolling employees in a two-day, customer service training program has negative short-term financial consequences (in the form of delayed revenues) but may have a positive long-term impact on business volume (i.e., increased revenues through greater customer satisfaction).

The usefulness of accounting as a symbolic system is that it is sufficiently general to permit analysis of practically any organizational behavior. The downside of using financial data for decision making is that, in focusing exclusively on the numbers, the unique strengths, weaknesses, and needs of the people most affected by the decisions are often overlooked.

The communication challenge inherent in managing costs is for the people who measure and care most about costs (e.g., the chief financial officer, controller, president, general manager) to communicate to all employees the need for cost control and the role individual employees can play in becoming more cost-conscious. Although decisions should not always be made on the basis of cost, they should be made with cost in mind. People need to know how their actions either directly or indirectly affect the organization's income statement.

Profit

Profit (or net income) is the difference between revenues and costs. When revenues exceed costs, a company is said to be profitable or "in the black"; when costs exceed revenues the company is losing money or is "in the red." In either case, revenues minus costs is often referred to as the *bottom line,* so named because it appears on the last line of the income statement (see Table 10.1).

A company's bottom-line profitability is *the* critical financial indicator of success or failure. It is particularly important in a capitalist system because profit is a major determinant of shareholder value, the current value of the business to those who own it. Ownership can be divided among just a few people (as in a privately held company), or it may be shared by hundreds or even thousands of stockholders (as in a publicly held company, such as IBM or General Motors, traded over one of the various stock exchanges around the world). The amount of profits alone is insufficient information to determine the overall financial health of a company (e.g., are profits of $400,000 good or bad? Compared to what?). For this reason, one typical way of expressing profitability is to divide a company's profit for the year by the total current value of the company at that time (which is called the company's net worth). Profit divided by net worth equals return on investment (ROI), which is the percent yield that investors are receiving for their investment.

Obviously, the higher the ROI the better, but realistic target percentages vary across industries. An aerospace or computer firm, for example, might aim at an ROI of 10 or 20 percent, whereas a retail food chain might shoot for 5 percent or less. Not uncommonly, many companies today run either at a loss or with ROIs of less than 5 percent. Compare these percentages with any savings account, which in 1992 would pay between 4 and 5 percent. Thus, while a company with ROI of 4 percent may do good work, the return is not sufficiently profitable for the shareholders, who would have done equally well if they had simply put their money in a federally insured bank account.

The main communication challenge involving profits is to educate all employees in the company as to what they are and where they come from. Those employees who understand the revenue, cost, and profit goals toward which they are working will have a better chance of asking the right questions that will help them make improvements. In the past, sharing financial information with employees has been frowned upon, partly because of legal restrictions and the potential effect on morale. But in nearly every case where this kind of information is provided to employees, positive gains are made. When people are trusted with complete financial information, they will be both more comfortable and more creative in dealing with difficult realities. If at that point they are still nervous, it will be with good reason, and not from an anxiety born of being kept in the dark.

Effective communication of financial information is no easy task; it requires honest leadership to be effective. Employees are naturally suspicious of accounting practices, and with good reason. Senior managers have been known to use financial data to manipulate employees, customers, lenders, and shareholders into accepting particular conclusions about the company's performance. Accountants are often asked to make financial statements look better or worse than they really are in order to prove a particular point. This is especially troubling to employees when they share in the profits of the company; the profitability figures must be seen as credible, for they are virtually impossible for employees to verify. A familiar example of creative accounting is the U.S. budget deficit; certain kinds of sensitive costs (such as the controversial savings and loan bailout) are routinely left out of the calculations.

Table 10.1 is an example of a simple income statement (sometimes called a profit and loss statement, or P & L) for a small restaurant. This statement tells the story of an organization that is bringing in business but having trouble controlling costs, such as the expense of buying the highest quality ingredients and of hiring a very experienced chef. The low level of profitability should be a warning signal to this company, because eventually a lack of profits shows up as a lack of cash, which is discussed next.

Cash Flow

Cash flow measures something very different from revenues, costs, or profits. Consequently, companies maintain cash flow records that are separate from income statements and accounts receivables sheets. To envision cash flow we can think about a checking account register. In general, as deposits and withdrawals are recorded, they are immediately added and subtracted from the balance, which is a fairly reliable indicator of the amount of cash on hand. The check register precisely reflects the flow of cash in and out of the account.

Cash flow is an emotional issue: it has a strong and predictable effect on the communication style of managers and salespeople. Responsible communication skills (e.g., active listening, empathy, building consensus) tend to disappear when a company is running out of cash. Managers become poorer managers, and salespeople become worse at selling. Anyone who has ever been approached by a salesperson who was obviously "pressing" to make the deal immediately, to help the company's (or their own) cash flow, knows how this hard sell feels, and also knows that it makes the prospective buyer want to run away, not buy.

In the final analysis, consistent, positive cash flow ensures that the doors of a business will be kept open on any particular day. Cash flow management is critical to business success. Obviously, neither cash without profits nor profits without cash will make it. Taken together, they define what it takes to remain a solvent and effective organization.

A final related communication concern is the widespread dissemination of information about what affects cash flow, which as a rule is a subject unclear to employees. Just as most people fail to realize how their decisions show up as costs or revenues to the company, they do not perceive the impact of their actions on cash flow. Decisions about when to buy a particular part; to offer early retirement; to pursue one type of customer over another; or even to select one type of business over another—all have implications for cash flow. Everyone who works for a company should understand the difference between cash flow and profits, and be able to assess the impact of their work on both.

Cash and profits are decidedly not the same thing. At any given moment, a company can be cash rich but unprofitable. Douglas Aircraft, for example, built MD-80 jets for

——————————————— ETHICS BOX 10.1 ———————————————

"THEY'LL NEVER NOTICE . . . "

Vince Pappazoni is a college student majoring in marketing. To acquire some practical experience in business—as well as to help finance his education—he took a job for the summer at a major department store in Atlanta as a sales associate. His boss, Robyn Jones, has been the manager of the gourmet items department for two years, and before that she was a sales associate, just like Vince.

One night Vince was approached by a customer who asked for a package that he said he had left at the counter earlier that day. Vince found the package, neatly wrapped and with the customer's name attached to it, beneath the sales counter. He gave it to the customer and said, "Thank you for shopping with us." The customer smiled and said, "Yeah, right. I'll remember that." Vince thought that was odd but didn't lose sleep over it.

Over the next month this same customer returned several times for packages left for him behind the counter. But he was not the only customer who seemed to consistently leave packages with sales associates in this department; there were others. Vince always smiled, thanked the customer for the business, and went on about his work.

Then one day Vince came to work and found an envelope with his name on it in the cash register. He opened the envelope and found five one-hundred dollar bills. Assuming some mistake had been made, he confronted his boss about it. She took him into her office quickly, and closed the door. "I thought you had figured it out," she whispered, conspiratorially.

"Figured what out?" asked Vince.

"The little deal we have going on here," she replied.

"What little deal?" Vince was becoming increasingly uncomfortable with this conversation.

"Well, I might as well tell you," Robyn confided. "We work a little scam in this department to offset our low wages." She grinned. "Sometimes we have friends come in and buy large-ticket items that we ring up as small-ticket items, or else we wrap up merchandise during our off-time and have friends pick it up after work. Because I am in charge of inventory, I chalk it up to theft, for which we are allotted a sizable budget each month. They'll never notice." She paused. "And because you have been helping out this month, the money in the envelope is your bonus."

Vince felt ill but didn't say anything. He needed the job to finish college, and he needed a good reference to get a job. Besides, who was he going to tell? It was his boss who was the ringleader! He left work that day feeling worse than he ever had felt in his life.

What should Vince do? Equally important, what should this company do to discourage future theft by employees? Assuming that in-house detectives and electronic surveillance either have not worked or are not options, what communication strategies might help?

———————————————————————————————————————

nearly ten years without turning a profit, but at $30 million apiece, they quite often experienced surpluses of cash. Alternatively, a company can be profitable but low in cash, as happens when there are many large receivables already recorded as income but yet to be paid. This is the origin of the expression "cash is king": your company may be very profitable, but until the money is collected, profitability doesn't pay the bills.

A final aspect of cash that explicitly involves communication is the initial capitalization of a start-up company. Imagine that in your hometown there is a great burger place that sells baked potatoes stuffed with ground beef. Every day since you left home for college, you have missed the taste of potato burgers and complained about the limited food options in your new town. One night, two friends are over and you have an idea: why not open a *Potato Burger* right here in Collegetown?

Most small businesses start this way, through some combination of personal experience, preference, and perceived demand. The thinking goes like this: "If I like it/need it so much, other people will like it too." If initial market research shows a potential customer base, the next challenge is to raise the money to begin building the business. This presents the first communication challenge facing the fledgling business, which is to persuade potential investors to part with their money (called the initial capitalization). Since costs left unchecked are sure to exceed revenues, a big question early in the process is: "How do we cover the initial costs of starting our business?" Over time, this question usually deteriorates into: "Which of my family and friends are rich and/or crazy enough to believe in me and lend me cash?"

Start-up businesses focus on family and friends because, with few exceptions, institutional lenders (e.g., banks, S&Ls) will not risk investing money in a new business. Venture capital firms, which in the past loaned money to start up companies (and launched, for example, the semiconductor and software booms in California), have of late withdrawn virtually altogether. While they may fund a company once it gets off the ground, they as a rule no longer invest in start-ups because of the risk and time required to manage the investment. Even the government sources of start-up capital, such as the Small Business Administration (SBA), have strict requirements for their loans. Most generally, the easiest business to get money for is one that has either been profitable for three years or more, or has a significant value of products in inventory that could be sold for cash by the investor should the business fail. Minority-run businesses also have an advantage in obtaining start-up capital. Businesses without inventory (e.g., those that provide service or information) and businesses that are less than three years old are low on the list of anyone's lending priorities. In summary, securing initial capital is the first significant communication challenge of the entrepreneur. Initial capitalization is crucial because it offsets the high costs of starting a business. Current wisdom suggests that a start-up firm needs enough cash in the bank to get through at least two years of losses.

Bankruptcy

When a business runs seriously short on cash, it will typically stop paying all but the most essential bills—payroll (employee salaries), taxes, phones, and rent. In a company in this position, customer service seems strained, inventory and selection are thin, and merchandise may be deeply discounted to raise cash. The pressure and stress of this situation makes recovery even less likely. Salespeople get desperate, and management may take cost-cutting to unrealistic extremes. Eventually, if revenues fail to increase significantly, more drastic measures may be necessary, the most common of which is bankruptcy.

The two types of corporate bankruptcy are named after chapters in the bankruptcy law: Chapter 7 and Chapter 11. The decision to file either one is prompted by a shortage of cash and a difficulty or inability to pay debts and/or meet payroll. Both types require the owners to turn the operation of the business over in part to the bankruptcy court, which then actively guides the owners in making financial decisions.

Chapter 7 bankruptcy is the death of a business. It means the end is *here,* and it involves selling everything down to the bare walls. Chapter 11, on the other hand, is much less catastrophic. Chapter 11 gives businesses a chance to reorganize their operations while not being obligated to pay any debts for a minimum of 120 days. This grace period provides breathing room to businesses which might yet find a way to get the needed cash to pay creditors and to remain in operation. Most of the bankruptcy stories in the news refer to Chapter 11 reorganizations; they are companies without cash looking for friendly buyers (sometimes called white knights) who will provide cash in return for some owner- ship position in the company. Companies can be profitable and still be forced to file bankruptcy, if they run out of cash. If they are very profitable, however, there is a fair chance they could borrow sufficient capital to avoid bankruptcy.

Especially in the case of Chapter 11 filings, the challenge of communicating with existing customers during bankruptcy is enormous. Chapter 11 does not mean the end of a business. It can even be a hopeful sign, an opportunity for major reorganization and upgrading of services. But customers don't usually understand this distinction and must be reassured of continuity of service. They must also be certain that someone will stand behind their purchase should a problem arise. In addition to customer communication, bankruptcy also requires constant, frank communication with creditors and lending insti- tutions. Without such open communication, these people will assume the worst and act accordingly, which itself can bring down the business. Unfortunately, although Chapter 11 saves some businesses, the majority eventually end up filing Chapter 7.

The overall number of corporate bankruptcies has declined since 1987, but the size of the companies that fail has changed dramatically. The typical bankrupt company in 1990 was fifty times as big, in numbers of employees, as the typical failure in 1980. Giant corporations are failing in the 1990s because they are unable to pay their enormous debts. As a direct consequence of the failure of larger companies, personal bankruptcies have risen dramatically, reaching a record 1 million in 1991.

Typically, a company's journey from health to bankruptcy begins with rising costs (e.g., inventory, employee salaries, and benefits) and falling revenues (e.g., decreased sales due to a recession; increased competition and price wars). These problems can be managed temporarily in various ways—through stepped-up advertising, special pricing incentives, and cost-cutting. Eventually, however, if allowed to continue, these trends end up as reduced profits, cash flow, and return on investment.

Simply showing reduced profits will not immediately force a company out of business. Hundreds of corporations today consistently lose money but remain in business; for example, car companies routinely post quarterly losses in the millions. In some cases, the losses exist only on paper, meaning that they involve some change in accounting procedure or tax writeoff. In other cases, changes in profitability can take a long time to show up as changes in cash flow. In general, the bigger the company is, the longer it can remain unprofitable but stay in business. When losses finally do show up as shortfalls of cash, things can turn ugly quickly. In the Pan Am bankruptcy, for example (which was Chapter 11), the struggling airline was within a week of running out of cash when it was bailed out by Delta.

This matter returns us to an observation we made in the first chapter concerning reduced slack. Businesses worldwide are increasingly unable to count on a long "float" between the time when a downturn occurs and when there is literally no money left to pay the bills. This leads to increased stress, which manifests itself as anxiety or urgency. *Anxiety* paralyzes and leads to a denial of reality, to an attempt to live in a dream world where things will "turn around soon" and be "just like they used to be." *Urgency* prompts us to stay ahead of the power curve, to develop creative, proactive ways of anticipating and addressing downturns in business, and to find new businesses to replace obsolete ones. Executives today should be warned to take the amount of time they think they have before hitting bottom, and then divide it in half. They should look carefully at a calendar and then move forward—with urgency.

Exceptions for the Truly Big   In a song with implications for business, Bob Dylan wrote, "steal a little and they throw you in jail, steal a lot and they make you king." Although no one is safe anymore, the rules continue to be stricter for small and midsized businesses than they are for large ones. Typically, this is a function of (1) the magnitude of their debt; and (2) the size of their contributions to local economies through employment and tax revenue.

For example, we watched with mixed emotions the rise and fall of Donald Trump's financial empire. We suspected he was in serious trouble when he wasn't able to make loan payments for many of his properties. After all, if *we* miss a few house payments, chances are we will lose our houses. But the rules of the game are different for truly large players. In effect, Trump doesn't "own" or hold title to many of his properties; they were bought, built, and financed through various lending agencies that would stand to "own" them should Trump be unable to pay on his loans. But this is the last thing they would want to happen, because then they would be stuck with them. An old saying in commercial lending is that with small loans, the bank owns you, but with truly big loans, you own the bank. Given the nature and size of Trump's debt, it is not in any lender's best interest to foreclose on his property. This gives Trump the upper hand and allows him to stall and renegotiate the terms of his debt. Meanwhile, if we are ten days late in paying a phone bill, our service is disconnected.

In the case of large debt, businesses often do not fail because the consequences to the lender are worse than allowing the business to drift, limp along, stall, or reorganize. But other reasons are involved. The classic American example is Chrysler Corporation, which the U.S. government bailed out because the consensus was that the social and economic implications of allowing this giant of American industry to fail would be too great. But the bailout required more money than it would have cost to support all existing Chrysler employees at their present salaries for the rest of their lives.

In a similar situation, the U.S. government recently acted to extend the time by two years that the McDonnell Douglas Corporation could pay on a $1.35 billion loan. It did so because the consequences of forcing the corporation to pay up were too great: bankrupting it would potentially lead to the closing of Douglas Aircraft, which is the largest employer in southern California. In addition to the obvious social costs associated with the resulting unemployment (with little hope of finding jobs in the declining aerospace market), such an action would have catastrophic effects on the city of Long Beach, a large part of whose tax base comes from the company. In addition, there would be pressure on local banks and savings and loans to foreclose on the homes of these laid-off employees. A complex picture emerges from this example: government, business, banks, and taxpayers are all part of a highly interdependent web of connections which at times can resemble a house of cards. When businesses grow to a certain size relative to their communities (e.g., greater than 10,000 employees in a big city like New York or Los Angeles), all the rules change, and stakeholders of various kinds are much less likely to let a business fail than they are to find ways to prop it up or bail it out.

For every large company that lenders or government save, many others are unceremoniously allowed to fail. For example, in the last 20 years many large companies have left small towns, taking most of the jobs in those towns with them. In such instances, it is seen as less expensive simply to cut one's losses and move on than to attempt to modernize and compete in the original location. The human cost may indeed be great, but by and large it is ignored unless it is large enough to command the attention of the federal government or the national news media.

The key terms, definitions, and communication implications of the various aspects of financial performance are summarized in Table 10.2.

TABLE 10.2
COMMUNICATING FINANCIAL PERFORMANCE

Key Terms	Definition	Communication Goals
Revenues	Monies that come into a business through the sale of a product or service.	Encourage sales personnel to (1) establish a comfortable rapport with clients, (2) develop listening and audience analysis skills, and (3) know how and when to ask for the order or close the deal.
Costs	Expenses incurred by a business in order to generate revenues.	(1) Communicate to all employees the full range of costs in the company, as well as how their decisions and behaviors affect these expenses, and (2) communicate to all employees the need for cost control and their role in becoming more cost-conscious.
Profit (Loss)	The difference between revenues and costs.	Education: Provide basic definitions (and corresponding data) to all employees in the company.
Cash flow	Up-to-the-moment indicator of the amount of cash on hand.	Education: Everyone who works for the company should understand the difference between cash flow and profits, and be able to assess the impact of their work on both.
Initial capitalization	Money obtained from investors to start a new business.	Persuasion: How can you secure the funds to cover at least two years of losses?
Bankruptcy	Chapter 7: The death of a business. Chapter 11: The business is given the opportunity to reorganize, not pay debts for 120 days (or more), and/or find new investors.	Communicating with existing customers, creditors, and lending institutions in a constant and frank way.

COMMUNICATING COMPETITIVE STRATEGY

Nothing is more important to the long-term success of a business than its competitive strategy. A strategy is a simple, clear statement of why customers should choose a company's products or services over those of the competition. Examples of simple strategies are cheapest, fastest, most reliable, friendliest, closest, best quality. Obviously, just communicating a strategy to customers is not enough; all aspects of the organization must be aligned with the strategy in order for it to be effective.

Given the straightforward nature of the concept, surprisingly, most organizations do not have a clear competitive strategy. Instead, most businesses grow up around the success of a product or product line, typically one that was introduced before significant competition emerged. When some leaders of successful companies are asked why a customer should choose them over a competitor, they are often completely stumped or give a long-winded reply. In technical terms, these companies, however successful, lack a competitive strategy.

Let's look at a detailed example of the conditions under which strategy might develop. Imagine for a moment that your potato burger business has taken off, and you are invited to a fancy reception held by the city's chamber of commerce. You put on your best suit, grab your business cards, and go to the party. What should you be prepared to say about your business? Common wisdom holds that you have approximately 15 seconds to explain what you do and what makes your business different and worthy of their attention. Further advice says that the person that you tell about your business in 15 seconds ought to be able to explain it (and want to explain it) to someone else later. If you can accomplish both, and if your message is memorable and distinct, your company likely has a strategy.

Over the years, as competition has increased overall, the markets for products and services have become more specialized. Competitive strategy today focuses mainly on identifying market niches, which are a specific segment of possible customers. For example, general-interest magazines like *Life* magazine are being replaced by literally hundreds of specialty magazines catering to individual interests. On television, mass-market broadcasting has rapidly been augmented by shows targeted at specific market segments. This approach is called narrowcasting. Witness, for example, the growth of cable television, which offers channels that are all sports, all comedy, all news, even all shopping. Many times a larger company cultivates two or more separate strategies in pursuit of multiple niches. MTV, for example, created VH1 as a separate channel to appeal to older audiences.

For communication specialists, crafting a competitive strategy is as pure an exercise in message design as one ever gets. Businesses that lack a clear strategy are more likely to fail than their more strategic counterparts. For the potato burger restaurant, perhaps the most obvious strategy is uniqueness. You serve something people can't find elsewhere: "The only place in town with burgers in our potatoes!" The success of this strategy lies in whether a niche market exists for such a product. Other companies don't have it so easy, and in trying to be all things to all people (e.g., "open long hours," "we deliver," "service with a smile," "lowest prices") end up unable to deliver fully on any of them.

Developing a strategy begins with the founder's intuition about a demand for a product or service, followed closely by an exhaustive analysis of the target market and relevant environment. This environment is enacted by the founder and includes not just potential customers but also various publics and stakeholders, including the community, govern-ment agencies, and the competition. Competitor analysis is especially important, since the idea for a product or service may have already been tried and failed, for good reasons; successful competitors unknown to you may exist in remote locations. In formulating a competitive strategy, prospective businesspeople must think not only about what they do well but also about how their strategy will be received by their various publics. Serious objections by any one public can sink their business.

An excellent, though unresolved, example can be found at a major medical center in the West. This hospital has received much of its funding from Jewish philanthropists, many of whom reside on its board of trustees. The medical staff is more noted for its cutting-edge technological care than for its bedside manner. The neighborhood is chang-ing, however, from predominantly Jewish to a broader ethnic mix. At the same time, the hospital is being pressured to become more cost-conscious and patient-focused. The twin foundations on which the hospital grew—the Jewish community and high-tech care—are being eroded. How can it remain competitive as a business?

With the arrival of a new president/CEO, hospital leadership decided to revise its competitive strategy to become more patient-focused and community-based, a "societal force for health." This change in direction has not been uniformly well received. Certain members of the board feel that the change in favor of a different ethnic base (the new local community) represents a betrayal of the Jewish community which has supported the hospital for years. The medical staff (an internal public) feels that the new strategy marks a reversal of what gave the hospital a competitive edge in the past—their technical excellence. The local community, however, is pleased with the change. Time will tell whether these different groups will be able to resolve their differences in such a way that will permit the hospital's new strategy to be successful.

Types of Business Strategies

A great deal of confusion surrounds the meaning of strategy when applied to business. Strategy is not the equivalent of a company's mission or vision, objectives or goals, with which it is often confused. Nor is strategy identical to tactics, which are the actions one takes to implement strategy. As stated above, in the business world competitive strategy has a particular meaning—that is, the reason why people should buy from you instead of from your competition.

The two basic types of strategies are lowest cost and differentiation (Porter, 1980). Adopting a lowest cost strategy means exactly what it says—a commitment to offer one's product or service at the lowest price in the marketplace. Discount appliance stores, no-frills airlines, and generic food products are examples of this strategy. They make no other claim except to say that they are the cheapest. For a large number of consumers, lowest cost is sufficient motivation to buy. Naturally, this strategy must be communicated loud and clear; what people must remember most is that no one can beat your prices. Potential customers must be won before they unwittingly pay more somewhere else.

Companies that choose the lowest cost strategy must live with many hardships. They must cut corners and reduce their costs in every conceivable way to maintain their cost advantage. For those companies located in an industrialized nation in a competitive global marketplace, the problem is to surmount high labor and material costs. Being lowest cost is a precarious position for yet another reason: if cost is your positioning, you have to be the lowest; simply being lower doesn't work. Those who are "stuck in the middle" cost-wise lose their advantage and whoever is lowest will attract the cost-conscious customers (Porter, 1980).

Businesses usually choose the second type of strategy, differentiation, when they can't, or won't, opt to be lowest cost. Differentiation means highlighting whatever makes one's product or service special. Are you the highest quality? The most reliable? Do you have the quickest delivery time? Are you open weekends? Do you offer the best warranty or service? More features and options? Do you cater to kids? Make the safest products? Are your products easiest to order? It's easy to see differentiation at work in the marketing of automobiles. Volvo's niche is safety, Hyundai's is lowest cost, BMW's is performance, and so on. Remember that differentiation as a strategy is also a communication issue; it's not so much how the product or service actually differs from its competition, but rather a company's ability to create the perception of that difference which they hope will be a competitive advantage. Differentiation is in large part a communicative act. Organizations can sometimes grow into a gap between communication and reality; for example, Ford declared quality "Job One" before it was able to build top-quality cars.

Developing a successful strategy is sometimes as simple as noticing an unfilled niche in the marketplace. A physician friend of ours in Santa Monica observed that none of the doctors' offices in the area were open on weekends or evenings, when people are most free to seek medical attention. He opened a family practice that has extended hours and has been wildly successful as a result. Most of the time, however, developing a strategy isn't so easy. Businesses often do battle over who can lay claim to a specific strategy or position. In Los Angeles, for example, three supermarkets are vying for the title of low-cost leader and run endless comparison studies to assert their superiority.

Overnight air delivery provides a more complicated illustration. Traditionally, Federal Express has pursued the differentiation strategy of most reliable; their commercials stress the embarrassment of not having a package show up should you be foolish enough to choose another company. (This is similar to IBM's claim that "no one ever lost their job for buying from IBM.") A new entry to the market is the United Parcel Service (UPS), which is trying a lowest cost strategy, maintaining that it can provide comparable services to Federal Express for less money. The future will show how many customers UPS can attract from FedEx using this strategy and whether UPS has the discipline to remain lowest cost in the industry. It will be fascinating to see whether FedEx tries to counter UPS by lowering its cost, or whether it sticks with its initial positioning of reliability. Practical wisdom suggests that FedEx should not try to compete on the basis of cost, but since the overall cost-sensitivity of customers is not well known in this service area, this advice may not hold. Will a customer choose an overnight delivery company based on price alone? How much of a discrepancy in price will a customer tolerate before making a switch? These are the kinds of questions that keep marketing strategists awake at night.

Similar battles for positioning can be observed among the major long-distance phone carriers—AT&T, Sprint, and MCI. Can anyone really tell who has the highest quality or who has the lowest cost? Each disputes the other's claims, or claims the competitive advantage for itself. Yet they all keep their prices closely in line with each other's. The history of airline deregulation in the United States illustrates the importance of strategy in a highly cost-sensitive service where brand loyalty is low. With deregulation, many new, smaller airlines entered the marketplace, undercutting prices dramatically on major routes. Much to the horror of the major carriers, many people would forego a $300 flight on American to fly People Express for $69, even if it meant paying for the peanuts. The fare wars began, and for a long time fares were ridiculously low—too low, in fact, for anyone to make a profit. One by one, the airlines that had tried to be lowest cost failed, taking some of the bigger carriers with them. Survivors quickly scrambled for a way to encourage brand loyalty and settled on frequent flyer programs. Prices went up again, and companies struggled to communicate differentiation strategies to consumers, such as "most on-time departures," and "best food."

One final caveat is necessary concerning business strategy. Just because a company chooses to make one aspect of its operation its competitive focus doesn't mean that it doesn't have other qualities; it simply doesn't communicate them to the public as competitive advantages. For example, Nordstrom emphasizes customer service, although it is vitally concerned with cost and quality, too. It doesn't highlight cost or quality simply because neither factor differentiates Nordstrom in the marketplace.

Know What Business You Are In   In summary, the overriding concern with strategy is an extension of the wise advice: "Know what business you are in." To this advice we add the further admonition to not only know what you do well, but also to be able to communicate to the public why they should rely on you for that product or service. A poorly communicated strategy is as bad as no strategy at all, since the major payoff of having a clear strategy derives from the customer's knowledge of what it is.

Two examples of the value of a clear strategy are instructive. Before air travel, people crossed the great oceans by boat, and many transportation companies existed to serve them. With the advent of passenger air travel, these businesses were threatened with obsolescence—but not all of them failed. Those that succeeded did so because of strategy. The cruise lines that defined their business as a form of entertainment survived; those that saw it narrowly as transportation failed.

A second example hits closer to home. McDonald's has always been a leader in competitive strategy, because it knows what business it is in—and it isn't hamburgers. McDonald's sells comfort, security, predictability, and safety. The location and cleanliness of stores, the appearance of the bathrooms, the rigid standards for food worldwide—all ensure safety and predictability. Recently, McDonald's has formalized this strategy, dubbing itself the world's community restaurant. The implications of such a strategy are different from those seen in the average restaurant chain. For example, McDonald's now has plans to open an experimental indoor playground called "Leaps and Bounds" which sells no food but is fully consistent with its strategy. If it had thought of itself as a burger restaurant, McDonald's could never have envisioned this opportunity. No competitive advantage outstrips truly knowing what business you are in and the reasons why people really buy your products or services.

Strategy and Business Life Cycle   Strategy changes as an organization ages and grows. Like people, businesses have life cycles (Kimberly & Miles, 1980), and the strategic and communicative challenges differ at each stage. At "birth," for example, a start-up company is concerned mainly with developing a strategy and finding a niche. The communication challenges include securing financial investment and making an initial foray into the marketplace.

In its childhood, the major challenge is managing growth and development. From a strategic perspective, in the pursuit of opportunities the growing organization tends to run in many different directions, dilute the basic strategy, and in general not have the discipline to stick with those activities in which it has the competitive advantage. The communication challenge here is to provide visionary leadership that provides a constant sense of focus and purpose.

When a company reaches adolescence, it encounters significant competition. As a rule, this means that the original strategic advantage—whether it be unique technology, best service, or unusual product—has been lost. The strategic challenge of adolescence is to recognize and fine tune your approach to the competition so that the strategic advantage is maintained. This usually requires significant focus on both internal and external communication: internal to streamline processes, cut costs, and develop new competencies, and external to continue to remind customers of their reasons for choosing you over the competition.

The final phase in an organization's life cycle, maturity, has become shorter and more difficult in recent years. The days when companies would mellow into venerable old institutions are gone. Instead, the strategic challenge of maturity is mainly one of renewal—of letting go of the old business in favor of a new one that is earlier in its life cycle. If they survive long enough, all businesses face this day of reckoning, and it is a difficult one. The communication challenges are gigantic: internally, to transform the organization from the old business to the new, and externally, to maintain a position in the marketplace while shifting into a newer business. J. C. Penney's recent attempt to upgrade its entire inventory and appeal to a different market niche is one such example.

Put differently, in maturity companies must come to terms with the legacy of their own success. It has often been said that, although it takes intelligence to overcome failure, it takes real genius to overcome success. One engineering firm has been so enormously successful in satisfying military customers with high-technology products that, in the face of a declining military budget and a mature product line, it is at a loss as to how to compete in the current business environment.

Finally, one company known for strategic excellence is Honda. When Honda entered the world marketplace in the 1970s, it did so with the tiny Honda Civic, which was not much more than a walled-in motorcycle engine. The genius of Honda's strategy since then has been its focus not on a particular product but on the same customers who purchased the first Civics—the baby boomers buying their first car. It has concentrated on transforming and upgrading its products to match these *customers'* life cycles. A few years after the Civic came the Prelude and Accord, which became available as these young adults moved into their thirties. More recently, the upscale Acura line was introduced for these same customers as they hit their forties and became more affluent. The key here is that Honda was wedded not to a particular product or service but to a strategic way of thinking about satisfying a well-defined market niche.

Implementing Competitive Strategy: Strategic Alignment

Perhaps you have had the experience of moving to a new town and setting out to start over, to radically change the way you present yourself to others. If before you were withdrawn and shy, the "new you" will be outgoing and social. If before you were always seen as a nosy pest, you resolve to mind your own business. Did it work? Our experience suggests that it probably didn't. The reason is that, to be believable, the way you think and talk about yourself has to be consistent with the way you really act. In most cases, your actions do indeed speak louder than your words, and people reach the same old conclusions about you.

A similar scenario applies in business. A company can strategize and communicate endlessly about an "environmentally conscious image" or "superior customer service," but unless customers see evidence of this emphasis, the words don't mean much and can even be highly ironic. Employees call this "walking the talk." To be convincing, the strategy communicated to various internal and external publics (e.g., employees, customers) must be aligned with other aspects of the organization. Strategic alignment is the modification of organizational systems (e.g., rewards, training) and structures (e.g., lines of authority, job design) to support the competitive strategy.

Strategic alignment is not simply cosmetic; it is *necessary* for a business to accomplish its strategy. To take a simple example, if a print shop advertises the lowest price and then proceeds to hire employees who are paid above the industry average, it is unlikely to achieve its strategy. Similarly, if a company that prides itself on being responsive to customers has a cumbersome automated phone system, it will not likely be able to successfully implement its service-based strategy.

Successful strategic alignment is difficult because it requires systems thinking; it forces a company to consider the relationship between its strategy and all the internal systems that will either encourage or prevent its strategy from succeeding. As noted in Chapter 4, most employees' biggest blind-spot is their inability to see themselves as part of a system. Similarly, most managers make decisions in isolation that ought to be motivated by the company strategy. Those few companies that pursue strategic alignment are invariably most successful if their strategy was well chosen to begin with.

7-S Model

The most commonly used model of strategic alignment is the 7-S model, developed by some of the original members of the consulting firm McKinsey & Company (see Figure 10.1, page 308). According to this model, the seven factors to be brought into alignment are strategy, superordinate goals, structure, systems, staffing, skills, and style. The lines indicate a need to promote consistency between each pair of factors. A lowest cost strategy may be consistent with a flat organizational structure, for example, but what are the implications of that structure for staffing and skills? These are the complex questions one asks when conducting strategic alignment.

The alignment process is best accomplished by thinking of organizations as communication systems. The fundamental principle of alignment is that information from each subsystem (each "S") both reflects and affects the whole in many ways. An organization that is out of alignment is one in which decisions are made in a vacuum, isolated from the other systems and decisions. Over time, organizational systems naturally drift out of alignment, as internal functions such as compensation practices and training courses become outdated and external changes in technology and market demographics require different internal responses. What is important to remember is that employees are extremely sensitive to alignment problems. If the company's mission statement promotes the values of trust and empowerment, for example, employees will be quick to point this

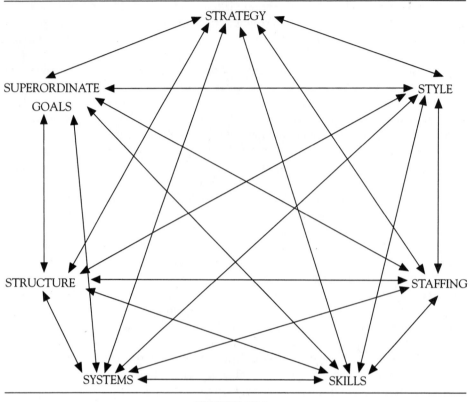

FIGURE 10.1
7-S Model of Strategic Alignment

out and complain if their ability to make decisions is severely limited. At Disneyland, employees objected to the apparent inconsistency between management proclamations of "the happiest place on Earth" and the treatment and compensation of employees (Smith & Eisenberg, 1987).

Strategy   As defined above, strategy is the competitive advantage of the business. Companies lacking a strategy or caught between strategies only succeed under conditions of minimal or nonexistent competition.

Superordinate Goals   These are specific targets on which all employees can focus, such as obtaining a certain return on investment or capturing a specific contract. In order to be effective, these goals must flow logically from strategy. Superordinate goals are more specific than a mission statement but not so specific that any employee would feel excluded from them. Superordinate goals are often stated ambiguously to allow room for innovation and creativity (Eisenberg, 1984).

Structure Structure refers to the formal reporting relationships prescribed by the organization in the organizational chart. (Informal relationships are typically treated under Systems.) Structure constrains to some degree who talks to whom and about what. It may be a symbolic representation of company values, as reflected in the height, breadth, and titles in the organizational chart. Ideally, structure should follow strategy.

Systems Systems are the ways information flows through various media, such as telephones, computers, or meetings. Systems include formal operating systems such as management information systems (MIS), informal standard operating procedures (cultural practices), and highly informal connections (emergent networks). Systems have obvious relevance for communication in that they deal with the adequacy of the distribution of information throughout the company. Certain strategies depend on certain types of systems to work. For example, a total quality strategy requires a shop floor control system that immediately surfaces defects and does not permit work to continue until they have been fixed.

Staffing Staffing refers to the people in the organization, their backgrounds, and how they are recruited and assigned to positions in the structure.

Skills Skills refers to the employees' level and range of talents and abilities, including both technical and interpersonal skills. Different skills are needed to accomplish different strategies. For example, a company striving to differentiate itself by providing superior customer service needs employees with superior interpersonal skills. Staffing practices (hiring and promotion) must also be brought in line with the desired skill base.

Style Style traditionally refers to management style, but it can also refer to an organization's prevailing attitude and treatment of employees, which may characterize the organizational culture. Style captures many of the remaining interpersonal factors that lead to the success or failure of a business. For example, a company with a laid-back culture that permits people to put off until tomorrow work that might be finished today is unlikely to survive in a competitive industry.

The Alignment Process The starting point in strategic alignment is to develop a strategy. Ideally, the strategy is based not on the company's present condition, but on reliable information about the future. The current organization is exactly the *wrong* place to start a program to reinvigorate and align a company, for it contains all the bad compromises and politically motivated decisions that were necessary to adapt to yesterday's business environment. Once a strategy is formed, it needs to be translated into superordinate goals so that it can be communicated to all employees. A strategy that has not been communicated internally and externally is useless.

Systems thinking suggests that structure should be examined next; will it support the goals and strategy? A specific example is useful in illustrating this point and the rest of the Ss. Recently, we witnessed the strategic alignment process in a major electronics firm that was seeking to make the transition from government business to the commercial marketplace. The company's strategy was to become customer-driven, which its competitors are not. What would it take to become customer-driven?

The first consideration was structure, which up until now consisted of many vertical silos—islands of expertise across which little communication ever passed. Over the years, people had grown comfortable building their own separate areas of influence, shielded from both customers and other employees. Nothing in the structure, neither the titles nor the departmental organization, reflected customer concerns. Consquently, the creation of a centralized customer program office was suggested that would act as a key interface for customer communication; a repair center was designed to meet existing customers' needs; and cross-functional teams were created to ensure horizontal communication.

Next up were systems, the analysis of which revealed two glaring problems of misalignment. First, the company had invested in an imposing voice-mail system that was keeping customers on hold for an eternity. Changes were made in the system to ensure that all customers could speak to a person in a specified amount of time; the marketing department was taken off the voice-mail system altogether during the day. (People were assigned to cover the phone.) Second, the overwhelming presence of military projects and schedules had created a norm in group meetings whereby issues would be tabled for the future rather than decided in a timely manner. This approach does not work in the commercial marketplace, which rewards quick action. With the help of the human resources department, the company's chief decision-making groups worked together to create a greater sense of urgency in its informal decision-making systems.

Staffing, skills, and style were the final considerations, focusing on putting the right people into the new organizational structure. The new incumbents needed to have the right qualifications, both in terms of technical and communicative skill, to succeed in the new structure and to enact the proposed strategy. Technically speaking, managers in the customer program offices needed to be able to speak with customers; interpersonally, they needed to cultivate a new style of working that was oriented toward customer-centered openness and empathy. Some of this was possible through training and education; those who were less open to change were reassigned to positions that were less visible to customers.

Sometimes alignment is done quietly and incrementally by a focused management team; at other times it is attempted with much fanfare as a high-profile intervention. One recent large-scale type of strategic alignment is total quality management (TQM). In implementing TQM, total quality becomes the company's strategy, and all other systems in the organization are modified in an attempt to support quality. For example, when a large computer manufacturer implemented TQM, it changed its objectives (superordinate goals), overhauled its organization (structure), got rid of managers who were from the "old school" (style), reevaluated all management for positions in the new structure (staffing), and trained all employees in, among other things, empowerment and teamwork (skills).

Alignment as large-scale intervention is very difficult and usually fails. There are so many different factors to keep track of all at once that maintaining strategic focus and performing any one function properly become difficult. In addition, most employees are suspicious of major interventions designed to promote radical change. Despite the usual disclaimers to the contrary, they worry that such programs are transitory and are often simply an opportunity to justify layoffs. Another way to sabotage strategic alignment is to overly focus on the alignment process itself and the external awards associated with achieving total quality. For example, the herculean efforts exerted by Florida Power & Light to win the Malcolm Baldrige Award (given for total quality) brought the company close to an organizational version of a nervous breakdown. FP&L "now has a complaint record worse than several other Florida utilities" (Sashkin, 1991, p. 164).

COMMUNICATING WITH PUBLICS: REPUTATION, IMAGE, AND IDENTITY

Today's sophisticated customer does not make financial decisions based solely on competitive advantage. Specifically, customers are increasingly sensitive to a company's reputation, where it invests its money, and how it fits into society as a whole. This section explores the nature of organizational reputation, image, and identity, and their relationship to organizational communication.

Reputation

Reputation is the perception by outsiders of an organization's overall quality (Fombrun & Shanley, 1990). Publics construct reputations on the basis of information from various sources, including interpersonal contacts, financial performance, and the media. As such, reputation is shaped largely by communication. "Just as firms compete for customers, so also do they vie for reputational status. Publics construct reputations from available information about firms' activities originating from the firms themselves, from the media, or from other monitors . . . reputations represent publics' cumulative judgments of firms over time" (Fombrun & Shanley, 1990, pp. 234–235).

Charles Fombrun and Mark Shanley (1990) have identified the types of information individuals use to develop impressions about reputation. Profitability impacts reputation, but so, too, do media visibility and perceptions of the firm's contributions to society. Reputation is an interpretive process in which people base their assessments on a mixture of information available in the environment about the organization. This information can, of course, come from performance data, but it can also derive from policy decisions and social networks.

A compelling strategy is not sufficient to command a superior reputation. Social performance is also important to reputation. For example, some people recently boycotted a restaurant because of its contributions to anti-abortion causes. Similarly, some switched gasoline credit cards after the Exxon *Valdez* oil spill. In both cases, some people viewed the quality of the product or service being offered as secondary to the overall reputation of the company.

For many companies, reputation is communicated through the corporate logo, a recognizable picture or design that stands for the company. Recently, many consumer products organizations have redesigned their logos to modernize them (e.g., Kentucky Fried Chicken), to appeal to contemporary tastes (e.g., Campbell's Soup, Del Taco), or to create a single, recognizable image worldwide (e.g., Pepsi, Coke, Procter & Gamble) (Horovitz, 1991).

In their studies of organizations and their environments, John Meyer and Richard Scott (1983) used the term *institutional organization* to refer to the kind of organization that is more accountable to issues of social legitimacy than to profitability. These researchers focused specifically on hospitals and schools, illustrating that public support for activities in both types of institutions was most critical to their survival, more so than traditional financial measures of effectiveness. Since Meyer and Scott did their work, more businesses have been held accountable to standards of social legitimacy. Many corporations and universities, for example, divested their financial holdings in South Africa in protest of apartheid. Other companies have begun using recycled materials in their products and packaging. These moves are often controversial, but they clearly indicate a need for companies to care more about their reputations.

A more striking example of the importance of reputation was the early demise of Uptown cigarettes. This product was developed for a niche market—upwardly mobile African-Americans. By all accounts, the strategy had a good chance of success, but the product was never brought to market. Government and other public interest groups strongly objected to targeting certain portions of the population for the purchase of products with potentially negative health effects. Although no legal action was ever taken, sufficient pressure was put on the manufacturer to withdraw the product.

Public Relations   Over the past century, an entire profession has developed whose mission is to manage the reputation of organizations. This profession is public relations. Public relations professionals are hired to scan the environment, monitor the public's interest, and find ways to develop public appreciation for the organization's position and performance (Heath & Nelson, 1986). According to George Cheney and Steven Vibbert (1987), public relations originated in attempts by American railroads at the turn of the century to explain and defend their actions. The next major turning point for the profession came in the 1920s, when the "father" of modern public relations, Edward Bernays, defined the task of its adherents as a two-way, interpretive one. Public relations work "interprets the client to the public, which he is enabled to do in part because he interprets the public to the client" (Bernays, 1923, p. 14). By the 1960s and 1970s, public relations became more professional, proactive, and strategic, making greater use of prepared media such as brochures, booklets, and press releases as well as informal networking with various interest groups. Over the years, public relations professionals have been recognized as agents who continuously monitor their symbolic environment and in doing so help create and shape this very environment (Cheney & Vibbert, 1987).

Seen in this way, the public relations function is highly rhetorical in that it entails communicating multiple messages with multiple goals to diverse audiences. Effective public relations requires striking a balance (1) between developing a distinct image while simultaneously being recognized as a cooperative member of society and the business community; and (2) between shaping the external public's perceptions and maintaining credibility with internal publics, the employees (Cheney & Vibbert, 1987). In both cases the type of communication required is not markedly different from that employed by any individual who walks a line between creativity and constraint.

Cheney and Vibbert highlight one unusual form of public relations—corporate issue advocacy—as having its origins in the 1973 oil embargo. According to these writers, oil companies had few good options at the time for communicating with the public and needed to remain in the public eye while not inviting criticism of current practices. One solution was campaigns like those mounted by Mobil and Phillips 66, both oil companies. Mobil began running full-page ads in major newspapers offering opinions about the politics of regulation and the free marketplace (Crable & Vibbert, 1983). Phillips 66 launched a campaign called "The Performance Story," which celebrated its most successful employees and the values that motivated the company. Other examples of corporate issue advocacy are Esprit's political videotapes of customers speaking in response to the question "What would you do to make the world better?" and Nike's TV spots that feature Spike Lee as a spokesperson for racial harmony.

As a result of the corporations' issue advocacy, the world is further permeated by corporate discourse, increasingly blurring distinctions between the corporate, the political, and the personal. Organizations recognize that the ultimate market position is to become an integral, everyday part of the consumer's life and routine. Hence, they vie for control over communicative arenas in which they can foster associations with public values *without* emphasizing their product or service. Because of the sheer economic power of some of these corporations, we must not overlook the positive contributions they can make to issues in the public interest (e.g., when McDonald's becomes a world leader in recycling). On the other hand, we must always remember that, within a capitalist system, all corporate communication must be seen as further positioning to sell a product or service, even if the product or service is not prominently featured. This is the corporate colonization that Stanley Deetz (1992) has written about with apprehension (see Chapter 6).

In sum, companies today must preserve their reputations if they are to survive. The public no longer makes decisions simply on the basis of products or services. Corporations can indeed improve quality of life through their contributions to the public dialogue, but these efforts must also be considered with some skepticism as further attempts to gain market position through improved reputation.

Image, Identity, and Action

Much of the writing on the subject of reputation focuses on the perceptions outsiders hold of an organization. In contrast, research on image and identity has to do more with insiders' (employees') perceptions of the company. Following Jane Dutton and Janet Dukerich (1991), an important distinction can be made between an organization's identity and its image: "An organization's identity describes what its members believe to be its character; an organization's image describes attributes members believe people outside the organization use to distinguish it . . . . image describes insiders' assessments of what outsiders think" (p. 547). Applying this definition, an employee at a Denny's restaurant may see the organization's identity as convenient, inexpensive, and friendly, and at the same time believe the chain has an (unjustifiably) negative image. In addition, his or her perception of the image may be different from the restaurant's reputation, which comes directly from outsiders (including customers).

These semantic distinctions show the relationships among a variety of essentially interpretive processes and associated actions. Dutton and Dukerich (1991) describe a case study where employees of the Port Authority of New York and New Jersey confronted the problem of homelessness in their facilities. In their analysis, the authors found that the organization put off dealing with the problem in any serious way until it began to threaten their identity. "In particular, (employees') sense of the Port Authority as a high-quality, first-class institution made the presence of homeless people problematic. . . . When the organization took actions that members saw as inconsistent with its identity, they judged the issue as more important" (Dutton & Dukerich, 1991, pp. 534, 545). In other words, identity-threatening events are an impetus for action.

Similarly, organizational members monitor the image of the company—"deterioration of an organization's image is an important trigger to action as each individual's sense of self is tied in part to that image" (Dutton & Dukerich, p. 520). In an extension of Cheney's (1983) use of the concept of identification, Dutton and Dukerich demonstrate how an individual's desire to identify with an organization can motivate action that will protect his or her preferred image of the company. Clearly, images, identities, and reputations are constructed largely through communication.

Corporate Crises   Our final consideration in the areas of organizational image and reputation has to do with corporate crises. The crises of recent memory (e.g, Union Carbide's Bhopal, Exxon's *Valdez,* Johnson and Johnson's Tylenol) have sensitized businesspeople and the public to both the inherent difficulties and the utter necessity of communicating effectively during a crisis. Johnson and Johnson's exemplary performance following the Tylenol poisoning, for example, has in the long run helped its reputation and even positioned the company as expert in dealing with such matters (Cheney & Vibbert, 1987).

There are many types of corporate crises, including scandals, safety incidents, and accidents. In a study of crisis communication (Marcus & Goodman, 1991), it was concluded that a tension exists between the types of messages that are comforting to the victims of the crisis and to the shareholders of the company. Not surprisingly, in the case of accidents, shareholders preferred the corporation to take a defensive posture, whereas victims preferred the organization to be more accommodating. In the case of scandals, however, both groups of stakeholders—shareholders and victims—felt that accommodation to the people affected by the impropriety was the appropriate response. This study further underscores a rhetorical view of crisis communication, which requires a recognition of multiple audiences and the types of messages and appeals that would be most appropriate to each.

SUMMARY

The financial side of organizations must be understood if we wish to become participants in the total business dialogue. Each of the financial indicators discussed here also has a communication component.

Both competitive strategy and strategic alignment require exceptional creativity. Once again, communication is key both to implementing strategy and facilitating alignment between strategy and other organizational systems.

Creativity, specifically communication, helps shape a company's image, identity, and reputation. Reputation is important. The motivation to take individual action increases sharply when serious discrepancies are found between an organization's present activities and its espoused image or identity.

CASE STUDY

The Case of the New
Communication Consulting Company

You have decided to form a new communication consulting company in your area. The idea you want to pursue is that to make businesses more competitive in the 1990s requires balancing creativity and constraint through programs that empower employees while holding them accountable for results. You believe you know how to do this by improving communication. You also want to emphasize the ethics of communication in everyday business activities.

You realize that a lot of consulting firms specialize (or claim to specialize) in communication. However, your particular market niche is going to be implementation. Rather than simply make recommendations about how a company can improve communication, you want to actually do on-site implementation of your ideas. You feel this is a strategic marketing decision, as well as being consistent with your emphasis on ethics and balance.

The model you want to use as your basic training product is ACE (see Chapters 6 and 7). You believe this should also help you attract customers due to its clarity and its basis in theory and research. Specifically, you wish to demonstrate how implementing the ACE model will result in improved financial performance.

Your task is to convince a few friends and relatives to help you start this new business. To do this, you will need to develop a business plan, a marketing plan, an alignment strategy, and a way of personally influencing them to invest in your idea. Given what you have read in this chapter (and elsewhere in this book), what should you do?

THE FUTURE OF
ORGANIZATIONAL
COMMUNICATION

In a world that is constantly changing, there is no one subject or set of subjects that will serve you for the foreseeable future, let alone for the rest of your life. The most important skill to acquire now is to *learn how to learn.*

—Naisbitt & Auberdene, 1985

In the Preface, we commented on how our world is littered with signposts from the past, former sites of significance that have passed into obscurity or nostalgia. Examples are easy to identify—Hollywood, the birthplace of cinema; Silicon Valley, the engine that launched the computer industry; and Japan, the country that rewrote the rule book for world-class manufacturing.

But what are the signposts of today that will leave a lasting impression on the future? Predicting the future is never easy. For every great social or technological development, there have been outspoken opponents ready and willing to recite all the reasons it will never work. History relegates these voices of protest to the margins, but in the midst of such debates it's hard to know how they will turn out. What will the future of organizational communication be like? What can we expect out of organizations in the twenty-first century? This chapter is an admittedly personal speculation about these possible futures. We explore a variety of directions we think communication in organizations might take, from the highly probable to the most uncertain and radical.

First, we offer a critical summary of the first ten chapters, identifying the major issues we believe will dominate organizational life in the future. Second, we focus on the need for organizations and their members to become adept at learning as a means of survival, including the learning of new skills, new technologies, and new ways of organizing. Third, we turn our attention to the moral dimensions of organizational communication, highlighting the importance of ethics and the physical environment. In closing, we return to our original question about creativity and constraint, and offer a means through communication of confronting the limitations of individualism and therefore of transcending this tension.

In our exploration of future possibilities for organizational communication, we above all wish to add our voices to the communal telling of what Charles Garfield (1992) calls the "New Story of Business." This story views organizations as living, dynamic ecosystems; promotes sustainable growth healthy to humans and the environment; explores workable alternatives to hierarchy; and supports forms of organizing in which all employees are treated as fully participating partners.

LOOKING BACKWARD: A CRITICAL SUMMARY OF THE TEXT

In Chapter 1, we stated our preference for questions over answers. While much valuable research has been summarized in this book, we still maintain that the best approach for a student of organizational communication is to concentrate on asking important questions while remaining open to alternative answers and interpretations. Provisional answers provide useful guidelines for action today, and perhaps tomorrow, too, but in our experience the most successful people engage in an ongoing questioning of their interpretive frameworks in order to determine how well they still work.

Also in Chapter 1, we introduced two forces that are shaping communication in organizations today: greater turbulence and competitiveness; and new priorities regarding work. Perhaps the toughest question facing business in the 1990s is whether forms of organizing that promote greater empowerment and more meaningful work also allow organizations to survive and prosper. Can organizations be successfully pro profits and pro people? Ethics Box 11.1 presents a scene from the movie *Other People's Money* which encourages further exploration of this question.

Chapter 2 traced the development of definitions of communication from the information transfer model to the use of dialogue to balance creativity and constraint. In presenting the dialogic model, we described how self, other, and context are constructed in communication, and specifically how individuals are situated in multiple contexts and are challenged to make sense out of them.

Since no definition is ever right or wrong—only more or less useful—the challenge remains to demonstrate the usefulness of the dialogic approach to communication. Attempts are well underway. For example, Patricia Geist and Jennifer Dreyer (1992) recast the doctor-patient relationship in terms of *participatory care*, which emphasizes the importance of doctors' (and other providers') understanding of patients' thoughts and feelings as a means of affording patients an "authentic voice" when conversing about their illness (Silverman & Bloor, 1990). Participatory care goes beyond the information transfer model of communication (which sees the provider's role as simply telling the patient "what they need to know") and focuses instead on the contribution of the patient's perspective to a jointly-arrived-at interpretation and course of action. Future research should investigate the kinds of dialogues that are possible in organizations, the conditions under which they flourish, and their consequences for organizations and their members.

Chapter 3 began our section on historical narratives about communication and organization, focusing on classical/scientific management and human relations/human resources approaches. We prefaced this review with the "Three Ps" of historical writing—partiality, partisanship, and problematic—and asserted that our goal should not be to select the single, best theory of organizational communication, but rather to consider all theories as potentially useful for understanding different situations.

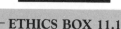

ETHICS BOX 11.1

SCENE FROM *OTHER PEOPLE'S MONEY* BY ALVIN SARGENT

The ultimate conflict between people and profits takes place at the point where a decision is made whether or not to close a plant. The movie *Other People's Money* is about one such proposed plant closing. This scene takes place toward the end, after Lawrence Garfinkle, a high-rolling investment banker, has secretly purchased enough shares of New England Wire and Cable to force a vote of the stockholders concerning the future of the company. Garfinkle wants to pay off the stockholders and liquidate the company; the current CEO, Andrew Jorgenson, believes that there is more to an organization than money and that the stockholders should vote to save the company. They take turns addressing the stockholders in a large town hall setting.

Jorgensen: It's nice to see so many familiar faces . . . so many old friends . . . many of you I haven't seen in four years. Thank you for coming and welcome to the 73d annual meeting of New England Wire and Cable—the 39th of which I am addressing you as your Chief Executive. Bill Coles, our able President, has told you about our year; what we accomplished—where we need to make future improvements—what our business goals are for the next year and the years beyond. I'd like to talk to you about something else. On this, our 73d year, I'd like to share with you some of my thoughts concerning the vote you are about to make in the company you own. We've had some very good years. We've had some very difficult ones as well. Though the last decade has been troubling for us it's been devastating for our industry.

Ten short years ago we were the 12th largest manufacturer of wire and cable in the country, the fourth largest in New England. We're now the 3d largest in the country and the largest in New England. We might not have flourished—but we survived. And we're stronger for it. I'm proud of what we accomplished. So we're at that point, where this proud company, which has survived the death of its founder, numerous recessions, a major depression and two world wars is in imminent danger of self-destructing this day in the town of its birth.

(*Points to Garfinkle*)

And there is the instrument of our destruction. I want you to see him in all his glory. Larry the liquidator—the entrepreneur in post-industrial America—playing God with other people's money. At least the robber barons of old left something tangible in their wake. A coal mine. A railroad. Banks. This man leaves nothing. He creates nothing. He builds nothing. He runs nothing. In his wake lies nothing but a blizzard of paper to cover the pain. If he said, "I could run this business better," well, that's something worth talking about. He's not saying that. He's saying, "I am going to kill you because at this particular moment in time you're worth more dead than alive." Well, maybe that's true. But it is also true that one day this industry will turn. One day when the dollar is weaker or the yen stronger or when we finally begin to rebuild the roads, the bridges, the infrastructure of our country, demand will skyrocket. And when those things happen we will be here and we will be stronger for our ordeal—stronger for having survived.

And the price of our stock will make his offer pale by comparison. God save us if you vote to take his paltry few dollars and run. God save this country if (*pointing to Garfinkle*) "that" is truly the wave of the future. We will then have become a country that makes nothing but hamburgers, creates nothing but lawyers, and sells nothing but tax shelters. And if we have come to the point in this country where we will kill something because at the moment it is worth more dead than alive, then turn around and take a good look at your neighbor. You won't kill him because it's called "murder" and it's illegal. This too is murder on a mass scale, only on Wall Street they call it "maximizing shareholder value," and they call it legal and they substitute dollar bills where a conscience should be. Damn it. A business is more than the price of its stock. It is the place where we make our living, meet our friends and dream our dreams. It is, in every sense, the very fabric that binds our society together. So let us, right now, at this meeting, say to every Garfinkle in this land, that here we build things, we don't destroy them. Here, we care for more than the price of our stock. Here . . . we care about people.

Garfinkle: Amen . . . and amen . . . and amen. Say "amen" someone, please (*to audience*).

You'll excuse me. I'm not familiar with the local custom . . . the way I was brought up you always said "amen" after you had a prayer. You hear someone praying, after he finishes, you say "amen" and drink a little wine.

Cause that's what you just heard—a prayer. The way I was brought up we called that particular prayer—the prayer for the dead. You just heard the prayer for the dead, and fellow stockholders, you didn't say "amen" and you didn't even get to sip the wine. So you don't think this company is dead? What about steel? You remember steel, don't you? Steel used to be an industry. Now heavy metal's a rock group. This company is dead, don't blame me, I didn't kill it. It was dead when I got here. It is too late for prayers, for even if the prayers were answered and a miracle occurred and the yen did this and the dollar did that and the infrastructure did the other thing we would still be dead. Know why? Fiber-optics. New technologies. Obsolescence. Fiber-optics. We're dead all right. We're just not broke. And you know the surest way to go broke? Keep getting an increasing share of a shrinking market. Down the tubes. Slow but sure. You know, at one time there may have been dozens of companies manufacturing buggy whips. And I'll bet you anything that the last one around was the one that made the best god damned buggy whip you ever saw. How would you have liked to have been a stockholder of that company? You invested in a business. And that business is dead. Let's have the intelligence, let's have the decency to sign the death certificate, collect the insurance, and invest the money in something with a future. Aha, but we can't, goes the prayer—we can't because we have a responsibility—a responsibility to our employees, our community. What will happen to them? I got two words for that—"Who cares?" Care about them? They didn't care about you. They sucked you dry. You have no responsibility to them. For the last ten years this company has bled your money. Did this community care? Did they ever say, "I know things are tough. We'll lower your taxes, reduce water and sewer?" Check it out. We're paying twice what we paid ten years ago. And our devoted employees, after taking no increases for three years, are still making twice what they made ten years ago. And our stock is one-sixth what it was ten years ago. Who cares? I'll tell you—me! I'm not your best friend—I'm your only friend. I care about you in the only way that matters in business. I don't make anything? I'm making you money. And lest we forget, that's the only reason any of you became stockholders in the first place. To make money, you don't care if they make wire and cable, fry chicken, or grow tangerines. You want to make money. I'm making you money. I'm the only friend you've got. Take the money, invest it somewhere else. Maybe—maybe you'll get lucky and it will be used productively—and if it is—you'll create more jobs and provide a service for the economy and God forbid—even make a few bucks for yourself. Let the government and the mayor and the unions worry about what you paid them to worry about. And if anyone asks, tell them you gave at the plant.

1. Make a list of all of the key points in each man's speech. What connections can you make between their arguments and the points made in this book?
2. Which speech do you find more convincing, and why? If you were a stockholder receiving this information, what would your vote be?

Although we have written about theory in this way for some time, the approach has recently gained in popularity. In the field of communication, for example, we have witnessed a significant rise in the number of individuals interested in what Wendy Leeds-Hurwitz (1992) calls social approaches. Assumptions common to social approaches are completely in line with the stance we have taken in this book:

> Common themes [of social approaches] include an acceptance of the social construction of reality (implying particular understandings of identity, self, and social roles); the implied need for taking a reflexive stance in research (for even researchers cannot stand outside of social constructions); a sociocultural, rather than an individual, focus for the study of communication (in turn requiring a particular definition of communication, an emphasis on the significance of context, and a frequent need to study actual behavior as it occurs); and investigation of symbols (whether or not these are explicitly named as topics of study) (Leeds-Hurwitz, 1992, pp. 131–132).

Chapter 3 also describes the emergence of classical approaches to understanding organizations, from empire to bureaucracy. An historical account of the human relations school followed, including subsequent research in the human relations tradition. While both classical and human relations approaches are out of style today in *theory* (the classical is seen as too hard, and the human relations as too soft), they continue to exert a strong influence on organizational practice. Perhaps this is because each approach reflects fundamental assumptions about human nature that are hard to give up. Recall, for example, the research on disciplining poor performers (Fairhurst, Rogers, & Sarr, 1987). Studies showed that while supervisors' first response to a performance problem is usually supportive, if unsuccessful this approach is quickly supplanted by a more authoritative style. In addition, you can still find managers who want to install employee suggestion programs primarily to "let them blow off some steam" and "feel like they are listened to."

Chapter 4 described the systems approach to organizational communication, beginning with historical background and continuing with basic systems terminology (e.g., goals, feedback, and the environment). Despite the complexities associated with researching systems theory, its current popularity in organizations is considerable. The perceived importance of the environment, for example, is steadily increasing as companies try to find better ways to understand and cope with turbulence. At the same time, most companies reflect a systems sensibility in their continuous improvement efforts, as they attempt to map out workflows, identify internal customers, and reduce process cycle-time.

The second half of Chapter 4 focused on the work of Karl Weick (1979), which serves as a bridge from systems to cultural approaches to organizational communication. While little research has successfully applied Weick's approach, his conceptualization of organizations as sense-making systems was a major theoretical development. In fact, Weick's work was arguably the most visible catalyst for the initial focus on meaning and interpretation in organizations (Putnam & Pacanowsky, 1983).

Alongside systems approaches, the other master metaphor in organizations today is organizational culture. In Chapter 5 we traced the history of thinking in this area. We reviewed the popular books of the early 1980s that celebrated organizational culture as a tool for inspiring excellence in organizations. Finally, we explored the culture metaphor for understanding organizations, revealing not only the existence of numerous definitions of culture, but also the myriad obstacles to "managing" organizational culture in any straightforward manner.

Despite arguments to the contrary (e.g., Smircich & Calas, 1987), the culture metaphor is far from dead; it has actually revitalized the way most people think about organizations. Naturally, as in any approach, there are hazards of oversimplification. The cultures approach is especially vulnerable to being coopted, inasmuch as unscrupulous managers attempt to get control of the corporate culture as a tool for maximizing profits (Smircich & Calas, 1987). Overall, however, the idea of culture has given people a way of talking about sources of uniqueness, tradition, and resistance to change that did not exist before.

Possibly the most important shift in thinking about organizational culture in recent years has been from a focus on shared values to a focus on practices. When the term *culture* was first introduced to business audiences, the tendency was to center on the powerful, defining effect that commonly held values could have on an organization. Lately, the focus on shared values has yielded to a focus on the rites, rituals, and everyday practices that make an organization unique (cf. Eisenberg & Riley, 1988). This shift is critical for communication, because it directs our attention to the issue of how social interaction enables people with diverse attitudes, values, and beliefs to organize successfully.

Chapter 6 provided an overview of two emerging approaches to the study of organizational communication: critical theory and postmodernism. The most important concept in critical theory is power, and we described the many levels and forms power can take. Clearly, this focus on power has not diminished over time. If anything, students of communication have become increasingly concerned with how relatively powerless individuals can resist corporate power and hegemony (Deetz, 1991).

Recent work by Charles Conrad (1990) links the idea of resistance to power with dialogue. Conrad begins with a quote from Stan Deetz and Dennis Mumby (1990): "In modern, 'deindustrialized' society, the value of labor and the nature of the production process are not as significant as having information and the opportunity to engage in meaningful discourse regarding decisions. . . . The modern problem is not monopoly capital but a monopoly of information and dialogue chances" (p. 29).

While power-resistance relationships can be regarded as dialogues between parties of unequal power, successful resistance can rarely be accomplished from *within* the dialogue (e.g., by standing up to your supervisor or by malicious obedience).

> Resistance which remains within the dialogue merely serves to reproduce these inequalities.
> To effectively challenge the rules and systems of the dialogue, communication must
> be addressed effectively to audiences who are independent of the meaning systems of the
> dialogue. . . . Societies are stable because each person simultaneously is part of a
> number of dialogues. When communication fails within one dialogue, actors can constitute
> audiences within other dialogues (Conrad, 1990, pp. 10, 14).

The main problem today, according to Conrad, is that the ability to move outside a dialogue, or to create alternative dialogues with different audiences, is disappearing. With the "corporate colonization of the life world" (Deetz, 1992), the power relationships promoted by corporations and capitalism are everywhere. As a result, "meaningful appeals across dialogues" (Conrad, 1990, p. 15) are much less likely.

The next section of Chapter 6 reviewed the basic threads that comprise postmodernism, focusing on the work of Jean-François Lyotard, Frederic Jameson, and Jean Baudrillard. Central to the idea of postmodernism is the critique of foundational beliefs about individuals, knowledge, and society. Each is "constructed" by people, and no single construction is in any sense privileged over another. Some strains of postmodernism further deconstruct the idea of the individual as agent of meaning or action. We relied heavily on the work of Stuart Clegg (1990) in applying these diverse ideas to the characteristics of organizations that might be classified as postmodern.

Postmodernism will likely continue to have an important, indirect effect on organizational theory and practice. A direct effect is less likely, mainly because the vocabulary of most postmodern writing is difficult to follow, and the sensibility at times quite bleak. Indirectly, however, we expect that a generation raised on MTV has internalized the postmodern aesthetic, which is inevitably reflected in their work. The interesting question that arises is whether this aesthetic will turn out to be more or less empowering. Will the reduced authority of history and tradition lead to a sense of possibility and opportunity, or will it simply reinforce the hegemony of organizations over individuals, for whom postmodernism says there is no firm source of truth, authority, or even personhood (Goodall, 1993)?

From the historical narratives we turned to the personal experience of work in Chapter 7. Beginning with an analysis of employee acculturation and the tendency for individuals to either cooperate or resist, we summarized the current research on factors shaping employee attitudes and behaviors. We considered the determinants of individual productivity, and in particular the role played by communication technology in affecting both productivity and quality of work life. We focused on alternatives to traditional business systems and procedures that provide employees greater voice and improve quality of work life. Interest in the experience of work will probably continue to increase, primarily because of changing priorities about quality of life, but also because so many people dislike their jobs (McClenahan, 1991). Turbulent economic times can be ideal for making such improvements. While on the one hand resources are scant, on the other hand people are searching for new ways of organizing for competitiveness. Radical innovations in communication could likely lead to significant cost-effective improvements.

Chapter 8 focused on the importance of interpersonal relationships in organizations. Few people in organizations understand the key role relationships can play in producing effective supervision, promoting social support, building personal influence, and ensuring productivity through smooth work flow. The second part of the chapter highlighted the role of communication in various types of relationships: with superiors, subordinates, peers, customers, and suppliers. We also described what can happen when relationships in organizations become more intimate, both when the feeling is mutual and when it is not. Finally, we reviewed the importance of communication skills such as assertiveness and active listening in maintaining good interpersonal relationships in organizations.

There will be a continued need for good interpersonal relationships in organizations of the future, from the standpoint of both the individual, who requires social support in an increasingly turbulent world, and the organization, which must maintain high levels of cooperation among all employees to effectively meet customer demands and remain competitive. Increasingly, no extra time is available for overly formal communication, or for individuals who cause problems because they lack the necessary skills to communicate with people. Those individuals who are aware that their personal influence and the success of the company depend on their ability to communicate informally in all directions of the organization are most likely to make it; everyone else will have problems.

In Chapter 9 we looked at larger numbers of communicators and focused on organizational groups, networks, and teams. We distinguished among different types of formal groups, characteristics of emergent networks, and kinds of teams that exist in organizations. We described the roles people play in groups, as well as the process by which groups communicate in attempting to make decisions. As in Chapters 7 and 8, the question of empowerment is again important here. Although many organizations aspire to self-managing teams, few can make them work.

We concur with most writers that the group is the fundamental unit of social organization. Activity in organizational groups is a microcosm of organizational culture and may even provide a reliable indication of the particular balance in that culture between creativity and constraint. Group communication in organizations will become even more important in the future. The details of what makes for a good work team, for example, are only now beginning to be worked out, with considerable difficulty and confusion. Teams and networks that cross organizations will become increasingly important, as global communication becomes both easier and more critical to our survival as a species.

In Chapter 10 we focused on the role of communication in the effectiveness of the organization as a whole. First, we defined effectiveness as having both a human and a financial side. We described the most common financial indicators of effectiveness—revenues, costs, profit, and cash flow—and in each case emphasized the key communication challenge facing the organization. Although a chapter of this kind is unprecedented in textbooks on organizational communication, we felt that it would provide the tools to engage in productive dialogue with the owners and managers of business. In our view, financial information is simply another potentially powerful context for interpreting organizational communication.

The ability to articulate the impact of communication on financial performance will be essential in the future. In organizations of the future, there will be no bystanders. Any function that cannot justify itself as supporting either the economic viability or social legitimacy of the company will be eliminated. This process is already well under way, and its effects are appearing in unlikely places, such as colleges and universities. As college course offerings are being reduced, subjects that are perceived as "marginal" (i.e., have failed to become connected somehow to economic or social legitimacy) are being dropped. A good argument can be made for the importance of just about any subject or discipline, but what is required is a willingness to (1) become an advocate for the value of what you do, and not assume that others "ought to understand" its inherent value; and (2) learn the language of the people who control the resources, the sources of money and legitimacy.

Chapter 10 continued with a discussion of competitive strategy and strategic alignment, and presented a closer look at how strategy changes throughout an organization's life cycle. Next came an examination of the process organizations go through to manage their reputations, both to external publics and to their own workforces. Taken together, emphases on competitive strategy and image management present some important issues for communication. On the one hand, to be successful a company must be able to clearly articulate its competitive advantage to customers. With regard to products with negative health effects (e.g., cigarettes, alcohol, junk food), it is in the company's best interest to use its image as its strategy. Seen this way, advertising and public relations accomplish at least two, somewhat different, objectives, both of which involve communication: they communicate characteristics of the product or service to publics; and they construct images to surround products, services, and the company as a whole which augment or substitute for strategy. (The respective themes and communication issues covered in Chapters 1–10 are presented in Table 11.1, pages 324–326.)

TABLE 11.1
CRITICAL SUMMARY OF CHAPTERS 1–10

Chapter	Themes	Communication Issues
1	(1) Asking new questions about work realities. (2) Two forces shaping communication in organizations today: greater turbulence and competitiveness; new priorities regarding work.	Do forms of organizing that promote greater empowerment and more meaningful work also allow organizations to survive and prosper?
2	(1) Development of four definitions of communication with emphasis on dialogic communication. (2) Self, others, and context as dialogic communication constructions. (3) Individuals as "situated" within multiple contexts and challenged with making sense out of them.	Can the concept of dialogue be useful as well as intellectually appealing?
3	(1) Classical (scientific management) and human relations/human resources narratives. (2) 3 "Ps" of historical writing. (3) Fundamental assumptions about the nature of humans, work, and society governed by issues of hierarchy (including empire and nationalism), strict divisions of labor, race, gender, and social class, and technologies (human and machine) derived from scientific rationality; worker motivation based on reward/punishment of behavior; symbolic dimensions of performance just beginning to be understood.	Can basic assumptions about hierarchy, scientific rationality, and divisions of labor, and so on, be productively discarded? Can dialogue be reframed as a meaningful way of inducing higher levels of commitment, performance, and satisfaction among workers and managers?
4	(1) Systems approach and the work of Karl Weick. (2) Singular importance of environment to models of organizing. (3) Organizations as sense-making systems.	Can systems theories be used to redefine workflows, identify internal customers, reduce process cycle time, improve feedback, and reduce friction and noise in the workplace? Can organizations as systems of meaning and interpretation reinvent the nature of cooperative organizing within competitive environments?
5	(1) Culture as master metaphor for understanding organizational realities. (2) Development of appreciation for the role of language in formation of cultures, subcultures, countercultures, rituals, rites, ceremonies, etc.	How does social interaction enable persons with diverse attitudes, values, and beliefs to organize successfully?

TABLE 11.1

(*continued*)

Chapter	Themes	Communication Issues
	(3) Move from culture as shared values to cultures as shared practices.	
6	(1) Two emerging approaches: critical theory and postmodernism. (2) Critical theory focus on power. (3) Postmodernism focus on critique of foundational narratives about individuals, knowledge, and society.	How can relatively powerless individuals resist corporate hegemony? Can organizations and societies find ways to sustain competing, diverse dialogues? What effects will the postmodern turn have on identity, power, and meaning in organizations? Can the postmodern be useful in finding ways to empower employees?
7	(1) Personal experience of work. (2) Acculturation and incentives for employees to cooperate or resist organizational goals and methods. (3) Role of new technologies in organizations and role of communication in dealing with the new technologies. (4) Importance of stress, burnout, and turnover to employee commitment, performance, and satisfaction.	How can communication be used to positively affect both productivity and quality of work life? How can dialogue be instrumental in dealing with employee resistance, stress, burnout, and turnover?
8	(1) Relational communication at work. (2) Key role played by interpersonal communication and relationships in effective supervision, promoting social support, building personal influence, and ensuring productivity through workflow. (3) Communication in relationships with superiors, subordinates, peers, customers, and suppliers. (4) Romance and sexual harassment. (5) The importance of building communication skills such as assertiveness and active listening.	How can communication be used to address key issues in professional relationships? How can dialogue be used to strengthen these relational ties in ways that also lead to improvement of productivity?
9	(1) Communication in groups, networks, and teams. (2) Characteristics of different types of groups, roles, and processes in groups that function in and across organizations. (3) The possibility of evolution to self-managing teams through empowered communication and increased responsibility and authority of groups.	What are the communication characteristics of a productive work team? How can teams and networks that function within and across organizations be used to improve information transfer, employee empowerment, and decision making?

TABLE 11.1
(continued)

Chapter	Themes	Communication Issues
10	(1) Communication effectiveness of the organization as a whole. (2) Effectiveness made up of both human and financial resources. (3) Vocabulary of financial indicators of effectiveness. (4) The need to clearly articulate financial performance across the organization and to external publics. (5) Competitive strategy and strategic alignment throughout an organization's life-cycle. (6) The importance of image as strategy.	How can financial performance be communicated throughout an organization as well as to external audiences? How can the articulation of financial performance be used to improve employee productivity and empowerment by reducing costs? What communication strategies can be used to improve the image and reputation of the company?

THE LEARNING ORGANIZATION

One excellent approach to the problems presented by our exceedingly complex world is to learn our way out. As we said at the outset, when the right answers about how to manage or how to compete change faster than we can keep up, the best strategy is to create a learning organization. Such an organization should be comprised of people who not only learn from past mistakes, but also question the assumptions that led to those mistakes in the first place (Argyris & Schon, 1978; Senge, 1991; Steier, 1989).

This sounds good in theory, but where does one begin in creating an organization whose members are willing to see the world in different ways, question assumptions, and devise new ways of doing business? Here we focus on three requirements for creating such an organization: (1) learning basic skills; (2) learning new technologies; and (3) learning new ways of organizing.

Learning Basic Skills

Most organizational practitioners, educators, and politicians have reached a consensus that the educational system in the United States does a poor job of providing students with even the most basic skills necessary for employment. In 1991 the U.S. Labor secretary's Commission on Achieving Necessary Skills reported three foundational abilities and five learning areas that have become increasingly important in the workplace (see Table 11.2). The description of skills and abilities as shown in the table emphasizes creativity and learning how to learn; it also stresses communication, including sociability, teamwork, negotiation, feedback, and use of new technologies. Unfortunately, few high school graduates are this well prepared. The situation is worse among minority populations

TABLE 11.2
NECESSARY WORKPLACE SKILLS

The Foundation

Basic: Reading, writing, mathematics, speaking, and listening.

Thinking: Creativity, making decisions, solving problems, seeing things in the mind's eye, knowing how to learn, reasoning.

Personal qualities: Responsibility, self-esteem, sociability, self-management, and integrity.

Job Skills

Resources: Allocating time, money, materials, space, and staff.

Interpersonal: Working on teams, teaching, serving customers, leading, negotiating, and working well with people from culturally diverse backgrounds.

Information: Acquiring and evaluating data, organizing and maintaining files, interpreting and communicating, and using computers to process information.

Systems: Understanding social, organizational, and technological systems, monitoring and correcting performance, and designing improving systems.

Technology: Selecting equipment and tools, applying technology to specific tasks, and maintaining and trouble-shooting technologies.

SOURCE: U.S. Labor Secretary's Commission on Achieving Necessary Skills, June 1991.

who make up the younger segment of the workforce, particularly in urban centers. If the problems of basic education in the United States are not addressed soon, there is no way to predict how low the standards might sink. In addition to their considerable impact on individual quality of life, this basic skills deficit will continue to have a devastating effect on business. Quality and customer service suffer in any industry that depends on the basic skills of its employees. Many, like McDonald's, have conceded the point and put pictures of food items rather than numbers on their cash registers. (McDonald's is also experimenting with picture menus for illiterate customers.) In a growing number of manufacturing organizations, interesting, complex, good-paying jobs are being redesigned into simple, low-paying, dead-end assignments for similar reasons. The result is a downward spiral of poor quality and service, de-skilling of jobs, lower wages, and still lower self-esteem.

One proposed solution to these problems is to establish programs in workplace literacy designed to provide remedial basic skills to employees. These programs vary widely in their focus and intensity. Some center on giving people the language skills they need to do the job (e.g., a carpenter learns all of the wood- and tool-related words and calculations). Others are more broadly concerned with teaching basic skills that are also helpful in life outside of work. Some claim to teach "basic skills" in 40 hours; others take 400. Some are sensitive to the differences in starting points among employees (e.g., a recent Guatemalan immigrant who is preliterate in both English and Spanish requires different instruction from a Mexican immigrant who is preliterate in English but fluent in Spanish), and others make no such distinctions. Some programs are offered by private companies, others by public agencies, and still others by corporations themselves for their own employees. This last route has had the most success so far. Some companies, like American

Honda and General Motors, actually maintain databases at some facilities that match employee education, skill level, and desired job opportunities. These programs are rare, however, and are perennially on the verge of being eliminated for financial reasons.

Even when they work well, basic skills programs do little to address the underlying issues of self-esteem, education, and opportunity in U.S. society. In the twenty-first century, we expect to see a tremendous amount of energy spent on teaching basic skills to employees. Unfortunately, much of this effort will make no difference unless the fundamental structure of the educational system is also addressed. Part of the solution may lie in revising our spending priorities as a nation. According to Laura Tyson (1991): "The share of the nation's economy invested by the federal government in education and training, children's programs, infrastructure, and civilian research and development has plummeted 40% since 1980. America ranks behind all its major competitors in each of these categories" (p. D2).

Learning New Technologies

The last decade marked a shift from an industrial age to an information age, but the meaning of this change is not entirely clear to the average person. While it has meant fewer industrial jobs and more information workers, the greatest impact has been an unprecedented increase in the rate at which information becomes obsolete.

This is not an abstract idea. In recent years, many people in their fifties, usually men, who after successful careers as engineers, accountants, or mechanics, suddenly find themselves laid off, with no prospect of finding a comparable job. The reason? Business conditions have changed—which often means that the technology in which they were expert has become obsolete.

But how did this happen? It is indeed a unique occurrence in history. Until recently, information aged at about the same rate as (or slower than) people. Thus, the knowledge engineers or doctors acquired in school could more or less serve them well throughout their careers. Certainly, there would be changes and developments to keep up with, but even a half-hearted effort would be enough. The fundamental technology underlying their work remained the same throughout their entire career.

This is no longer the case. The "life cycles" of technologies and businesses can no longer be counted on to exceed employee life cycles. In the computer and aerospace industries, for example, the half-life or perishability of a set of skills is presently five to ten years and shrinking fast. As a result, many people in their forties and fifties are discovering that little of their technical knowledge matters much anymore and that what is more important than their old set of skills is their ability to learn a new set, and *fast*. Learning, once primarily an activity of the young, is becoming a lifelong project—and the cornerstone of global competitiveness and economic success.

In the twenty-first century, recertification and reeducation will be common in all professions, which will in turn alter the fundamental role of primary and secondary education. The education people receive in the first 20 years of their lives will be focused not so much on conveying information (which won't be relevant for long in any case), but on helping people learn how to think and how to learn.

Still, certain content areas will grow in importance. Many people speculate about the technologies of the future that will impact the business world. And while such projections are extremely perishable, two broad-ranging technological developments will very likely have a major impact on organizations, at least until the year 2000. These two developments are biotechnology and virtual reality.

Biotechnology   Biotechnology is the purposeful creation or modification of genetic material (DNA) for commercial applications. Over the past decade enormous amounts of time and money have been invested in these techniques. For example, pharmaceutical companies have developed gene therapies for certain diseases; by the time this book is published, the first genetically altered tomato should be available in your local market. The gene that determines the speed of ripening was modified to produce a tomato that rots more slowly. Finally, the U.S. Army is setting up a gene bank for all of its members to facilitate positive identification of soldiers. But to what other uses could a gene bank be put?

The possibilities are both amazing and frightening (as are the legal and ethical challenges to this line of work), but biotechnology seems destined to have a major impact on organizations. A recent example of a contract between Merck pharmaceuticals and the government of Costa Rica reveals some of the complexities associated with biotechnology. In the past, large drug companies have explored the undeveloped areas of countries like Costa Rica for sources of new products. Under the new agreement, Costa Rica agrees to send small parcels of biological samples—bushels of twigs, packages of ground-up caterpillars—to Merck, for them to consider using in research and development. For any product that Merck develops based on a Costa Rican sample, the country receives a percentage of the profits. It is estimated that if ten products can be found based on Costa Rican samples, their percentage of profits from Merck alone will more than double their total current income as a nation from traditional exports.

This example raises many interesting questions and possibilities. First, it establishes a country's "ownership rights" over its biological resources. But who, in fact, owns the land, the plants, and animals? Is it the government, or the people themselves, or neither? Second, once Merck identifies a biological specimen that can successfully be developed into a product, there is no further need for material. Based on the genetic code found in the sample, scientists can synthesize as much as they need. This means that the Costa Ricans are not selling material resources as much as they are trading in *information*—biological information that in turn provides the clues for genetic engineering. The whole arrangement seems wildly postmodern and calls into question all of the old boundaries that have traditionally been drawn between individuals, biology, governments, businesses, and information.

In their award-winning book, Stan Davis and Bill Davidson (1991) place this move toward biotechnology in an appealing historical framework. They argue that we are presently in the second half of the information economy and that the next big shift (which will occur around 2020) will be to a bioeconomy, in which genetics will be as central to business as information is today. Their advice to organizations is simple, if challenging: To be successful in the twenty-first century, companies should find a connection between their present strategy, product, or service and biotechnology. They make a persuasive case that the most successful corporations of the past two decades are those that went into the information business. In most cases, even when this business was a sideline at first (as in the airlines' computerized reservation systems and TRW's entry into the credit reporting business), it soon outpaced the company's other businesses (Davis & Davidson, 1991).

Virtual Reality   Virtual reality is a technology that allows an individual to experience imaginary worlds in striking detail, complete with sight, sound, and other sensations. In some instances, the participant puts on wraparound goggles or a headset that simulates reality by changing sensory inputs as the wearer moves the eyes or head. Familiar precursors to virtual reality are computer-aided design (CAD) and holography. Computer-aided design allows engineers, artists, and designers to design in three dimensions. Once they have done their initial drawing, these sophisticated programs allow them to rotate the object in any direction, thus giving a better sense of how it will actually fit together and behave when built. The time savings alone from CAD has been enormous.

Holography is a kind of advanced photography/image projection that also simulates three dimensions, either on a flat surface or suspended in the air in front of you. Holograms can be found in arcade games, on credit cards, or on the rides at Disneyland. In the near future, holograms will be used for teaching and design. Virtual molecules will appear as three-dimensional and spin in space in your chemistry classroom or in an engineer's drafting "box."

As is true for the bioeconomy, imagining the next step for virtual reality—where you could actually "drive" in a virtual car or "walk through" a prehistoric scene in your science class—is still very difficult. But writers like Harold Rheinhold (1991) have already chronicled many working examples of virtual reality, and there will be many more. One involves airplane pilot training in which flying conditions are simulated using virtual reality technology instead of old-fashioned flight simulators. With the growth of this technology, changes in entertainment, education, and health care will be truly amazing.

Learning New Ways of Organizing

As we suggested in Chapters 8 and 9, contemporary organizations are struggling to make empowerment a reality. Perhaps the hardest part of this process is discovering or creating alternatives to traditional hierarchy that really work. While quite a number of companies are implementing some form of self-managing, semiautonomous work teams, others are going further to redesign the corporation. This section focuses on two of the more radical bodies of work that offer alternatives to hierarchy: participative action research and ecofeminism.

Participative Action Research   Perhaps the most exciting work on alternative organizational forms is being conducted in Scandinavia. Consider Skaltek AB, a Swedish company that designs and manufactures packaging machines for the wire industry. Skaltek has 90 employees and annual revenues of $17 million. The company's founder, Oystein Skalleberg, started the company in 1972 in a small basement shop with the assumption that, given the right setting, human potential was unlimited. This is what Skaltek AB looks like today:

> No hierarchy or titles exist at Skaltek. Members of the staff are called "responsible persons," not "employees." Openness is total; everyone in the company has access to all

information. Each morning the entire staff meets for discussion and exchanges information about the volume of orders, the cash situation, and similar matters.

  Control, as such, does not exist, not even quality control. Everyone is—and perceives himself or herself to be—personally responsible. On each unit of the packaging machines that are manufactured there is a little aluminum label on which is written: "Quality-Security. I am responsible," along with the signature of the person who has done the work. If there are any questions about the work later in the production chain, people don't turn to a foreman or supervisor but go directly to the one "responsible" (Osterberg, 1992, p. 10).

The natural reaction to this scenario is skepticism—can it really work? What about hiring and firing, grievances and compensation? Who sets the strategy and direction for the firm? And so on. Many of these concerns are legitimate. Firms of this kind often have very low profit margins by American standards, in that they operate within a cultural environment that values full employment more than profit maximization. But some of these companies do survive, and even thrive, with a noticeable absence of much of what we would consider normal organizational characteristics. This fact alone should cause us to question our traditional assumptions about what an organization has to look like to be effective.

Obviously, not all Scandinavian companies follow this model, but most are interested in moving work life in this direction—toward increased democracy, political equality, and social justice. Notable among Scandinavian advocates of this change in organizations are participative action research (PAR) professionals who conduct research projects in organizations that are explicitly designed to bring about social change. In Norway, for example, participative action researchers share the following four assumptions (adapted from Elden & Levin, 1991, p. 129):

1. A commitment to democratization and economic improvement—people have the right to good-quality jobs.
2. A vision of the good organization as maximizing human potential, equalizing power, and promoting self-management and workplace democracy.
3. A view of the "researcher" as co-learner rather than expert in charge of change.
4. An extensive appreciation for and connection with the political infrastructure that supports greater democratization of workplaces, including specific labor legislation, agreements, and traditions.

PAR should be of interest to students of organizational communication for two reasons. First, it embodies many of the values of greater power-sharing and employee voice that are associated with effective communication. Second, PAR is interesting because the research process explicitly involves dialogue between the researcher and the organization as a means of creating new interpretive frameworks. According to Max Elden and Morten Levin (1991):

Empowering participation occurs between insiders and outsiders in what we call cogenerative dialogue. Both insiders and outsiders operate out of their initial frames of reference but communicate at a level where frames can be changed and new frames generated. Exchange on a level that affects one's frame of reference is a much more demanding form of communication than mere information exchange (p. 134).

In other words, we learn from PAR not only that dialogic models of communication are being tried in organizations, but also that one successful process for turning more traditional organizations toward empowered participation is itself dialogic.

Ecofeminism: The Partnership Way   Ecofeminism blends ecology and feminism and is based on a reinterpretation of history (Eisler, 1987; Milbrath, 1989). Archaeological evidence presented by these writers supports the idea that before the dominator societies of today, there existed partnership societies, which were characterized by an equal relationship between the sexes, with neither dominating the other; and nature as a source of nurturance, and not as something to be dominated. The view of power in partnership societies was power to nurture and to actualize, and not to dominate (Eisler, 1987). Furthermore, ecofeminists believe that life on earth is "an interconnected web, *not* a hierarchy." They advocate a "decentralized global movement that is founded on common interests yet celebrates diversity and opposes all forms of domination and violence" (King, 1989, pp. 19–20). By emphasizing opposition to "all" forms of domination and violence, ecofeminism moves the locus of concern from "men over women" to "men over the world"; that is, the domination of women and the exploitation of nature are seen as part of the same problem—the problem of hierarchy. Ecofeminism is a call to reclaim both women and nature from their status as "the original others" back into the web of life.

Communication researchers Connie Bullis and Hollis Glaser (1992) champion ecofeminism as a framework for identifying and promoting emergent, alternative forms of organizing that are decentralized, small, and egalitarian, and focus on local concerns. There is an urgent need to demonstrate how these ecofeminist recommendations might work in practice.

MORAL DIMENSIONS OF ORGANIZATIONAL COMMUNICATION

In this section we focus on ethics and responsibility to the planet. Both topics are of growing concern and will hold much currency in the future. In each case, we examine the role played by communication in facilitating moral judgment.

Ethics of Organizational Communication

Consider the following statistics: "Between 1975 and 1985, two-thirds of Fortune 500 firms were convicted of serious crimes, ranging from fraud to the illegal dumping of hazardous wastes. A much larger number were convicted of misdemeanors after extensive plea bargaining, and a still larger number settled suits out of court" (Conrad, 1990, p. 15).

Ethical issues pervade organizational behavior. Throughout this text, we have posed ethical problems connected with the issues under discussion. An increasing number of business schools and corporations are requiring their students and employees, respectively, to take courses in ethical decision making. Apparently, the ethical abuses of the past two decades have left people searching for a new moral foundation in the workplace.

W. Charles Redding (1991) has sounded the ethics alarm for organizational communication:

> The preponderance of everyday problems that plague all organizations are either problems that are patently ethical in nature, or they are problems in which deeply embedded ethical issues can be identified. . . . if we take a close look, we can discover, in almost every act of human communication, an ethical dimension (pp. 1–2).

One possible reason why unethical communication has become commonplace is the increased pressure to compete. The nature of organizing itself may be another contributing factor. As companies grow from individuals to dyads to groups, and then into organizations and interorganizational fields, increasing levels of hierarchy and role differentiation often lead to lies, distortion, turf building, and coverup. Redding has developed a preliminary typology of unethical messages in organizations, which appears in Table 11.3.

In tracing the roots of the ethics problem, Redding cites James Patterson and Peter Kim (1991): "Lying has become a cultural trait in America. Lying is embedded in our national character . . . Americans lie about everything—and usually for no good reason" (p. 49). Terence Mitchell and William Scott (1990) take a similar position as they confront "the ethic of personal advantage," which they feel is the cause of American decay. Three themes comprise this ethic: "(1) a present versus a future orientation; (2) an instrumental as opposed to a substantive focus; and (3) an emphasis on individualism contrasted with community" (pp. 25–26).

We agree that perhaps the greatest weakness of businesspeople in the past two decades has been short-term thinking, or the willingness to trade off long-term value for immediate gain. This explains our feeling of culture shock when the host of a new restaurant in Venice, California—a place where the "hot" new restaurant changes weekly—announced

TABLE 11.3
TYPOLOGY OF UNETHICAL MESSAGES

Type	Examples
Coercive	An employee criticizes the boss's "pet" development program in a meeting and is fired on the spot for her remarks.
Destructive	A supervisor makes a sexist joke at the expense of an employee.
Deceptive	Federal Aviation Administration (FAA) employees falsifies employee work records to justify the firing of air traffic controllers during their 1981 strike.
Intrusive	Electronic surveillance of employees is conducted through hidden video cameras.
Secretive	The asbestos industry suppressed information that left little doubt about the health hazards posed by their product.
Manipulative/exploitative	Management threatens union members with a plant closing if they don't ratify a contract.

SOURCE: Redding, WC (1991). Unethical messages in the organizational context. Paper presented at the Ann. Convention of the ICA, Chicago, IL.

that the owners were planning for it to be a success for at least 300 years, which was how long their other restaurants had prospered in Japan. This long-term thinking is reflected in their approach to customer service. They aim to bring not just you, but also your children's children back for more.

Similarly, we have observed the self-serving attitudes that lead individuals in organizations to spend more time covering up and taking care of themselves than reaching out to create a supportive community. We were intrigued by Michael Lerner's (1992) contention that the looters in the 1992 Los Angeles riots were merely "living out the cynical American ethos" (B7). According to Lerner, we live in a culture of looting, where the highest goal is to "look out for number one" and to "get what you can when you can. Any cost to others is acceptable as long as you don't get caught or don't hurt your own future chances. . . . Within this ethos, concern for the future—of the planet, of one's own country or even of one's own children—seems naive and silly, something to be left to 'do-gooders.' The ethos of looting becomes the 'common sense' of the society" (B7).

The goal of ethics education in this area should be to build moral character, which requires above all the ability to hear and understand perspectives that are different from one's own. Unfortunately, most business ethics courses treat the subject as a series of problems to be solved, which results in the student learning a set of rules necessary for ethical behavior. These rules, after a while, take on a life of their own and do little to enhance moral character. As an alternative for teaching ethical behavior, Mitchell and Scott (1990) suggest moral discourse, which to us sounds a lot like dialogue:

> Moral discourse is a process of rhetorical engagement by students and professors in free and open forums of conversation and debate. One tries to persuade others of the truth of his or her point of view on moral issues. In the process, widely divergent opinions are expressed and each individual is exposed to alternative propositions about values. The whole point is to provide knowledge of moral options and the opportunity to choose among different value systems. . . . The function of ethics courses should be to instill an open, moral, loving, humane, and broadly informed mentality, so that students may come to see life's trials and business's ethical challenges as occasions to live through with integrity and courage (p. 29).

Responsibility to the Planet

One outgrowth of the self-serving values described here has been the deterioration of our physical environment. Red tides, deforestation, acid rain, toxic waste—these and hundreds of other byproducts of human industry deplete the world's resources at a rate that is far outstripping our ability to replace them (Mitchell & Scott, 1990). The actions that follow from our inability or refusal to see the world as an interconnected system have come home to roost. Reports of growing cancer rates in areas known for industrial pollution are on the increase. It would not be an overstatement to say that business organizations have the potential to be among the most thoughtless and brutal enemies of nature on the planet. Consider Charlene Spretnak's (1991) dark postmodern vision:

> Within the value structure of the intensification of competition in production and consumption that will characterize the focus of life in the global market and mass culture that are presently being constructed, the felt connections between the person and the family, the community, the bioregion, the country, other peoples, other species, the Earthbody, and the cosmos merely get in the way (p. 9).

ETHICS BOX 11.2

THE FUTURE IS US

Jason had gotten through most of his life on a series of small, but increasingly significant, lies. At first, when he was small, they were about things such as who ate all of the ice cream, or how he had managed to get so dirty while playing outside. By the time he was in high school, the lies had expanded somewhat to cover his poor performance in some classes ("the teacher has it in for me") and whether he was cheating on his girlfriend (he was but claimed he wasn't).

In college a lot of Jason's small untruths developed into one much larger one—the story he told about his life to people who didn't know him. Because he had gone almost 3,000 miles away from home to attend school, his invention of important family connections, the tragic, often bizarre deaths of family members and friends, and the level of his excellence in high school sports escalated. Although he knew he was lying, he also knew that the lies he told made his life seem richer and more meaningful than it had actually been. And they had also contributed—he believed—to his admission to a top fraternity, which in turn helped his election to class president.

Now Jason was ready for graduation and his first "real" job. Recently, he had done a lot of soul-searching and had admitted, at least to himself, that his lying was wrong. He felt, at the end of his seemingly collegiate career, that most of his accomplishments had been gained illegitimately, based more on his story of who he was than on anything an examination of the facts could bear out. He was ashamed of himself, and, ironically, of what he had achieved. He resolved to change.

Through a fraternity contact, he was scheduled for an interview with a top international firm. The night before his interview, his frat brother told him that he was being interviewed largely because of the connections he had bragged about his family having back home. The company believed that someone well-connected would be valuable in their acquisition of a firm in that part of the country, and that Jason could be instrumental in smoothing the local political waters because of those contacts. The problem was, he did not have those contacts—they were part of his lie. On the other hand, he really wanted this job and believed that his developed rhetorical abilities could help him through almost any situation. And at home there were some friends who might be able to help out. Perhaps he could pull it off, after all.

Let's assume for a moment that you are Jason. What should you do? What would you do?

An exploitative view of our natural world simply cannot last; it is unsustainable. We are beginning to see clearly the limits to such mindless growth. James Robertson (1985) foresees two possible futures: we can either follow the current, hyperexpansionist (HE) path, or we can reflect seriously on our current assumptions and forge a sane, humane, ecological (SHE) future. Adopting the second alternative will require us to reclaim the various forms of "caring labor"—nurturing, helping, loving others—that have been devalued in hyperexpansionist economic systems (Rose, 1983).

The reintegration of caring labor into the economic mainstream, however, will not be enough to promote a stable ecological future. Basic socioeconomic and political systems must also be scrutinized and reformed. Consider the development of the U.S. economy over the past 50 years. In 1952, in response to a precipitous drop in gross national product and rising unemployment following World War II, the U.S. government was forced to admit that full employment was, at least in the foreseeable future, an unattainable goal. The chosen solution to this problem was to spend unprecedented amounts of money on the development of the military, which both created jobs and brought into being the powerful military-industrial complex. In this new economy, the military became a major customer of many of our largest corporations, and a substantial portion of the nation's budget was allocated to support the military. Regardless of one's politics, it is undeniable that the tradeoffs involved in supporting such an economy have been enormous. For example, the cost of developing one Intercontinental Ballistic Missile (ICBM) could feed 50 million children, build 160,000 schools, and open 340,000 health care centers (Sivard, 1983).

Given these tradeoffs, how is it that the military economy has persisted for so long? Perhaps it is because this economy favors individuals who *own* businesses in the United States, those 2 percent of American families who control 54 percent of American assets. The current trend to shift resources away from the military in the wake of the Cold War raises many other questions about national and international priorities and about quality of life in society. To take a highly critical view, shifting funds from the military to health and education may create a monster for those in power—a healthy, educated underclass that wants more money, better jobs, and a real voice in government. In any case, changes internal to organizations may have little impact on overall quality of life until underlying issues of economic priorities are addressed at a societal or global level.

In some respects, correctives to the abuses discussed so far are forthcoming. According to Spretnak (1991), "The notions that industrialized societies somehow live on top of nature, rather than embedded within its finely balanced complexities, and that humans have no inherent connectedness with one another are being rejected as ignorant fabrications, which have led to heinous deeds" (pp. 1–2). Questions of environmental impact and the sustainability of the habitat are on almost everyone's agenda—the environmental conference in Rio de Janeiro in 1992 being one well-known example. In populous states like California, agencies such as the Air Quality Management District are becoming increasingly powerful in regulating environmentally sensitive business practices, such as recycling, hazardous waste disposal, and the air pollution associated with employee commuting. Individual companies have also taken up specific environmental initiatives. For example, Ben & Jerry's Ice Cream, Patagonia, and Del Monte Foods were among the companies represented at a recent environmental conference in San Francisco. The purpose of the conference was to bring environmentally smart changes into these companies and their products. Many fast-food outlets are replacing their old packaging with recyclables. An organization called the Elmwood Institute has even prepared a guide for organizations to conduct their own "eco-audit" as a means of evaluating the degree to which their practices are ecologically sound.

Organizational responses to environmental issues revolve around time and hard choices. The timing question is whether we can respond soon enough to acid rain, defoliation, air or ocean pollution. The question of choice is a stickier one, and it follows the pattern of creativity and constraint we have described. Every decision made in an organization has a potential environmental impact. Hence, each decision ought to be accompanied by a risk analysis and a choice—"how much is too much?" What actions will not be tolerated under any circumstances?

Most of these choices involve significant economic and personal tradeoffs. Yet by making intelligent decisions today, we create our collective future as a species. The twenty-first century will be characterized by more conscious attention to and discussion of the choices affecting our habitat and future as a species. Although we may spend our lives in and out of organizations and institutions, we are above all residents of the world, and we forfeit our residency when we stop talking about the things that matter most.

Not all responses to environmental problems originate from within formal organizations. Some of the most creative approaches involve the reorganization of communities, with significant implications for the relationship among work, family, and society. One intriguing example is the eco-village. Eco-villages are "cooperative communities that aim to live in harmony with nature by growing their own food, generating their own energy, and handling their own wastes" (Walljasper, 1992). Unlike the communes of the 1960s, eco-villages provide separate dwellings, yards, and cars, and residents are free to work away from the village if they choose. At the same time, they lower living costs while raising living standards through the clustering of 20 to 50 residences in one compact community. Once again, Scandinavia is at the forefront of this trend; 80 eco-villages are being planned in Sweden, with 10 now under construction (Walljasper, 1992). Perhaps the greatest advantage of this living arrangement is a renewed sense of community: "Eco-villages reconcile our need for community and routine with our taste for adventure and sophistication. There's room for both here" (Berg, in Walljasper, 1992, p. 142).

In some ways, the movement toward promoting sustainability is an extension of the best parts of systems theory, of a recognition that to survive, we must attend to the needs and requirements of the whole. Spretnak (1991) calls this the "ecologizing of consciousness":

> The ecologizing of consciousness is far more radical than ideologies and strategies of the existing political forms . . . seem to have realized. They often try to tack ecology onto programs born on instrumental rationality, scientific reductionism, and the modern belief that further advances in the manipulation of nature for human ends will deliver a future filled with peace, freedom, and goodwill. It seems quite unlikely that political versions of democracy that are steeped in these values of modernity that have proven so deficient can serve as the vehicles of transformation to carry humans into our new relationship with the entire Earth community and our own potential. It is already clear that visionary political developments lag behind the ecological and spiritual awakening. Increasingly, moral authority lies less in official position than in wisdom, in *an experiential sense of the interrelated nature of our reality* (p. 229, italics added).

A QUESTION OF BALANCE REVISITED: REFIGURING IDENTITY THROUGH COMMUNICATION

When we set up the creativity-constraint tension at the outset of this book, we knew that we had created a useful, but essentially artificial, conceit. Certainly, we live our lives through institutions (schools, organizations, marriage, etc.), and the main activity involved in each of them appears to be maintaining a give and take between autonomy and dependence, freedom and conformity. Life, it seems, is a question of balance.

Or is it? Also in the spirit of this book, we must point out that the idea of a balance between creativity and constraint, between the individual and the organization, is also only one interpretation, a human construction. This distinction weakens a bit as you press on it—precisely what *is* an organization, without individuals? What *are* individuals, apart from organizations? This final section, then, addresses the critique of individualism itself, of the idea that humans are isolated, separate entities who variously choose to interact (or not to interact) with other, similarly isolated creatures.

We begin with the work of Robert Bellah and his colleagues, first in *Habits of the Heart* (1985) and, more recently, in *The Good Society* (Bellah et al., 1991). These researchers maintain that the language and ideology of individualism, as it appears most frequently in our families and offices, is a significant obstacle to what we desire most, which is community. They further connect an emphasis on individualism with the tendency toward exploitation. Those who feel that existence is separate and against the world are most capable of destroying part of it and themselves in the process. Bellah et al.'s (1991) good society is consistent with the ecofeminist ideal:

> Americans have pushed the logic of exploitation about as far as it can go. It seems to lead not only to failure at the highest levels, where the pressure for short-term payoff in business and government destroys the capacity for thinking ahead, whether in the nation or in the metropolis, but also to personal and familial breakdown in the lives of our citizens. In this book we have repeatedly called for a new paradigm, which we can now call the pattern of cultivation . . . it would be the attempt to find, in today's circumstances, a social and environmental balance, a recovery of meaning and purpose in our lives together, giving attention to the natural and cultural endowment we want to hand down to our children and grandchildren, and avoiding the distractions that have confused us in the past (p. 271).

In their vision of a good society, Bellah et al. (1991) give primacy to the ability to pay attention. Their fundamental assumption is that the source of our current difficulties is our inability to face reality and instead to get distracted or to engage in elaborate denial over what to others is as plain as day. While we take exception to their implication that there is "a" single reality to face, we see important similarities between this argument and Mitchell and Scott's (1990) critique of the ethos of personal advantage—the root of this way of thinking is an inability to be open to alternative world-views, to engage in dialogue. At a still deeper level, we agree with Bellah et al. that many of our problems as a species lie less in the need to learn more about how to live than in keeping still long enough to understand what our bodies and hearts have known all along. Toward the end of their book, Bellah et al. (1991) hint at the possible rewards of closer attention to life:

> We can indeed try genuinely to attend to the world around us and to the meanings we discover as we interact with that world, and hope to realize in our own experience that we are part of a universal community, making sense of our lives as deeply connected to each other. As we enlarge our attention to include the natural universe and the ultimate ground that it expresses and from which it comes, we are sometimes swept with a feeling of thankfulness, of grace, to be able to participate in a world that is both terrifying and exquisitely beautiful. At such moments we feel like celebrating the joy and mystery we participate in (p. 285).

As we read this paragraph, we are filled with hope but frustrated in knowing what to do next. How can the experience of work be infused with such revelations? What does this all have to do with organizations? Vigilant attention seems key, but if we feel like isolated individuals fighting against the world, or against the boss, how does this opening up to the whole take place?

Not surprisingly, we feel it can happen through communication. We cope with our alienation—from love, work, or society—by constructing stories that we come to know as our "selves," our identities. More often than not, these stories have to do with our social roles, our success or failure within organizations and other social institutions. In time, we become attached to these stories, which seem to define us against a fearful sea of otherness. We use these stories to guide, justify, and explain both who we are and what we do. We attach ourselves to issues of personality and consequently find it increasingly hard to work together (Sennett, 1978).

What postmodernist approaches (see Chapter 6) do best is to reveal that these consistent, unified identities are human *constructions*, no more, no less. They come to us from our families and friends, and although they may start out innocently, if they are taken too seriously, they end up as traps. Studies on the "Pygmalion effect" in organizations support the idea of the self-fulfilling prophecy. That is, if you take two employees of equal ability, label one "smart" and the other "stupid," the chances are good that people will treat them accordingly, which in turn will affect their actual performance. Average employees who are singled out and treated as "smart" do indeed get smarter. The person we think we are (and who others think we are) makes a big difference in what we become.

Simply put, the stories we tell about ourselves (our identities or personalities) are not us (Hyde, 1991). Instead, we are expressions of a larger whole, the interconnected web of life described above, and we are capable of doing many things that might initially seem out of character. An overly rigid view of one's identity leads to an unwillingness to engage in dialogue and the pernicious belief that we exist "in" and against the world, which in turn prompts us to defend against and exploit what we can of other people and of nature (Bellah et al., 1991). An alternative metaphor for thinking about ourselves is as waves in the ocean. We don't say a wave is *in* the ocean; rather, it comes *out of* (while remaining part of) the sea (Bateson & Bateson, 1987; Watts, 1966). From this interpretive framework, our individual identities seem small, our potential infinite. While rational language may be able to sever in concept the connection between the individual self and the world, in lived experience they are inseparable (Jackson, 1989).

Nevertheless, it is true that in everyday communication we reinforce each other's belief that we *are* the stories we tell about ourselves and that we must defend these stories against the world. As such, we act in defensive and aggressive ways, which in many cases create the very conditions that we fear. For example, a person who is sure that her co-workers hate her will act in a way that is hesitant, aloof, even suspicious—which in turn leads to considerable negative reactions.

How can people come to envision themselves not as isolated units, but as part of an interconnected web or whole? For some of us the answer lies in religion (from the Latin religare: "binding into one"), but in practice there is often little connection between religious experience and religious institutions. For others, such realization follows a life crisis, such as the loss of a loved one or a serious illness. Tragically, a jolt of this magnitude is often needed to force a reintegration of self into the world, to open a person's heart to what heretofore seemed wholly "other."

But perhaps there are less dramatic routes to the same destination. It is our conviction that quality dialogue—in which individuals are respectful of the validity of others' lived experiences and mindful of the constructed nature of our own stories—is the cornerstone of our future. Without such dialogue and the community it inspires, all talk of diversity, cooperation, and ecology will be for naught. We must position ourselves in the world through communication, and in doing so take responsibility for its future. The future of organizational communication starts now, and there is a role in it for each of us. Following Conrad (1990): "Identity formation/enactment is the site of a constant struggle between alternate definitions of one's self, each of which imbeds an actor in societal power relationships in different ways" (p. 9). In the end, how we position ourselves in the world through communication is critical not only to our felt power as individuals, but also, as a result, to the future of our organizations, societies, and the world.

Which brings us to this final thought: If each of us is an expression of the whole, then creativity and constraint are inseparable parts of the same activity. Rather than seeing human activity as consisting of individuals balancing between themselves and the world, we see only activity: communicating, organizing, and life itself.

> When I walk several hours the Earth becomes sufficient to my imagination, and the lesser self is lost or dissipates in the intricacies, both the beauty and the horror, of the natural world. I continue to dream myself back to what I lost, and continue to lose and regain, to an Earth where I am a fellow creature and to a landscape I can call home. When I return I can offer my family, my writing, my friends, a portion of the gift I've been given by seeking it out, consciously or unconsciously. The mystery is still there (Harrison, 1991).

CASE STUDY

The Case for the Future

Now that you have finished the final chapter of this book, the time has come to move from textbook case studies to direct observation, analysis (and, perhaps, intervention) in organizations in your community. Here are some ideas to get you started:

1. Select an organization, or industry, in your area. Based on your understanding of the new moral and ethical imperatives for the future of organizations, perform an eco-profile on the ways these local organizations and industries impact the quality of planetary life.

2. Collect materials about a local organization or industry's development of training programs for its employees, including those sponsored at your school. Find out what employers believe to be important areas of new understanding and skills for employees, as well as their plans for incorporating these understandings and skills in their operations.

3. Stage a debate in your class—or in public—on the topic: Resolved: That male-dominated thinking has led to the current deterioration of the planet. Make sure that your debaters provide not only a sensible analysis of the issues, but also productive alternatives for change.

4. Organize a community study group dedicated to "Redefining the Meaning of Work"; be sure to invite a cross-section of your community to participate.

These are just a few ideas to get you started. We hope you generate more of your own! In the spirit of continuing the dialogue between our readers and ourselves, please write us with your results, suggestions, or issues you feel ought to be raised.

And good luck! May your lives be long and full of meaningful communication and work!

Eric M. Eisenberg
H. L. Goodall
c/o St. Martin's Press
175 Fifth Avenue
New York, N.Y. 10010

REFERENCES

Ackoff, R. (1957). Towards a behavioral theory of communication. *Management Science* 4:218–234.

Adams, J. (1980). Interorganizational processes and organizational boundary activities. In L. L. Cummings & B. Staw, eds., *Research in organizational behavior.* Vol. 2 (pp. 321–355). Greenwich, Conn.: JAI Press.

Adorno, T. (1989). *Kierkegaard: The construction of the aesthetic.* Minneapolis: University of Minnesota Press.

Ahrne, G. (1990). *Agency and organization.* London: Sage Publications.

Albrecht, K. (1992). *The only thing that matters: Bringing the power of the customer into the center of your business.* New York: HarperBusiness.

Albrecht, T., & Adelman, M. (1987). *Communicating social support.* Beverly Hills, Calif.: Sage Publications.

Albrecht, T., & Hall, Bradford. (1991). Facilitating talk about new ideas: The role of personal relationships in organizational innovation. *Communication Monographers,* 58: 273–288.

Aldrich, H., & Pfeffer, J. (1976). Environments of organizations. *Annual Review of Sociology* 2: 79–105.

Alexander, G., & Giesen, B. (1987). From reduction to linkage: The long view of the micro-macro debate. In J. Alexander, ed., *Action and its environments.* New York: Columbia University Press.

Altman, S., Valenzi, E., & Hodgetts, R. (1985). *Organizational behavior: Theory and practice.* New York: Academic Press.

Anderson, J. (1987). *Communication research: Issues and methods.* New York: McGraw-Hill.

Arendt, H. (1971). *The life of the mind.* San Diego: Harcourt Brace Jovanovich.

Argyris, C. (1957). *Personality and organization.* New York: Harper & Row.

Argyris, C., & Schon, D. (1978). *Organizational learning: A theory of action perspective.* Reading, Mass.: Addison-Wesley.

Ashford, S., & Cummings, L. (1983). Feedback as an individual resource: Personal strategies of creating information. *Organizational Behavior and Human Performance* 32: 370–398.

Atwood, M. (1990). Adolescent socialization into work environments. Unpublished Master's thesis, Department of Occupational Science, University of Southern California.

Axley, S. (1984). Managerial and organizational communication in terms of the conduit metaphor. *Academy of Management Review* 9: 428–437.

Aydin, C. (1989). Occupational adaptation to computerized medical information systems. *Journal of Health and Social Behavior* 30: 163–179.

Aydin, C., & Rice, R. (1992). Bringing social worlds together: Computers as catalysts for new interactions in health care organizations. *Journal of Health and Social Behavior* 33: 168–185.

Bachrach, P., & Baratz, M. (1962). Two faces of power. *American Political Science Review* 56: 947–952.

Baird, J. (1977). *The dynamics of organizational communication.* New York: Harper & Row.

Baker, B. (1991). Safety risks: The price of productivity. *Los Angeles Times,* October 6, pp. 35–36.

Bakhtin, M. (1981). *The dialogic imagination.* Trans. Caryl Emerson and Michael Holquist. Austin: University of Texas Press.

Bakhtin, M. (1984). *Problems of Dostoevsky's Poetics.* Trans. M. Holquist. Austin: University of Texas Press.

Bakhtin, M. (1986). *Speech genres and other late essays.* Trans. C. Emerson. Minneapolis: University of Minnesota Press.

Bales, R., & Strotdbeck, F. (1960). Phases in group problem solving. In D. Cartwright & A. Zander, eds., *Group dynamics: Research and theory* (pp. 624–638). New York: Harper & Row.

Barley, S. (1983). Semiotics and the study of occupational and organizational culture. *Administrative Science Quarterly* 23: 393–413.

Barley, S. (1986). Technology as an occasion for structuring: Evidence from observations of CT scanners and the social order of radiology departments. *Administrative Science Quarterly* 31: 78–108.

Barnard, C. (1938–1968). *The functions of the executive.* Cambridge, Mass.: Harvard University Press.

Bastien, D., & Hostager, T. (1988). Jazz as a process of organizational innovation. *Communication Research* 15: 582–602.

Bateson, G. (1972). *Steps to an ecology of mind.* New York: Ballantine.

Bateson, M. C., & Bateson, G. (1987). *Angels fear: Towards an epistemology of the sacred.* New York: Bantam Books.

Baudrillard, J. (1983). *Simulations.* New York: Semiotext.

Baudrillard, J. (1988). *America.* London: Verso.

Baudrillard, J. (1990). *Cool memories.* London: Verso.

Bavelas, A. (1951). Communication patterns in task oriented groups. In D. Lerner & H. Laswell, eds., *The policy sciences* (pp. 193–202). Stanford, Calif.: Stanford University Press.

Bellah, R., Madsen, R., Sullivan, W., Swidler, A., & Tipton, S. (1985). *Habits of the heart.* Berkeley: University of California Press.

Bellah, R., Madsen, R., Sullivan, W., Swidler, A., & Tipton, S. (1991). *The good society.* New York: Alfred A. Knopf.

Bell-Detienne, K. (1992). The control factor: An empirical investigation of employees' reaction to control in an organizational work environment. Unpublished doctoral dissertation, Communication Arts & Sciences, University of Southern California.

Bendix, R. (1956). *Work and authority in industry.* New York: John Wiley.

Benne, K., & Sheats, P. (1948). Functional roles of group members. *Journal of Social Issues* 4: 41–49.

Bennis, W., & Nanus, B. (1985). *Leaders: Strategies for taking charge.* New York: Harper & Row.

Benson, T. (1981). Another shootout in cowtown. *Quarterly Journal of Speech* 67: 347–406.

Berger, P., & Berger, B. (1983). *The war over the family.* Garden City, N.Y.: Anchor Doubleday.

Berger, P., & Luckmann, T. (1967). *The social construction of reality.* Garden City, N.Y.: Anchor.

Berlo, D. (1960). *The process of communication.* New York: Holt, Rinehart & Winston.

Bernays, E. (1923). *Crystallizing public opinion.* New York: Boni & Liveright.

Best, S., & Kellner, D. (1991). *Postmodern theory: Critical integrations.* New York: Guilford Press.

Beyer, J., & Trice, H. (1987). How an organization's rites reveal its culture. *Organizational Dynamics* 15: 4–35.

Bhabha, H. (1990). Dissemination: Time, narrative, and the modern nation. In H. Bhabha, ed., *Nation and narration* (pp. 291–322). London: Routledge.

Bingham, S. (1991). Communication strategies for managing sexual harassment in organizations: Understanding message options and their effects. *Journal of Applied Communication Research* 19: 88–115.

Blake, R., & Mouton, J. (1964). *The managerial grid.* Houston, Tex.: Gulf.

Blumer. H. (1969). *Symbolic interactionism: Perspective and method.* Englewood Cliffs, N.J.: Prentice-Hall.

Bochner, A. (1982). The functions of human communication in interpersonal bonding. In C.

Arnold & J. Waite-Bowers, eds., *Handbook of rhetorical and communication theory* (pp. 544–621). Boston: Allyn-Bacon.

Boje, D. (1991). The storytelling organization: A study of story performance in an office-supply firm. *Administrative Science Quarterly* 36: 106–126.

Boland, R., & Hoffman, R. (1983). Humor in a machine shop. In L. Pondy, P. Frost, G. Morgan, & T. Dandridge, eds., *Organizational symbolism* (pp. 187–198). Greenwich Conn.: JAI Press.

Brass, D. (1984). Being in the right place: A structural analysis of individual influence in an organization. *Administrative Science Quarterly* 29: 518–539.

Brown, M., & McMillan, J. (1991). Culture as text: The development of an organizational narrative. *Southern Communication Journal* 57: 49–60.

Browning, L. (1992). Reasons for success at Motorola. Paper presented at the applied communication pre-conference of the International Communication Association, Miami, May.

Browning, L., & Hawes, L. (1992). Style, process, surface, context: Consulting as postmodern art. *Journal of Applied Communication Research* 19: 32–54.

Buber, M. (1985). *Between man and man.* 2nd ed. New York: Macmillan.

Buckley, W. (1967). *Sociology and modern systems theory.* Englewood Cliffs, N.J.: Prentice-Hall.

Bullis, C., & Tompkins, P. (1989). The forest ranger revisited: A study of control practices and identification. *Communication Monographs* 56: 287–306.

Burke, K. (1969). A rhetoric of motives. Berkeley: University of California Press.

Burke, K. (1966). *Language as symbolic action.* Berkeley: University of California Press.

Burke, K. (1989). *On symbols and society.* Chicago: University of Chicago Press.

Burke, R., Weir, T., & Duwors, R., Jr. (1979). Type A behavior of administrators and wives' reports of marital satisfaction and well-being. *Journal of Applied Psychology* 64: 57–65.

Burke, W. (1986). Leadership as empowering others. In S. Srivasta, ed., *Executive power* (pp. 51–77). San Francisco: Jossey-Bass.

Burrell, G. (1988). Modernism, postmodernism, and organizational analysis 2: The contribution of Michel Foucault. *Organization Studies* 9: 221–235.

Calder, B. (1977). An attribution theory of leadership. In B. Staw & G. Salancik, eds., *New directions in organizational behavior.* Chicago: St. Clair Press.

Calvert, L., & Ramsey, V. (1992). Bringing women's voice to research on women in management: A feminist perspective. *Journal of Management Inquiry* 1: 79–88.

Campbell, J., Campbell, R., & Associates. (1988). *Productivity in organizations.* San Francisco: Jossey-Bass.

Carlsson, C., & Leger, M. (1990). *Bad attitude: The processed world anthology.* London: Verso.

Cartwright, D. (1977). Risk taking by individuals and groups: An assessment of research employing choice dilemmas. *Journal of Personality and Social Psychology:* 361–378.

Cascio, W. (1986). *Managing human resources.* New York: McGraw-Hill.

Chandler, C., & Ingrassia, P. (1991). Shifting gears. *The Wall Street Journal,* April 11, p. 1.

Cheney, G. (1983). The rhetoric of identification and the study of organizational communication. *Quarterly Journal of Speech* 69: 143–158.

Cheney, G., & Vibbert, S. (1987). Corporate discourse: Public Relations and issues management. In F. Jablin, L. Putnam, K. Roberts, & L. Porter, eds., *Handbook of organizational communication* (pp. 165–194). Newbury Park, Calif.: Sage Publications.

Clegg, S. (1989). *Frameworks of power.* Newbury Park, Calif.: Sage Publications.

Clegg, S. (1990). *Modern organizations.* Newbury Park, Calif.: Sage Publications.

Clifford, J. (1983). On ethnographic authority. *Representations* 1: 118–146.

Clifford, J., & Marcus, G. (1985). *Writing culture: The poetics and politics of ethnography.* Berkeley: University of California Press.

Cohen, H. (1985). The development of research in speech communication: An historical perspective. In T. Benson, ed., *Speech communication in the 20th century* (pp. 282–298). Carbondale: Southern Illinois University Press.

Compo, S. (1990). *Life after death.* Winchester, Mass.: Faber & Faber.

Conger, J., & Kanungo, R. (1988). The empowerment process: Integrating theory and practice. *Academy of Management Review* 13:471–482.

Connor, S. (1989). *Postmodernist culture: Theories of the contemporary.* New York: Basil Blackwell.

Conquergood, D. (1991). Rethinking ethnography: Towards a critical cultural politics. *Communication Monographs* 58: 179–194.

Conquergood, D. (1992). Ethnography, rhetoric, and performance. *Quarterly Journal of Speech* 78: 80–97.

Conrad, C. (1983). Organizational power: Faces and symbolic forms. In L. Putnam & M. Pacanowsky, eds., *Communication and organizations* (pp. 173–194). Beverly Hills: Sage Publications.

Conrad, C. (1985). Chrysanthemums and swords: A reading of contemporary organizational communication theory and research. *Southern Speech Communication Journal* 50: 189–200.

Conrad, C. (1990). Nostalgia and the nineties. Paper presented at the conference on Organizational Communication in the 1990s: A research agenda, Tempe, Arizona.

Conrad, C. (1991). Communication in conflict: Style-strategy relationships. *Communication Monographs* 58: 135–155.

Contractor, N. (1992). Self-organizing systems perspective in the study of organizational communication. In B. Kovacic (ed.), *Organizational communication: New perspectives.* Albany: SUNY Press.

Contractor, N., & Eisenberg, E. (1990). Communication networks and the new media in organizations. In J. Fulk & C. Steinfeld, eds., *Organizations and communication technology* (pp. 143–172). Newbury Park, Calif.: Sage Publications.

Contractor, N., Eisenberg, E., & Monge, P. (1992). Antecedents and outcomes of interpretive diversity in organizations. Unpublished manuscript, Department of Communication, University of Illinois, Urbana, Illinois.

Contractor, N., & Seibold, D. (1992). Theoretical frameworks for the study of structuring processes in group decision support systems. Unpublished manuscript, University of Illinois, Urbana, Illinois.

Cooper, C. J. (1984). Executive stress: A ten country comparison. *Human Resource Management* 23: 395–407.

Cooper, R., & Burrell, G. (1988). Modernism, postmodernism, and organizational analysis: An introduction. *Organizational Studies* 9: 91–112.

Crable, R., & Vibbert, S. (1983). Mobil's epideictic advocacy: "Observations" of Prometheusbound. *Communication Monographs* 50: 380–394.

Csikszentmihalyi, M. (1990). *Flow: The psychology of optimal experience.* New York: Harper & Row.

Cummings, T. (1978). Self-regulating work groups: A socio-technical synthesis. *Academy of Management Review* 3: 625–634.

Cusella, L. (1987). Feedback, motivation, and performance. In F. Jablin et al., eds., *Handbook of organizational communication* (pp. 624–678). Beverly Hills, Calif.: Sage Publications.

Czarniawska-Joerges, B. (1988). Dynamics of organizational control: The case of Berol Kemi Ab. *Accounting, Organizations, and Society* 11: 471–482.

Daniels, T., & Spiker, B. (1991). *Perspectives on organizational communication.* Dubuque, Iowa: Wm. C. Brown.

Dansereau, F., & Markham, S. (1987). Superior-subordinate communication: Multiple levels of analysis. In F. Jablin et al., eds., *Handbook of organizational communication* (pp. 343–388), Beverly Hills, Calif.: Sage Publications.

Davis, S., & Davidson, B. (1991). *2020 Vision.* NY: Simon and Schuster.

Davis, K. (1953). Management communication and the grapevine. *Harvard Business Review* 31: 43–49.

Davis, K. (1972). *Human behavior at work.* New York: McGraw-Hill.

Deal, T., & Kennedy, A. (1982). *Corporate cultures.* Reading, Mass.: Addison-Wesley.

deCerteau, M. (1984). *The practice of everyday life.* Berkeley: University of California Press.

Deetz, S. (1991). *Democracy in an age of corporate colonization.* Albany, N.Y.: SUNY Press.

Deetz, S., & Mumby, D. (1990). Power, discourse, and the workplace: Reclaiming the critical tradition. In J. Anderson, ed., *Communication Yearbook 13* (pp. 18–47). Newbury Park, Calif.: Sage Publications.

Derrida, J. (1972). Structure, sign, and play in the discourse of the human sciences. In R. Macksay & E. Donato, eds., *The structuralist controversy: The language of criticism and the science of man.* Baltimore: Johns Hopkins University Press.

Derrida, J. (1976). *Speech and phenomenon.* Evanston, Ill.: Northwestern University Press.

Desmonde, W. (1962). *Magic, myth, and money: The origin of money in religious ritual.* New York: Free Press of Glencoe.

Dessler, G. (1982). *Organization and management.* Reston, Va.: Reston.

Dillard, J., & Miller, K. (1988). Intimate relationships in task environments. In S. Duck, ed., *Handbook of personal relationships* (pp. 449–465). New York: John Wiley.

Dillard, J., & Segrin, C. (1987). Intimate relationships in organizations: Relational types, illicitness, and power. Paper presented at the Annual Conference of the International Communication Association, Montreal, Canada.

Domanick, J. (1992). You talk with people; you don't talk to them. An interview with new LAPD police chief Willie Williams. *Los Angeles Weekly,* April 24–April 30, p. 14.

Donnellon, A. (1992). Team work: Linguistic models of negotiating difference. In B. Shepard et al. eds., *Research and negotiations in organizations.* Vol. 4. Greenwich, Conn.: JAI Press.

Donnellon, A., Gray, B., & Bougon, M. (1986). Communication, meaning, and organized action. *Administrative Science Quarterly* 31: 43–55.

Downs, C., Clampitt, P., & Pfeiffer, A. (1988). Communication and organizational outcomes. In G. Goldhaber & G. Barnett, eds., *Handbook of organizational communication* (pp. 171–212). Norwood, N.J.: Ablex.

Drucker, P. (1957). *The landmarks of tomorrow.* New York: Harper & Row.

Drucker, P. (1992a). *Managing for the future: The 1990's and beyond.* New York: Truman Talley Books/Dutton.

Drucker, P. (1992b). There's more than one kind of team. *The Wall Street Journal,* Feb. 11, p. 16.

Dutton, J., & Dukerich, J. (1991). Keeping an eye on the mirror: Image and identity in organizational adaptation. *Academy of Management Journal* 34: 517–554.

Edwards, L. (1991). Samurai hackers. *Rolling Stone,* September 19, pp. 67–69.

Eisenberg, E. (1984). Ambiguity as strategy in organizational communication. *Communication Monographs* 51: 227–242.

Eisenberg, E. (1986). Meaning and interpretation in organizations. *Quarterly Journal of Speech* 72: 88–98.

Eisenberg, E. (1990). Jamming: Transcendence through organizing. *Communication Research* 17: 139–164.

Eisenberg, E., Farace, R., Monge, P., Bettinghaus, E., Kurchner-Hawkins, R., Miller, K., & Rothman, L. (1985). Communication linkages in interorganizational systems: Review and synthesis. In B. Dervin & M. Voight, eds., *Progress in Communication Sciences* 6: 231–258. Norwood, N.J.: Ablex.

Eisenberg, E., Monge, P., & Farace, R. V. (1984). Coorientation on communication rules in managerial dyads. *Human Communication Research* 11: 261–271.

Eisenberg, E., Monge, P., & Miller, K. (1983). Involvement in communication networks as a predictor of organizational commitment. *Human Communication Research* 10: 179–201.

Eisenberg, E., & Phillips, S. (1991). Miscommunication in organizations. In N. Coupland, H. Giles, & J. Wiemann, eds., *"Miscommunication" and problematic talk* (pp. 244–258). Newbury Park, Calif.: Sage Publications.

Eisenberg, E., & Riley, P. (1988). Organizational symbols and sense-making. In G. Goldhaber & G. Barnett, eds., *Handbook of organizational communication* (pp. 131–150). Norwood, N.J.: Ablex.

Eisenberg, E., & Riley, P. (1991). A closed-loop model of communication, empowerment, urgency and performance. Unpublished working paper, University of Southern California.

Eisenberg, E., & Witten, M. (1987). Reconsidering openness in organizational communication. *Academy of Management Review* 12: 418–426.

Eisler, R. (1987). *The chalice and the blade.* San Francisco: HarperCollins.

Elden, M., & Levin, M. (1991). Cogenerative learning: Bringing participation into action research. In W. F. Whyte, ed., *Participatory action research* (pp. 127–142). Newbury Park, Calif.: Sage Publications.

Eliot, T. S. (1949). *Notes toward the definition of culture.* New York: Harcourt, Brace.

Emerson, C. (1983). Bakhtin and Vygotsky on internalization of language. *Quarterly Newsletter of the Laboratory of Comparative Human Cognition* 5: 9–13.

Emery, F., & Trist, E. (1965). The causal texture of organizational environments. *Human Relations* 18: 21–32.

Etzioni, A. (1961). *A comparative analysis of complex organizations.* New York: Free Press of Glencoe.

Etzioni, A. (1988). *The moral dimension: Toward a new economics.* New York: Free Press.

Evered, R., & Tannenbaum, R. (1992). A dialog on dialog. *Journal of Management Inquiry* 1: 43–55.

Fairhurst, G., & Chandler, T. (1989). Social structure in leader-member interaction. *Communication Monographs* 56: 215–239.

Fairhurst, G., Green, S., & Snavely, B. (1984). Face support in controlling poor performance. *Human Communication Research* 11: 272–295.

Fairhurst, G., Rogers, E., & Sarr, R. (1987). Manager-subordinate control patterns and judgments about the relationship. *Communication Yearbook* 10: 395–415.

Farace, R., Monge, P., & Russell, H. (1977). *Communicating and organizing.* Reading, Mass.: Addison-Wesley.

Farley, L. (1978). *Sexual shakedown: The sexual harassment of women on the job.* New York: McGraw-Hill.

Featherstone, M. (1988). In pursuit of the postmodern. *Theory, Culture, and Society* 5: 195–216.

Feldman, S. (1991). The meaning of ambiguity: Learning from stories and metaphors. In P. Frost et al., eds., *Reframing organizational culture* (pp. 145–156). Newbury Park, Calif.: Sage Publications.

Feldman, M., & March, J. (1981). Information in organizations as signal and symbol. *Administrative Science Quarterly* 26: 171–186.

Fenster, M. (1991). The problem of taste within the problematic of culture. *Communication Theory* 1: 87–105.

Ferguson, K. (1984). *The feminist case against bureaucracy.* Philadelphia: Temple University Press.

Ferguson, T., & Dunphy, J. (1992). *Answers to the mommy track: How wives and mothers in business reach the top and balance their lives.* New Horizon Press.

Fiedler, F. (1967). *A theory of leadership effectiveness.* New York: McGraw-Hill.

Fisher, A. (1980). *Small group decision making.* 2nd ed. New York: McGraw-Hill.

Fisher, W. (1984). Narration as a human communication paradigm: The case of public moral argument. *Communication Monographs* 51: 1–22.

Fombrun, C., & Shanley, M. (1990). What's in a name: Reputation building and corporate strategy. *Academy of Management Journal* 33: 233–258.

Foster, H. (1983). *The anti-aesthetic: Essays on postmodern culture.* Port Townshend, Wash.: Bay Press.

Foucault, M. (1972). *The archaeology of knowledge.* London: Tavistock.

Foucault, M. (1979). *The birth of the prison.* Hammondsworth, England: Penguin.

Franklin, B. (1970). *The complete Poor Richard almanacs published by Benjamin Franklin.* Barre, MA: Imprint Society.

Freeman, S. (1990). *Managing lives: Corporate women and social change.* Amherst: University of Massachusetts Press.

French, R., & Raven, B. (1959). The bases of social power. In D. Cartwright & A. Zander, eds., *Group dynamics* (pp. 601–623). New York: Harper & Row.

Friedman, M. (1992). *Dialogue and the human image.* Newbury Park, Calif.: Sage.

Friere, P. (1968). *Pedagogy of the oppressed.* Berkeley: University of California Press.

Frost, P., Moore, L., Louis, M., Lundberg, C., & Martin, J. (1991). *Reframing organizational culture.* Newbury Park, Calif.: Sage Publications.

Fulk, J., & Mani, S. (1986). Distortion of communication in hierarchical relationships. *Communication Yearbook 9* (pp. 483–510). Newbury Park, Calif.: Sage Publications.

Fulk, J., Schmitz, J., & Steinfeld, C. (1990). A social influence model of technology use. In J. Fulk & C. Steinfeld, eds., *Organizations and communication technology* (pp. 143–172). Newbury Park, Calif.: Sage Publications.

Futrell, C., & Parasuramann, A. (1984). The relationship of satisfaction and performance to salesforce turnover. *Journal of Marketing* 48: 33–40.

Gabarro, J., & Kotter, J. (1980). Managing your boss. *Harvard Business Review* 58: 92–100.

Galbraith, J. (1973). *Designing complex organizations.* Reading, Mass.: Addison-Wesley.

Garfield, C. (1992). *Business in the ecological age.* San Francisco: Berrett-Koehler. (Audiotape.)

Geertz, C. (1973). *The interpretation of cultures.* New York: Basic Books.

Geist, P., & Dreyer, J. (1992). A dialogical critique of the medical encounter: Understanding, marginalization, and the social context. Paper presented at the Annual Meeting of the Speech Communication Association, Chicago.

Gergen, K. (1985). The social constructionist movement in modern psychology. *American Psychologist* 40: 266–275.

Gersick, C. (1988). Time and transition in work teams: Toward a new model of group development. *Academy of Management Journal* 31: 9–41.

Gersick, C. (1991). Revolutionary change theories: A multi-level explanation of the punctuated equilibrium paradigm. *Academy of Management Review* 16: 10–36.

Gibson, J., & Hodgetts, R. (1986). *Organizational communication: A managerial perspective.* New York: Academic Press.

Gibson, D., & Rogers, E. (in Press). *Synergy on trial: Texas high tech and the MCC.* Newbury Park, Calif.: Sage Publications.

Giddens, A. (1979). *Central problems in social theory.* London: Hutchinson.

Ginsberg, E. (1982). The mechanization of work. *Scientific American* 247: 66–75.

Gitlin, T. (1987). *The sixties: Years of hope, days of rage.* New York: Bantam.

Glaser, H., & Bullis, C. (1992). Ecofeminism and organizational communication. Paper presented at the Speech Communication Association Annual Meeting, Chicago.

Goldstien, I., & Gilliam, P. (1990). Training systems issues in the year 2000. *American Psychologist* 45: 134–140.

Goodall, H. L. (1989). *Casing a promised land.* Carbondale: Southern Illinois University Press.

Goodall, H. L. (1990a). Interpretive contexts for decision-making: Toward an understanding of the physical, economic, dramatic, and hierarchical interplays of language in groups. In G. M. Phillips, ed., *Teaching how to work in groups* (pp. 197–224). Norwood, N.J.: Ablex.

Goodall, H. L. (1990b). Theatre of motives. In J. Anderson, ed., *Communication Yearbook* 13 (pp. 69–97). Newbury Park, Calif.: Sage Publications.

Goodall, H. L. (1991a). *Living in the rock n roll mystery.* Carbondale: Southern Illinois University Press.

Goodall, H. L. (1991b). Unchained melodies: Toward a poetics of organizing. Blair Hart lecture on communication, Department of Communication, University of Arkansas, Fayetteville, Arkansas.

Goodall, H. L. (1993). Empowerment, culture, and postmodern organizing: Deconstructing the Nordstrom's Employee Handbook. *Journal of Organizational Change Management* 5: 25–30.

Goodall, H. L., Wilson, G., & Waagen, C. (1986). The performance appraisal interview: An interpretive reassessment. *Quarterly Journal of Speech* 72: 74–87.

Gouldner, A. (1971). *The coming crisis of Western Sociology.* New York: Basic Books.

Graen, G. (1976). Role making processes within complex organizations. In M. Dunnette, ed., *Handbook of industrial and organizational psychology* (pp. 1201–1245). Chicago: Rand McNally.

Graen, G., & Ginsburgh, S. (1977). Job resignation as a function of role orientation and leader acceptance: A longitudinal investigation of organizational assimilation. *Organizational Behavior and Human Performance* 19: 1–17.

Graen, G., Liden, R., & Hoel, W. (1982). Role of leadership in the employee withdrawal process. *Journal of Applied Psychology* 67: 868–872.

Graen, G., & Schiemann, W. (1978). Leader member agreement: A vertical dyad linkage approach. *Journal of Applied Psychology* 63: 206–212.

Gramsci, A. (1971). *Selections from the prison notebooks.* London: Lawrence & Wishart.

Granovetter, M. (1973). The strength of weak ties. *American Journal of Sociology* 78: 1360–1380.

Grant, L. (1992). Breaking the mold: Companies struggle to reinvent themselves. *Los Angeles Times,* May 3, pp. D1, D16.

Gray, B., Bougon, M., & Donnnellon, A. (1985). Organizations as constructions and destructions of meaning. *Journal of Management* 11: 83–98.

Greenblatt, S. (1990). Culture. In F. Lentricchia & T. McLaughlin, eds., *Critical terms for literary study* (pp. 225–232). Chicago: University of Chicago Press.

Gronn, P. (1983). Talk as the work: The accomplishment of school administration. *Administrative Science Quarterly* 28: 1–21.

Grossberg, L. (1991). Review of theories of human communication. *Communication Theory* 1: 171–176.

Grossman, H., & Chester, N. (1990). *The experience and meaning of work in women's lives.* Hillsdale, N.J.: Lawrence Erlbaum.

Habermas, J. (1972). *Knowledge and human interests.* London: Heinemann Educational Books.

Habermas, J. (1981). Modernity versus postmodernity. *New German Critique* 22: 3–14.

Hackman, R., and associates. (1990). *Groups that work (and those that don't): Creating conditions for effective teamwork.* San Francisco: Jossey-Bass.

Hackman, R., & Oldham, G. (1975). Development of the Job Diagnostic Survey. *Journal of Applied Psychology* 60: 159–170.

Hackman, R., & Suttle, J. (1977). *Improving life at work: Behavioral science approaches to organizational change.* Santa Monica, Calif.: Goodyear Publishing.

Hage, J., & Aiken, M. (1970). *Social change in complex organizations.* New York: Random House.

Hall, K., & Savery, L. (1987). Stress management. *Management Decision* 25: 29–35.

Hamper, B. (1991). *Rivethead.* New York: Warner Books.

Harrigan, B. (1977). *Games mother never taught you: Corporate gamesmanship for women.* New York: Warner Books.

Harrison, J. (1991). *Just before dark*. Livingston, Mont.: Clark City Press.

Harrison, T. (1985). Communication and participative decision-making: An exploratory study. *Personnel Psychology* 38: 93–116.

Hart, R., & Burks, D. (1972). Rhetorical sensitivity and social interaction. *Speech Monographs* 39: 75–91.

Harvey, D. (1989). *The conditions of postmodernity*. London: Basil Blackwell.

Hassan, I. (1971). *The dismemberment of Orpheus: Toward a postmodern literature*. Madison: University of Wisconsin Press.

Hassan, I. (1987). *The postmodern turn: Essays in postmodern theory and culture*. Columbus: Ohio State University Press.

Hawes, L. (1974). Social collectivities as communication: Perspective on organizational behavior. *Quarterly Journal of Speech* 60: 497–502.

Hawking, S. (1988). *A brief history of time*. New York: Bantam.

Hayes-Bautista, D. (1988). *The burden of support: Young Latinos in an aging society*. Stanford, CA: Stanford University Press.

Hearn, J., Sheppard, D., Tancred-Sheriff, P., & Burrell, G. *The sexuality of organization*. Newbury Park, Calif.: Sage Publications.

Heath, R. (1980). Corporate advocacy: An application of speech communication perspectives and skills—and more. *Communication Education* 29: 370–377.

Hebdige, D. (1979). *Subculture: The meaning of style*. London: Methuen.

Helgeson, S. (1990). *The female advantage: Women's ways of leadership*. New York: Doubleday.

Hellweg, S. (1987). Organizational grapevines: A state of the art review. In B. Dervin & M. Voight, eds., *Progress in the communication sciences* 8. Norwood, N.J.: Ablex.

Herbst, P. (1976). *Alternatives to hierarchies*. Leiden: M. Nijhoff Social Sciences Divison.

Herzberg, F. (1966). *Work and the nature of man*. New York: Collins.

Hirokawa, R., & Rost, K. (1992). Effective group decision making in organizations. *Management Communication Quarterly* 5: 267–388.

Hirschman, A. (1970). *Exit, voice, and loyalty*. Cambridge, Mass.: Harvard University Press.

Hoffman, L. (1982). *Foundations of family therapy*. New York: Basic Books.

Hollander, E., & Offerman, L. (1990). Power and leadership in organizations. *American Psychologist* 45: 179–189.

Holquist, M. (1990). *Dialogism: Bakhtin and his world*. London: Routledge.

Holt, G. (1989). Talk about acting and constraint in stories about organizations. *Western Journal of Speech Communication* 53: 374–397.

Horovitz, B. (1991). Firms focus on logos to project right image. *Los Angeles Times*, October 1, p. D6.

Hochschild, A. (1979). Emotion work, feeling rules and social structure. *American Journal of Sociology* 85: 551–575.

Hochschild, A. (1983). *The managed heart: Commercialization of human feeling*. Berkeley: University of California Press.

House, R. (1971). A path-goal theory of leader effectiveness. *Administrative Science Quarterly* 16: 321–338.

Huber, G. (1990). A theory of the effects of advanced information technologies on organizational design, intelligence, and decision-making. In J. Fulk & C. Steinfeld, eds., *Organizations and communication technology* (pp. 237–274). Newbury Park, Calif.: Sage Publications.

Hume Corporation (1987). *Improving your financial profile*. USA: Hume Corp.

Hunger, R., & Stern, L. (1976). Assessment of the functionality of superordinate goals in reducing conflict. *Academy of Management Journal* 16: 591–605.

Hyde, B. (1990). Already always listening. Personal communication.

Hyde, B. (1991). Speaking being: Ontological rhetoric as transformational technology. Paper presented at the Thirteenth Annual Conference of the Association for Integrative Studies, St. Paul, Minnesota.

Ilgin, D., & Knowlton, W., Jr. (1980). Performance attributional effects on feedback from supervisors. *Organizational Behavior and Human Performance* 25: 441–456.

Infante, D., & Gordon, W. (1985). Superior's argumentativeness and verbal aggressiveness as predictors of subordinate's satisfaction. *Human Communication Research* 12: 117–125.

Infante, D., Trebing, J., Sheperd, P., & Seeds, D. (1984). The relationship of argumentativeness to verbal aggression. *Southern Speech Communication Journal* 50: 67–77.

Israel, et al. (1989). The relation of personal resources, participation, influence, interpersonal relationships and coping strategies to occupational stress, job stress, and health: A multivariate analysis. *Work and Stress* 3: 163–194.

Ivancevich, J., & Matteson, M. (1980). *Stress and work: A managerial perspective.* Glenview, Ill.: Scott, Foresman.

Jablin, F. (1979). Superior-subordinate communication: The state of the art. *Psychological Bulletin* 86: 1201–1222.

Jablin, F. (1985). Task/work relationships: A life-span perspective. In M. Knapp & G. Miller, eds., *Handbook of interpersonal communication* (pp. 615–654). Newbury Park, Calif.: Sage Publications.

Jablin, F. (1987). Organizational entry, assimilation, and exit. In F. Jablin, L. Putnam, K. Roberts, & L. Porter, eds., *Handbook of organizational communication* (pp. 679–740). Newbury Park, Calif.: Sage Publications.

Jackson, M. (1989). *Paths toward a clearing.* Bloomington: Indiana University Press.

Jackson, S. (1983). Participation in decision-making as a strategy for reducing job-related strain. *Journal of Applied Psychology* 68: 3–19.

Jacobson, R. (1992). Colleges face new pressure to increase faculty productivity. *Chronicle of Higher Education* 38 (32): 1, 16.

Jameson, F. (1984). Postmodernism, or the cultural logic of late capitalism. *New Left Review* 146: 53–92.

Janis, I. (1972). Victims of groupthink. 2nd revised ed. Boston: Houghton Mifflin.

Jencks, C. (1977). *The language of postmodern architecture.* New York: Pantheon.

Johnson, B. (1977). *Communication: The process of organizing.* Boston: Allyn-Bacon.

Jones, B. (1972). Sex in the office. *National Times* 12 (June).

Jones, E., Jr. (1973). What it's like to be a Black manager. *Harvard Business Review* (July/August).

Kanter, R. M. (1977). *Men and women of the corporation.* New York: Basic Books.

Kanter, R. M. (1989). The new managerial work. *Harvard Business Review* (November-December): 85–92.

Karasek, R. (1979). Job demands, job decisions, latitude and mental strain: Implications for job redesign. *Administrative Science Quarterly* 24: 285–308.

Katz, D., & Kahn, R. (1966–1978). *The social psychology of organizations.* New York: John Wiley.

Katzell, R., & Thompson, D. (1990). Work motivation. *American Psychologist* 45: 144–153.

Keeley, M. (1980). Organizational analogy: A comparison or organismic and social contract models. *Administrative Science Quarterly* 25: 337–362.

Kelly, J. (1982). *Scientific management, job redesign, and work performance.* London: Academic Press.

Keys, B., & Case, T. (1990). How to become an influential manager. *Academy of Management Executive* 4: 38–50.

Kiesler, C. (1971). *The psychology of commitment.* New York: Academic Press.

Kilmann, R., & Thomas, K. (1975). Interpersonal conflict handling behavior as a reflection of Jungian personality dimensions. *Psychological Reports* 37: 971–980.

Kimberly, J., & Miles, R. (1980). *The organizational life cycle.* San Francisco: Jossey-Bass.

King, Y. (1989). The ecology of feminism and the feminism of ecology. In J. Plant, ed., *Healing the wounds: The promise of ecofeminism.* Philadelphia: New Society Publishers.

Kipnis, D., & Schmidt, S. (1982). *Profile of organizational influence strategies.* San Diego, Calif.: University Associates.

Kipnis, D., & Schmidt, S. (1983). An influence perspective on bargaining. In M. Bazerman & R. Lewicki, eds., *Negotiating in organizations* (pp. 303–319). Beverly Hills, Calif.: Sage Publications.

Kipnis, D., Schmidt, S., & Braxton-Brown, G. (1990). The hidden costs of persistence. In M. Cody & M. McLaughlin, eds., *The psychology of tactical communication.* Philadelphia: Multilingual Matters.

Kipnis, D, Schmidt, S., & Wilkinson, I. (1980). Intraorganizational influence tactics: Explorations in getting one's way. *Journal of Applied Psychology* 65: 440–452.

Knorr-Cetina, K., & Cicourel, A. (1981). *Advances in social theory and methodology.* Boston: Routledge & Kegan Paul.

Kobasa, S., Maddi, S., & Kahn, S. (1982). Hardiness and health: A prospective study. *Journal of Personality and Social Psychology* 42: 168–177.

Kreps, G. (1991). *Organizational communication: Theory and practice.* 2nd ed. New York: Longman.

Krippendorff, K. (1985). On the ethics of constructing communication. ICA Presidential Address, Honolulu, Hawaii.

Krivonos, P. (1982). Distortion of subordinate to superior communication in organizational settings. *Central States Speech Journal* 33: 345–352.

Kuhn, T. (1972). *The structure of scientific revolutions.* Chicago: University of Chicago Press.

Laing, R. D. (1965). *The divided self.* Harmondsworth, England: Penguin.

Larkey, P., & Sproull, L. (1984). *Advances in information processing in organizations.* Vol I. Greenwich, Conn.: JAI Press.

Larson, J. Jr., (1989). The dynamic interplay between employees: feedback-seeking strategies and supervisors' delivery of performance feedback. *Academy of Management Review* 14: 408–422.

Lavie, S. (1990). *The poetics of military occupation: Mzeina allegories of identity under Israeli and Egyptian rule.* Berkeley: University of California Press.

Lawler, E., III. (1986). *High involvement management.* San Francisco: Jossey-Bass.

Lawrence, P., & Lorsch, J. (1967). *Organization and environment: Mapping differentiation and integration.* Boston: Graduate School of Business Administration, Harvard University.

Leavitt, H. (1951). Some effects of certain communication patterns on group performance. *Journal of Abnormal and Social Psychology* 46: 38–50.

Leeds-Hurwitz, W. (1992). Social approaches to interpersonal communication. *Communication Theory* 2: 131–138.

Lerner, M. (1992). Looters were living out the cynical American ethos. *Los Angeles Times,* May 14, p. B7.

Levering, R., Moskowitz, M., & Katz, M. (1984). *The 100 best companies to work for in America.* Reading, Mass.: Addison-Wesley.

Liden, R., & Graen, G. (1980). Generalizability of the vertical dyad linkage model of leadership. *Academy of Management Journal* 23: 451–465.

Likert, R. (1961). *New patterns of management.* New York: McGraw-Hill.

Lipsitz, G. (1990). *Time passages: Collective memory and American popular culture.* Minneapolis: University of Minnesota Press.

Locke, E., & Latham, G. (1984). *Goal setting: A motivational technique that really works!* Englewood Cliffs, N.J.: Prentice-Hall.

Loher, B., Noe, R., Moeller, N., & Fitzgerald, M. (1985). A meta-analysis of the relation of job characteristics to job satisfaction. *Journal of Applied Psychology* 70: 280–289.

Long, R. (1987). *New office information technology.* London: Croom Helm.

Louis, M. (1980). Surprise and sense-making: What newcomers experience in entering unfamiliar organizational settings. *Administrative Science Quarterly* 23: 225–251.

Luhmann, A. D., & Albrecht, T. L. (1990). The impact of supportive communication and personal control on job stress and performance. Paper presented at the International Communication Association, Chicago.

Lukes, S. (1974). *Power: A radical view.* London: Macmillan.

Lunneborg, P. (1990). *Women changing work.* Westport, Conn.: Greenwood Press.

Lyotard, J. (1984). The postmodern condition: A report on knowledge. Trans. G. Bennington and B. Massumi. Minneapolis: University of Minnesota Press.

Manning, P. (1977). *Police work.* Cambridge, Mass.: MIT Press.

March, J. (1965). Introduction. In J. March, ed., *Handbook of organizations* (pp. ix–xvi). Chicago: Rand McNally.

March, J., & Olsen, J. (1976). *Ambiguity and choice in organizations.* Bergen, Norway: Universitets-forlaget.

March, J., & Simon, H. (1958). *Organizations.* New York: John Wiley.

Marcus, G., & Fischer, M. (1986). *Anthropology as cultural critique.* Chicago: University of Chicago Press.

Marcus, A., & Goodman, R. (1991). Victims and shareholders: The dilemmas of presenting corporate policy during a crisis. *Academy of Management Journal* 34: 281–305.

Martin, J., & Myerson, D. (1988). Organizational culture and the denial, channeling, and acknowl-edgment of ambiguity. In L. Pondy, R. Boland, & H. Thomas, eds., *Managing ambiguity and change.* New York: John Wiley.

Martin, J., & Siehl, C. (1983). Organizational culture and counter-culture: An uneasy symbiosis. *Organizational Dynamics* 12: 52–64.

Maruyama, M. (1963). The second cybernetics: Deviation-amplifying mutual causal processes. *American Scientist* 51: 164–179.

Maslach, C. (1982). *Burnout: The cost of caring.* Englewood Cliffs, N.J.: Prentice-Hall.

Maslow, A. (1965). *Eupsychian management.* Homewood, Ill: R.D. Irwin.

Maslow, A. (1970). *Motivation and personality,* 2d edition. NY: Harper & Row.

May, S. (1988). The modernist monologue in organizational communication research: The text, the subject, and the audience. Paper presented at the Annual Convention of the International Communication Association, San Francisco.

Mayo, E. (1945). The social problems of industrial civilization. Cambridge, Mass.: Graduate School of Business Administration, Harvard University.

McClenahan, J. (1991). It's no fun working here anymore. *Industry Week,* March 4, pp. 20–22.

McDonald, P. (1988). The Los Angeles Olympic Organizing Committee: Developing organizational culture in the short run. *Public Administration Quarterly* 10: 189–205.

McGregor, D. (1960). *The human side of enterprise.* New York: McGraw-Hill.

McLuhan, M. (1964). *Understanding media: The extensions of man.* New York: McGraw-Hill.

McPhee, R. (1985). Formal structures and organizational communication. In R. McPhee & P. Tompkins, eds., *Organizational communication: Traditional themes and new directions* (pp. 149–177). Beverly Hills, Calif.: Sage Publications.

Mead, G. (1934). *Mind, self, and society.* Chicago: University of Chicago Press.

Mead, (1991). The new old capitalism: Long hours, low wages. *Rolling Stone,* May 30, n605, p. 27(3).

Metcalfe, J. (1976). Organizational strategies and interorganizational networks. *Human Relations* 29: 327–343.

Meyer, J., & Rowan, B. (1977). Institutionalized organizations: Formal structure as myth and ceremony. *American Journal of Sociology* 83: 340–363.

Meyer, J., & Scott, W. (1983). Organizations and environments. Newbury Park, Calif.: Sage.

Milbrath, R. (1989). *Envisioning a sustainable society.* Albany, N.Y.: SUNY Press.

Miller, G. R. (1991). Applied communication in the 21st century. Paper presented at the SCA/University of South Florida Conference on applied communication in the 21st century, Tampa, Florida.

Miller, J. G. (1978). *Living systems*. New York: McGraw-Hill.

Miller, K., Ellis, B., Zook, & Lyles, J. (1990). An integrated model of communication, stress, and burnout in the workplace. *Communication Research* 17: 300–326.

Miller, K., & Monge, P. (1985). Social information and employee anxiety about organizational change. *Human Communication Research* 11: 365–386.

Miller, K., Stiff, J., & Ellis, B. (1988). Communication and empathy as precursors to burnout among human service workers. *Communication Monographs* 55: 250–265.

Miller, V., & Jablin, F. (1991). Information seeking during organizational entry: Influences, tactics, and a model of the process. *Academy of Management Review* 16: 92–120.

Minh-Ha, T. (1991). *When the moon waxes red: Representation, gender, and cultural politics*. New York: Routledge.

Mintzberg, H. (1973). *The nature of managerial work*. New York: Harper & Row.

Mitchell, T., & Scott, W. (1990). America's problems and needed reforms: Confronting the ethic of personal advantage. *The Executive* 4: 23–35.

Mitroff, I., & Kilmann, R. (1975). Stories managers tell: A new tool for organizational problem-solving. *Management Review* 64: 18–28.

Monge, P., Bachman, S., Dillard, J., & Eisenberg, E. (1982). Communicator competence in the workplace: Model testing and scale development. *Communication Yearbook* 5, (pp. 505–528). New Brunswick, N.J.: Transaction Books.

Monge, P., Cozzens, M., & Contractor, N. (1992). Communication and motivational predictors of the dynamics of organizational innovation. *Organizational Science* 3: 250–274.

Monge, P., & Eisenberg, E. (1987). Emergent communication networks. In F. Jablin et al., eds., *Handbook of organizational communication* (pp. 204–342). Beverly Hills, Calif.: Sage Publications.

Monge, P., Farace, R., Eisenberg, E., Miller, K., & Rothman, L. (1984). The process of studying process in organizational communication. *Journal of Communication* 34: 22–43.

Morgan, G. (1986). *Images of organization*. Newbury Park, Calif.: Sage Publications.

Morrill, C. (1991). Little conflicts: The dialectic of order and change in professional relations. In D. Kolb & J. Bartunek, eds., *Disputing in the crevices: New perspectives on organizational conflict*. Newbury Park, Calif.: Sage Publications.

Morrison, A., & Von Glinow, M. A. (1990). Women and minorities in management. *American Psychologist* 45: 200–208.

Morrison, E., & Bies, R. (1991). Impression management in the feedback-seeking process: A literature review and research agenda. *Academy of Management Review* 16: 522—541.

Moskowitz, M., & Townsend, C. (1991). The 85 best companies for working mothers. *Working Mother* (October): 29–64.

Mouritsen, J., & Bjorn-Andersen, N. (1991). Understanding third-wave information systems. In C. Dunlop & R. Kling, eds., *Computerization and controversy: Value conflicts and social choices* (pp. 308–320). San Diego, Calif.: Academic Press.

Moyers, B. (1989). *A world of ideas*. New York: Doubleday.

Mumby, D. (1987). The political function of narratives in organizations. *Communication Monographs* 54: 113–127.

Myerson, D. (1991). "Normal" ambiguity? A glimpse of an occupational culture. In P. Frost et al., eds., *Reframing organizational culture* (pp. 131–144). Newbury Park, Calif.: Sage Publications.

Naisbett, J., & Auberdene, P. (1990). *Megatrends 2000*. N.Y.: Morrow.

Newton, I. (1803). *The mathematical principles of natural philosophy* Trans. Andrew Motte. London: H. D. Symonds.

Ochs, E., Smith, R., & Taylor, C. (1989). Detective stories at dinnertime: Problem solving through co-narration. *Cultural Dynamics* 2: 238–257.

Odiorne, G. (1986). The crystal ball of HR strategy. *Personnel Administrator* 31: 103–106.

Offerman, L., & Gowing, M. (1990). Organizations of the future: Changes and challenges. *American Psychologist* 45: 95–108.

Okabe, R. (1983). Cultural assumptions of east and west: Japan and the United States. In B. Gudykunst, ed., *Intercultural communication theory* (pp. 212–244). Newbury Park, Calif.: Sage Publications.

Oldham, G., & Rotchford, N. (1983). Relationships between office characteristics and employee reactions: A study of the physical environment. *Administrative Science Quarterly* 28: 542–556.

Oliver, C. (1990). Determinants of interorganizational relationships: Integration and future directions. *Academy of Management Review* 15: 241–265.

Ong, W. (1958). *Ramus, method, and the decay of dialogue.* Cambridge, Mass.: Harvard University Press.

Ortner, S. (1980). Theory in anthropology since the sixties. *Journal for the Comparative Study of Society and History:* 126–166.

Osborn, J., Moran, L., Musselwhite, E., & Zenger, J. (1990). *Self-directed work teams.* Homewood, Ill.: Business One Irwin.

Osterberg, R. (1992). A company without hierarchy. *At Work: Stories of Tomorrow's Workplace* 1: 9–10.

Ouchi, W. (1981). *Theory Z.* Reading, Mass.: Addison-Wesley.

Pacanowsky, M. (1988). Communication in the empowering organization. In J. Anderson, ed., *Communication Yearbook* 11 (pp. 356–379). Newbury Park, Calif.: Sage Publications.

Pacanowsky, M., & O'Donnell-Trujillo, N. (1983). Organizational communication as cultural performance. *Communication Monographs* 50: 126–147.

Papa, M. (1989). Communicator competence and employee performance with new technology: A case study. *The Southern Communication Journal* 55: 87–101.

Papa, M. (1990). Communication network patterns and employee performance with new technology. *Communication Research* 17: 344–368.

Parks, M. (1982). Ideology in interpersonal communication: Off the couch and into the world. In M. Burgoon, ed., *Communication Yearbook* 5 (pp. 79–108). New Brunswick, N.J.: Transaction Books.

Parsons, C., Herold, D., & Leatherwood, M. (1985). Turnover during initial employment: A longitudinal study of the role of causal attributions. *Journal of Applied Psychology* 70: 337–341.

Patterson, J., & Kim, P. (1991). *The day America told the truth.* Englewood Cliffs, N.J.: Prentice-Hall.

Percy, W. (1991). *Sign posts in a strange land.* New York: Farrar, Straus, Giroux.

Perrow, C. (1986). *Complex organizations: A critical essay.* 3rd ed. New York: Random House.

Peters, T. (1987). *Thriving on Chaos.* New York: Alfred A. Knopf.

Peters, T., & Waterman, R. (1982). *In search of excellence.* New York: Harper & Row.

Phillips, G. (1991). *Communication incompetencies: A theory of training oral performance behavior.* Carbondale: Southern Illinois University Press.

Phillips, G., & Goodall, H. L. (1983). *Loving and living.* Englewood Cliffs, N.J.: Prentice-Hall.

Phillips, G., & Wood, J. (1982). *Communication in human relationships.* New York: Macmillan.

Poole, M. S. (1981). Decision development in small groups I: A comparison of two models. *Communication Monographs* 48: 1–24.

Poole, M. S. (1983). Decision development in small groups II: A study of multiple sequences in decision making. *Communication Monographs* 50: 321–341.

Poole, M. S. (1992). Structuration and the group communication process. In L. Samovar & R. Cathcart, eds., *Small group communication: A reader.* 6th ed. Dubuque, Iowa: William C. Brown.

Poole, M. S., & Desanctis, G. (1990). Understanding the use of group decision support systems: The theory of adaptive structuration. In J. Fulk & C. Steinfeld, eds., *Organizations and communication technology* (pp. 173–193). Newbury Park, Calif.: Sage Publications.

Poole, M. S., & Roth, J. (1989). Decision development in small groups V: Test of a contingency model. *Human Communication Research* 15: 549–589.

Porter, M. (1980). *Competitive strategy.* New York: Free Press.

Pritchard, Robert, Jones, S., Roth, P., Steubing, K. (1988). Effects of group feedback, goal setting, and incentives on organizational productivity. *Journal of Applied Psychology* 73: 337–358.

Putnam, L. (1982). Paradigms for organizational communication research: An overview and synthesis. *Western Journal of Speech Communication* 46: 192–206.

Putnam, L. (1985). Contradictions and paradoxes in organizations. In L. Thayer, ed., *Organization and communication: Emerging perspectives* (pp. 151–167). Norwood, N.J.: Ablex.

Putnam, L., & Pacanowsky, M. (1983). *Communication and organizations: An interpretive approach.* Beverly Hills, Calif.: Sage Publications.

Putnam, L., & Poole, M. S. (1987). Conflict and negotiation. In F. Jablin et al., eds., *Handbook of organizational communication* (pp. 549–599). Newbury Park, Calif.: Sage Publications.

Pynchon, T. (1973). *Gravity's rainbow.* New York: Viking Press.

Quick, J., & Quick, J. (1984). *Organizational stress and preventative management.* New York: McGraw-Hill.

Quinn, R. (1977). Coping with Cupid: The formation, impact, and management of romantic relationships in organizations. *Administrative Science Quarterly* 22: 30–45.

Raban, J. (1991). *Hunting mister heartbreak: A discovery of America.* San Francisco: HarperCollins.

Rabinow, P., & Sullivan, W. (1986). *Interpretive social science—a second look.* Berkeley: University of California Press.

Rafaeli, A., & Sutton, R. (1987). The expression of emotion as part of the work role. *Academy of Management Review* 12: 23–37.

Rafaeli, A., & Sutton, R. (1991). Emotional contrast strategies as means of social influence: Lessons from criminal interrogators and bill collectors. *Academy of Management Journal* 34: 749–775.

Ray, E. (1987). Supportive relationships and occupational stress in the workplace. In T. Albrecht & M. Adelman, eds., *Communicating social support* (pp. 172–191). Newbury Park, Calif.: Sage Publications.

Redding, W. C. (1972). *Communication within the organization.* New York: Industrial Communications Council.

Redding, W. C. (1985a). Rocking boats, blowing whistles, teaching speech communication. *Communication Education* 34: 245–258.

Redding, W. C. (1985b). Stumbling toward identity: The emergence of organizational communication as a field of study. In R. McPhee & P. Tompkins, eds., *Organizational communication: Traditional themes and new directions* (pp. 15–54). Beverly Hills, Calif.: Sage Publications.

Redding, W. C. (1991). Unethical messages in the organizational context. Paper presented at the Annual Convention of the International Communication Association, Chicago.

Redding, W. C., & Tompkins, P. (1988). Organizational communication—Past and present tenses. In G. Goldhaber & G. Barnett, eds., *Handbook of organizational communication* (pp. 5–33). Norwood, N.J.: Ablex.

Reddy, M. (1979). The conduit metaphor—a case of frame conflict in our language about language. In A. Ortony, ed., *Metaphor and thought* (pp. 284–324). Cambridge, England: Cambridge University Press.

Rheinhold, H. (1991). *Virtual reality.* New York: Summit Books.

Richards, I. A. (1936). *The philosophy of rhetoric.* New York: Oxford University Press.

Richards, W. (1985). Data, models, and assumptions in network analysis. In R. McPhee & P. Tompkins, eds., *Organizational communication: Traditional themes and new directions* (pp. 109–128). Newbury Park, Calif.: Sage Publications.

Richmond, V., Davis, L., Saylor, K., & McCroskey, J. (1984). Power strategies in organizations: Communication techniques and messages. *Human Communication Research* 11: 85–108.

Richmond, V., & McCroskey, J. (1979). Management communication style, tolerance for disagreement, and innovativeness as predictors of employee satisfaction: A comparison of single-factor, two-factor, and multiple-factor approaches. In D. Nimmo, ed., *Communication Yearbook* 3 (359–374) New Brunswick, N.J.: Transaction Books.

Rider, A. (1992). Wishful thinking. *Los Angeles Times* Magazine, September 15, p. 10.

Riley, P., & Eisenberg, E. (1991). The ACE model of management. Unpublished working paper, University of Southern California.

Rilke, R. (1984). Letters to a young poet. Trans. Stephen Mitchell. New York: Random House.

Roberts, K., & O'Reilly, C. (1974). Failures in upward communication: Three possible culprits. *Academy of Management Journal* 17: 205–215.

Robertson, J. (1985). *Future work: Jobs, self-employment, and leisure after the industrial age.* New York: Universe Books.

Rogers, E., & Kincaid, D. (1981). *Communication networks: Toward a new paradigm for research.* New York: Free Press.

Rose, D. (1989). *Patterns of American culture.* Philadelphia: University of Pennsylvania Press.

Rose, H. (1983). Hand, brain, and heart: A feminist epistemology for the natural sciences. *Signs* 9: 81.

Rosen, M. (1985). Breakfast at Spiro's: Dramaturgy and dominance. *Journal of Management* 11: 31–48.

Rosen, M. (1991). Scholars, travelers, thieves: On concept, method, and cunning in organizational ethnography. In P. Frost et al., eds., *Reframing organizational culture* (pp. 271–284). Newbury Park, Calif.: Sage Publications.

Rosenberg, B., & White, D. (1957). *Mass culture.* Glencoe, Ill.: Free Press.

Rosenmann, R., Brand, R., Jenkins, C., Friedman, M., Straus, R., & Wurm, M. (1975). Coronary heart disease in the western collaborative group study: Final follow-up experience of 8.5 years. *Journal of the American Medical Association* 233: 872–877.

Ross, R. (1989). *Small groups in organizational settings.* Englewood Cliffs, N.J.: Prentice-Hall.

Rounds, J. (1984). Information and ambiguity in organizational change. *Advances in information processing in organizations* 1: 111–141.

Roy, D. (1960). Banana time: Job satisfaction and informal interaction. *Human Organization* 18: 156–180.

Rummler, G., & Brache, A. (1991). *Managing the white space in your organizational chart.* New York: Free Press.

Sahlins, M. (1976). *Culture and practical reason.* Chicago: University of Chicago Press.

Said, E. (1978). *Orientalism.* New York: Pantheon.

Said, E. (1984). *The world, the text, and the critic.* Cambridge, Mass.: Harvard University Press.

Sailer, H., Schlachter, J., & Edwards, M. (1982). Stress: Causes, consequences, and coping strategies. *Personnel* (July-August) 59: 35–48.

Salancik, G., & Pfeffer, J. (1978). A social information processing approach to job attitudes and task design. *Administrative Science Quarterly* 23: 224–252.

Sartre, J. P. (1973). *Existentialism and humanism.* Trans. P. Mariet. London: Methuen.

Sashkin, M. (1991). *Total quality management.* Brentwood, Md.: International Graphics, Inc.

SCA. (1991). *Pathways to careers in communication.* Annandale, Va.: SCA.

Scandura, T., Graen, G., & Novak, M. (1986). When managers decide not to decide autocratically. *Journal of Applied Psychology* 71: 1–6.

Schall, M. A. (1983). A communication-rules approach to organizational culture. *Administrative Science Quarterly* 28: 557–581.

Scheidel, T., & Crowell, L. (1964). Idea development in small discussion groups. *Quarterly Journal of Speech* 50: 140–145.

Schein, E. (1969). *Process consultation: Its role in organizational development.* Reading, Mass.: Addison-Wesley.

Schein, E. (1988). *Organizational culture and leadership: A dynamic view.* San Francisco: Jossey-Bass.

Schein, E. (1991). The role of the founder in the creation of organizational culture. In P. Frost et al., eds., *Reframing organizational culture* (pp. 14–25). Newbury Park, Calif.: Sage Publications.

Schuler, R., & Jackson, S. (1986). Managing stress through PHRM practices: An uncertainty interpretation. *Research in Personnel and Human Resource Management* 4: 183–224.

Scott, J. (1990). *Domination and the arts of resistance: Hidden transcripts.* New Haven, Conn.: Yale University Press.

Scott, W. R. (1964). Theory of organizations. In R. Faris, ed., *Handbook of modern sociology* (pp. 485–529). Chicago: Rand McNally.

Scott, W. R. (1981). Organizations: Rational, natural, and open systems. Englewood Cliffs, N.J.: Prentice-Hall.

Seabright, M., Levinthal, D., & Fichman, M. (1992). Role of individual attachments in the dissolution of interorganizational relationships. *Academy of Management Journal* 35: 122–160.

Selznick, P. (1948). Foundations of the theory of organizations. *American Sociological Review* 13: 25–35.

Selznick, P. (1957). *Leadership in administration.* New York: Harper & Row.

Senge, P. (1991). *The fifth discipline: The art and practice of the learning organization.* New York: Doubleday/Currency.

Sennett, R. (1978). *The fall of public man.* New York: Vintage.

Shockley-Zalabak, P. (1991). *Fundamentals of organizational communication.* New York: Longman.

Shorris, E. (1981). *Scenes from corporate life.* New York: Penguin.

Silverman, D., & Bloor, M. (1990). Patient-centered medicine: Some sociological observations on its constitution, penetration, and cultural assonance. *Advances in Medical Sociology* 1: 3–25.

Silverstien, S. (1992). Sabbaticals are costly for women. *Los Angeles Times,* January 1, p. D1.

Simon, H. (1957–1976). *Administrative behavior.* 3d. ed. New York: Free Press.

Sink, D. (1985). *Productivity management.* New York: John Wiley.

Sivard, R. (1983). *World military and social expenditures 1983.* (p. 26). Washington, D.C.: World Priorities.

Smircich, L., & Calas, M. (1987). Organizational culture: A critical assessment. In F. Jablin et al., eds., *Handbook of organizational communication* (pp. 228–263). Newbury Park, Calif.: Sage Publications.

Smith, A. (1898). *Wealth of nations.* London: G. Routledge.

Smith, D. (1972). Communication research and the idea of process. *Speech Monographs* 39: 174–182.

Smith, H. (1982). *Beyond the postmodern mind.* New York: Crossroad.

Smith, M., Cohen, B., Stammerjohn, V., & Happ, A. (1981). An investigation of health complaints and job stress in video display operations. *Human Factors* 23: 387–400.

Smith, R. (1990). In pursuit of synthesis: Activity as a primary framework for organizational communication. Doctoral dissertation, Department of Communication Arts and Sciences, University of Southern California, Los Angeles.

Smith, R., & Eisenberg, E. (1987). Conflict at Disneyland: A root metaphor analysis. *Communication Monographs* 54: 367–380.

Somervell, D., & Toynbee, A. (1947). *A study of history.* New York: Oxford University Press.

Spencer, D. (1986). Employee voice and employee retention. *Academy of Management Journal* 29: 488–502.

Spretnak, C. (1991). States of grace. San Francisco: HarperCollins.

Staimer, M. (1992). U.S. workers get little vacation. *USA Today.*

Stallybrass, P., & White, A. (1986). *The politics and poetics of transgression.* Ithaca, N.Y.: Cornell University Press.

Steelman, J., & Klitzman, S. (1985). *The VDT: Hazardous to your health.* Ithaca, N.Y.: Cornell University Press.

Steers, R. (1977). Antecedents and outcomes of organizational commitment. *Administrative Science Quarterly* 22: 46–56.

Steers, R. (1981). *Introduction to organizational behavior.* Santa Monica, Calif.: Goodyear.

Steier, F. (1989). Toward a radical and ecological constructivist approach to family communication. *Journal of Applied Communication Research* 17: 1–26.

Steier, F., & Smith, K. (1992). The cybernetics of cybernetics and the organization of organization. In L. Thayer, ed., *Organization-communication: Emerging perspectives.* Norwood, N.J.: Ablex.

Steiner, G., & Ryan, W. (1968). *Industrial project management.* New York: Crowell-Collier and Macmillan.

Stewart, T. (1991). GE keeps those ideas coming. *Fortune,* August 12, Vol. 124 n4, p. 40(8).

Stoller, P. (1989). *The taste of ethnographic things.* Philadelphia: University of Pennsylvania Press.

Strine, M., & Pacanowsky, M. (1985). How to read interpretive accounts of organizational life: Narrative bases for textual authority. *Southern Speech Communication Journal* 50: 283–297.

Sullivan, J. (1988). Three roles of language in motivation theory. *Academy of Management Review* 13: 104–115.

Sundstrom, E., DeMeuse, K., & Futrell, D. (1990). Work teams: Applications and effectiveness. *American Psychologist* 45: 120–133.

Sussman, G. (1976). *Autonomy at work.* New York: Praeger.

Sutton, R., & Rafaeli, A. (1988). Untangling the relationship between displayed emotions and organizational sales: The case of convenience stores. *Academy of Management Journal* 31: 461–487.

Swidler, A. (1986). Culture as action. *American Sociological Review* 51: 273–286.

Tamaki, J. (1991). Sexual harassment in the workplace. *Los Angeles Times,* October 10, p. D2.

Taylor, F. (1913). *The principles of scientific management.* New York: Harper.

Taylor, F. (1947). *Scientific Management.* New York: Harper & Brothers.

Thomas, L. (1975). *The lives of a cell.* New York: Penguin.

Thompson, J. (1967). *Organizations in action.* New York: McGraw-Hill.

Tichy, N. (1983). *Managing strategic change.* New York: John Wiley.

Tjosvold, D. (1984). Effects of leader warmth and directiveness on subordinate performance on a subsequent task. *Journal of Applied Psychology* 69: 422–427.

Tjosvold, D., & Tjosvold, M. (1991). *Leading the team organization.* New York: Lexington Books.

Tompkins, P. (1987). Translating organizational theory: Symbolism over substance. In F. Jablin, L. Putnam, K. Roberts, & L. Porter, eds., *Handbook of organizational communication* (pp. 70–96). Newbury Park, Calif.: Sage Publications.

Tompkins, P., & Cheney, G. (1981). Communication and unobtrusive control. In R. McPhee, & P. Tompkins, eds., *Organizational communication: Traditional themes and new directions* (pp. 179–210). Newbury Park, Calif.: Sage Publications.

Torbert, W. (1991). *The power of balance.* Newbury Park, Calif.: Sage Publications.

Tracy, K., & Coupland, N. (1990). Multiple goals in discourse: An overview of issues. *Journal of Language and Social Psychology* 9: 1–13.

Tracy, K., & Eisenberg, E. (1991). Giving criticism: A multiple goals case study. *Research on Language and Social Interaction* 24: 37–70.

Trice, H., & Beyer, J. (1984). Studying organizational cultures through rites and ceremonies. *Academy of Management Review* 9: 653–669.

Trist, E. (1981). The evolution of socio-technical systems. *Occasional Paper* No. 2. Toronto: Quality of Work Life Centre.

Trujillo, N. (1985). Organizational communication as cultural performance: Some managerial considerations. *Southern Speech Communication Journal* 50: 201–224.

Trujillo, N., & Dionisopoulos, G. (1987). Cop talk, police stories, and the social construction of organizational drama. *Central States Speech Journal* 38: 196–209.

Turnage, J. (1990). The challenge of new workplace technology for psychology. *American Psychologist* 45: 171–178.

Turner, B. (1990). *Organizational symbolism.* Berlin: Walter de Gruyter.

Tyson, L. (1991). U.S. needs new spending priorities. *Los Angeles Times,* November 10, p. D2.

Van Maanen, J. (1979). *Qualitative methodology.* Beverly Hills, Calif.: Sage Publications.

Van Maanen, J. (1988). *Tales of the field: On writing ethnography.* Chicago: University of Chicago Press.

Van Maanen, J. (1991). The smile factory: Work at Disneyland. In P. Frost et al., eds., *Reframing organizational culture* (pp. 58–76). Newbury Park, Calif.: Sage Publications.

Van Maanen, J., & Barley, S. (1984). Occupational communities: Cultural control in organizations. In B. Staw & L. Cummings, eds., *Research in Organizational Behavior* Vol. 6 (pp. 265–287). Greenwich, Conn.: JAI Press.

Von Bertalanffy, L. (1968). *General systems theory.* New York: George Braziller.

Vroom, V. (1964). *Work and motivation.* New York: John Wiley.

Waldera, L. (1988). The effects of influence strategy, influence objective, and leader-member exchange on upward influence. Unpublished doctoral dissertation, George Washington University.

Waldron, V. (1991). Achieving communication goals in superior-subordinate relationships: The multi-functionality of upward maintenance tactics. *Communication Monographs* 58: 289–306.

Waller, R. (1986). Women and the typewriter during the first 50 years: 1873–1923. *Popular Culture* 10: 39–50.

Walljasper, J. (1992). At home in an eco-village. *Utne Reader* 51: 142–143.

Wanous, J. (1980). *Organizational entry: Recruitment, selection, and socialization of newcomers.* London: Addison-Wesley.

Watts, A. (1966). *The book: On the taboo against knowing who you are.* New York: Pantheon.

Watzlawick, P., Beavin, J., & Jackson, D. (1967). *The pragmatics of human communication: A study of interactional patterns, pathologies, and paradoxes.* New York: Norton.

Weber, M. (1946). From Max Weber: Essays in sociology. Eds. Hans Gerth & C. Wright Mills, New York: Oxford University Press.

Weick, K. (1976). Educational organizations as loosely coupled systems. *Administrative Science Quarterly* 21: 1–19.

Weick, K. (1979). *The social psychology of organizing.* 2nd ed. Reading, Mass.: Addison-Wesley.

Weick, K. (1980). The management of eloquence. *Executive* 6: 18-21.

Weick, K. (1984). Theoretical assumptions and research methodology selection. In F. McFarlan, ed., *Proceedings of the information systems research challenge* (pp. 111–132). Boston: Harvard Business School Press.

Weick, K. (1990). The vulnerable system: An analysis of the Tenerife air disaster. In P. Frost et al., eds., *Reframing organizational culture* (pp. 117–130). Newbury Park, Calif.: Sage Publications.

Weil, S. (1977). *The Simone Weil Reader.* Edited by George Panichas. New York: McKay.

Wellins, R., Byham, W., & Wilson, J. (1991). *Empowered teams.* San Francisco: Jossey-Bass.

Wenberg, J., & Wilmot, W. (1973). *The personal communication process.* New York: John Wiley.

Wentworth, W. (1980). *Context and understanding.* New York: Elsevier.

Whalen, S., & Cheney, G. (1991). Contemporary social theory and its implications for rhetorical and communication theory. *Quarterly Journal of Speech* 77: 467–479.

Whyte, W. F. (1948). *Human relations in the restaurant industry.* New York: McGraw-Hill.

Wilensky, Harold. (1967). *Organizational intelligence.* New York: Basic Books.

Wilkins, A. (1984). The creation of company cultures: The role of stories and human resource system. *Human Resource Management* 23: 41–60.

Wilkins, A., & Dyer, W. (1988). Toward culturally sensitive theories of culture change. *Academy of Management Review* 13: 522–533.

Williams, M. (1977). *The new executive woman: A guide to business success.* New York: New American Library.

Wilson, G., & Goodall, H. L. (1991). *Interviewing in context.* New York: McGraw-Hill.

Wood, J. (1977). Leading in purposive discussions: A study of adaptive behavior. *Communication Monographs* 44: 152–165.

Woods, J. (1991). The corporate closet: Heterosexual hegemony in a white-collar world. Presented as part of the panel "In or Out? The ethics and politics of disclosure and exposure of sexual orientation" at the International Communication Association, Chicago.

Zedeck, S., & Mosier, K. (1990). Work in the family and employing organization. *American Psychologist* 45: 240–251.

Zeithaml, V., Parasuraman, A., & Berry, L. (1990). Delivering quality service: Balancing customer perceptions and expectations. New York: Free Press.

Acknowledgments (continued from copyright page)

Ethics Box 3.2, from *The Oppressed Middle: Politics of Middle Management: Scenes from a Corporate Life* by Earl Shorris, ©1981. Reprinted by permission of the author and Roberta Pryor, Inc.

Table 4.2, "Evolution of the Hierarchy of Systems Thinking," from *General Systems Theory* by Ludwig von Bertalanffy, © 1968. Reprinted by permission of George Braziller, Inc.

Table 4.3, from *Communicating and Organizing* by Richard V. Farace, Peter R. Monge, and Hammish M. Russell, © 1977. Reprinted by permission of McGraw-Hill, Inc.

Table 4.5, from *The Fifth Discipline* by Peter Senge. Copyright © 1990 by Peter M. Senge. Used by permission of Doubleday, a division of Bantam Doubleday Dell Publishing Group, Inc.

Figure 4.1, "Model of Organizing," from *The Social Psychology of Organizing* by Karl Weick, © 1979. Reprinted by permission of McGraw-Hill, Inc.

Table 5.1, "Definition of Man," by Kenneth Burke. Adapted with permission from *The Hudson Review*, vol. xvi, No. 4 (Winter 1963–64). Copyright © 1964 by The Hudson Review, Inc.

Table 5.4, from *Tales of the Field: On Writing Ethnography* by John Van Maanen. Copyright © 1988, The University of Chicago Press. Reprinted by permission of The University of Chicago Press.

Table 5.7, Martin and Myerson table from *Reframing Organizational Culture* by Peter Frost, et al., (eds.), © 1991. Reprinted by permission of Sage Publications, Inc.

Table 5.6, from "How an Organization's Rites Reveal Its Culture," by Janice M. Beyer, et al. Reprinted by permission of publisher, from *Organizational Dynamics*, Spring/1987 ©1987. American Management Association, New York. All rights reserved.

Figure 6.1, reprinted by permission of Lindsley Armstrong.

Figure 6.2, *Nordstrom Employee Handbook* reprinted by permission of Nordstrom.

Table 6.4, from *Modern Organizations* by Stuart Clegg, © 1990. Reprinted by permission of Sage Publications, Inc.

Figure 9.2, from W. Richard Scott, *Organizations: Rational, Natural, and Open Systems*, 3d ed., © 1992, p. 160. Reprinted by permission of Prentice-Hall, Englewood Cliffs, New Jersey.

Figure 9.4, reprinted with the permission of The Free Press, a Division of Macmillan, Inc., from *Industrial Project Management* by George Steiner and William Ryan. Copyright © 1968 by The Trustees of Columbia University in the City of New York.

Figure 9.5, Figure 9.6 from *Empowered Teams: Creating Self-Directed Work Groups that Improve Quality, Productivity, and Participation* by Richard S. Wellins, William C. Byham, and Jeanne M. Wilson. Copyright © 1991 by Jossey-Bass Inc., Publishers. Reprinted by permission.

Ethics Box 11.1, reprinted by permission of Applause Books, New York, from *Other People's Money*, by Jerry Sterner. Copyright © 1989 by Jerry Sterner.

INDEX